P9-AEY-500

FRANCO-ITALIAN RELATIONS

FRANCO-ITALIAN RELATIONS

1860-1865

The Roman Question and the Convention of September

LYNN M. CASE

AMS PRESS
NEW YORK

Reprinted with permission of the University of Pennsylvania Press
From the edition of 1932, Philadelphia
First AMS EDITION published 1970
Manufactured in the United States of America

International Standard Book Number: 0-404-01405-4

Library of Congress Catalog Card Number: 75-121289

AMS PRESS, INC.
NEW YORK, N.Y. 10003

To My Wife

DORIS FELLOWS CASE

"La questione romana è una di quelle che un secolo pone e solo un altro risolve."

—CESARE CANTÙ

TABLE OF CONTENTS

PREFACE

THE principal problem involved in the relations of France and Italy between 1861 and 1865 was the solution of the Roman question. There have been three important definitive attempts to solve this difficult problem. The first was a French-Italian attempt in the form of the Convention of 15 September 1864, the second was a purely Italian effort by the Law of Papal Guaranties of May 1871, and the third was the Italian-Vatican endeavor by the Lateran Treaties of 1929. To appreciate the significance of the latest arrangement a knowledge of the two previously attempted solutions is necessary. It is the purpose of this work to relate the negotiation of the Convention of September as a step in the direction of a comprehensive study of both French-Italian relations and the Roman question.

To limit the discussion of the French-Italian relations to the negotiation of this Convention does not eliminate much from a full account of the diplomacy between France and Italy from 1860 to 1865. On the other hand it contributes the added advantage of unity. The history of the Convention of September covers the decade from 1860 to 1870, but because of the limitations of space and material it is necessary to restrict the discussion in the present work to the five years (1860-1865) when the Convention was formulated, negotiated, and concluded.

Since the close of the World War the documentary material of the French and Italian foreign offices is being made progressively much more available. In addition the publications of private correspondence and memoirs are steadily filling in the gaps. Thus it will soon be possible to trace definitively the history of the relations between these two Latin Powers from 1860 to 1914. The correspondence of the French Foreign Office has been made available up to the year 1871; the publication of the official French documents entitled *Les origines diplomatiques de la guerre de 1870-1871* is of great help for the years 1861-1871; and a similar, more complete official collection of the *Documents diplomatiques français 1871-1914* will admirably complete the material to 1914. The Italian sources, which are nearly complete for the years from 1860-1865, include the *Carteggio Cavour-Nigra*, *Carteggio Cavour-Vimercati-Pantaleoni-Passaglia*, and Bianchi's *Storia documentata* for the period to June 1861; the various collections of private correspondence such as Chiala's *Lettere di Cavour*, the *Carteggio Minghetti-Pasolini*, and Ricasoli's *Lettere;* as well as the memoirs of Pasolini, those of Minghetti in his *Convenzione di settembre*, the collection of documents in Bollea's *Silloge*, and many other works. These are soon to be supplemented by the official publication of the Italian diplomatic correspondence from 1861 to 1915.

In the preparation of this work I have encountered many of the difficulties which beset American historians who attempt investigations in Europe. The problems of making the most of one's limited time, of familiarizing oneself with foreign libraries and archives, of making new and necessary acquaintances, and of financing the costly journeys abroad create burdens in addition to those inherent in the primary task of research. The degree of success with which I was able to cope with those problems is largely due to the many friendships begun and continued during the progress of my studies and to the benevolent and helpful attitude of the many libraries and archives in which I worked. Indeed scholarship seems to know no national boundaries, and one of the compensations for the difficulties of studying in Europe is the international comradeship formed between brothers of one family of letters.

To the staffs of the British Public Record Office and the British Museum for their help and consideration I wish to express my thanks; likewise to the staffs of the *Archives du ministère des affaires étrangères*, the *Bibliothèque nationale*, and the *Archives nationales*. Particularly am I indebted to M. Pingaud, Director of the *Archives du ministère des affaires étrangères*, for his personal interest. M. Doysié was also very kind to me during my labors at the *Quai d'Orsay*. But among my many friends in France I am most deeply obligated to M. Ernest d'Hauterive who went to the trouble of making important investigations into the private and quite inaccessible Bonaparte archives at Prangins the results of which were obviously extremely valuable.

In Italy the officials and attendants of the government libraries of the *Biblioteca nazionale dell'Università di Torino* and the *Biblioteca del Senato* in Rome were characteristically Italian in their enthusiastic coöperation with me in my work. Senator Einaudi and Professor Sarfatti of Turin were especially kind to me during my early days in Italy and I value highly their friendship and thoughtfulness. Likewise Professor Luzzio of the same university, Mr. Eduardo Giretti of Bricherascio, and Mr. Ratti, Italian Consul in Philadelphia, have befriended me on several occasions.

In the United States I am very grateful to the staffs of the University of Pennsylvania Library and the New York Public Library, especially to Mr. Lydenberg, Assistant Director of the latter. I am under particular obligations to the University of Pennsylvania which, by its award of the Harrison Fellowship, aided me in financing the cost of my European researches. I am likewise grateful to Professor R. F. Nichols and Doctor J. P. Nichols for their constant encouragement and helpful counsel. Professor D. Vittorini went to considerable trouble to check my translations from the Italian, a service which I deeply appreciate. However, having pursued this study under the direction of Professor William E. Lingelbach, I am more especially indebted to him for his inspiring guidance, helpful interest, and kindness in reading the manuscript and in giving valuable criticisms and suggestions. The author, nevertheless, assumes complete responsibility for the final form of the text and translations.

L. M. C.

Houston, Texas
1 October 1931

ABBREVIATIONS

Aff. Etr. Archives du ministère des affaires étrangères.

C.P. Correspondance politique.

M.D. Mémoires et documents.

"Da Aspromonte a Mentana." An anonymous documentary article published in the *Nuova Antologia*. See chapter I, p. 7, note 4.

Doc. Guerre 1870. The official collection of French documents on the diplomatic origins of the Franco-Prussian War. See chapter VII, p. 288, note 56.

F.O. Public Record Office. British Foreign Office Correspondence.

Ques. romana. Two volumes of Cavour's correspondence on the Roman question (1860-1861) with Pantaleoni, Passaglia, Vimercati, and others. These are taken principally from the official archives in Turin and Rome. See chapter I, p. 26, note 70.

R.P. Public Record Office. Russell Papers.

PART I

THE PERIOD OF CAVOUR

CHAPTER I

FRANCE AND ITALY'S UNIFICATION IN 1860

AFTER many attempts and failures the national movement toward Italian unification which had received its encouragement during the days of the First Empire was beginning to show some definite results in the second half of the nineteenth century. In 1821 Austria intervened by force and restored absolutist régimes in both Naples and Piedmont where constitutional governments had been granted after revolutionary uprisings. In 1831 revolts broke out anew, this time in the Papal States, Parma, and Modena. Austria intervened again and successfully restored the old order. However, on this occasion France under Louis Philippe, opposing the policy of foreign intervention, but more especially jealous of Austrian predominance in Italy, sent troops to Ancona under the double guise of friendship for the Liberals and as a protection to the Pope's person. The French force was withdrawn in 1838.

The liberal and nationalistic spirit of revolt was not indeed killed in Italy. It needed only the news of the fall of Louis Philippe in France and Metternich in Austria in 1848 in order to spur the Italians on to form a united constitutional state by force. This time the whole Peninsula rose in unison: Lombardy, Venice, Piedmont, the Central States, and Naples. Even the Pope himself, Pius IX, at that time more liberal in his attitude, joined the movement to drive the Austrians from Italian soil. But this Italian revolt of the spring of 1848 was put down by the Austrian forces under Radetzky after the Pope had withdrawn his support.

Later, however, in the autumn of 1848 revolts of a more republican character broke out again in Italy. This time the Italians turned against Pius IX, drove him from Rome, and established the Roman Republic under Garibaldi and Mazzini. Still this more radical revolution had even less success. The

Bourbons in Naples restored order without concessions; Austria reduced the liberal forces in the north; and Louis Napoleon came to the aid of the Pope, drove out Garibaldi, and restored the Pontiff in his territories. This last element of intervention was the beginning of what was to become Europe's all-important Roman question. Napoleon continued his military occupation in and around Rome after all disorders had ceased, partly as a check on Austria and partly as a move to win the support of clerical opinion at home.

After Cavour came into power in Sardinia, and after that state's coöperation in the Crimean War, the relations between Napoleon III and Sardinia became more intimate. Motivated largely by the desire to eliminate Austria as a power in Italy, Napoleon III joined Sardinia again in the Austro-Sardinian War of 1859. This struggle left Austria only Venetia in Italy, and gave Sardinia not only Lombardy but also eventually Tuscany, Parma, Modena, and the Romagna.

Finally in 1860 Garibaldi with his expedition of the Thousand left Genoa for Sicily. There he overthrew the power of the Bourbons, proceeded to the Peninsula, gained Naples, and threatened to retake Rome from the Pope. At this point Cavour openly interfered and gained the acquiescence of Napoleon III to a plan for Sardinia to move south and check Garibaldi before the latter should move against the Pope. Of this French acquiescence more will be said further on. It suffices to say at this juncture that Sardinia invaded and occupied the Papal territory except Rome and the Patrimony of St. Peter, met Garibaldi, persuaded him to return to his island of Caprera, and joining her troops with Garibaldi's men, proceeded to besiege Francis II, the young King of Naples, at Gaëta. With the fall of Gaëta the whole Italian Peninsula with the exception of Rome and Venetia became united under the liberal constitution of Sardinia. The problem of adding Rome and Venice to this union developed more distinctly what has been known in diplomatic circles as the Roman and Venetian questions.

On the Roman question three parties had very decided and

different opinions. Italy demanded the French evacuation of Rome and the Patrimony, the incorporation of the imperial city into the union as its capital, the forfeiture of all temporal power by the Pope, and the annexation of the Patrimony itself as a part of Italy. The Pope, on the other hand, not only insisted on Rome and the Patrimony, and his age-old temporal power, but he demanded the restitution of all his lost territory of Umbria, the Marches, and even the Romagna. France, finding herself between the two contestants, took a firm stand for the Pope's possession of Rome and the Patrimony. The French Emperor opposed Rome as capital of Italy, but would not support the Pope's claim to his lost territories. France was willing, even desirous, to withdraw her troops from all Italian territory as soon as Italy and the Pope would come to an agreement or as soon as Italy would effectively guarantee the Pope's safety and actual possessions.

In addition to these three principals in the dispute, Great Britain conceived an interest in the problem. Jealous of French influence in the Mediterranean and hoping to find in the new Italy a friendly power to counteract France, she tended to develop this Italian friendship by favoring Rome as the capital and the destruction of the temporal power. England vigorously opposed the French occupation of Rome because it gave France a foothold on the Peninsula, weakened Italy, and better commanded the Mediterranean. Furthermore, the English policy of friendliness to Austria as a check both on France and Russia preferred the agitation of the Roman to that of the Venetian question. Austria opposed the Italian union, upheld the most extravagant claims of the Papacy, and did not object to France's occupation as long as it was only intended for the Pope's protection. But Austria seemed to be following a policy of non-aggression and non-intervention as long as she was not attacked by her southern neighbor.

After this brief summary of the course of Italian unification and the swift survey of the positions of the more important countries in the Roman question, the ground is prepared for a clearer understanding of the more intricate details of French and Italian relations during the dramatic events of 1860.

After eleven years of military occupation in Rome, both France and the Vatican became tired of such a makeshift situation. Early in 1859 the Pope proposed to France the arrangement for evacuation to begin at the end of the same year, but the outbreak of the Austro-Sardinian War precluded any discussion of the subject. French troops would not be withdrawn from Rome while Austria was attacking France's Italian ally.[1] At the end of that short struggle the negotiation with the Pope on the question of withdrawal was again taken up. This time Napoleon suggested that the troops of the King of the Two Sicilies be substituted for the French. The Vatican was quite ready to agree to such an arrangement but Naples declined to accept such a duty.[2] After the Neapolitan refusal a purely French-Vatican accord was reached on 12 May 1860 which provided that the French troops would gradually depart between the last of May and the last of August.[3] The Emperor felt that since Lamoricière, a Legitimist French general, had taken command of the Papal army, the defense of Rome could be assured without French aid. This may have been as much an expression of spite as of reassurance on the part of the Bonaparte because the Pope selected a Bourbonist instead of a friend of the actual régime in France.

The Franco-Vatican agreement had hardly been signed when Garibaldi began his expedition to Sicily. This positively forestalled any evacuation on the part of the French. It is now reasonably sure that if Garibaldi had waited six months before launching his scheme, there would have been no French troops in Rome. Two years later Napoleon III declared to Pepoli that "if he (Garibaldi) had delayed his Sicilian expedi-

[1] *Aff. Etr., C.P., Rome,* 1028: pp. 38-41; *M.D., Rome,* 124: year 1864 n.d. This contained a report on France and the Roman question from 1831-1864. See Also *Livre Jaune,* (1860), pp. 114-115; (1864), pp. 35-39.

[2] E. Bourgeois, et E. Clermont, *Rome et Napoleon III (1849-1870), étude sur les origines et la chûte du Second Empire* (Paris, 1907), p. 203. *Livre Jaune,* (1860), pp. 97-99.

[3] *Livre Jaune* (1860), pp. 115-117.

tion for two months, he would no longer have found the French army in Rome. . . ."[4] That France would have returned to Rome in this emergency is not certain, but her action later, in 1867, would seem to indicate that her troops would have been again on the Tiber by the time Garibaldi had arrived in that vicinity.

The spectacle of Garibaldi moving toward the Continent from Sicily while the French troops still remained in Rome made the English very uneasy. The British Government began to press France for some indication of an early departure just when Garibaldi was publicly declaring his intention to attack the Pope. Napoleon III was put in a position of abandoning the Pope under English pressure, which French public opinion would never allow, or give Great Britain the advantage of seeming to the Italians to be their more sincere friend. The fretfulness of the Emperor's note to Persigny in London reveals his mood in this situation.

As to South Italy, I am free from all engagements, and I ask nothing better than to come to an agreement with England on this point, as on others; but *au nom du ciel,* may the eminent men in charge of the English Government put narrow jealousies aside; let us understand each other in a straightforward fashion like the honest people that we are and not like robbers who are trying to outwit each other.

To sum up, this is my innermost thought: I desire that Italy

[4] Pepoli to Rattazzi, Paris, 15 Aug. 1862, (Anonymous), "Sulla via di Roma—Da Aspromonte a Mentana," *Nuova Antologia,* Ser. IV, LXXXV, (1 Jan. 1900), pp. 25-27. On the negotiation of this agreement and its failure see also: Drouyn de Lhuys to Sartiges, Paris, 12 Sept. 1864, *Aff. Etr., C.P., Rome,* 1028: pp. 38-41; *M.D., Rome,* 124: (year 1864), n.d.; *Livre Jaune* (1864), pp. 35-39. The Emperor told Vimercati: "Quinze jours plus tard et mon armée d'occupation était rappelée et quittait les États pontificaux d'après la demande du Saint-Père: tous mes embarras auraient été finis et l'Italie auriat été libre de s'arranger comme elle le voulait." (Anon.), "Da Aspromonte," *loc. cit.,* pp. 9-11. Rouher wrote a similar statement to Minghetti: "Si le Royaume de Naples eût été attaqué par Garibaldi un mois plus tard, notre armée s'éloignait de Rome sur la demande du Saint-Père. . . ." Paris, 15 April 1864, Marco Minghetti, *La convenzione di settembre 1864, un capitolo dei miei ricordi.* Edited by the Prince of Camporeale. (Bologna, 1899), pp. 21-23. Joseph Grabinski, "Nouvelles révélations sur la politique napoléonienne en Italie, 1860-1864. Lettres inédites du Prince Napoléon et de Napoléon III à propos du livre de Minghetti sur la Convention de Septembre," *Le Correspondant,* Sér. II, CLIX, 864-865. Bourgeois et Clermont, *Rome et Napoleon III,* p. 203.

should obtain peace, no matter how,[5] but without foreign intervention, and that my troops should be able to quit Rome without compromising the security of the Pope.[6]

This letter, defining Napoleon's policy of non-intervention in Italian affairs, was made public, and caused some speculation, especially in Rome. Gramont, French Ambassador at the Vatican, wrote:

> The Vatican approves it in a general way, but they are alarmed by the expression, *n'importe comment.* On the contrary in their eyes that's the whole question, and the important point is to know just *how* Italy will obtain peace.[7]

Indeed, instead of talking of evacuation the Vatican was now thinking entirely in the terms of reënforcements from France. When the Papal Nuncio asked Thouvenel, the French Foreign Minister, what could be expected in the line of support in case of attack, he was told that France would let them know later but that they could certainly count on some protection.[8] Finally

[5] N'importe comment.

[6] St. Cloud, 25 July 1860, a translated copy found in *R.P.*, LXII. H. d'Ideville, *Journal d'un diplomate en Italie, 1859-1862, 1862-1866. Notes intimes pour servir à l'histoire du Second Empire* (2 vols., Paris, 1872-1873), I, 319-320. On 13 July 1860 the Emperor revealed his early attitude toward the Garibaldian expedition and Sardinian intervention in an interview solicited by Nigra after instructions from Cavour. He wanted Cavour to keep Sardinia carefully within the accepted practice of international law. Napoleon suggested the following line of conduct for Cavour: 1) coöperation with the King of Naples, 2) armistice and plebiscite for Sicily, 3) Sardinian and Neopolitan joint request to the Pope for reforms. "If the King of Naples does not accept, he will put himself in the wrong. . . ." "If the King of Naples falls from his own weight, if Sicily votes for annexation [to Sardinia], if Umbria and the Marches do the same, *we'll see.*" The Emperor's description of his attitude was suggestive rather than definite. "I (the Emperor) do not like the Bourbons of Naples. . . . As for the Pope, he has lost my sympathies." The Emperor would withdraw his troops from Rome just as soon as Lamoricière had developed the semblance of an army. He was not against the principle of Italian unity. Nigra to Cavour, Paris, 13 July 1860, *Il Carteggio Cavour-Nigra dal 1858-1861.* A cura della R. Commissione Editrice. Vol. IV, *La liberazione del Mezzogiorno.* (Bologna, 1929), IV, 75-78. Later when Naples refused Cavour's offer of coöperation, it became necessary for Cavour to determine the Emperor's meaning of "we'll see." This was done at the Chambéry interview for the account of which see below.

[7] Rome, 7 Aug. 1860, L. Thouvenel, *Le secret de l'Empereur* (2 vols., Paris, 1889), I, 164-167.

[8] Thouvenel, *Secret,* I, 174-176. Thouvenel's memorandum of the interview, Paris, 10 Aug. 1860.

as the Garibaldi danger came nearer, Gramont, sharing the excitement of the Papal Court, advised France to give the Pope a definite assurance of aid, and take the responsibility for domestic order as well as for that on the frontiers.[9]

But before making the Pope any blanket promise, Napoleon seemed to want to make himself a little more sure on the Sardinian side. His eyes roved toward Turin and London as well as toward Rome. Should he blindly support a government which seemed on its last legs and lose at the same time all the favorable sentiment in Italy which he had gained the year before? Gramont, although seemingly anti-Sardinian and pro-Vatican, had just recently written in regard to the Roman Government that "never have I seen such symptoms of decay so clearly outlined as at this moment. Only internal discord was lacking and that was now appearing on all sides."[10] If Rome was bound to lose, France should not be too far involved in the interests of the Pope whatever her own Catholic opinion might be. Above all France did not wish to drive Sardinia into the arms of Great Britain through neglect.

Cavour was too shrewd a diplomat not to take advantage of the Anglo-French *défiance*. He sent a note to England containing a dispatch from Nigra, Sardinian minister in Paris, in which French hatred for Garibaldi was clearly shown. This was calculated to make the English more favorable to the unification movement. Cavour ended with the words: "If England opposes, France will not intervene, and events will run their natural course."[11] On the other hand Cavour instructed Nigra to explain to France England's enthusiasm for Garibaldi. This would make the French more favorable toward any anti-Garibaldian move that Sardinia might propose.[12]

Whatever may have been Napoleon III's reason for selecting one place for a summer vacation in preference to another,

[9] Rome, 18 Aug. 1860, Thouvenel, *Secret,* pp. 179-185.

[10] Rome, 7 Aug. 1860, *ibid.,* pp. 164-167.

[11] Turin, 1 Aug. 1860, N. Bianchi, *La politique du Comte de Cavour de 1852 à 1861* (Turin, 1885), pp. 379-380.

[12] 23 Aug. 1860, L. C. Bollea, *Una silloge di lettere del Risorgimento. . . .* (Turin, 1919), p. 325.

at least the fact is that when Italy was becoming Europe's most serious problem, the Emperor decided to take a rest and retired to the Savoyard Alps at Chambéry. He had his Minister of Foreign Affairs, Thouvenel, telegraph to Cavour to send some one there to "regulate the transfer of the port of Eveiller."[13] Whatever purpose France may have hinted for the interview, Cavour seemed to ignore it and sent Farini and Cialdini "to pay [Italy's] compliments to the Emperor."[14]

From the time of Garibaldi's departure, Cavour had been deliberating on a policy for Sardinia whereby he could take full advantage of the situation in Italy without bringing all of Europe down about his head. His playing of France and England against each other was one phase of that plan. That the rest of the plan was well developed by the time the Emperor decided to go to Chambéry is now certain.[15] Before these envoys of Sardinia went to Chambéry, however, they consulted with Dr. Conneau, a great friend of the Emperor and a member of the French Senate. Conneau, who was well informed on the political situation in France and the attitude of the Emperor, advised them to explain the plan fully to the Emperor. Conneau was one of the staunchest French advocates of Italian unification, and it does not seem probable that he would have advised such open frankness if it would have worked to the harm of Italy. But, unless the Emperor was in a very pro-Italian frame of mind when he went to Chambéry, it would have been dangerous to reveal so completely Italy's intentions.[16]

The compliments, whatever they may have been, were

[13] Paris, 20 Aug. 1860, *Aff. Etr., C.P., Italie,* 350: p. 159.

[14] Talleyrand to Thouvenel, Turin, 23 April 1860, *Aff. Etr., C.P., Italie,* 350: p. 160. Farini stated this also in the Italian Parliament: "Andai a visitare Sua Maestà l'Imperatore di Francia per complimentarlo in nome di Sua Maestà il Re." Arbib, "Sulla via di Roma—la questione in Parlamento," *Nuova Antologia,* Ser. IV, LXXXV, (16 Feb. 1900), 680-681.

[15] Cowley to Russell, Paris, 25 Sept. 1860, *F.O., France,* 1346: no. 1251. Cavour to Nigra, Turin, 29 Aug. 1860, Luigi Chiala, *Lettere edite ed inedite del Conte Camillo di Cavour* (7 vols., Turin, 1883-1887), VI, 583, Farini said in Parliament that "il governo del Re aveva di già presa la risoluzione che condusse poi ad effetto." Arbib, *loc. cit.,* 680-681.

[16] Cavour to Nigra, Turin, 29 Aug. 1860, Chiala, *Cavour lettere,* VI, 583. Matteo Mazziotti, "Un fervido amico dell'Italia in Francia. Enrico Conneau," *Nuova Antologia,* Ser. VI, CCXX, (1922), 106.

quickly paid and the envoys did not delay in obeying the directions of Cavour and the advice of Conneau. "I frankly related," Farini reported, "what were the opinions and decisions of the Government."[17] Cialdini and Farini proceeded to tell the Emperor that Sardinia after 1859 had determined to consolidate her powers in the neighboring states which had voluntarily placed themselves under King Victor-Emmanuel and to leave to time the solution of the Neapolitan and Venetian questions. They had therefore seen the proceedings of Garibaldi with deep concern, and had done their utmost to prevent his expedition to Sicily and later to Naples. But their remonstrances had been answered by the production of a letter on Garibaldi's part from the King which too clearly proved that Victor-Emmanuel approved of Garibaldi's policy. Under these circumstances no choice had been left Cavour but to accept that policy or to resign. Two considerations had deterred him from the latter course. First, because of the lack of men, it looked as if Garibaldi might be easily seized and hanged, which, Cavour felt, would have relieved Italy of a very troublesome individual. Secondly, in case of Cavour's resignation the Government would have inevitably fallen into the hands of the friends of Garibaldi and Mazzini. Cavour preferred, therefore, to share the responsibility of the King's acts. But events had not gone as he had expected. Garibaldi, and indirectly the Republican Party, was succeeding. This movement had to be counteracted. Now, they continued, if contagious outbreaks should occur in the Marches and Umbria, Sardinia would occupy them, not as a conquest, but for the preservation of liberty and order, and without prejudice to the future wishes of the populations. They would sink Lamoricière in the sea and capture Ancona. Already Garibaldi was threatening Rome. When Naples should show no more resistance, when the insurrections began to appear in the Papal States, and when the Pope appeared to be in danger, then Sardinia would march against Garibaldi and either defeat him or dissuade him from his project. Persano, they continued, had

[17] Arbib, *loc. cit.*, pp. 680-681.

already been ordered to move the fleet to Naples. All this time the person of the Pope and his possession of Rome and the Patrimony of St. Peter would be solemnly protected, while an attack on Venice would be avoided. Then after peace and order had been established, if it were found necessary, Europe could decide by Congress what would be the disposition of the revolutionized provinces.

Napoleon III listened carefully to their story and proposal. There was an evidence of a suppressed smile at the suggestion of sinking Lamoricière, but the whole matter was very serious and needed at that moment a quick decision, which he was never accustomed to make. It has been thought that he realized how he had compromised himself with Europe and Italy by taking Nice and Savoy. Now, if he deserted Italy a third time, he would not even have *her* friendship. Furthermore, it has been suggested that the hostility of the Pope of late to the Emperor's Government was rankling in his soul.[18] Finally the Emperor cautiously approved of Sardinia's proposed policy.[19] Nevertheless he warned that Cavour should be sure that the King of Naples had been vanquished beyond hope, that revolts had voluntarily broken out in the Marches and Umbria, and that the Pope would not otherwise be molested. Above all no attack should be made against Austria, and finally nothing definitive should be established without the decisions of a Congress. Of course the whole proceeding was quite irregular. France would have to be entirely out of the picture. He would have to wash his hands completely of the affair. In fact he might even have to oppose them publicly, but that opposition would not be in the form of force as long as Sardinia adhered to this program. At the departure of Cialdini and Farini there may have been a final warning. What Sardinia was then contemplating was fraught with many unknown dangers, especially from the direction of Aus-

[18] These are suggestions of Professor Charles Seignobos, author of vol. VII of Mr. Ernest Lavisse's *Histoire de France contemporaine* (Paris, 1921), VII, 125.

[19] "The Emperor expressed his acquiescence in this line of policy," were the words Cowley used to report what Thouvenel said. *F.O., France,* 1346: no. 1251.

tria. It would be the duty of Cavour to assure himself of the right moment and the appropriate steps. In any case the scheme, once launched, should be carried through swiftly.[20]

It had done no harm to be frank and soon two very excited and exultant officials scurried back to Turin bearing the happy secret between them.[21]

The Chambéry interview took place on the 28th of August, but it was not until two days later that the Emperor telegraphed the following summary to Thouvenel, his Minister of Foreign Affairs:

> Mr. Farini spoke to me with great frankness. Here is his aim and that of Cavour: to get the movement under control (*s'emparer du mouvement*); to keep the Patrimony of St. Peter for the Pope; to prevent any attack on Venice; to invoke the concurrence of Europe for a settlement of Italian affairs as soon as Naples and the Marches are in their power.[22]

Emperor Napoleon neglected to add what he had said or done but the apologetic tone of his telegram no doubt convinced Thouvenel of the Emperor's tacit approval.

[20] Cialdini during the excitement of the resulting campaign boasted that Napoleon III had said just before parting, "Bonne chance et faites vite." Another reported Cialdini as describing it in the words "Fate, ma fate presto." Gramont to Thouvenel, Rome, 6 Oct. 1860, Thouvenel, *Secret,* I, 236-238. Seignobos in Lavisse, *France contemporaine,* VII, 125. Antonin Debidour, *Histoire des rapports de l'Eglise et de l'Etat en France de 1789 à 1870* (Paris, 1898), pp. 565-566. Cavour had been wont to describe the position of Napoleon as evasively wishing him "good luck," and it is likely that Cialdini carelessly combined the Emperor's last advice and Cavour's apt phrase into "Bonne chance et faites vite." At any rate it is quite probable that Napoleon's last words were not intended to infuse any definite bravado into Sardinian policy. See Cavour to Nigra, Turin, 29 Aug. 1860, Chiala, *Cavour lettere,* VI, 583.

[21] Full accounts of the Chambéry meeting from different sources do not conflict greatly with each other, but it is not until they each have been examined that one can piece together the whole story of the incident. The principal references are as follows: French Foreign Office Circular, Paris, 18 Oct. 1860, *Livre Jaune,* (1860), pp. 162-163. Chiala, *Cavour lettere,* VI, 583. Paul Matter, *Cavouret l'unité italienne* (3 vols., Paris, 1922-1927), III, 380-381. The most complete account was given later by Thouvenel to Cowley who reported it home to Lord Russell. *F.O., France,* 1346: no. 1251. Farini later before the Italian Parliament declared that "l'Imperatore di Francia non mi diede consigli, molto meno mi impose condizioni. Ministro del Re Vittorio Emanuele, non avrei accettato condizioni da nessuno. . . ." Arbib, *loc. cit.* But this denial on the part of Farini does not overcome the more definite admissions of the French, especially when we realize the delicate point Farini was trying to defend before the Chamber.

[22] Annecy, 30 Aug. 1860, *Aff. Etr., C.P., Italie,* 350: p. 173, telegram in cipher.

Cavour was very pleased with the result of the conference. "The Emperor was perfect," he wrote to Nigra.

> [He] approved everything. . . . The results of Farini's interview must not be made known: I shall say here that the Emperor is washing his hands of Italian affairs, but at the same time wishes us good luck. The supreme moment[23] has arrived.[24]

In an interview with Rayneval, the French chargé in Turin, Cavour interpreted Napoleon's attitude as that of hands-off. He would not take any responsibility for what might happen, and had warned Piedmont to be moderate and not to attack Austria. Cavour assured Rayneval that on the latter subject "we shall be as prudent as possible."[25]

But Cavour also was prudent about putting too much faith in the reports of the Emperor's decision. It either seemed too good to be true, or else he began to suspect the enthusiastic accounts of Cialdini and Farini. He decided to send Arese to interview Napoleon III again. Arese was a great friend of the Emperor and a loyal Italian patriot. In addition he was moderate in his manner of thought and expression. A verification by him would give Cavour a more sure footing to begin operations.

> Go to Thonon. Describe situation Italy after Villafranca and Nice. Underhand war continued after Villafranca by Austrian enlistments in Rome and Naples. Alliance almost formed between Pope, Austria, and Bourbons. Opinion very much aroused all over Italy from danger of this league. After cession Nice impossible to hold back Garibaldi. Admit that the Government let him go (*l'a toléré*), even supported him. But has energetically stopped and checked Mazzinian expeditions. Impossible to allow one's self to be outdistanced by demagoguery in Naples. Annexation once made, will try not to attack Rome nor Austria. Emperor will save Italy by delaying aggression until spring. If necessary, we will fight Austria alone. Sure Emperor will not let France's only ally be destroyed by coalition.[26]

[23] "Nous touchons au moment suprême."

[24] 29 Aug. 1860, Chiala, *Cavour lettere,* VI, 583.

[25] Rayneval to Thouvenel, Turin, 31 Aug. 1860, Matter, *Cavour et l'unité italienne,* III, 380-381.

[26] Cavour to Bruno (for Arese), Turin, 31 Aug. 1860, telegram, Chiala, *op. cit.,* III, 360-361.

By adding the above array of arguments to those already used by Cialdini and Farini, Arese obtained the same success. Cavour wrote Farini:

> Had a talk with Arese. From what he says the Emperor confirmed what he told you. Only he appeared to Arese more explicit in his disapproval of our attitude toward the Neapolitan Government.[27]

Before any public move was made by Cavour, on 3 September, rumors reached Rome of the understanding arranged at Chambéry. A letter from Turin quoted Farini who had boasted that the Emperor had agreed to the annexation of the Papal States if Rome were left to the Pope, and that France would not interfere materially nor diplomatically. This rumor was generally believed, and the Papal Court was filled with consternation.[28]

At the same time that the reports were coming in to Thouvenel from Annecy and Rome, Austria, aroused by the events in Italy and the rumors which were current, began to feel out the position of France in regard to Austrian intervention. Rechberg, Austrian Foreign Minister, had his ambassador in Paris approach Thouvenel with the proposal that Austria should have a free hand in Italy should she be attacked by Sardinia in Venetia. Austria also complained of the undecided stand that France was taking under the present circumstances.[29]

Almost simultaneously with this step by Austria there came a note from Lord John Russell, British Secretary of State for Foreign Affairs, indicating that Great Britain did not believe that Austria would invade Italy

> but if the King of Sardinia is prepared to . . . seek to involve Europe in war, on his head be the consequences of a policy alike inconsistent with wisdom and with honor.[30]

Thouvenel remarked that it was Great Britain who was pushing Austria against France in this manner: British statesmen

[27] Turin, 6 Sept. 1860, Chiala, *op. cit.*, III, 372. See also Cavour to Nigra, Turin, 12 Sept. 1860, *ibid.*, p. 383.

[28] Gramont to Thouvenel, Rome, 4 Sept. 1860, Thouvenel, *Secret,* I, 185-186.

[29] Thouvenel to Gramont, 9 Sept. 1860, Thouvenel, *Secret,* I, 187-191.

[30] London, 7 Sept. 1860, *Aff. Etr., C.P., Rome,* 1015: pp. 166-167, copy in English; *C.P., Angleterre,* 718: p. 74, copy in French.

wished to embarrass France by the prospect of a general war on the one hand and by a big revolutionary explosion on the other.[31]

Under the weight of the triple burden of ignorance of the Emperor's commitments, the rumors of Sardinian intentions, and the pressure from Austria and England, Thouvenel finally applied for instructions from the Emperor who was making a tour of southern France. The Emperor's reply on the eve of the Sardinian invasion is significant:

> In reply to the dispatch from Vienna here is my idea: If Austria is attacked unjustly, I will not defend Piedmont; but if after a victory, Austria violates the treaty of Villafranca, I will take Piedmont's part. As to the latter I wish to write the King the following: 'I am forced to acquaint you with my intentions; if as Farini said, your troops enter the Papal States only after an insurrection and in order to restore order there, *I have nothing to say;* but if while my soldiers are at Rome, you attack the Church's territory, I shall be compelled to withdraw my minister from Turin and put myself in opposition (*Je suis forcé . . . de me placer en antagoniste*).'
>
> If you approve this language, write Talleyrand to come to Nice, and I shall give him the letter.[32]

Cavour had already made the first move in his long meditated plan. On September 7 he sent his ultimatum to Antonelli, Papal Foreign Secretary, calling on him to disband his foreign troops in the regions of the Marches and Umbria or Sardinia would invade those territories. Antonelli, of course, refused to heed the ultimatum. Cavour's demand was only intended as a pretext and Antonelli's reply was all that could have been expected from a self-respecting state. On the 10th the Sardinian army moved against Lamoricière and within a month Umbria and the Marches were under Sardinian control.

Talleyrand immediately reported Cavour's decision to Paris:

> According to Cavour, the Piedmontese Government, being unable to check Garibaldi's march either at Naples or in the Romagna, must bar his way in the Abbruzzi and also stop Lamoricière's army from massacring the insurgent populations.[33]

[31] Thouvenel, *op. cit.*, I, 187-191.

[32] Marseilles, 8 Sept. 1860, *Aff. Etr.*, *C.P.*, *Italie*, 350: p. 197. Thouvenel, *Secret*, I, 192-193.

[33] 8 Sept. 1860, *Aff. Etr.*, *C.P.*, *Italie*, 350: p. 194.

On the same day Victor-Emmanuel sent a personal note to the French Emperor justifying Sardinia's move:

> My troops have not crossed the frontiers. Since yesterday insurrections have broken out at many places in the Marches and Umbria. Provisional governments have been named at Urbino and Città della Pieve. They have sent me deputations which are on their way to Turin. I shall accept their protection. I have sent Count Della Minerva to Rome, demanding dissolution of foreign troops.
>
> Garibaldi has declared to a delegation from the city of Naples that he wants to attack Rome. I am going to publish a proclamation in which I declare that Rome must not be attacked. Your Majesty will understand the necessity of stopping Garibaldi [and] sending my troops to the Neapolitan frontier. This is all according to the program explained by Mr. Farini (*tout ceci est conforme au programme exposé par M. Farini*).[34]

Thouvenel was furious when he heard of the action which Cavour had taken. He hurriedly wrote the Emperor that France should take a strong stand since her honor was seriously involved. On the following day he asked the Emperor for the authority to demand that Turin should not follow up the ultimatum or else France would withdraw her minister.[35]

The Emperor's immediate reply was an announcement of a dispatch which he was sending to Victor-Emmanuel. It read as follows:

> Your Majesty knows how devoted I am to the cause of Italian independence, but I could not approve of the means used today to achieve it, for these means go counter to the proposed purpose. If it is true that without legitimate reason Your Majesty's troops are entering the States of the Pope, I shall be forced to oppose it (*de m'y opposer*). I am even giving an order this day for increasing the Roman garrison. Mr. Farini had explained your Majesty's policy to me quite differently (*bien différemment*).[36]

Thouvenel, by that time thoroughly aroused by the state of affairs, suspected that it all took place "as a consequence of the much too generous concessions made by the Emperor to

[34] 8 Sept. 1860, *Archivio di Stato di Torino, carte Cavour,* quoted from Bollea, *Silloge,* pp. 335-336.

[35] 8 Sept. 1860, *Aff. Etr., C.P., Italie,* 350: p. 196. Thouvenel, *Secret,* I, 193-194. 9 Sept. 1860, Thouvenel, *Secret,* I, 195-196.

[36] Marseilles, 9 Sept. 1860, *Aff. Etr., C.P., Italie,* 350: p. 199. Thouvenel, *Secret,* I, 196-197.

Farini."[37] On the other hand the Emperor was not at all in accord with Thouvenel's demand for active opposition. In the French Foreign Office Archives is found a telegram from Napoleon to his minister which was deciphered as follows:

> I fear from your dispatches that you are taking things in Turin too seriously. I mean to threaten but not to act.[38]

Thus we have the Emperor's own interpretation of *de m'y opposer* which he had sent to Turin. It is also evident that his attitude was in conformity with his understanding with Farini whether Sardinia's action was or not. In other words the Emperor seemed "devoted" enough to the Italian cause not to take advantage of their departure from the original agreement.

Thouvenel, left alone with the responsibility of upholding France's honor, had taken the step on his own authority of ordering Talleyrand's recall from Turin unless France was assured that Sardinia would not execute the ultimatum of the 7th.[39] Then on the following day came the Emperor's "threaten but do not act." Seeing that Napoleon's plan and his own were not in accord, Thouvenel wrote the Emperor for an explanation of just what his intentions were. The telegraphed reply found in code in the Foreign Office Archives reveals an added link in the train of the French Emperor's policy toward Sardinia.

> The explanation of my dispatches is that I thought threats enough. Since they are not, here is what I am deciding: Mr. Talleyrand will leave Turin as Drouyn de Lhuys left London in 1850 as a sign of disapproval but not of complete rupture.[40]

Talleyrand saw Cavour at nine on the morning of the 11th and delivered Thouvenel's terse note. Cavour said that he would have to go against Garibaldi. If he had to fight Austria alone, he preferred to "fall fighting." One thing he declared, "The

[37] Thouvenel to Gramont, Paris, 9 Sept. 1860, Thouvenel, *Secret,* I, 188.

[38] "Je veux menacer mais pas agir." Toulon, 11 Sept. 1860, *Aff. Etr., C.P., Italie,* 350, p. 211.

[39] 10 Sept. 1860, *Aff. Etr., C.P., Italie,* 350: p. 203. *Livre Jaune,* (1860), p. 161.

[40] Emperor to Thouvenel, Nice, 12 Sept. 1860, *Aff. Etr., C.P., Italie,* 350: p. 214.

Sardinians would retreat before any opposing French force and refuse to fight them." Since Talleyrand could not change Cavour's determination, he left for Nice to see the Emperor, leaving the legation in charge of Rayneval.[41]

Cavour took Talleyrand's withdrawal calmly seeing in it only an evidence of Napoleon's promised outward opposition.

> It is clear to me that France must not seem to be our accomplice in this expedition. . . . We might be scolded by the Emperor without being disapproved. The Emperor had approved our plan without reserve. He had discussed its chances and even indicated our army's field of operation. It appears probable to me that Mr. Thouvenel, while being aware of the secret thoughts of the Emperor, felt it necessary to separate in a more striking fashion France's policy from that which circumstances force on us.[42]

The Sardinian Minister was pleased to hear that France had sent more troops to Rome. That fact would make Garibaldi more pro-Sardinian and less bold to go against Rome. On every occasion the Italians let it be known that France was really backing the movement. Cialdini was telling the surrendering officers of the Papal troops that the Emperor had said, "Good luck and work fast." The Prince de Ligne repeated the story to Pius IX and Antonelli. Nigra was circulating similar reports in Paris, while D'Azeglio was performing a like service in London.[43] Gramont wrote that "there was not a person (in Rome) who was not convinced of our (France's) complicity with the Piedmontese."[44]

At the time of the first attack by Sardinia a false report was circulated in Rome that France was going to evict the invaders by force. But as time went on and no move was made by the French troops and as the inactivity of Napoleon became apparent, the Pope's and the Curia's anger became more intense. Gramont began to report this attitude in his dispatches to

[41] Talleyrand to Thouvenel, Turin, 11 Sept. 1860, *Aff. Etr., C.P., Italie,* 350: p. 206. *Livre Jaune,* (1860), p. 162. Thouvenel, *Secret,* I, 206-207.

[42] Cavour to Nigra, Turin, 12 Sept. 1860, *Aff. Etr., C.P., Italie,* 350: p. 221. Bollea, *Silloge,* pp. 337-338. Chiala, *Cavour lettere,* IV, 2-4.

[43] Gramont to Thouvenel, Rome, 6 Oct. 1860, Thouvenel, *Secret,* I, 236-238. Cowley to Russell, Chantilly, 4 Sept. 1860, *R.P.,* LV.

[44] Thouvenel, *Secret,* I, 210.

Thouvenel. The Pope had seen Goyon, the French general in Rome, and had declared that the Catholic world would brand His Holiness as a conspirator with France against the Church if he allowed France to continue to protect him after she assumed so vacillating a position. Gramont greatly feared that the Pope would flee and make it appear that French protection was not trusted.[45]

But Thouvenel had already told England that France's position would be one of protecting the Pope in Rome only.[46] Three days later on 24 September he instructed Gramont to inform the Pope of this decision and warn the Holy Father of the dangers to him and the Church should he flee, concluding that France would withdraw should the Pope leave. The latter should tolerate the present situation until a congress could settle the tangled question.[47]

Cavour thought that both England and Prussia were elated at the French rupture:[48] the former because her only rival for Italian favor had been eliminated, the latter because France was thereby alienating her only friend on the Continent. The subsequent attitude of Napoleon, however, could not have been too reassuring to either.

During the month of September 1860 while Napoleon seemed to be winking at the Sardinian invasion of the Church States and Naples, French public opinion was judged to be apathetic to the cause of the Pope. Thouvenel warned Rome that the Pontiff was respected but the *Sovereign* Pontiff was not popular. This feeling was to him quite apparent. French opinion was quite willing to have their army protect the person of the Pope in Rome and leave to a future congress the settlement of the whole question, but it was opposed to a material intervention to regain the lost territories. If the Pope should flee, sincere Catholics would be aroused but there would be an unfavorable reac-

[45] 15 Sept. 1860; 20 Sept. 1860; Thouvenel, *Secret,* I, 198-201, 213.

[46] Cowley to Russell, Paris, 21 Sept. 1860, *Parl. Papers,* (1861), LXVII, 81.

[47] 24 Sept. 1860; 28 Sept. 1860; *Livre Jaune,* (1860), pp. 118-119, 120.

[48] Cavour to Nigra, Turin, 14 Sept. 1860, Bollea, *Silloge,* p. 340. Chiala, *Cavour lettere,* IV, 7.

tion in French public opinion because of that evidence of lack of faith in French policy. They must understand in Rome that "we are no longer in the days of the crusades."[49]

It was well known that Napoleon III kept his ear to the ground for every indication of French opinion. It was not surprising that he should continue the policy of the July Monarchy in requiring regular reports of the state of public opinion from the *procureurs-généraux*, French district attorneys in each judicial division of the country. In November 1849 he exhorted them to send reports every month but by 1858 quarterly reports became the rule and included economic and moral as well as political surveys.[50] The first part of October was the period when the last quarterly reports of 1860 were due. As these began to come in, the Government's conception of the state of French opinion was considerably changed. Only from Aix were there reports of a lack of interest in the Papal cause. Around Bourges opinion was only calmed by the prompt withdrawal of the French minister from Turin, and the dispatch of reënforcements to the Pope. Even in radical Bordeaux general opinion was reported as against the progress of Sardinia in achieving too solid a union on France's south-west boundary. Agens also appeared concerned over a united Italy but more so over the temporal power of the Pope. In Picardy the clericals were declared to be the strongest group. In the *Midi* around Montpellier the moderate people stressed their interest in the Pope and added considerable weight to the Legitimist outcries. The whole report from Brittany dealt with the Roman question and showed that the *Bretons* were decidedly for the Pope in his struggle against Sardinia. From Normandy they summarized opinion in the following manner:

> The solution of the Roman question incontestably causes concern among all serious people from the triple point of view of the pre-

[49] "Le vent n'est plus aux croisades." For the above estimates of French opinion see: Thouvenel to Gramont, Paris, 23 Sept. 1860; same to same, 2 Oct. 1860, Thouvenel, *Secret*, I, 220-221, 231-233.

[50] *Rapports des procureurs-généraux, Ministère de Justice,* 376: circulars, Garde des Sceaux to procureurs-généraux, 21 Feb. 1853, no. 8167a.

ponderance of English influence, the excessive expansion of Piedmont, and the threatened annihilation of the Pope's temporal power.[51]

The British Ambassador reported home a statement by Thouvenel after the Emperor's return to Paris:

The Emperor had become very morose and conversed very little on Italian affairs. . . . His Majesty's perplexity as to what course he shall take is very great. . . . He sees that he is fast losing ground in public estimation in France, and the whole of continental Europe is afraid of him and is suspicious of his policy. This crisis, Thouvenel thinks, cannot be continued. The Emperor must take a resolution one way or the other, and either identify himself with the revolution in Italy or step in to put it down. The Emperor is profoundly disgusted with the proceedings of the Sardinian Government. . . .[52]

Prince Napoleon[53] on his return to Paris stressed the growth of opposition to the Bonapartes in the country but he interpreted it according to his desires and concluded that it was because of its pro-Italian sentiment. He insisted that the Emperor should join whole-heartedly with the Italian cause.[54]

The Emperor was more inclined to heed the ominous signs written in the reports of the *procureurs* than the partisan advice of his cousin. He began cautiously to draw out of his shell of obscurity and ride with the wind. He engaged his pamphleteer, La Guéronnière, to write an article against Sardinia for the semi-official newspaper, *Le Constitutionnel.* This turned out to be very severe toward Sardinia. It was reported that it went beyond Napoleon's intentions, but one incident seems to prove the contrary. La Guéronnière is reported to have submitted his article to Napoleon before publication and the Emperor returned it with the remark: "Fine but not sharp enough."[55]

[51] *Rapports des procureurs,* Caen, 12 Oct. 1860, 375: v. 4; Aix, 6 Oct. 1860, 370: v. 4, no. 4577; Bourges, 3 Oct. 1860, 374: v. 3; Bordeaux, 5 Oct. 1860, 374, v. 3; Agens, 6 Oct. 1860, 370: v. 3; Amiens, 9 Oct. 1860, 371: v. 4; Montpellier, 10 Oct. 1860, 380: v. 4; Rennes, 12 Oct. 1860, 386: v. 4.

[52] 19 Oct. 1860, *R.P.,* LV.

[53] Prince Jerome Napoleon, cousin of the Emperor and son-in-law of Victor-Emmanuel II of Sardinia.

[54] *R.P., ibid.*

[55] "Très bien mais pas assez incisif." Taken from the Journal of Le Comte Horace de Viel-Castel, (19 Oct. 1860); quoted from Thouvenel, *Secret,* I, 253.

The article was published on 12 October under the name of L. Boniface. It began by recognizing the right of the Neapolitans to revolt but denied that Sardinia had any more right to intervene than Austria would have had. It could excuse a revolutionary Garibaldi if he disregarded international law but not a leading European state such as Sardinia. "From every point of view it is impossible not to deplore Piedmont's conduct." It would be Europe's duty "to rectify the breach of the law and recall those governments who have departed from it to a respect for the laws by which all states are obligated."[56]

> The Emperor (remarked Cavour) has his press thunder against us. I am sure his cannon are only loaded with powder. Prince Napoleon applauds us and urges us on to shoot far (*tirar di lungo*).[57]

On the very eve of the Sardinian invasion of the Church States Austria had approached France to sound out the latter's attitude toward Austrian intervention. Thouvenel said that Rechberg, Austrian Foreign Minister, "aimed at nothing less than to obtain full and complete liberty to act as he pleased in Italy after he repulsed an attack against Venetia."[58] Napoleon had replied that he would not defend Piedmont if she attacked Austria, but he would go to her assistance if Austria should violate the treaty of Villafranca after a victory.[59]

But the steady progress of the Italian revolution began to alarm the monarchs of all the Northern Powers. The Czar told Montebello, the French ambassador in St. Petersburg, that he observed that France had said that she would oppose Sardinia's invasion of the Church States. "I am awaiting with impatience the consequences of that declaration. Your position in Europe will depend a lot on what you are going to do." This seemed to have influenced the sending of reënforcements by France to

[56] *Le Constitutionnel,* 12 Oct. 1860.

[57] Cavour to Farini, Turin, 13 Oct. 1860, Chiala, *Cavour lettere,* VI, 616.

[58] Thouvenel to Gramont, Paris, 9 Sept. 1860, Thouvenel, *Secret,* I, 187-191.

[59] Napoleon to Thouvenel, Marseilles, 8 Sept. 1860, *Aff. Etr., C.P., Italie,* 350: p. 197. Thouvenel, *Secret,* I, 192-193.

Rome.[60] However, when these reënforcements appeared to be limited in their activity to the protection of the city of Rome and when France seemed otherwise to encourage the revolutionary movement indirectly, the Czar invited the Emperor of Austria, the Prince-Regent of Prussia, and Thouvenel to come to Warsaw to confer on the matter. Thouvenel declined personally to attend the conference but accepted the suggestion that the Emperor write his opinion personally to the Czar and allow the Czar to present the French point of view.[61]

The Emperor's note explained in more detail his earlier policy in regard to Austria and Sardinia. France would not support a Sardinian attack against Austria as long as no other German power intervened in the conflict. Russia and France should prevent a return of Austrian influence in Italy by demanding the maintenance of the arrangements of Villafranca and Zurich. A future congress to be called by Russia and France should determine the status of the various Italian states "from the double point of view of the rights of the sovereigns at present dispossessed and *necessary concessions to assure the stability of the new order of affairs.*" If Sardinia should lose the Central States in the final readjustment, this fact should not put in question the French possession of Nice and Savoy.[62]

Cavour had not seemed worried about the unfavorable actions of the Emperor. He had kept a placid countenance when Russia had withdrawn her minister and Prussia had declined to recognize the new state of Italian affairs. But he became decidedly alarmed before the prospects of a conference of monarchs including Austria. "The only point on the diplomatic horizon where menacing clouds are likely to gather is at Warsaw," he wrote to the King on 10 October.[63] He begged Gropello, his chargé in Paris, to keep him informed of any news

[60] Montebello to Thouvenel, St. Petersburg, 15 Sept. 1860, F. C. Roux, "La Russie et la politique italienne de Napoleon III," *Revue historique*, (1910-1911), 105: p. 288.

[61] 25 Sept. 1860, *Aff. Etr., C.P., Russie*, 222: pp. 109-110.

[62] *Ibid.* Annex to Thouvenel to Montebello, 25 Sept. 1860. Also Napoleon III to Alexander II, Paris, 20 Oct. 1860, *Aff. Etr., C.P., Russie,* 222: pp. 153-154.

[63] Chiala, *Cavour lettere,* IV, 37.

from Warsaw. On the same day he wrote to Prince Napoleon asking that he help to gather any possible information for him on the Warsaw conference.[64]

The conference took place during the days between 22 and 26 October where a decision of watchful waiting was the result.[65] Thouvenel in an official memorandum, summed up the positions assumed by the Powers at the Warsaw Conference.

To sum up, extremely grave events had occurred in the Peninsula, but the attitudes of the respective Powers . . . had not altered in the least. Austria had renewed the assurance of her intention not to abandon her watchful attitude. Russia, whose policy, formulated because of Piedmont's conduct, had been as close to France's as possible, had openly declared at Warsaw that under all circumstances she would keep a strict neutrality as long as she judged none of her interests endangered (*lesés*). Neither did Prussia encourage any thought of aggression. She had been limited in case of a war in north Italy to the incontestable right of the Germanic Confederation to adopt precautionary measures which her safety might require. As to England, who took no part in the interview of Warsaw and therefore was not informed of the attitude which we announced there, her maxims in regard to non-intervention, similar to those of the Government of the Emperor, could be considered as a guaranty of her intentions. All the powers agreed that this principle (non-intervention) was the one which divided them the least and that the maintenance of the general peace was dependent on it.[66]

Cavour was much relieved by the results of this meeting and he credited France with successfully manoeuvring the Powers into a hands-off policy.[67] But France, who had twice previously warned Austria not to begin an aggressive war or France would reserve full liberty of action in such a case,[68] also warned Ca-

[64] Cavour to Gropello, Turin, 15 Oct. 1860, Chiala, *Cavour lettere,* IV, 34-40. Cavour to Prince Napoleon, *ibid.,* VI, 617-619; F. Masson, "Lettres du Prince Napoléon à Victor-Emmanuel II et à Cavour," *Revue des deux mondes,* Ser. VII, XIV, (1923), 372-374; A. Comandini, *Il principe Napoleone nel risorgimento italiano* (Milan, 1922), pp. 193-194.

[65] For brief accounts of this conference see A. Debidour, *Histoire diplomatique de l'Europe,* Ser. I, II, 224; and Charles Seignobos in Lavisse, *Histoire de France contemporaine,* VII, 126.

[66] Memorandum of Thouvenel to Flahault, Jan. 1861, *Aff. Etr., C.P., Angleterre,* 719: pp. 44-66.

[67] "Grâce au ciel et à l'attitude résolue de la France le péril était conjuré pour le moment." Cavour to Nigra, Turin, 30 Oct. 1860, Matter, *op. cit.* III, 410.

[68] Roux, *loc. cit.,* p. 289.

vour against attacking Austria under pain of losing French support.[69]

The danger of a recurrence of Austrian supremacy in Italy had moved the French Emperor to take a slightly more pro-Sardinian attitude at Warsaw. Since he had gained his point with the Powers, he could as a matter of compensation take a sterner attitude toward Sardinia.[70] This would also stem the tide of resentment at home. Consequently a Bonaparte took the singular step of aiding the Bourbon King of Naples, Francis II, while he was being besieged at Gaëta by the combined Italian forces.

As early as September 26th on his return from the south of France the Emperor conceived the idea of sending a fleet to Gaëta to forestall a Sardinian attack by sea on the remnants of Francis II's army.[71] As the reports of antagonistic public opinion promoted by Legitimist agitation began to come to the Ministry of Justice during the first two weeks of October, it became apparent that something more should be done against Sardinia as a part of Napoleon's plan to oppose publicly the invasion of South Italy. What could be more convenient than to make a gesture of sympathy to this representative Legitimist on the Neapolitan throne? On the day following the article in the *Constitutionnel* Thouvenel announced that Rear-Admiral de Tinan would be ordered to Gaëta to prevent a Sardinian blockade or attack.[72] At the end of the month after the Warsaw conference de Tinan was instructed as to the exact policy of the

[69] Thouvenel to Rayneval, Paris, 6 Nov. 1860, *Aff. Etr., C.P., Italie,* 350: pp. 301-302.

[70] "The Emperor sent [Vimercati] back to explain to us by word of mouth the motives for his conduct toward the King of Naples. It appears that in order to spare our heads from the storm which was being formed at Warsaw, he (the Emperor) promised Russia to help her protégé (Francis II) with his fleet." Cavour to Victor-Emmanuel II, Turin, 16 Dec. 1860, *La questione romana negli anni 1860-1861. Carteggio del conte di Cavour con Pantaleoni, Passaglia, Vimercati.* A cura della commissione reale editrice. (2 vols., Bologna, 1929), [hereafter referred to as *Ques. romana*], I, 135.

[71] Emperor to Prince Napoleon, St. Cloud, 26 Sept. 1860, Ernest d'Hauterive, "Lettres du Prince Napoléon et Napoléon III," *Revue des deux mondes,* XX, (1924), 82-83.

[72] Thouvenel to Gramont, Paris, 13 Oct. 1860, Thouvenel, *Secret,* I, 242-245.

French Government in regard to Gaëta. He had been sent only to assure Francis of a dignified escape. The Rear-Admiral should try to persuade Francis to capitulate. At Warsaw Austria was persuaded to refrain from an attack so that Francis could not expect help from that source. The King was to be reminded that the bad season would soon be on them and the French squadron would be compelled to retire anyway.[73] This last warning would seem to indicate an intention on the part of the French to retire their squadron from Gaëta at an early date.

Both Sardinia and Great Britain were alarmed by this new French move. Great Britain was favorable to the Italian unification movement; her statesmen were out of sympathy with the Bourbon régime in Naples; and she was fearful of an increase of French control of the Mediterranean. Therefore Russell was pleased to find another suitable occasion to champion the Italian cause. Time and again Russell took up with Thouvenel the question of evacuating Gaëta and each time the French Minister explained that France was there only for the personal safety of Francis II, that Tinan was instructed to dissuade the King from further resistance, and that the French Government hoped England would not continue the pressure because it would give the impression that France was submitting to British dictation.

At the same time the Northern Powers tried to counteract the English influence by having their Paris ambassadors press the Emperor to keep his fleet at Gaëta. When their pressure was the most severe, the French showed signs of being more reluctant to leave Francis II.

Sardinia sent Vimercati to Paris during the last part of November (1860) to persuade France to recede from Gaëta. Victor-Emmanuel II even wrote a personal letter to the Emperor. Finally an armistice was arranged by the French between the besiegers and the besieged to last from 10 to 19 January. The French would retire all but one ship on the 14th. That ship would only remain to see that the armistice was observed and

[73] Thouvenel to Tinan, Paris, 30 Oct. 1860, Thouvenel, *Secret,* I, 269-271, (text in full); *Livre Jaune,* (1860), pp. 160-163.

would leave on the 19th if Francis took up arms again after that period.[74]

As the end of the period of truce approached, de Tinan tried in vain to persuade Francis II to leave. On the other hand the ministers of Prussia, Austria, and Russia at Gaëta encouraged the King to continue the conflict. Although these representatives declined to remain with Francis, he finally decided to follow their advice. De Tinan left on the *Bretagne* on the 19th and kept the *Mouette* in readiness in the port of Naples for Francis' use should he plan to escape.

Sardinian hostilities began again, this time by land and sea, and within less than a month surrender was inevitable. Negotiations began on 12 February 1861 and the capitulation followed immediately. Francis II escaped on a French ship and sought refuge finally in Rome under the protection of Pius IX, who had twelve years before been protected by the Bourbon family in the same port of Gaëta.[75]

Since the Gaëta affair is not as directly connected with the theme of this work as some other events, a general account of it will have to suffice. It is enough to observe that the Emperor entered on that venture to satisfy his home opinion and to gratify the other European courts.[76] At the same time Napoleon thought it would be interpreted in Italy only as a part of his aforementioned *public* censure. Panizzi wrote Cavour:

> The Emperor replied that all that had been done was in agreement with the King's Government, and that it would be wrong to consider him solely responsible for what had happened. . . . The

[74] For documentary accounts of the Gaëta phase of the Italian struggle see the following collections: *Aff. Etr., C.P., Italie,* 351: pp. 2-3, 4, 6-9, 30; *C.P., Angleterre,* 718: pp. 160, 213-214, 228; 719: pp. 34-35; *C.P., Rome,* 1016: pp. 203-204. *F.O., France,* 1329: nos. 1058, 1076; 1330: nos. 1240, 1274; 1347: no. 1389; 1348: no. 1408; 1350: nos. 1576, 1615; 1351: nos. 1636, 1673; 1372: no. 1638; 1383: nos. 44, 56. *R.P.,* LV, 17, 20, 24 Dec. 1860. Chiala, *Cavour lettere,* IV, 113; VI, 633, 659, 665. Thouvenel, *Secret,* I, 351-352. Comandini, *op. cit.,* pp. 199-200. Bianchi, *Politique de Cavour,* pp. 390-393, no. 198. *Ques. romana,* I, 97-208, *passim.*

[75] Thouvenel, *Secret,* I, 359-360. *F.O., France,* 1384: no. 108. *Aff. Etr., C.P., Italie,* 351: p. 95.

[76] After the Warsaw Conference the French Ambassador to Prussia wrote that the Gaëta policy of the Emperor "has been viewed here with great satisfaction." Belcastel to Thouvenel, Berlin, 6 Nov. 1860, Thouvenel, *Secret,* I, 293-297.

King knows how the Emperor feels on all that has taken place. But he knows also what the Emperor especially hopes for.[77]

Considering the possible motives which actuated Napoleon's Gaëta policy, it does not seem that England's suspicions of a French attempt to gain more of a foothold on the Mediterranean is justified. The temporary nature of the expedition in the minds of the French would seem to weaken the argument of Mr. Debidour that it was because of English pressure that the Emperor receded from his position.[78] No doubt the English pressure was one influence to hasten the evacuation of Gaëta, but other reasons should be taken into consideration. We know that the expedition was sent with instructions to encourage surrender. If the expedition were to serve as an *outward* manifestation of ill-will toward Sardinia, it is not likely that it was intended to remain long. Furthermore, the French Government was becoming greatly concerned with the approaching Italian elections. If the French prolonged the Gaëta impasse, it might swell the ranks of the Mazzinian radicals. Thouvenel remarked that

the Emperor thinks that the Italian elections should not take place under the influence of a hostile feeling toward France which would play into the hands of the Garibaldians and Mazzinians.[79]

These reasons in addition to the fact of severe weather during the winter and spring would seem to indicate many other factors were as responsible as the English for the French withdrawal. It is likely that Thouvenel stressed the argument of the Italian Parliament to counteract the rumors of English pressure, but the cry of English pressure was greatly exaggerated

[77] Another of those enigmatic statements which were so necessary while the Emperor was trying to make his action an enigma to the Powers. Panizzi to Cavour, London, 7 Dec. 1860, Chiala, *Cavour lettere,* IV, 113-114.

[78] Antonin Debidour, *Eglise et Etat à 1870,* p. 567; *Histoire diplomatique,* Ser. I, II, 226-227.

[79] Thouvenel to Gramont, Paris, 6 Jan. 1861, Thouvenel, *Secret,* I, 342-343. In another note to Flahault, Thouvenel said: "It seems to me that today all depends on the composition of the future Italian Parliament, and we did well, as I see it, to come to a decision as to our squadron in order to remove from the Mazzinians a pretext of bellicose and demagogic declamations on the eve of the elections." *ibid.,* I, 346. This attitude in France is substantiated again in Vimercati to Cavour, Paris, 13 Jan. 1861, *Ques. romana,* I, 191-192.

at the time by the political opponents of the day who desired to make capital of it. It is quite likely that it is from that campaign that the general tendency arose of crediting England with the responsibility.

The Gaëta affair closes the narrative of Italian unification of 1860. While only indirectly concerned with Franco-Italian relations on the Roman question, yet this phase has been given enough discussion to make the French, English, and European positions on Italian affairs stand out more clearly, and will enable the observer to appreciate better the events connected with the later attempts to obtain the French evacuation of Rome.

CHAPTER II

ITALIAN-VATICAN NEGOTIATIONS 1860-1861

THE Peninsula had barely come under Sardinia's control, Cavour had scarcely made sure of France's policy of non-intervention, and the results of the Warsaw Conference were still unknown when the New Italy began to be concerned with the question of obtaining Rome as its capital. Bixio had written Cavour on this subject and the Italian statesman had replied that he was "ready to negotiate immediately provided that negotiations rested on bases acceptable to Italian nationality." But he feared that it would need more than six months to calm the Pope and take cognizance of the new European situation.[1] However, on that same day, 18 October, Cavour took the first step in negotiating with the Vatican for that very purpose. He wrote Dr. Pantaleoni, an influential physician in Rome, that he thought of sending some one to Rome to arrange an exchange of prisoners. At the same time he would have this person find out whether Rome was ready to negotiate on the questions of sovereignty and independence. He ended by asking the doctor "whether this attempt seemed to him to have some probability of success."[2]

Pantaleoni's reply was significant. He declared that in Rome there was so much bitterness that there was little hope of successful negotiations at present. As the Pope and his advisers cooled down, they might relent little by little.

> But there is another way more determined and bold, which, although it might fail right now in Rome, by chance might promise easier and more speedy success in future negotiations, and that is to make from now on the most generous offers of conciliation, claiming that we are ready to accept all the conditions that can be demanded in order to assure spiritual independence showing what great evils there would be for religion, especially in Italy, if Rome opposed all honest conciliation. Sure of a refusal from Rome, the knowledge of such an act

[1] 18 Oct. 1860, Chiala, *Cavour lettere,* IV, 49-50.

[2] *Ques. romana,* I, 60-61. Chiala, *Cavour lettere,* IV, 50-51. N. Bianchi, *Storia documentata della diplomazia europea in Italia, 1814-1861* (8 vols., Turin, 1865-1872), VIII, 694-695. D. Pantaleoni, *L'Idea italiana della soppressione del potere temporale dei Papi* (Turin, 1884), pp. 159-160.

would unmask at one stroke the hypocrisy, ambition, and avarice of the priests, who go about under the mantle of religion. On the one hand the public opinion of the honest and truly religious men in Europe would be gained, and on the other hand the responsibility for the harm which would result for the Church would be thrown on Rome, and the Italians would be set on the real road whereby Rome would be obliged to yield to the necessity of coming to an agreement. The decision at this point of the advisability of that line of policy rests with you alone, my dear Count, since you have well in hand the facts which determine just how far France will go hand in hand with us on the Roman question, and whether there is a possibility of a Congress in which one could help to force the question by a decisive act approved by European public opinion.[3]

This letter of Pantaleoni's was only one in what was to become a long negotiation in the form of exchanged notes. From its tone it would seem at the beginning that there was some insincerity on the Italian side. "Sure of a refusal from Rome" seemed to be the basic axiom. And closely allied with it was the idea of "unmasking Roman hypocrisy" before France and Europe.

By the end of October the good news from Warsaw had arrived and had relieved Cavour of the fear of an Austrian invasion. Thereupon he began immediate negotiations for the reciprocal release of Roman and Italian prisoners. Mr. de Corcelle was sent to Turin from Rome. At this conference Cavour intimated that an arrangement with France for the evacuation of Rome in return for the guaranty of Papal sovereignty over a trans-Tiber city might be a future possibility.[4] This could have been little more than a daydream of the Sardinian Minister, but it was used to try to break down the morale of the Papal Court.

During all this time Pantaleoni had been spurred on by Cavour's encouragement to sound out the Curia as to possibilities of negotiating. He had approached Father Passaglia, a friend, who was influential at the Court both as an expounder of the dogma of the Immaculate Conception and as a member of a Theological and Canonical Council. These two, the physician for Italy and the priest for the Church, drew up a scheme for political and

[3] Rome, about 26 Oct. 1860, Chiala, *Cavour lettere,* IV, 52-55. Pantaleoni, *op. cit.,* pp. 160-163. Similar ideas were expressed by Pantaleoni to Cavour in a note of 23 Oct. 1860, *Ques. romana,* I, 63-66.

[4] Gramont to Thouvenel, Rome, 10 Nov. 1860, Thouvenel, *Secret,* I, 320.

ecclesiastical reconciliation. They then sent it to Cavour for his advice and approval. The ecclesiastical part does not concern to any great degree the subject of this work, but it is of special interest to study the political clauses and Cavour's reactions to them. The latter are given in parentheses after each clause.

1. The Pope shall be recognized as a nominal sovereign although sovereignty shall not be exercised over any territory. (I approve.)

2. His person shall therefore be inviolable and shall not be subject even civilly to any prince. (I approve.)

3. For the double reason of rightful recompense and of national gratitude and veneration there shall be assigned to him as his own such amount of landed property (*beni stabili*) as by common consent may seem sufficient not only for the necessities but also for the dignity of the Most Holy Pontiff and his Court. (I approve in principle but I reserve the discussion on the nature of the property. I do not believe that it is indispensable that all this property be in land or all located in Italy. Indeed, it appears to me that it would be better for the dignity and independence of the Pontiff if he had acquired property elsewhere and if he could dispose of it as he pleased, that is as real or movable property, to the extent of the amount assigned to him.)

4. This property shall be declared immune from all taxation and from all political action by the Government. (I approve the tax exemption, but there must be clarifications as to the immunity from any political action by the Government. What does that clause mean? Under no guise can it be permitted that such territory become a place for sheltering criminals or delinquents, or that it be immune from regulations concerning police, justice, and hygiene, etc.)

5. An equal inviolability is accorded to the Conclave, at the time of a vacant See and to the Chamberlain and officials who represent the Pope before the former is convoked. (I approve, and what is more, in the case of a conclave I propose the abolition of the veto exercised by certain states.)

6. The Holy Pontiff shall be most free to send for ecclesiastical purposes legates, nuncios, and other ministers, whose inviolability shall be observed as long as they keep to the ecclesiastical nature of their missions. (I approve as far as it concerns our own state within the limits of the ordinary diplomatic customs.)

7. All Christians, without exception, shall be allowed the freest access to the Pontiff for ecclesiastical matters. (I approve and for non-Christians as well, subject to the surveillance of the laws of the State. The residence of the Pope can not serve as an asylum for delinquents, neither from our country nor from another.)

8. The above provisions shall form a part of the fundamental laws of the Kingdom and shall be regarded as resulting from a bilateral

contract and in compensation for the renunciation of the exercising and possessing of temporal dominion. (I approve.)

9. In case of difficulties the guaranty of the Catholic Powers could even be invoked. (I accept good offices or mediation, but I can admit neither guaranty nor any similar obligation which would serve as a pretext for conflicts or foreign intervention.)[5]

Both the political and ecclesiastical provisions were constructed on the basis of a free Church in a free State. Although the Pope was to lose his temporal power, the State was to sacrifice its policy of religious supervision. Whereas the spiritual authority of the Church in other Catholic states was restricted by concordats, in Italy it would be unlimited.

With this plan as a working basis Passaglia then approached one of the more liberal Cardinals, Santucci. He presented the latter a memorandum in which he stated that the whole Catholic world was gradually losing sympathy with the political principles of the Papacy. In Spain, Portugal, France, Belgium, Italy, Bavaria, Austria, and South America liberal governments were being given the hearty support of devout Catholics. In Belgium and Poland the clergy furnished the leaders of the liberal movement. The clergy was becoming divided in its attitude toward the policy of the Popes. It should also be remembered that it was the political opposition that caused the Lutheran schism in Germany. Certainly the Church did not want the same to happen throughout Italy and Europe. The Russian and Greek Churches were quite as strong spiritually without their temporal power as they had been with it. Lastly, little independence could be enjoyed when it had to be supported by the presence of a foreign army. It was the duty of the liberal cardinals to prevail in the counsels to the Pope over the influence of the blind Jesuitical forces who would lead the Holy Father to his downfall by fostering an uncompromising attitude.[6]

It was just at this time that Cavour actually received from

[5] *Ques. romana,* I, nos. 67, 75, 79. Chiala, *Cavour lettere,* IV, 102-103, (28 Nov. 1860). Pantaleoni, *op. cit.,* pp. 169-170. An English translation is also found in Hudson to Russell, Turin, 27 April 1861, *R.P.,* LXVIII.

[6] Memorandum presented to Santucci about 11 Dec. 1860. Pantaleoni, *op. cit.,* pp. 173-186. A more accurate copy was found in the Italian Foreign Office Archives and published in *Ques. romana,* I, 121-131.

Napoleon III a plan of solution for the Roman question. Vimercati was engaged by the Emperor to deliver the plan in person to Cavour. The nature of the plan was to return to the Pope the Marches and Umbria and then arrange for Victor-Emmanuel to rule all the Church territory as the vicar of the Pope. Italian soldiers would replace the French as protectors of the Church and the Pope.[7]

Cavour sent Vimercati back with a reply which rejected the French plan in preference to that sent to Pantaleoni. Cavour wanted some assurance that Rome would become the Italian capital. He also declared that the Italians would not now countenance the return of Umbria and the Marches to the Pope after Castelfidardo. The Italians had become convinced of the need of abolishing the temporal power. Therefore any veiled suzerainty such as the vicariat plan inferred would be inacceptable. Besides neither the Pope nor any of the factions of the Curia would accept the Paris plan which did not offer fuller spiritual independence.

> The Paris plan is therefore doubly defective in our opinion. It accords too much to the partisans of temporal power, and it does not accord enough to those who believe in the necessity of its abolition. The Turin plan starts from an opposite point of view. It proposes the abolition of the temporal power . . . but in compensation [it] would give to the Church and to its Chief the greatest liberty of action in spiritual matters.

Cavour then proceeded to describe in detail the plan which he had sent to Pantaleoni as well as the steps which had been taken in Rome up to that time.[8]

Realizing the importance of the new French element in the situation Cavour wrote Passaglia to keep the negotiations quiet and not to go too fast pending word from Paris. On the other hand it began to appear that Cavour became more sincere about the seriousness of these negotiations. If he gained French cooperation in this project and at the same time obtained all that he desired, there would be no object in desiring to put the Roman

[7] Memorandum from Napoleon III to Cavour, Paris, about 15 Dec. 1860, *Aff. Etr., M.D., Rome,* 124: after 28 July 1859. *Ques. romana,* I, 132-135.

[8] Turin, about 22 Dec. 1860, *Ques. romana,* I, 140-144.

Court in a bad light. A purely Italian-Vatican accord would be still more in harmony with the policy of foreign non-intervention. Thus Cavour even went so far as to obtain from the majority of his cabinet the permission to make the acceptance of the aforementioned plan a Cabinet question before Parliament.[9]

Rumors about the negotiations were beginning to leak out, however, in both Italy and France. Cowley, British Ambassador to Paris, suspected that Napoleon wished to keep his fleet at Gaëta in order to have more influence on the Pope to help some negotiations in progress between Italy and Rome.[10] Gramont warned Thouvenel against aiding this rumored negotiation because the loss of the temporal power would be a gain for Italian unity, which in turn would be a menace to French security.[11] But contrary to this advice Napoleon encouraged Cavour to continue the negotiations although he saw little chance that they would succeed.[12]

The gentle and sincere Cardinal Santucci, disliking the more worldly and aggressive Jesuit element, was thoroughly moved by the clever arguments of the Pantaleoni-Passaglia memorandum. No doubt the emotional state caused by the Christmas celebrations added to his alarm, so that, the Christmas and New Year activities once over, he determined to introduce the subject of conciliation to Pius IX. The evening of 10 January was the time of the usual Thursday audience that Santucci had with the Pope. This time instead of giving the Holy Father general advice on matters of contemporary concern the aged Cardinal informed the Pope of the Pantaleoni arrangement which he had been given in a friendly and confidential way. He observed that it provided for the abolition of the temporal power but gave in return precious concessions which ought to serve at least as an acceptable basis for negotiations. The Pope was much moved

[9] Cavour to Pantaleoni, Turin, 27 Dec. 1860, Chiala, *Cavour lettere,* IV, 136-138. Bianchi, *Storia documentata,* VIII, 695-696. Pantaleoni, *op. cit.,* pp. 187-189.

[10] Cowley to Russell, Paris, 24 Dec. 1860, *R.P.*, LV.

[11] 29 Dec. 1860, Thouvenel, *Secret,* I, 335-337. Chiala, *Pagine,* I, 17.

[12] Conneau to Vimercati, Paris, 13 Jan. 1861, *Ques. romana,* I, 191. "L'Imperatore . . . mi ha caricato dirle . . . , etc."

and immediately called in Antonelli. The latter observed that their vows as cardinals forbade negotiating on the subject of territorial cessions. But they were all favorably enough disposed so that Antonelli and Santucci asked to be loosed from their vows in that respect and the Pope after some reflection assented. They were to ask Italy to send official representatives, some one known and respected by the Vatican, preferably no lawyer nor ecclesiastic.[13]

At this juncture Cavour received word that the Emperor approved of the negotiations.[14] Napoleon had only approved the negotiations and not the plan, a typical Napoleonic precaution, but Cavour interpreted it as an approval of his plan. He replied that he was pleased with France's approval, he reiterated his determination to keep in agreement with French policy, and ended by assuring the Emperor that this plan contained nothing dangerous to France. In fact Cavour saw eventually in this arrangement a modification in the relations between state and clergy generally. Especially it would benefit France by enabling her to retire from Rome.[15]

The French Government took a greater part in the Turin-Rome negotiations than just that of a benevolent observer. First Napoleon sent some private agents to Rome to sound out the Vatican on its views of his own plan. These reported back that Rome considered such terms as "impossible." "This step was taken semi-officially and secretly, and the refusal . . . was formal."[16] It was after this news that the Emperor indicated his willingness to have Cavour try out his plan in Rome. After the French withdrawal from Gaëta and the frequent manifestations

[13] Relazione fatta dal Nigra, 17 April 1861, *Carteggio Cavour-Nigra,* IV, 369-371. Teccio (for Pantaleoni) to Cavour, Rome, 13 Jan. 1861, Chiala, *Cavour lettere,* IV, 149.

[14] "L'Empereur Napoléon répond qu'il verra avec plaisir que l'on poursuive les négociations avec Rome, qu'il souhaite leur succès mais qu'il en espère peu." Vimercati to Cavour, Paris, 13 Jan. 1861, *Ques. romana,* I, 191. E. Artom, *L'Opera politica del Senatore I. Artom nel risorgimento italiano* (Bologna, 1906), p. 187.

[15] Cavour to Vimercati, Turin, 16 Jan. 1861, Chiala, *Cavour lettere,* IV, 152-154. *Ques. romana,* I, 200.

[16] Vimercati to Cavour, Paris, 27 Dec. 1860, 30 Dec. 1860, *Ques. romana,* I, 152, 159.

of the Papal displeasure toward France, Thouvenel, Persigny, and the Emperor decided to aid Cavour indirectly in his negotiations with Rome by inferring that France would not back Rome in its uncompromising attitude. This was to be done by the preparation and publication of a brochure. Persigny wrote it in quite strong terms and ended with quite definite conclusions. The Emperor finally decided to omit the conclusion, which might make it too emphatic. But he left it so that the reader would be forced to form the same conclusions as Persigny had written. There is no doubt as to the Emperor's coöperation in drawing up this pamphlet, neither is there any question as to its purpose. The Emperor told Vimercati in an audience of 9 February:

> I shall see with the greatest pleasure the conclusion of the arrangement which you are about to make and a pamphlet which is going to appear has been written for the purpose of helping you to succeed.[17]

Persigny, being the Minister of Interior, did not publish the brochure himself. He let one of his subordinates, La Guéronnière, have the credit of being its author but no one doubted but that it was inspired by the Emperor. Persigny had given it the title *Le Pape et l'Empereur* but that was thought to be too pointed. So, out of deference to the wishes of the Emperor, the title was modified to *La France, Rome, et l'Italie.* It appeared on 15 February 1861 and created quite a sensation.

Its purpose was to show that the Emperor was not so blindly attached to the Pope that he would support him under all circumstances. It was to convey the idea that the Emperor would be very displeased if the Pope did not come to an agreement with Italy, and to suggest that France would abandon Rome if the Pope did not accept a reasonable compromise. It can be seen that such an attitude would help considerably to strengthen the Italian position and weaken that of the Pope in the Roman negotiations. Yet, while the tone of the eventual pamphlet was

[17] Vimercati to Cavour, Paris, 9 Feb. 1861, *Ques. romana,* I, 274.

distinct enough to show its inclinations, it was too mild to cause great concern.

> Italy is a great interest of civilization and European order. She found her place only in history; but she made it in active politics and the diplomacy of nations. It is as difficult to conceive of Italy without the Pope as to conceive of the Pope without Italy. They are both connected by historical tradition and by the universal respect of Catholic nations for the Head of the Church. When the Emperor went against Austria, it was his intention to reëstablish this precious connection. The day when this great purpose will have been accomplished the Pope will be seen to recover in modern society an authority as high as his origin and his mission. . . . In the meantime and in spite of so many refusals by France to intervene, in spite of so many injustices, which have not diminished his devotion, the Emperor, we are convinced, will leave his sword in Rome to protect the security of the Holy Father. Faithful to his double rôle of sovereign elected by the national will and of eldest son of the Church, he can not sacrifice Italy to the Roman Court nor deliver the Papacy into the hands of revolution.[18]

This brochure failed to frighten the Pope and Antonelli into an accommodation with Italy, but it succeeded in showing the Emperor's interest in Italy and in exciting the attention of ministries and chanceries throughout Europe. Lord Russell remarked that "in these days pamphlets are events,"[19] and this latest one proved no exception to the rule.[20]

After Santucci's conference with Pius IX and Antonelli, Passaglia was also to have a conversation with them. Cavour was so informed and he waited to hear the results of this. No news came and the Sardinian minister began to be worried. Time and again he wired Pantaleoni for the promised information without any results.[21] Finally after more than ten days of such suspense on 31 January he began to distrust Rome's intentions. To Vimercati he wrote: "Nothing very definite from Rome on our negotiations. . . . I am advancing with the greatest reserve

[18] L. E. A. Vicomte de la Guéronnière, *La France, Rome, et l'Italie* (Paris, Dentu, 1861).

[19] Russell to Cowley, London, 24 Dec. 1860, *F.O., France,* 1330: no. 1273.

[20] Documentary accounts of the writing and publishing of this pamphlet can be found in Vimercati's dispatches in *Ques. romana,* I, 202, 211-212, 274, 280, 294, 297.

[21] Chiala, *Cavour lettere,* IV, 151, 157. Bianchi, *Storia documentata,* VIII, 697. Pantaleoni, *op. cit.,* pp. 190-191.

and looking closely to right and to left in order not to make a *faux pas*."[22]

It was sometime during this period of anxiety and doubt that Cavour started another channel of negotiation with Rome.[23] Omero Bozino, a lawyer of Vercelli, had gone to Rome on business. Since Bozino was acquainted with Isaia, the secretary to Cardinal D'Andrea, one of the cardinals more favorable to Italy, he had been able to gain some more light on the situation in accord with the suppositions of the Emperor's agents. The Abbott Isaia, after conferring with Bozino, had gone to Aguglia, a confident of Antonelli's, who in turn had acquainted Isaia confidentially with some of Antonelli's personal obstacles to a successful rapprochement. Through the indirect agencies of Aguglia and Isaia, Bozino had been given some very delicate information. With the return of Pius IX to Rome in 1849 under French protection Antonelli had come into power. He had at once set about to put his family and their friends into very lucrative offices by which through doubtful procedures they had been able to enrich themselves magnificently.

> In order to realize to a greater degree his plan, he put his most devoted satellites at the head of the public administrations instructing them to put some of the income from those offices to his account and he agreed to allow them to keep a part for themselves. So it was seen that Luigi Antonelli, his brother, was put at the head of the Roman municipality; his other brother, Filippo, was made president of the Bank; the lawyer Massani was put in charge of the Loan Office; Monsignor Ferrari, the Finance Department; Marquis Ferrajoli, the Tobacco Office; and they worked out all by such arrangements the plans of Antonelli so that in a few years they made him one of the richest proprietors in Europe.[24]

[22] Turin, 31 Jan. 1861, Chiala, *Cavour lettere,* IV, 161-162. Bollea, *Silloge,* pp. 425-426.

[23] Cavour had received on 24 Dec. 1860 a note from Vimercati which reported a conversation with the Emperor: "Secret agents sent to Rome (by France) declare that Cardinal Antonelli *for certain conditions entirely personal* could not only enter into the designs of the Emperor but help in the accomplishment of his projects. The Emperor seems not to wish to stop at any sacrifice in this matter." *Ques. romana,* I, 146.

[24] This revelation was found in the papers of Bozino many years after the annexation of Rome by Italy. It was never divulged by Bozino or other Italian negotiators, although Cavour's correspondence shows that they knew of it. So this secret could not have been manufactured to put Antonelli in

It was explained to Bozino that such a system would be in danger of apprehension if Italy took over the civil government. In order to protect the Antonelli name and interests it was proposed that

1. A veil be thrown over the contracts and administrations held by the Antonelli brothers in the various departments (*corpi morali*); their administration of them was even to be approved.
2. Cardinal Antonelli be paid 3,000,000 scudi for the expenses of the negotiation.
3. Decorations and honors be distributed to the brothers of Cardinal Antonelli.[25]

Bozino on his return immediately wrote Cavour recounting the whole episode, and added that Antonelli would probably be willing to treat on the basis of the following terms: 1) The Pope should recognize the Kingdom of Italy by crowning Victor-Emmanuel and permitting the capital to be in Rome. 2) The Pope should have suzerainty of the Patrimony with the Italian King as Vicar. 3) Assurance should be given to cardinals without bishoprics of an income of at least 10,000 scudi. 4) The right of the Italian cardinals to sit in the Italian Senate should be granted. 5) A civil list should be furnished to the Pope.[26] It must be noted that apparently Antonelli had had very little to do with this negotiation up to this point. There had only been indirect suggestions by his private secretary to D'Andrea's private secretary.

Cavour, on learning of the nature of the Bozino negotiation, requested the latter to come to Turin and report orally.[27] This additional phase of the negotiations having been brought to light, it is easier to understand some rather cryptic phrases in Cavour's subsequent correspondence. To Vimercati on 6 Febru-

a bad light. On the other hand it reveals how well the Italians could keep a secret when they wanted something very much. This was published by G. C. Faccio in an article entitled "Tentativi di Cavour per risolvere la questione romana nel 1860-1861," *Nuova Antologia,* (1 June 1912), pp. 416-417.

[25] *Ibid.*

[26] Orvieto, 27 Jan. 1861, *Ques. romana,* I, 222-223.

[27] 2 Feb. 1861, *ibid.,* I, 258. N. Argenti, "Una fase poca nota nella questione romana," *Nuova Antologia,* (Sept. 1911), pp. 133-135.

ary he reported that "the Pope is undecided; one day he says *no*, the next *yes*. Antonelli is quite perturbed."[28] On 11 February, when Cavour discussed in a letter to Pantaleoni the use of money for bribing, he wrote:

> I give you permission to spend as much as you think necessary to gain the friendship of lower officials of the Curia. But when it becomes necessary to have recourse to such means on a large scale for the big fish (*pesci grossi*), let me know about it and I will set about arranging it but by some other channel than that of the negotiators, who from my way of thinking should remain strangers to this less beautiful part of our undertaking.[29]

After his verbal conference with Bozino, Cavour wrote him the following veiled instructions:

> I beg you to pass on to your correspondent in Rome (Isaia) a letter of the following tenor: 'Having talked with Count Cavour, I am convinced that he is disposed to enter into serious negotiations. . . . The Count has a high opinion of the ability (*abilità*) and resourcefulness of Cardinal Antonelli. I believe therefore that he can be easily induced to do all that may be opportune, either for the above-mentioned Eminence or for his family in order to make them favorable to the projected work of pacification.'[30]

On 19 February Bozino reported news from Isaia in Rome to the effect that Aguglia had seen Antonelli and had actually opened negotiations. The bases of the Vatican-Italian accord were similar to those suggested previously by Isaia to Bozino with some additional terms which would protect the ecclesiastical interests and activities of various religious orders, provide for the going and coming of diplomatic representatives to and from the Pope, guarantee the absolute freedom of the Italian clergy in religious affairs, insure the *status quo ante 1859* in case of the disruption of the Italian union, and finally furnish some solemn guaranties of fulfillment and execution. "Then only would [Antonelli] permit the formal negotiations with our lawyer (Aguglia)."[31]

[28] Turin, 6 Feb. 1861, Chiala, *Cavour lettere,* IV, 166-167. Bollea, *Silloge,* p. 427.

[29] Chiala, *Cavour lettere,* IV, 170-171. Pantaleoni, *op. cit.,* pp. 195-196.

[30] 14 Feb. 1861, Chiala, *Cavour lettere,* IV, 173. *Ques. romana,* I, 290-291.

[31] Isaia to Bozino, Rome, 17 Feb. 1861, *Ques. romana,* II, 12-13; I, 298-299.

Eventually a courier arrived from Pantaleoni (31 January 1861) with news of the other phase of the negotiations. It was reported to Cavour that six cardinals (D'Andrea, De Silvestri, Amat, Boffondi, De Pietro, and Santucci) were favorable to the project. The Pope was undecided and Antonelli perturbed.[32] He also learned that Passaglia was leaving for Turin to confer on what future steps to take. However, Bozino's information made Cavour more cautious. He tried to delay Passaglia's departure, but by the time his telegram arrived, it was too late to prevent it.[33]

Although Cavour invited Passaglia to his own home, the priest stayed at a hotel and tried to keep his mission a secret. He conferred with Cavour and Minghetti and came to an agreement with both as to the articles to form the bases of the negotiations. He returned to Rome on 12 February 1861 with an outline of the revised project.[34]

The new bases of agreement worked out together by Cavour, Minghetti, and Passaglia contained two major concessions to the Church on political matters which had not been included in the former proposal of 28 November 1860. The first concession gave positive guaranties of power and income to the College of Cardinals. They were to have the titles and honors of princes; the Pope was to be given enough extra property to furnish a sufficient income for the cardinals; and finally, a certain number of cardinals would be appointed to the Italian Senate by the King with the possibility of an additional income from this office.[35]

The second concession, which was not as apparent as the first, dealt with the possibility of negotiating on the basis of the Leonine City plan. The lack of the positiveness of this conces-

[32] See note no. 24. 19, 22 Jan. 1861, *Ques. romana,* I, 206-208, 212-214.

[33] Chiala, *Cavour lettere,* IV, 165, 166. *Ques. romana,* I, 258, 259, 261, 269.

[34] Cavour to Pantaleoni, Turin, 11 Feb. 1861, Chiala, *Cavour lettere,* IV, 170-171; Pantaleoni, *op. cit.,* pp. 195-196; *Ques. romana,* I, 278-279. Cavour to Nigra, Turin, 14 Feb. 1861, Chiala, *Cavour lettere,* IV, 172; Bollea, *Silloge,* p. 430. Gramont to Thouvenel, 23 Feb. 1861, *Aff. Etr., C.P., Rome,* 1016: pp. 420-430.

[35] Project and annexed instructions, Cavour to Pantaleoni and Passaglia (Bianchi and Artom copies), 21 Feb. 1861, *Ques. romana,* I, 314, 316, 322, 327.

sion was due to the fact that it was not to be a part of the proceedings unless the regular proposal of the abolition of the temporal power failed. The Leonine City plan was essentially that of the recent Vatican City arrangement of 1929. According to this plan the Pope would be sovereign over a certain area of Rome on the right bank of the Tiber. In Minghetti's first memorandum of 1 February after the clause dealing with property to be consigned to the Pope, Cavour noted that "if the Pope asks to be allowed to keep his sovereignty over the Leonine City, you may negotiate on the question."[36] This note gives a clue to the position which Cavour was assuming. However, in the final instructions the Sardinian Prime Minister did not mention this compromise on the question of the temporal power. While the instructions were based on the "renunciation of the temporal power,"[37] on the other hand Cavour left his representatives enough latitude to admit a discussion on this minimum vestige of temporal power. In the first place the Pope was assured of the possession of the Vatican and certain palaces "which were not to be subject to the jurisdiction of the state." This renunciation of jurisdiction was not to be granted until some treaty had been made for the return of fugitive criminals, and, according to the Bianchi copy, "in case the Papal delegates made too extreme demands in regard to the palaces [the Turin delegates were] to ask for new instructions."[38] The Artom copy, which certainly reflects Cavour's ideas at one stage of their formulation, is more specific, and declared that "whenever the Pope asked that his sovereignty over the Leonine City be preserved, the proposal may be received *ad referendum*."[39] Thus it is seen that although Cavour did not exactly concede to the Pope the Leonine City, he at least was ready to accept negotiations on that question.

Passaglia acquainted Antonelli with the new concession on the 21st. On 19 February Passaglia had seen D'Andrea to ask

[36] "Potrà trattarsi." *Ques. romana,* I, 253.
[37] Bianchi and Artom copies of instructions, *Ques. romana,* I, 312, 321.
[38] *Ques. romana,* I, 314, 316.
[39] "Si potrà accogliere la proposta *ad referendum.*" Instructions (Artom copy), *Ques. romana,* I, 327.

him to bring his colleagues together to consider the question of reconciliation. D'Andrea had spoken to Cardinals Boffondi and De Silvestri on the 20th and to Santucci on the 21st and they had concurred on the advisability of negotiating. Santucci had seen the Pope on the 21st but the Pope was so aroused over the arrival of vanquished Francis II that the timid Cardinal had deemed it prudent not to discuss the subject. Isaia repeated the account of a conversation between Aguglia and Antonelli in which Antonelli said, after his audience with Passaglia on the 21st, that he was tired out by the conversation over religious matters. Furthermore, the Cardinal Secretary of State had expressed the fear that the Pope might refuse to negotiate if he were approached at this particular moment since he had been so deeply moved by the arrival of Francis II.[40]

Cavour held to his policy of engaging France as a potential auxiliary in these negotiations by keeping the Emperor informed.

> The Emperor is informed of everything. He takes the liveliest interest in this attempt and had it stated time and again through Conneau that he would be most happy if this accord could enable him to withdraw the French troops from Rome. He even offered to employ his secret channels of influence over Antonelli to aid our project, but I am going slowly in accepting this offer of which I shall take advantage only in case of necessity. . . .[41]

As the Sardinian Prime Minister began to draw up the final instructions and draft project for the pending negotiations, he dutifully sent copies and summaries to Napoleon with the request to keep them absolutely secret, especially from Gramont.[42]

The information furnished by Cavour to France was kept quite consistently secret from Gramont. There were enough rumors abroad at the time to justify Thouvenel in asking Gramont whether he had heard of negotiations.[43] But Gramont re-

[40] Passaglia to Cavour, Rome, 23 Feb. 1861, Thouvenel, *Secret,* II, 4-9. Argenti, *loc. cit.,* p. 135.

[41] Cavour to Nigra, Turin, 22 Feb. 1861, Chiala, *Cavour lettere,* IV, 178-179. Bollea, *Silloge,* p. 431. *Carteggio Cavour-Nigra,* IV, 342-343.

[42] Cavour to Vimercati, Turin, 21 Feb. 1861, Chiala, *Cavour lettere,* IV, 177-178. Bollea, *Silloge,* p. 431.

[43] 20 Jan. 1861, Thouvenel, *Secret,* I, 359-360.

plied on 26 January that there was not a word of truth in such rumors.[44] None the less Gramont began to investigate more thoroughly and found that there was a certain amount of activity but no direct negotiations. On 9 February he reported the consultations between Pantaleoni and Passaglia. This was only to get the advice of a great canonist on the ecclesiastical law involved. Gramont admitted that the Pope and Antonelli had been engaged in conversations, but these had nothing official in them. Passaglia had seen Santucci and the latter had seen the Pope, but it seemed to be only a question of religious matters. The Pope was severe with Santucci saying that he was always ready to negotiate with any sovereign, with the Sultan of Turkey or the King of Sardinia, on purely religious questions in their lawfully possessed territories, but he would not discuss either religious or political questions with Victor-Emmanuel if they pertained to the territories stolen from others. The French Ambassador went on to tell of Passaglia's trip to Turin. He had asked for the Pope's permission but the Holy Father refused to allow or prohibit the journey. The Pope had declared that "he knew that Count Cavour was all ready for, and resigned to, a refusal and this refusal was one of the arguments to be used against Rome." Gramont agreed with this Papal prediction and added further that France had better be on her guard because the next Piedmontese move was to get France to promise to leave Rome if this refusal were given.

Gramont was also assured by the Vatican that a public denial would soon be published.[45] This came out on 16 February which would make it seem that Gramont's informant, if not Antonelli, was one very close to that Cardinal. The public denial published in the *Giornale di Roma* read as follows:

> There are many diffused declarations and letters from France which pretend to confirm that the Holy See is secretly treating with the Piedmontese Government on the present troubles in Italy. This is absolutely without foundation; and the very persecution from which the Church is now suffering (ecclesiastical laws in the Marches, Um-

[44] 26 Jan. 1861, Thouvenel, *Secret,* I, 364.
[45] *Aff. Etr., C.P., Rome,* 1016: pp. 333-340.

bria, and Naples) is enough in itself to refute the above-mentioned rumors which have been started (*divulgata*) perhaps purposely.[46]

Napoleon III was so desirous of the success of the Italo-Vatican negotiations that he wrote directly to Pius IX asking him to consider favorably the possibility of a reconciliation with Sardinia. But the Pope in his reply of 14 February refused to come to any terms with Sardinia while his territory was being held by that government. He indirectly blamed France for the loss of the territory and declared that he could not give up territory belonging to the Church. Plebiscites could not determine ownership because what God had given only God could take away.[47]

Up to this time Gramont had not been informed of what Paris knew about the negotiations.[48] But on the 10th of February Thouvenel wrote him some of the information on the negotiations. "They continue to assert that confidential conversations are in progress . . . and that Cardinal Antonelli is less opposed to [them] than is generally supposed."[49] This circumspect statement from home arriving soon after the dispatch of his report of the Vatican denials to Paris (9 February) distressed Gramont. Had both Paris and the Vatican been deceiving him? Cowley wrote home from Paris that Thouvenel admitted that Gramont had not previously known of the Turin-Vatican negotiations and "is evidently furious at having been kept in the dark."[50] In this mood Gramont went directly to Antonelli soon after Passaglia reported to the Cardinal on his mission from Turin. This was before the 23rd and not on the 28th as Argenti claimed.[51] Then it was that Antonelli positively denied his negotiations with Turin and recounted his disapproval of Passaglia's treating on political questions and his indignation at Cavour's disguised threat. In turn he implicated the Emperor

[46] *Giornale di Roma,* 16 Feb. 1861.
[47] *Aff. Etr., M.D., Rome,* 124. Thouvenel, *Secret,* I, 446-456.
[48] Argenti, *loc. cit.,* p. 136.
[49] Thouvenel to Gramont, Paris, 10 Feb. 1861, Thouvenel, *Secret,* I, 401-403.
[50] Cowley to Russell, Paris, 18 Feb. 1861, *R.P.,* LVI.
[51] Argenti, *loc. cit.*

in the movement by citing Passaglia's declaration that "the propositions . . . were concerted with Emperor Napoleon."[52] From this time on Antonelli declined to negotiate further with any Turin representatives for fear of compromising himself at home and abroad.[53]

Thouvenel fathered the Vicariat plan which would in addition give the Pope the islands of Sardinia and Elba as the property necessary for his support.[54] Cowley knew of this plan in March when he said that "the Emperor still hopes upon his project of a direct understanding between Rome and Turin by the cession of the island of Sardinia to the Pope." This was shown to Palmerston who noted at the end that France would like the Pope to go to Sardinia so she could follow him and take possession of that Mediterranean island.[55] As a matter of fact the Emperor did make a suggestion of the transfer to the Pope of the island of Sardinia to Vimercati through Conneau, but the proposal was never intended to be anything more than a suggestion.[56] So much apprehension was aroused over this rumored plan in Italy and in England that Cavour had to deny the seriousness of any such proposal.[57]

After Passaglia had left Turin, Cavour intended to draw up the new terms into a definitive proposal, enclose official credentials for Pantaleoni and Passaglia, include confidential letters to Antonelli, D'Andrea, and Santucci, and finally to dispatch at the same time secret instructions to Pantaleoni, Passaglia, and Isaia to guide them in the double negotiations. Minghetti had gone to Milan with the King and his absence delayed the instructions because Cavour depended on Minghetti almost exclusively

[52] Gramont to Thouvenel, Rome, 23 Feb. 1861, *Aff. Etr., C.P., Rome,* 1016: pp. 420-430.

[53] Argenti, *loc. cit.*

[54] "Copie sur une minute de M. Thouvenel." *Aff. Etr., C.P., Rome,* 1017: pp. 106-107.

[55] Cowley to Russell, Paris, 1 March 1861, *R.P.*, LVI.

[56] Conneau to Vimercati, Paris, 25 Feb. 1861, *Ques. romana,* II, 10-11. Including a photostatic copy of Conneau's autographed letter.

[57] Cavour to D'Azeglio, Turin, 16 March 1861, Bianchi, *Politique de Cavour,* pp. 406-407. *Parl. Papers,* (1861), LXVII, 1-2. Cavour to Vimercati, Turin, 10 April 1861, *Ques. romana,* II, 134. Chiala, *Cavour lettere,* IV, 208-209.

for advice on this question.[58] The lack of an English courier delayed the instructions for a further period but finally the whole group of important documents were sent on 21 February 1861 in the care of Father Molinari, a Rosminian monk.[59]

This packet of documents contained instructions and credentials for Pantaleoni and Passaglia and a letter for Antonelli requesting him to consent to negotiate by appointing his official delegates. Two other letters of a similar nature for Cardinals D'Andrea and Santucci were also in the collection.[60] Cavour wrote Nigra the following day that "the instructions . . . were drawn up by Minghetti and myself and in such a way as to be able to be published in case of an obstinate refusal on the part of the Roman Court to welcome the proposals."[61] Thus Cavour was preparing for either eventuality.

It was at this stage of the negotiations that Bozino's activities again came into prominence. Bozino, after consulting Cavour, had replied to Isaia's letter of 17 February mentioning Aguglia by name and discussing "pecuniary clauses of the most delicate nature."[62] This letter had been stopped by Antonelli in the Roman post-office, and he became very much alarmed because they were mentioning names of persons so close to him and in connection with suggestions of bribery.[63] He thereupon reprimanded Aguglia for the lack of secrecy and declared he would no longer negotiate.[64]

[58] Cavour to Pantaleoni, 11 Feb. 1861, Chiala, *Cavour lettere,* IV, 170-171. Pantaleoni, *op. cit.,* pp. 195-196.

[59] Cavour to Teccio, Turin, 20 Feb. 1861, Chiala, *Cavour lettere,* IV, 176. Pantaleoni, *op. cit.,* p. 197. Cavour to Pantaleoni, Turin, 21 Feb. 1861, F. Salata, *Storia diplomatica della questione romana* (1st vol., Bologna, 1929), I, 16-17.

[60] Cavour to Pantaleoni, Antonelli, D'Andrea, and Santucci, Turin, 21 Feb. 1861, Salata, *op. cit.,* I, 16-20. *Ques. romana,* I, 307-331.

[61] Chiala, *Cavour lettere,* IV, 178-179. *Carteggio Cavour-Nigra,* IV, 342-343. Bollea, *Silloge,* p. 431.

[62] Reported in Passaglia to Cavour, Rome, 26 Feb. 1861, *Ques. romana,* II, 19-20.

[63] "Antonelli ha fermato alla posta la lettera del Vercellese che veniva al basso agente di Roma, e truovandovi (*sic*) discorso di milioni, o ha simulato, o ha veramente preso collera al vedere che si parlasse così allo scoperto, e pare che abbia o rotto con quel basso agente o al meno lo abbia minacciato di rompere." Pantaleoni to Cavour, Rome, 3 March 1861, *Ques. romana,* II, 29.

[64] Faccio, *loc. cit.,* pp. 425-427.

In the early part of February Cavour had instructed Teccio, his consul in Rome, to request that Father Bertetti, General of the Rosminians, "let Father Molinari return to Rome," "not as a negotiator, but to bring our instructions to Passaglia and Pantaleoni and let them know our thoughts fully."[65] Thus it was that the Curia knew of the significance of Molinari's voyage at a time when Antonelli was on the point of putting an end to the negotiations. Bertetti was ordered to go to Civita-Vecchia and prevent Molinari from coming directly to Rome. Bertetti obeyed and Molinari was obliged to go on to Naples with the instructions, project, and credentials. This delaying of the instructions by sending Molinari around to Naples seems to have been a part of a scheme of Antonelli to have the negotiations fail through the appearance of dilatoriness on the part of Cavour. Both he and the Pope began to complain of the delay in the arrival of the Passaglia-Pantaleoni instructions and credentials, and they intimated that they suspected bad faith on the part of the Piedmontese Government.

In the meantime Pantaleoni and Passaglia were sending frantic telegrams and letters to Cavour asking him to hurry credentials and instructions, inquiring as to the causes of the delay, complaining about evidences of separate negotiations with the Vatican by Bozino and Manteucci, and warning him that the anti-Church policy in the ecclesiastical affairs of the Marches, Umbria, and Naples was compromising the possibilities of opening negotiations.

To all these communications Cavour replied by explaining the flight of Molinari to Naples with the necessary papers, and denying any serious negotiations by Bozino and Manteucci. He persisted in the right to regulate ecclesiastical affairs according to the Sardinian program untii negotiations should produce a compromise to the possible benefit of the Church.

The credentials and instructions sent by Cavour on 21 February did not arrive in Rome by the way of Naples until 14 March. By the time that Antonelli and the Pope were informed

[65] "Connaître le fond de nos pensées." 5 Feb. 1861, *Ques. romana,* I, 262.

of the receipt of full powers by the Sardinian representatives, the former were so firmly resolved not to continue the negotiations that they not only refused to treat but threatened Pantaleoni with arrest and caused him to flee for safety on 21 March. Passaglia was able to linger in Rome six months longer but he too, after a longer series of incidents displeasing to the Vatican had occurred, had to flee from Rome in the guise of a shepherd.

Poor Santucci in attempting to stem the tide of Papal wrath unfortunately chose the day to visit the Pope in the service of the cause of reconciliation just when the Pope was about to refuse emphatically to negotiate. The Pope so upbraided and threatened him that he never recovered from the shock of the interview. The elderly Cardinal gradually became demented and died five months later. On the same day, 18 March 1861, in a consistorial allocution Pius IX declared that he would not negotiate with the Sardinian Government so long as it possessed any of the former Church territory.

In spite of the discouraging aspect of the Roman negotiations both Cavour and Napoleon continued in apparent hopes of success from a reconciliation until the first part of April. But Antonelli's rupture of the Bozino negotiations, his publication of the denial in the *Giornale di Roma,* his expulsion of Pantaleoni from Rome, and the Pope's allocution finally bore down upon the Italians and French the realization of the finality of the *non-possumus.*[66]

Many commentators on this negotiation have suggested what they considered to be the cause for its failure. Although each opinion usually suggested a different cause, a careful examination of the available documentary material tends to confirm the conclusion that nearly all these suggested causes had some weight in the final decision. Antonelli was certainly fearful that his se-

[66] The facts on this negotiation and especially on the last phase can be found in the following references: *Ques. romana,* I, 307-331; II, 12-85, *passim.* Raffaele de Cesare, *The Last Days of Papal Rome 1850-1870* (N.Y., 1909), pp. 297-310. Relazione fatta . . . dal Nigra . . ., 7 April 1861, *Carteggio Cavour-Nigra,* IV, 369-371. Faccio, *loc. cit.,* pp. 416-420. Argenti, *loc. cit.,* Chiala, *Cavour lettere,* IV, 136-138, 187-191, 192-194. Pantaleoni, *op. cit.,* p. 200. Thouvenel, *Secret,* II, 7-8. Bianchi, *Storia documentata,* VIII, 695-696. Arbib, *loc. cit.,* p. 675. Bollea, *Silloge,* p. 435.

cret proposals might be revealed. When Gramont pressed him for an explanation, the Cardinal Secretary of State no doubt chose the easiest and most pleasant way out of the difficulty by denying the negotiations and thereafter he remained consistent by not pursuing them further. Cavour's veiled threat through Passaglia that not only the Church but even the persons of the Pope and Cardinals might be endangered by any resultant religious revolt, if it did not arouse Antonelli, at least served as a pretext for great indignation. There is ample testimony from many sides that the arrival of Francis II in Rome had a very adverse effect on the course of the negotiations by engaging the sympathies of the Pope and many others of influence in the Roman Court. Finally, and of equal importance, was the knowledge that Spain, Austria, and other Catholic Powers were considering the calling of a congress to settle the Roman question.[67] Such a meeting would avoid the humiliation of having to treat with Sardinia alone. It might also enable the Church to preserve more of its power and territory. Besides, the Vatican could not help but suspect that the whole Sardinian program was insincere in that it only wanted to force the Church into a bad light. Nor were these suspicions entirely unfounded. The simultaneous appearance of all these factors would seem to give an inevitable trend towards the *non-possumus*. That Pius and Antonelli gave the Sardinian proposals as much attention as they did, is probably to be explained largely by the natural desire to burn no bridges behind them in a period so full of uncertainty.

[67] Antonelli told Passaglia that he positively would not negotiate. When Passaglia observed that the nationalist movements in the Catholic countries were desirous for an understanding between Italy and the Pope, Antonelli replied, "You are mistaken, my professor, . . . this very morning the Spanish Government announced to me that it had taken on itself the task of persuading the Catholic Powers that the temporal power is absolutely necessary for the free independence of the Pope . . . and that they should undertake to resist the plan of Piedmont . . . by protests and every other opportune means." Passaglia to Cavour, Rome, 6 April 1861, *Ques. romana,* II, 117.

CHAPTER III

CAVOUR'S NEGOTIATIONS WITH FRANCE

AS FRANCE and Italy became more and more certain of the impossibility of a reconciliation with Rome, they began to consider seriously the advisability of an independent Italian-French agreement on the Roman question. In a letter of 14 February the Pope had declared to Napoleon III that he positively would not negotiate with Italy until that Government had restored all the stolen territory to the Church.[1] Cavour himself was informed of the absolute refusal of the Pope just a week before the French offered him a definite proposal.[2] To the Sardinian statesman even a partial solution by joint French and Italian action would be preferable to one by a European congress. Italy especially did not want a congress since it might easily become an occasion for encouraging outside intervention in the Italian Peninsula.

Before the Emperor would treat with Italy separately on the Roman question, however, he took time to consult public opinion at home and scrutinize the diplomatic situation abroad. The reports of the *procureurs* for the first of the year 1861, while showing many evidences of Clerical sympathies, were not as positively pro-Vatican as they had been the previous autumn. From Agens came the news that the majority was opposed both to the Italian union and to English influence but was desirous of some definite action. The region around Besançon showed a general state of irritation toward the Emperor because he seemed to abet the spoliation of the Pope's territory by Italy. Montpel-

[1] *Aff. Etr., M.D., Rome,* 124: (14 Feb. 1861).

[2] On 19 March Passaglia reported to Cavour a conversation with Antonelli which showed distinctly the Cardinal's firm determination not to treat. He would consult the Pope, however, before giving a final answer. "Ed ekli (Antonelli) a me: no, Professore, *no si può trattare.* Udite per la seconda e per la terza volta queste parole. . . . Avendomi ripetuto che udirebbe Sua Santità, mi aggiunse che egli medesimo mi avrebbe presso sè richiamato probabilmente lunedì." *Ques. romana,* II, 67. Finally on 6 April Passaglia wrote that the Pope himself positively refused to negotiate: "Sua Eminenza . . . recisamente asserì, che la Santa Sede . . . era . . . risolutissima a non trattarne col Governo di Sua Maestà." Same to same, *ibid.,* p. 116.

lier reported the active opposition of the combined Clericals and Legitimists, while in Brittany, although they favored Italy's independence from Austria and did not respond to the Pope's call for men and money, yet they were opposed to Italy's union and preferred the separation of the Papal States and Naples from the North. In Bordeaux the Clerical party had quieted down and in Lyons a desire for France to extricate herself from Italian affairs was mingled with the disapproval of the Pope's attitude of *non-possumus*. Part of the account from Lyons ran as follows:

> Wise and reflective men . . . proclaim that the Emperor has done everything possible to reconcile two powers necessary to Italy and they greatly deplore the blindness of the Court of Rome. The largest number desire that . . . [the Government] continue to protect the Holy Father, and defend his religious interest without openly opposing the unification movement.[3]

These reports were not as unanimously favorable to the Pope and anti-Italian as the October ones had been. It seemed as if at least a slight reaction had taken place. The date of the convening of the legislature was nearing. This might also give an indication of public opinion and enable the Emperor to suggest the trend of his policy.[4]

At the opening of the sessions of the French Senate and Legislative Body (lower house) it was the custom for the Emperor to address it on the state of the nation and the policy of the Government. The Government toward the end of January 1861 began, therefore, to consider seriously its policy toward Rome and Italy. It was decided that the Emperor would be rather laconic. He was only to say that extra troops had been sent to protect the Pope when he had suddenly found himself in a more dangerous position. Any further explanation was to

[3] *Rapports des procureurs*, Agens, 7 Jan. 1861, 370: v. 4; Besançon, 19 Jan. 1861, 373: v. 5; Montpellier, 8 Jan. 1861, v. 4; Rennes, 18 Jan. 1861, 5 Feb. 1861, 386: v. 4; Bordeaux, 10 Jan. 1861, v. 3; Lyons, 1 Jan. 1861, 7, 22 Feb. 1861, 379: v. 5.

[4] The Emperor had given the legislature the right to discuss and reply to his address by a decree of 24 Nov. 1860. This gave the groups a chance to criticize and defend the Imperial policy. Permission to publish the debates was also given at this time.

be given by members of the Government in the debates.[5] The Emperor delivered his address on 4 February:

> . . . If France had sympathies with all that is great and noble, she did not hesitate to condemn all that violates the law of nations and justice. . . . In Italy . . . my Government in accord with its allies felt that the best way to avoid greater dangers was to have recourse to the principle of non-intervention, which leaves each country master of its own destinies, localizes questions, and stops them from degenerating into European conflicts. . . .
>
> I shall not let myself be sidetracked by any . . . extremes of excitement. It suffices for the country's greatness to maintain its rights where they are unquestioned, to defend its honor where it is attacked, to lend assistance where it is implored in the name of a just cause.

He barely mentioned the reënforcements for the Pope, as Thouvenel had predicted, and excused his withdrawal from Gaëta with the reason that the presence of the fleet "gave rise to erroneous interpretations," "obliged us every day more and more to depart from the system of neutrality . . . because, you know, in politics they hardly believe in any purely disinterested action."[6]

He had suggested a veiled censure of Sardinia for "violating the law of nations and justice," but had balanced that with a defense of non-intervention. The question of temporal power had not been mentioned. England was no doubt the one he had in mind as one of those who believed in no disinterested action. In all, it was a colorless speech taking its cue from a rather colorless public opinion.

The evidence of the state of parliamentary opinion began to show up in the debates on how to phrase the address in reply to the Emperor's speech. The friends of the Government wanted as little as possible said on the Roman question so as to leave the Emperor free in the future. Some statement as to the support of the Pope's spiritual authority was thought by this group

[5] Thouvenel to Gramont, Paris, 3 Feb. 1861, Thouvenel. *Secret,* I, 387-389.

[6] Emperor's speech to the Legislature, Monday, 4 Feb. 1861, *Moniteur universel.*

to be enough. However, a bare majority seemed to favor a definite declaration in favor of the temporal power.[7] In the original motion sent to the bureau, it was worded so as to hope that His Majesty "will continue to maintain and defend . . . the independence and sovereignty of the Holy See."[8]

In all the controversy at this time Prince Jerome Napoleon took an active part. He was a member of the Senate bureau charged with wording the section of the address on Rome and Italy. There he warmly defended the Italian cause.[9] At Court he began to defend and expand a plan for the solution of the Roman question similar to the present Vatican City arrangement. He was even suggesting the possibility of being sent to Turin and Rome to sound them out on such a proposal.[10] After La Rochejacquelein, one of the most fiery Clericals of the Senate, had delivered a rather scathing speech on the Italian situation, Prince Napoleon became very much aroused. It is said that he went to the Emperor and asked permission to reply and to have *carte blanche* as to what he should say. The Emperor is supposed to have consented providing the Prince avoided personalities.[11]

It was quite an event in the Senate, when the rights of public debate had been so recently extended, to see the cousin of the Emperor rise to make a formal speech. Considerable interest was aroused from the fact that it was suspected he would oppose La Rochejacquelein and that he might be reflecting the opinion of the Emperor. His speech, delivered on 2 March, lasted over three hours and was spoken in a very vigorous manner interspersed with clever repartee in reply to frequent interruptions. He denounced the governments and policies of Austria, the Pope, and the Bourbons of Naples. He cited document after document to show that the Bourbons had been against liberty, the interests of the Church, and the interests of France while the

[7] Cowley to Russell, Paris, 11 Feb. 1861, *F.O., France,* 1385: no. 214.
[8] Cowley to Russell, Paris, 18 Feb. 1861, enclosure, *R.P.,* LVI.
[9] *F.O., ibid.*
[10] Cowley to Russell, Paris, 25 Feb. 1861, *F.O., France,* 1386: no. 275.
[11] Cowley to Russell, Paris, 5 March 1861, *R.P.,* LVI.

Bonapartes had always favored liberty, the *spiritual* interests of the Church, and the welfare of France. Then, with the permission of the curious Senate, he launched forth into an explanation of his idea of a solution of the Roman question. Although he favored the abolition of the temporal power, he now sacrificed it for the Vatican City idea.

> Glance at a map of Rome and you will see an extraordinary thing that nature has done. The Tiber dividing that city: on the right bank you see the Catholic city, . . . on the left bank you see . . . all the great imperial relics.

The Pope's spiritual and temporal authority should be guaranteed in the Vatican City and his possession of ecclesiastical property on the left side should be permitted. Imperial Rome should go to Italy and become its capital. The Pope should be furnished a generous civil list by the Catholic powers and given special and mixed jurisdiction over contested matters.

> History gives us an example of this neutrality: Washington, that federal city which has been for a long time the object of respect from the whole American continent. You will have, in like manner, an oasis of Catholicism in the midst of worldly tempests.[12]

The speech made a great sensation and started much speculation as to how much it reflected the Emperor's opinion. Although the Emperor did not want himself committed to so radical and positive a plan, he put himself in a difficult position by immediately sending a note of congratulation to the Prince.

> Although I do not share all your opinions, I wish to congratulate you, however, on the immense success you obtained yesterday in the Senate.[13]

The Emperor did not mean this note to be made public, but in some way it reached the outside world and caused both the Emperor and the Prince much embarrassment. Cowley thought that the Emperor really approved the ideas in the Prince's speech because despite the fact that Billault, the parliamentary spokesman of the Government, on the following day said that "the Government recognized nothing and adopted nothing which

[12] *Moniteur,* 2 March 1861.
[13] D'Hauterive, *op. cit.,* pp. 212-213. Comandini, *op. cit.,* pp. 208-209.

might be said by any other person than their own agent," he did not use one word which might be interpreted as a disapproval of Prince Napoleon's speech.[14] Thouvenel also was evasive at first in his attitude toward the Prince's suggestion:

> Although Prince Napoleon said some fine things and showed evidence of great talent, you will easily understand that I decline any solidarity with some (*quelques-unes*) of his ideas.[15]

In his next communication to Flahault, Thouvenel revealed the general position of the Ministry to the proposals of the Prince and at the same time gave evidence that France despaired of the Italian-Vatican negotiations.

> Among the ministers M. de Persigny is the only one I know who approved it.
>
> I foresee no solution of the Roman question which is a big internal embarrassment. To abandon the Pope is just as difficult as to support him, and an accord between him and Victor-Emmanuel is impossible.[16]

Another evidence of a little more Clerical color to the ministerial complexion is found in the fact that while Billault at an earlier date had avoided any definite statement as to the Papacy, he came out about 24 March strongly favoring the continuance of the French occupation of Rome.[17] Gropello, Sardinian chargé in Paris, wrote confidentially to Cavour that "the speech (Prince Napoleon's) . . . was the revelation of the intimate thoughts of the Emperor. . . . Some people in the Prince's entourage slipped me a word on this subject."[18] It appears from the above facts that the Emperor knew of the Prince's ideas, allowed him to expound them, and warily congratulated him on some indefinite parts of it. All this was no doubt in order to gain a more definite idea of public opinion. The Prince would resemble a decoy. The Emperor was going to burn no bridges when public opinion was so uncertain. If he commended the speech, his ministers were

[14] Cowley to Russell, Paris, 4 March 1861, *F.O., France,* 1385: no. 318.

[15] To Flahault (in London), Paris, 5 March 1861, Thouvenel, *Secret,* I, pp. 467-469.

[16] 11 March 1861, Thouvenel, *Secret,* I, 487-488.

[17] Cowley to Russell, Paris, 25 March 1861, *F.O., France,* 1388: no. 460.

[18] Paris, 9 March 1861, *Carteggio Cavour-Nigra,* IV, 356.

allowed to disapprove it. Thus uncertainty responded to uncertainty.

Nevertheless the tone of the Senate became more certain when on 9 March it passed the Roman clause of the address with the words:

> Your filial affection for a holy cause . . . has been evinced unceasingly in the defense and maintenance of the *temporal* power of the Sovereign Pontiff, and the Senate does not hesitate to give its most entire approval to all the acts of your loyal, moderate, and persevering policy.[19]

This was entirely out of line with the desire of the Ministry and in stressing the temporal power was unsympathetic with the Prince's position if not with his plan.

The effect on Thouvenel of the debates and vote of the Senate was quite marked. He had previously been rather neutral with a slight tendency in favor of Italy. He now interpreted the Senate's pro-Vatican position as a reflection of French public opinion. He declared that the Emperor could not withdraw from Rome and that Italy would have to be satisfied and organize what she had already obtained. "The best way to conquer Rome would be by the moral example of a contented unity of the rest of Italy."[20]

While Napoleon's Government was trying to discover which way the wind of public opinion was blowing in order to set their sails in that direction, a definite blast came up from across the Channel. As early as the dispatch of De Tinan to Gaëta, Russell was grumbling about the French occupation of Rome. He failed to see the reason for so much fuss over the temporal power and independence of the Pope when the Papacy was actually dependent on France for what little temporal authority remained.[21] But the British Foreign Secretary was not willing to press the matter on France during the last part of 1860.[22]

[19] *Moniteur,* 9 March 1861.

[20] Cowley to Russell, Paris, 25 March 1861, *R.P.*, LVI; 26 March 1861, *F.O., France,* 1388: no. 463. For a complete discussion of the Parliamentary debates see Maurain, pp. 486-498.

[21] Russell to Cowley, London, 3 Nov. 1860, *F.O., France,* 1329: no. 1077.

[22] Russell to Cowley, London, 1 Dec. 1860, *R.P.*, CIV.

Cowley had a conversation with the Emperor on 11 January in which the Emperor intimated that the most he could do for Italy was to withdraw his troops from Rome. The Emperor wished Sardinia might persuade the Pope to allow the substitution of the Sardinian garrison for the French. Cowley told the Emperor he "might just as well think of jumping over the moon." Cowley suggested the evacuation of Rome by a similar method as that of Gaëta. "[His Majesty] appears to have some scheme in his head . . . by which he hopes to bring the Pope and Victor-Emmanuel to terms."[23] This report interested Russell so much that he forwarded it to the Queen.[24]

If the Emperor was in the process of thinking out a prospective solution, Russell had evidently decided that it was time for England to depart from her attitude of watchful waiting and strike while the iron was hot. Seizing upon the French idea that the first step of the solution must be an arrangement for the French evacuation of Rome, Russell dispatched a vigorous note to Paris to that effect. He said that he had forborne to say anything definite on the subject before but the situation in Rome was becoming so bad that he could refrain no longer. The Papal army which they intended to increase, made up of adventurous mercenaries, was found to be lawless and dishonest. Supplies were secretly being sent over the boundary to aid the brigands against the Sardinian forces of order. The Italians were not allowed to go at war against the Pope because of the French occupation.

> The Emperor wishes not to interfere and yet his authority is used to prevent the Italians from settling their own affairs. . . . That [the French troops] remain there indefinitely to keep an ecclesiastical fiction, to the great detriment and danger of the Italian people, seems neither just nor reasonable.[25]

Cowley took the matter up with Thouvenel but the latter would say very little on the subject except that he felt sure that the reports sent to London must have greatly exaggerated the

[23] Cowley to Russell, Paris, 11 Jan. 1861, *R.P.*, LVI.
[24] Russell to Cowley, Pembroke Lodge, 12 Jan. 1861, *R.P.*, CIV.
[25] Russell to Cowley, London, 25 Jan. 1861, *F.O., France,* **1372**: no. **107**.

conditions in Rome.[26] Russell was also at this time relaying reports from Odo Russell in Rome giving information about the Sardinian-Vatican negotiations. When Gramont was questioned about the matter, he charged that England was helping Sardinia to circulate these rumors in order to put the Curia in a bad light.[27]

Cowley had an interview with Napoleon III about the first of March at which time the Emperor appeared very desirous of an arrangement between Italy and the Pope by the cession of the island of Sardinia to the latter.[28] When Cowley observed that that settlement could not possibly endure, the Emperor replied, "If it only lasts a year or two, that is all that is necessary." The British Ambassador explained that the Emperor inferred that he would no longer feel responsible for the Pope if he could once withdraw his army.[29] This attitude on the part of Napoleon is significant in the light of future negotiations. Time and again on later occasions it will be seen that he favored temporary expedients in order to get out of Rome and at the same time delude the French people and the Pope into thinking that such arrangements would be permanent. It is just as possible, however, that the Emperor indicated such a motive to the English and Italians with the insincere purpose of reassuring them of his desire to withdraw at any cost.

Toward the end of March Cavour gave his declarations in the Italian Parliament in favor of Rome as capital with the consent of France.[30] This statement together with the apparent failure of the negotiations in Rome, led many to think that France and Italy would soon attempt to settle the question by

[26] Cowley to Russell, Paris, 29 Jan. 1861, *F.O., France,* 1384: no. 159.

[27] Gramont to Thouvenel, Rome, 9 Feb. 1861, *Aff. Etr., C.P., Rome,* 1016: pp. 333-340. Cowley to Russell, Paris, 5 Feb. 1861, *R.P.,* LVI.

[28] Napoleon III had actually suggested through Conneau to the Italian chargé the transfer of the island of Sardinia to the Pope in exchange for Rome. "Esso (the Emperor) ha aggiunto che se il Re alle condizioni indicate aggiungesse la sovranità della Sardegna, l'Imperatore pensa che la cosa potrebbe avere più di probabilità di riuscire." Conneau to Gropello, Paris, 25 Feb. 1861. *Ques. romana,* II, 10.

[29] Paris, 1 March 1861, *R.P.,* LVI.

[30] This is discussed more fully on pp. 64-65.

themselves.[31] At the same time Cowley reported that while at a reception at the Tuileries he found "that His Majesty is at a complete non-plus as to what to do in Italy."[32] The possibility of a Franco-Italian accord and the apparent imperial *tabula-rasa* led Russell to follow up his January protest with a definite proposal of a temporary expedient. In order to encourage quiet in Rome and Italy, Russell said, the French should only occupy Rome, Cività-Vecchia, and the territory joining the two. Viterbo and Terracina would then become Italian. This would quiet the Italians for a while during the early critical days and still the French would be strongly enough situated to hold their position.[33]

The reception of this proposal was very cool. Thouvenel told Cowley that England was preventing evacuation rather than helping it by her dispatches because if the French public saw the French policy conforming itself to the desires of the British, it would swell the ranks of the Clericals and prevent the withdrawal from Rome.[34] As a matter of fact negotiations had already begun between Paris and Turin on the Roman question. Cowley heard rumors of them and informed his Government of as much as he knew.[35] While Lord Russell continued to insist on the feasibility of his proposals,[36] yet the continued reports which he received from many quarters of the Franco-Italian negotiations caused him to desist his pressure in deference to this hopeful sign.

While examining closely the situation as it was just prior to the negotiations between Cavour and France, we should not ignore the events in the newly assembled Italian Parliament. On 21 February 1861 the bill for recognizing Victor-Emmanuel II as King of Italy instead of King of Sardinia was presented to

[31] Odo Russell to Russell, Rome, 30 March 1861, *R.P.*, LXXV. "When Paris and Turin begin to negotiate about Rome I dare say I may have some useful and curious things to write you from here."

[32] Paris, 1 April 1861, *R.P.*, LVI.

[33] To Cowley, London, 5 April 1861, *F.O., France,* 1374: no. 412.

[34] Cowley to Russell, Paris, 12 April 1861, *R.P.*, LVI, Thouvenel to Flahault, Paris, 21 Feb. 1861, Thouvenel, *Secret,* I, 441-442.

[35] Paris, 23 April 1861, *R.P.*, LVI.

[36] To Cowley, London, 17 April 1861, *F.O., France,* 1375: no. 463; 24 April 1861, *R.P.*, CIV.

the Senate amid great enthusiasm. By the 17th of March both houses had passed it and it was proclaimed by royal decree.[37] The formal consummation of Italian unity had hardly been removed from the legislative calendar when it became apparent that the question of Rome was to take its place in the parliamentary discussions. The Pope on the following day (18th) had issued his consistorial allocution refusing negotiations with Italy. This was followed in less than a month by a vigorous protest against the proclamation of the Kingdom of Italy.[38] This had led Cavour to feel the impossibility of negotiations with Rome and to turn to Parliament and France for another means of attacking the problem.

Very early in 1860 before Garibaldi's expedition Zanolini in the Sub-Alpine Parliament had proclaimed the idea that "Rome should be the capital of a great kingdom and not of a small state."[39] In October of the same year after the success of Garibaldi had been assured, Cavour was moved to take up that thorny question in the Chamber:

> For the last twelve years the polar star of Victor-Emmanuel has been the aspiration of national independence. What will be this star in regard to Rome? (Movement of attention.) Gentlemen, I tell you openly, our star is to have the Eternal City, on which twenty-five centuries have accumulated every species of glory, become the splendid capital of the Italian Kingdom. (Tremendous and prolonged applause.)[40]

These would seem rather strange words from the man who one month before had agreed with Napoleon III at Chambéry that Sardinian troops were to go to check Garibaldi in order to preserve Rome for the Pope. Yet the French Emperor had continued his Chambéry program of public opposition and secret acquiescence.

At last in March 1861, with apparently little hope of a suc-

[37] Cavour to Nigra, Turin, 22 Feb. 1861, Chiala, *Cavour lettere,* IV, 178-179; *Carteggio Cavour-Nigra,* IV, 342-343, no. 1266.

[38] Arbib, *loc. cit.,* p. 675. Antonelli circular, Vatican, 15 April 1861, *Aff. Etr., C.P.,* Rome, 1017: pp. 152-153.

[39] Arbib, *loc. cit.,* pp. 674-675.

[40] Chiala, *Pagine di storia,* I, 17-18. Matter, *Cavour et l'unité italienne,* III, 432.

cessful direct arrangement with the Vatican, Cavour was to follow Pantaleoni's early advice and reveal the attempted negotiations with the Vatican, put that party in a bad light, and win the good will of France. He engaged his friend, Audinot, to interpellate him in the Chamber on the Roman question.[41] After declaring his belief that Rome should be Italy's capital, Audinot turned to Cavour with these words:

> Word has gone around of negotiations with the Roman Court. . . . What are these negotiations . . . and is there any truth in these rumors?
>
> [The] principle of non-intervention is being observed neither in Rome nor the Patrimony of St. Peter. . . . I ask the President of the Council whether he has begun negotiations so that this principle . . . will be applied to the advantage of the Romans?
>
> As a third question I ask the President of the Council what are his governing principles in the solution of the great problem presented by the temporal and spiritual power of the Pope?[42]

Cavour arose and answered point by point the prearranged questions of his friend. ". . . Without Rome as capital of Italy, Italy can not be constituted." He intimated that Turin should be the capital until Rome was annexed after which the northern city should relinquish the honor. He continued by recounting the attempted negotiations directly with Rome and its failure. He declared that the Church should be freed from the temporal power. Cavour cleverly propounded the theory that the Pope was right in insisting that the temporal power would not admit of democratic reforms. But in that case the temporal power should be surrendered and its place should be taken by a new arrangement embracing a free Church in a free State. As to the means of attaining these ends he concluded:

> We must go to Rome, but with two conditions, we must go there in accord with France, and . . . without lessening the independence of the Papacy . . . without the power of the civil authority being extended to control that of the spiritual.[43]

[41] Rayneval (French chargé) to Thouvenel, Turin, 23 March 1861, *Aff. Etr., C.P., Italie,* 351: pp. 170-171. Grabinski, "Lettres prince Napoléon et Napoléon III," *loc. cit.,* p. 644.

[42] *Atti ufficiali del Parlamento italiano* (*1861-1874*), Chamber, 25 March 1861, pp. 134-135.

[43] *Ibid.,* pp. 135-137.

On the following day, 26 March, Boncampagni made the motion that—

> The Chamber, having heard the ministerial declaration, and confident that the dignity, position, and independence of the Pontiff and the complete liberty of the Church will be assured, that the application of the principle of non-intervention may take place in conjunction with France, and finally that Rome, acclaimed capital by national opinion, may be delivered to Italy; passes to the order of the day.[44]

After Cavour asked for the support of this motion in preference to others of a more violent nature, it was passed on 27 March.[45] On 9 April Cavour made similar declarations in the Senate, but by that time little thought remained of a direct arrangement with Rome.[46] Consequently his words were intended more for the French. "I want my attitude (*manière de voir*) on the Roman question to become popular in France." Through his correspondence with Prince Napoleon, Vimercati, and Conneau he continued his attempts to move France to help solve the problem independently of Rome.[47]

It will be of interest to see what was the Vatican's attitude toward France at the time of the Italian move to woo the French from Rome. One would expect to see an especially benevolent attitude on the part of the Pope toward the Emperor in order to forestall the Italian manœuvres. But, on the contrary, the Holy Father seemed angry with France. The Pope and his Court showed themselves extremely chagrined by the fact that the French limited their protection of the Holy See to Rome and the Patrimony. The Vatican had hoped that the

[44] *Atti ufficiali,* 26 March 1861, p. 144. Arbib, *loc. cit.,* p. 678. "*Delivered* to Italy" was changed to "*joined* to Italy."

[45] *Ibid.,* 27 March 1861, p. 156. Arbib, *loc. cit.,* pp. 678-679.

[46] Rayneval to Thouvenel, Turin, 10 April 1861, *Aff. Etr., C.P., Italie,* 351: p. 222.

[47] Cavour to Prince Napoleon, Turin, 2 April 1861, Frédéric Masson, "Lettres et dépêches au Prince Napoléon (1857-1861) de Cavour et Victor-Emmanuel," *Revue des deux mondes,* (1-15 Feb. and 15 March 1923) Ser. VI, XIV, p. 387; *Carteggio Cavour-Nigra,* IV, 367; to Conneau, Turin, 2 April 1861, Chiala, *Cavour lettere,* IV, 203-204; *Carteggio Cavour-Nigra,* IV, 366-367; to Vimercati, Turin, 2 April 1861, Bollea, *Silloge,* pp. 436-438; Turin, 10 April 1861, Chiala, *Cavour lettere,* IV, 208-209; Bollea, *Silloge,* pp. 441-442.

French would stop the Italians or attack them and drive them out of the Church territory. The failure of the French to give unlimited military support to the Holy Father caused keen disappointment. A short time before 20 September 1860 Pius IX told Goyon, the French military commander in Rome, that by consenting to France's continued protection while the Emperor was winking at the invasion, the Bishop of Rome would be betraying all the Catholics of the world.[48] This aroused Thouvenel who, although he was becoming more anti-Sardinian, wondered how long France would continue to protect that nest (*foyer*) of hatred of the Emperor.[49] Four days later Thouvenel was complaining that the Emperor was very much affected by the rumor that Mérode, the Papal Secretary of War, had called Goyon to his face "the last faded finery which his master used to cover up his infamy." The Emperor, Thouvenel continued, was beginning to hope that the Pope would flee from Rome and give the French an excuse to recall their troops.[50]

By the last of November 1860 rumors reached Rome by the way of England, who seemed to be informed by Persigny or Prince Napoleon, that the Emperor was contemplating an early withdrawal of the army from Rome. This gossip did not tend to soothe the temper of His Holiness. At the New Year's reception when Goyon and his army officers presented themselves to Pius IX, the latter blessed *France* and the *French army* for their services rendered to the Catholic Faith but he never mentioned the Emperor. Goyon, however, in thanking His Holiness for the blessing took occasion to mention that the army was only fulfilling the wishes of the Emperor. This reply disconcerted the Pope to no small degree.[51]

These successive incidents caused the Emperor to become aroused in his turn. Upon receipt of news of the latest incident he addressed a rather sharp note of complaint to the Pope.

[48] Gramont to Thouvenel, Rome, 20 Sept. 1860, Thouvenel, *Secret,* I, 213.

[49] Thouvenel to Gramont, 6 Nov. 1860, Bourgeois et Clermont, *Rome et Napoleon III,* p. 204.

[50] Same to same, Paris, 10 Nov. 1860, *ibid.,* Thouvenel, *Secret,* I, 281-283.

[51] Goyon to Gramont, Rome, 2 Jan. 1861, *Aff. Etr., C.P., Rome,* 1016: pp. 216-217.

> Although Rome has become the center of all the enemies of my Government, I have nevertheless maintained my troops in Rome. . . . But how has my conduct been appreciated? They have called me the opponent of the Holy See; they have stirred up against me the most fanatical of the French clergy. It now seems as if Rome has become a den of conspirators against my Government.[52]

The Pope was astonished by the Imperial remonstrance. Perhaps he had never anticipated such plain talk from that quarter. It had the effect, however, of modifying his resentful tone. "This time," Pius remarked, "the Emperor's language is so clear and precise, he says so frankly what he dislikes, that one can now believe him when he says, at other times, that he is deeply attached to the Papacy and to the preservation of its temporal power."[53] This statement seems almost to betray a fear that the Emperor's attachment might not continue, which would explain the quieting effect on the Pope's belligerent attitude.

It was just at the time of this episode that it became quite evident that the Pope would not negotiate with Cavour. Even Gramont, who was anti-Sardinian, began to suggest a separate French agreement with Turin.

> You will have to end up by making some temporary arrangement, without the Pope's participation, which, while reserving questions and principles, will permit [him] to live a real life until things take some shape.[54]

But from then on the Curia seemed to vent its spleen on the Emperor's representative rather than on the Emperor himself. Gramont had reported the anti-Bonaparte feeling shown at the Vatican on the occasion of a Breton pilgrimage to the Holy See. This report, when published in France, greatly embarrassed its author in Rome. Hence a bitter and vile campaign of abuse was directed at Gramont. The tone of Gramont's account of his treatment would almost mislead one to think him pro-Italian and more anti-Church than Garibaldi, when, as a matter of fact, he was just the reverse.

[52] 8 Jan. 1861, Bourgeois et Clermont, *Rome et Napoléon III,* pp. 204-205.

[53] Gramont to Thouvenel, Rome, 2 Feb. 1861, Thouvenel, *Secret,* I, 384-385.

[54] To Thouvenel, Rome, 16 Feb. 1861, Thouvenel, *Secret,* I, 430.

It seems to me that the Emperor and his Government have nothing to gain in not defending their representative a little when they cover him with insults which is not possible for him to bear up under. Here I am called a political spy on the Vatican, an anti-Catholic, and personal enemy of the Pope! Is it possible, you know better than any other, to push further such baseness and ingratitude? And, too, these insults and slanders which are arising from the most ignoble cesspool to invade all the *salons,* even to come to the throne and altar, these infamous lies will be accepted with joy by the enemies of the Emperor and of France! . . . It's too much to have to agree that to serve France in Rome one has to lose his reputation and to see himself insulted publicly out of all bounds of decency. . . .

As long as the Emperor thinks it necessary I shall remain at my post; but if the conveniences of the service permit it, I would be very grateful to be changed.[55]

When it is remembered that both Goyon and Gramont were so favorable to the Pope as to desire France to reacquire his lost territory, and when it is considered that both of these men were antagonists of each other in Rome, it can be easily seen what a profound impression their joint protests against the Roman Court must have made on the mind of the Emperor. Added to this adverse feeling was the keen disappointment of the Emperor at the Pope's flat refusal to negotiate with Sardinia.

At the beginning of April the reports of provincial public opinion were due. The eagerness of the Imperial Government to consult these can be easily imagined. In them they hoped to read the effects of the parliamentary debate, the reaction to the Prince's proposal, the opinion on Cavour's newly stated French and Roman policy, and the consequences of the anti-imperial campaign in Rome. A few of the districts seemed to retain a very definite pro-Catholic sympathy, but in many others there was an appreciable shift in favor of Italy. Most of the reports showed a demand for some early solution. From Agens came the frank statement that a majority was against the Imperial policy in Italy. The people were led to oppose Prince Napoleon's plan because England seemed to favor it. They wanted to see

[55] Gramont to Thouvenel, Rome, 19 Feb. 1861, Thouvenel, *Secret,* I, 434-439.

an early solution, however. Normands, it was reported, were concerned more over the Roman question than over any other. "While it receives no definitive solution, future eventualities are to be feared. . . ." Besançon this time was not so Clerical. The peasants were only demanding that Rome be preserved for the Pope, while the masses as well as many others were greatly impressed by the speech of Prince Napoleon. Reports from the Paris district showed the Italian question to be the most promiment. The lower classes were indifferent, the bourgeoisie was not at all concerned over the temporal power of the Pope, and the clergy and upper classes had little influence. The report from Aix reflected the general shift of opinion by this significant passage:

> The line of conduct of the Government between these two extreme theories (clerical reaction and republican radicalism), its watchful attitude, and especially the speech of Prince Napoleon has simply resulted in a shift of . . . the center of support to the Imperial institutions. . . . The Legitimist and religious element . . . shows a keen irritation. But the ground lost on this side has been greatly (*largement*) compensated by the conquests made among the Orleanist, liberal, skeptic, and Voltairian bourgeoisie, and among the moderate republicans.

The Legitimists and Clericals were having difficulty in the Aix district to raise money or recruits for the Pope's cause. From Amiens they reported the popularity of Prince Napoleon's speech. Demonstrations by the Clericals had been unsuccessful. "The bourgeoisie and merchants which form the only considerable part of this city by their number and importance have remained and still remain most definitely unmoved (*étrangers*) by this demonstration." From Bordeaux an appreciable abandonment of the cause of temporal power was announced. "Its definite downfall will no longer excite emotion." Prince Napoleon's speech made a very favorable impression on the masses. The working class of Lyons had sympathy only with the Italian cause. All classes were pleased with the Prince's speech but the moderates felt that his tone was a little too violent. However, the reports from the superstitiously and devoutly Catholic Brittany must have made one of the strongest impressions on the Imperial Government. Here it was reported that even a priest of St. Croix de Vitré preached that the temporal power was unnecessary. On the north shore peasants were heard to say "that they could not understand why the Pope wished to be mayor and priest at the same time." The mass of the people favored Prince Napoleon's speech and at Nantes the more they learned of the situation the less they were influenced by the clergy.[56]

Hence it came about that in the four months preceding the opening of negotiations directly with Italy the Emperor had been under influences from many quarters to push him on to this step. By encouraging Prince Napoleon's action in Parliament, he had already shown a tendency to favor Italy. Although the results of the debates had led him and his ministers to be more cautious, other forces had caused them eventually to become more pro-Italian. England's pressure, however unpleasant, could not be ignored. Cavour's seductive approaches seemed to charm the Emperor as much now as at Plombières. The ungrateful attitude of the Pope and his Court made the duty of protecting him more and more distasteful. All that held the Emperor back from making some arrangement for withdrawal was the fear of the power of the Clericals at home. Then in the early days of April Napoleon seemed to receive reassurances from that quarter. In the ordinarily Catholic districts the Clerical influence was diminishing; in the anti-Clerical districts the lack of sympathy for the Pope's cause seemed decidedly more pronounced. Prince Napoleon's speech was being generally applauded. Even Brittany was showing amazing signs of a shift to opposition to the temporal power. All, Clericals as well as anti-Clericals, were demanding an early definitive solution. In the light of these forces and these opinions it is not surprising that by the middle of April the Emperor had taken the first steps toward a purely Franco-Italian agreement.

[56] *Rapports des procureurs,* Agens, 6 April 1861, 370: v. 4; Caen, 8 April 1861, 375: v. 4; Besançon, 6 April 1861, 373: v. 5; Paris, 28 May 1861, 384: v. 8; Aix, 7 April 1861, 370: v. 4; Amiens, 1 April 1861, 371: v. 4; Bordeaux, 9 April 1861, 374: v. 3; Lyons, 8 March 1861, 379: v. 5; Rennes, 22 March, 19, 23 April 1861, 386: v. 4.

Long before Prince Napoleon made his famous speech in the Senate, he was chafing under the inaction of the French Government on the Roman question. He was convinced that the French people generally wanted not only an immediate solution but also one favorable to Italy. His preferences easily led him to feel that it would harm Italy to withhold Rome from her and it would soon deprive France of her only possible Mediterranean ally. Thus it was that as soon as Gaëta had been evacuated by the French fleet, the Palais-Royal[57] became the center of agitation on the Roman question.

The Prince was eager to go to Italy, reconnoitre the situation, and perhaps in conference with Cavour work out some acceptable scheme. On 5 January the Prince wrote Cavour that

> it is necessary to attack the Roman question and let Venetia wait. There's no Italian unity without Rome. I am still thinking of my trip (to Italy). . . . I have no definite plan in mind for Rome and I shall decide on nothing before having seen you. . . . [58]

As early as 17 January rumors were circulating in Turin of the Prince's possible visit.[59] Some time during the last of January or the first part of February the Prince actually approached the Emperor with the request that he be allowed to visit Italy. The Emperor, however, declined to give the suggestion his approbation. Finally on 18 February the Prince addressed a long note to his cousin. He complained that France held no more future for him. "My position seems very agreeable, but it does not satisfy me because I can do nothing that my name requires." Then too, the Patterson trial had left him in a disagreeable atmosphere from which he needed a few weeks' escape. The most natural thing would be for him to take his wife to visit her family.[60] From Turin he would go alone to visit the rest of Italy except Rome and Venice "to investigate conditions (*pour m' in-*

[57] Residence of Prince Jerome Napoleon.

[58] *Carteggio Cavour-Nigra,* IV, 300.

[59] Rayneval to Thouvenel, Turin, 17 Jan. 1861, *Aff. Etr., C.P., Italie,* 351: p. 24.

[60] Princess Clothilda was the daughter of Victor-Emmanuel II. Her betrothal to Prince Napoleon had been a part of the Plombières agreement which obliged France to aid Sardinia against Austria in 1859.

struire)." His father-in-law's Government lacked men. In Italy he might find in peace or in war a place to win glory and renown. "I am not moved in the least by bitterness, but a great deal by dullness."[61]

The Emperor replied immediately with a very definite disapproval. The Prince's reaction to this was to write another very strong note on the Roman question. The very subject-matter of the second note would seem to indicate that the Roman question was uppermost in the Prince's mind in regard to his proposed Italian tour. He stressed the necessity of a French solution of the Roman question before the Italian Parliament had made too extreme declarations. "You must decide yes or no on the temporal power of the Pope in Rome." "Tell the Pope to come to an agreement with the King of Italy because it is your will, or you will make a treaty with Victor-Emmanuel." This treaty should be on the basis of assuring the person, independence, and spiritual power of the Pope. After this France would evacuate the territory, turning the Pope over to the protection of the Italian soldiers after receiving certain guaranties. The Prince used all the events of the preceding months as arguments. "France seems like a forsaken husband whose wife tells him just where to get off,[62] never follows his advice, and compromises him in a bad affair in spite of himself and his friends." "The great cause of Italy, of liberty, of French interests, of changes in the map of Europe to our benefit, all will be spoiled for the sake of an obstinate old man and a weak Clerical party who would have you assassinated if they could."[63]

Thus in this letter we see the germ of the future French proposal to Italy. This came two weeks before the Prince made the Vatican City proposal in the Senate and two months before he forwarded the Emperor's proposal to Cavour. As will be seen,

[61] Prince Napoleon to Napoleon III, Paris, 18 Feb. 1861, D'Hauterive, *op. cit.*, pp. 200-202.

[62] This American colloquial expression seems to fit more exactly than any other the meaning of the French phrase, *dont la femme l'envoie promener.*

[63] Paris, 19 Feb. 1861, *ibid.*, pp. 204-207.

the April proposal was in the nature of a return to the suggestion in the above letter.

The Emperor replied three days later by flatly refusing to allow the Italian trip. He curtly stated that the Prince could only help France by not embarrassing her Emperor. He claimed that Jerome, being like the former Bourbon princes of the blood, should not complain. He could not be a prince and minister too.[64]

The Prince had the last word in these exchanges when he retorted in a despairing note that he had hoped to be the head of the navy or hold some high position in the Imperial Guard. But now he would abandon all his projects and never trouble His Majesty again although he wanted very much to be kept informed on the Imperal policies.[65]

With much the same effect of rubbing salt into an open wound a letter from Cavour arrived about a week later. After thanking the Prince for his work for Italy in the Senate committee and after expressing the hope of a pro-Italian speech in the forthcoming debates, the Sardinian Prime Minister hoped "Your Highness will realize your plan of a trip" when "I would be so happy to talk over with Your Highness the great political questions whose solutions can not be delayed indefinitely."[66] This letter seems to indicate again that the Roman question was involved in the projected voyage.

The Prince wrote both Victor-Emmanuel and Cavour that he could not make the proposed journey. To the latter he stated:

> The Emperor sees grave inconveniences in it and opposes it firmly. In Court circles I am detested and pursued with an intense hatred. They harm me all they can. I hold up under it all with great patience. These gentlemen will not have gained anything anyway by stopping me from seeing you.

He admonished Cavour to hurry the proclamation of the Kingdom so that France could be asked to recognize it. He intimated

[64] To Prince Napoleon, Paris, 22 Feb. 1861, D'Hauterine, *op. cit.*, pp. 208-209.

[65] Paris, 22 Feb. 1861, *ibid.*, pp. 209-210.

[66] Turin, 23 or 24 Feb. 1861, Masson, *loc. cit.*, pp. 383-384; *Carteggio Cavour-Nigra,* IV, 343-344; Comandini, *op. cit.*, pp. 207-208.

that both Persigny and Thouvenel were well disposed toward Italy.[67]

Both Victor-Emmanuel and Cavour expressed their disappointment at the failure of the plan of a journey by Prince Napoleon and Clothilda. The former declared in addition that he did not desire to go to Rome quickly and that he would let the Prince know when to approach the Emperor.[68] On the other hand Cavour's reply contained the wish that the Prince might accompany the King into Rome "in a not far distant time."[69] It was evident that the King and Cavour disagreed on the Roman policy in the same way that the King and his future prime ministers were to disagree.

The new Italian Kingdom was decreed on 17 March and Cavour's national cabinet was announced on the 23rd. After the vote of the Chamber on the Roman question on the 27th Cavour began to think seriously of a way to approach France for recognition and evacuation. Three letters, all written to Paris on 2 April, contained suggestions of the new pre-occupation.[70]

Hudson, the British-Minister in Turin, had the most confidential relations with Cavour and the latter told him a day or so after these notes had been dispatched "that he was going to write to the French Government upon the Roman question and make a proposal for the settlement of the question: but that his letter was not yet completed."[71] A few days later Cavour was shown a letter from Vimercati to Castelli in which the former had shown the difficulty of the French Government in the face of Clerical opposition. This Paris informant emphasized the necessity of "finding some way by which the Emperor can withdraw his troops from Rome. That is the *sine qua non* for gaining the Emperor's open support to our cause and to reës-

[67] 6 March 1861, *Carteggio Cavour-Nigra,* IV, 355.

[68] 12 March 1861, Comandini, *op. cit.,* p. 211; Masson, *loc. cit.,* pp. 385-386.

[69] 16 March 1861, Masson, *loc. cit.,* pp. 386-387; Chiala, *Cavour lettere,* VI, 692-693; *Carteggio Cavour-Nigra,* IV, 360.

[70] To Prince Napoleon, Turin, Masson, *loc. cit.,* p. 387; *Carteggio Cavour-Nigra,* IV, 367. To Conneau, Turin, *Carteggio Cavour-Nigra,* IV, 366-367. To Vimercati, Turin, Bollea, *Silloge,* pp. 436-438.

[71] Hudson to Russell, Turin, 6 April 1861, *R.P.,* LXVIII.

tablish French sympathy. Instead of going to Rome in just one step, we must go in two, but we must absolutely satisfy the Emperor." The Emperor, according to Vimercati, was sincerely desirous of ending his Roman occupation.[72]

Vimercati must have been in communication with Prince Napoleon at that time because on the very next day the Prince addressed a very similar note to Cavour himself. This letter declared that Cavour's ideas as expressed in Parliament were good in theory but bad in practice. It had not convinced the Pope and had not converted the Clericals.

> Find an arrangement that the Emperor can accept for the Pope and which has us leave Rome, that's what is especially necessary. . . . Above all, we must leave Rome! This arrangement will last as long as it can, I am not concerned about that, as long as it permits the Emperor to withdraw his troops, *then you can do as you please with the Pope.*[73] . . .Why don't you think of recognition as the first point? . . . Find a transaction that Italy can accept *for a few weeks*[73] and which will satisfy the Emperor for an evacuation, the problem of the day is right there.[74]

On the tenth Cavour wrote Vimercati in a tone similar to that of the Prince. He insisted that in order to overcome the excesses of the Mazzinians, the intrigues of the French Clericals, and the Pope's *non-possumus* the Emperor should openly recognize Italy. A firm policy on Napoleon's part would quiet the dangerous elements on all sides and gain an enormous support from the Italians.[75]

Cavour could not have received the Prince's note of the 8th until the 10th. Therefore his reply to Vimercati of the 10th could not have arrived in Paris until 12 April. But this could have had little bearing on the plan evolved on that last-mentioned day since it only spoke of recognition. It was on the evening of the 12th that Prince Napoleon interviewed the Emperor and went away with an outline of the famous plan.

[72] Vimercati to Castelli, Paris, 8 April 1861, Chiala, *Cavour lettere,* VI, 697.

[73] Author's italics.

[74] *Carteggio Cavour-Nigra,* IV, 372-373.

[75] Cavour to Vimercati, Turin, 10 April 1861, Chiala, *Cavour lettere,* IV, 208-209; Bollea, *Silloge,* pp. 441-442.

A great deal of speculation has arisen over the authorship of this plan which became the basis of the French-Italian negotiations and was later embodied in the Convention of 15 September 1864. Because Prince Napoleon was the channel of the negotiations during their early stages, and because the plan was drawn up at a conference between him and the Emperor, many have attributed the authorship to him. On the other hand in consideration of the fact that Thouvenel was Minister of Foreign Affairs, he has often been given credit for originating the plan. Nevertheless, in view of the fact that the Emperor often carried on important negotiations independently of his Foreign Office, many have been wont to indicate him as the real author. A consideration of the successive steps of this negotiation in the light of the new and more complete documentation will clarify this point to a considerable degree.

At first sight many evidences point to the possibility of the Emperor's initiation of the plans. It was he who approved the final draft of the Prince's letter to Cavour in the following words: "You have well analyzed our conversation of yesterday."[76] The Prince in his letter to Cavour began by saying: "I believe that I can point out to you the general ideas of the Emperor."[77] Thouvenel's own son, who had access to his father's papers, gave the Emperor the credit for conceiving the plan in his book, *Pages d'histoire du Second Empire.* In this work the editor stated that

> the arrangement came in reality from the Emperor Napoleon III himself and was communicated to Count Cavour by Prince Jerome. . . .[78]

In spite of the above statements, however, one would not be convinced that the Emperor was not influenced by either Cavour, the Prince, or Thouvenel to adopt such a plan after one of them had developed it. This question, therefore, leads the in-

[76] Napoleon III to Prince Napoleon, Paris, 13 April 1861, D'Hauterive, *op. cit.*, p. 216. Bollea, *op. cit.*, pp. 442-443. Grabinski, *loc. cit.*, p. 649.

[77] Comandini, *op. cit.*, pp. 216-217.

[78] L. Thouvenel, *Pages d'histoire du Second Empire d'après les papiers de M. Thouvenel, ancien ministre des affaires étrangères* (Paris, 1903), p. 312, note.

vestigator back before the events of the Prince-Emperor interview of 12 April. It now becomes a question of whether Cavour, Prince Napoleon, or Thouvenel originated the terms and persuaded the Emperor to adopt them.

There are many indications which seem to point to the fact that Prince Napoleon might have been the real source of proposals. His agitation for a solution, his former suggestion of these terms in February, his conference with the Emperor, and his communications with Cavour, make an array of circumstantial evidence impossible to overlook. Furthermore, Comandini, who had access to the Prince's correspondence, declared that the Convention came "in reality from [the Prince's] brain and was put into the Emperor's. . . ."[79] Ricasoli, who was consulted by Cavour on receipt of the plan, declared later that

> Prince Napoleon was the author of this plan, which he promised to have accepted by the Emperor to whom he had already communicated it without the Emperor having given his own opinion.[80]

But, on the contrary, there is reason to doubt the validity of the assertions favorable to Prince Napoleon. Although Comandini had access to most of the Prince's correspondence, and although he was trying in his work to produce every evidence of the service rendered by Prince Jerome to the Italian cause, yet he gave no document in his collection which would corroborate his statement. Neither in Thouvenel's correspondence nor in the official French and Italian documents is there the least indication of the Prince's authorship. Neither do the D'Hauterive nor the Masson documents reveal any such evidence. In fact Mr. D'Hauterive kindly went to the trouble to check again for the author the Prince's correspondence and found no document to sustain such a claim. The Cavour correspondence on this matter has been completely revealed now by the publication of

[79] "Uscita, in realtà, dal suo (Prince's) cervello e fatta entrare in quello di Napoleone III. . . ." Comandini, *op. cit.*, p. 62.

[80] "Il principe Napoleone era l'autore di quel disegno, che dichiarava impegnarsi di farlo accettare dall'Imperatore al quale lo aveva già comunicato senza che l'Imperatore avesse profferito il suo proprio giudizio." Ricasoli to C. Bianchi, Brolio, 27 June 1863, *Lettere e documenti del Barone Ricasoli. Pubblicate per cura di Marco Tabarini ed Aurelio Gotti* (11 vols., Florence, 1887-1896), VII, 164-168.

the Italian documents in the *Archivio di Stato di Torino* and the *Archivio del Ministero Esteri*, where we find that no document was sent him which declared the Prince to be the author. Neither is there any letter in Ricasoli's volumes of *Lettere* to show that Ricasoli was so informed. We are left to conclude that because the Prince wrote the letter at the Emperor's request and stated that the Emperor had not given his positive consent, therefore Ricasoli assumed that the Prince was the author and that he would persuade the Emperor to make the final favorable decision.

The above would amount to nothing more than flimsy negative proof if there did not exist some more positive evidence that Thouvenel was the real author of the proposals. Contrary as this conclusion may seem to the statements of Thouvenel's son, new documents revealed in the *Carteggio Cavour-Vimercati, etc., Questione romana* fill in gaps in the story which give serious proof of Thouvenel's authorship. On 4 April, one week before the Prince interviewed the Emperor, Thouvenel had a conversation with Vimercati which the latter reported to Cavour as follows:

This morning I handed Mr. Thouvenel the part of your letter which dealt with Roman affairs. The Minister was not the least astonished to see your proposals (to Rome) quite (*à peu près*) rejected.

He does not agree with you on the publication of the negotiations, especially the way you propose (publication of a summary letter written by Pantaleoni).

'France,' he said, 'can not lend her support, even in appearance, to propositions which she would be pleased to see succeed, but which she did not consider of the kind for her to formulate herself. Note well that the difficulties of France in proposing this plan herself does not come from a regard for the Papacy, but simply from the opposition it would excite at home.

'All the reports which we receive from the provinces[81] are such as to suggest to us the prudent step of advising Mr. Cavour to go to Rome and bring about there the accomplishment of his vast and intelligent views, but take this journey in two stages.

[81] Thouvenel is here evidently referring, in part at least, to the reports of the *procureurs*. This reference is not only significant as to the importance of the reports generally but also as to their importance in determining the policy of France in this negotiation. Thouvenel's plan follows immediately after this statement in the very same document.

'The Emperor is sad: I have all I can do to prevent him from making a decision which would be inopportune at this moment,[82] but right now I see the need for providing means for obtaining a solution, I can not yet tell you what one (*laquelle*).'

Seeing the danger of having the former Paris plan brought up, I (Vimercati again) told His Excellency that it was impossible for the King's Government to enter even in preliminary discussions on this plan, which would not have as a base the absolute separation of Church and State. Mr. Thouvenel replied, 'As to the Emperor's project, I think, myself, that it is inapplicable. My opinion now is that you can no longer treat, nor make any direct engagement, with the Court of Rome. You have got to find a way by which, without going back to past conditions, and negotiating with France, you can promise us not to take from the Pope his present territory while he remains in Rome, which would not prevent you from negotiating and making your principles prevail with the passing of time. Both Piedmont and Rome would be expected to take their proportional share of the public debt.'

Having asked Mr. Thouvenel who would guard the Pope in Rome after the departure of the French troops, he told me that he (the Pope) would be permitted to form an army of not more than 10,000 men. 'I understand very well,' he added, 'that this state of things would not be durable, but it's precisely on the short period of time that leads one to think that Cavour would accept this plan, all the more because the Pope's health is so seriously threatened and because when the See became vacant, France and Italy in accord would be able to elect an Italian Pope who might accept the proposals laid down by Cavour.'[83]

Thouvenel also expressed the wish to see Cavour personally in the near future. Vimercati begged Cavour to indicate clearly the course he should follow in this serious matter.

Cavour's letters during the next week seem to give very little notice to Thouvenel's plan. On the 7th he wrote Vimercati that a delegation of Roman nobles was going to present a petition to the Emperor.

After that the Emperor could propose a provisional arrange-

[82] This would seem to indicate that the Emperor was not of Thouvenel's mind up to one week before the proposal. Yet, as we shall see, it was Thouvenel's plan which the Emperor eventually suggested to Cavour through Prince Napoleon.

[83] A comparison of these statements of Thouvenel with the Prince's letter of the 12th will show striking resemblances. Vimercati was in as close touch with the Prince as with Thouvenel, and if the Prince had mentioned this plan on about the 4th, Vimercati would no doubt have mentioned the fact in this account or later. But the subsequent correspondence only mentions Thouvenel.

ment, and during its duration negotiations could continue. We would accept it in principle and would discuss its mode of execution.[84]

On the 8th Vimercati reported that the Emperor had asked both Thouvenel and Persigny to formulate plans for a solution of the Roman question. Persigny's plan was the Vicariat but with the title of viceroy for Victor-Emmanuel instead of vicar. This was to be an Italian-Vatican agreement with the understanding that France would withdraw her army if the Pope rejected it. Thouvenel's plan was similar to the one explained on the 4th. One modification was to the effect that the Franco-Italian agreement including the Italian respect for the Pope's present territory would provide for the French evacuation only after the Vicariat had been proposed and rejected by the Pope. Vimercati begged Cavour to draw up a plan which the Emperor could accept. Vimercati would communicate it secretly to the Emperor and let it appear that the Emperor was proposing it.[85] Cavour was preoccupied with the controversy with Garibaldi in the Parliament which seems to have prevented him from acting immediately. His correspondence between the 11th and the 13th contained no plan for Vimercati.

Then on the day after the Prince's interview with the Emperor Vimercati wired Cavour as follows: "Yesterday evening I saw the Emperor. I am leaving this evening with a letter for Turin, sent by him."[86] Thus it is seen that Vimercati was with the Emperor the same evening, perhaps at the same time, that the Prince had the interview and Vimercati was charged with the task of delivering the important document.

In the light of the documents it would seem that Thouvenel arrived at the conception of the plan independently of the Emperor, Prince Napoleon, Cavour, Vimercati, and Persigny. The plan was given to the Emperor by Thouvenel at the former's request and soon thereafter Vimercati and Prince Napoleon were called in to coöperate by being the channels of communication.

[84] 7 April 1861, *Ques. romana,* II, 118.
[85] Paris, 10 April 1861, *ibid.,* pp. 130-133.
[86] 13 April 1861, *ibid.,* p. 138.

The Prince must have spent several hours of the night between the 12th and the 13th wording the letter to Cavour. On the 13th he sent a copy to the Emperor who observed:

You have well analyzed our conversation of yesterday. However, have Cavour understand in a post-script that these propositions are only bases of a treaty which it will be necessary to examine deeply with a view to all its difficulties.[87]

The Prince's note, authorized by the Emperor and delivered by Vimercati, is reproduced here almost in full because of its evident importance and its significant relation to later negotiations.

My dear Count,

I understand all the importance of your letter, the difficulty of your situation in face of the moral opposition of France which does not recognize the King of Italy and that a part of public opinion is believed to favor the pretensions of Prince Murat; in face of the conduct of General Goyon who has the King of Naples review his troops and treats this prince as the legitimate king of the Two Sicilies; and finally in face of Austria who may attack you at any moment. You do not need to have me make known my personal opinion which I have manifested clearly on all these questions. It is the intentions of the Emperor that it is important for you to know.

Although what I am writing has nothing official in it, I believe I can point out to you the general ideas of the Emperor which will aid you perhaps in finding a solution for the evacuation of Rome, so desirable from the French and Italian points of view.

To solve the question, it must first be well stated. Now here is how the question appears to me. The Emperor who has occupied Rome for twelve years does not want to have the evacuation of that city have the character of an abandonment of his policy (*un démenti donné à sa politique*), nor a retreat before an Italian unity which has been made without his approval (*en dehors de ses conseils*).

The desire of the Emperor is to leave Rome and get out of an inconsistent position. You have an interest of the first order to obtain this evacuation. That, I believe, ought to make you pass over secondary and especially temporary[88] difficulties. The application of

[87] Napoleon III to Prince Napoleon, Paris, 13 April 1861, D'Hauterive, *op. cit.*, p. 216; Bollea, *Silloge*, pp. 442-443. Grabinski, *loc. cit.*, p. 649.

[88] From these passages and from the Emperor's letter of approval we see that the Emperor really was willing to have the Pope lose Rome by internal revolution. There will be many other occasions to show this same attitude in 1864. He was giving the Italians a chance to gain Rome by two steps instead of one. He was calling Italy's bluff about the desire of the

the policy of non-intervention to Rome and the Patrimony of St. Peter can serve as a basis of an arrangement. Considering the Pope as an independent sovereign, toward whom non-intervention ought to be observed, France would evacuate Rome, and Austria could not replace her there; but the Italian Government should undertake toward France not only not to attack the Government of the Pope directly by regular troops, but also not to let him be attacked indirectly by volunteers led by Garibaldi or others.

This engagement is in conformity with your declarations before Parliament where you said that the Roman question is not one of those to be solved by force.

Non-intervention consists in guaranteeing a sovereign state, considered as independent, from all foreign attack. If with time, the situation of the five or six hundred thousand subjects who remain under its authority becomes intolerable, the Government of the Emperor can not be thought obliged to guarantee the Pope against his own subjects.[88] It is a question which it is not useful to include in a direct arrangement between France and Italy. The Government of the Emperor having obtained a formal guarantee on your part to respect the territory which the Pope still governs today, can consider his mission in Rome at an end.[89]

. . . .

I therefore sum up as follows:

1. A direct arrangement will be concluded between France and Italy.

2. France having guaranteed the Pope against all foreign attack, will withdraw her soldiers from Rome.

3. Italy promises not to attack the present territory of the Pope and to prevent even by force all outside attacks against the same.

4. The Italian Government denies itself the right to object to the organization of a Papal army composed of foreign Catholic volunteers, as long as that army does not exceed 10,000 men.[90]

5. Italy declares herself ready to enter into an agreement with the government of the Pope for the proportional part which would fall to it of the burdens of the former States of the Church.

This arrangement appears to me to be equally advantageous to both France and Italy. The Emperor would remain toward European public opinion in conformity with the program which he had de-

---

Romans to join the union and calling the Pope's bluff about being an independent temporal sovereign.

[89] The paragraph following this is less important and is summarized again in the last part of the quotation.

[90] Here was the possibility of frustrating Italian hopes of a successful internal revolution. On the other hand it was an indirect step by foreign powers to limit the sovereignty of the Pope in the matter of the size of his army. In the final treaty of 1864 the size of the Pope's army in definite numbers was not stipulated.

termined previously, to maintain the temporal power of the Pope in Rome and in the Patrimony of St. Peter. Italy would have the immense advantage of being recognized by France, of having the natural and indispensable alliance completely reëstablished with us, and finally if the temporal government of the Pope should fall with time, this proof must be made before public opinion and must be well shown that it will not be overthrown by an outside force, but by its own internal difficulties.[88]

In a word it leaves the Pope face to face with his population. If some day Rome becomes the capital of Italy, it must not be by foreign conquest, but by the evident and perseverant will of her own inhabitants and by the impotence of the government of the priests.[88]

I understand, my dear Count, how great are the domestic difficulties which you have to overcome in respect to your Parliament, Garibaldi and his volunteers, and the whole party which wishes immediate unity. But believe me, and my opinion could not be suspected by you, you will obtain no more from the Emperor.[91]

If an arrangement is not made at the earliest possible time which permits us to leave Rome, the situation will become worse and worse in Italy and in France as well as in the relations of the two countries. The moment when Austria will attack you will come. France will be in an inconsistent position, all will be left in the air, and the great cause won in 1859 may be lost.

I count on your tact as a statesman to bring you to understand how important it is to obtain the evacuation of Rome by an arrangement which will satisfy France.

If you reply that you think you can accept these bases, send your letter to the Emperor and I have reason to expect that he will authorize his Minister of Foreign Affairs to conclude this arrangement as soon as possible.

P.S.[92] These proposals are at present only the bases of a treaty which will have to be examined closely with a view to all its difficulties.[93]

[91] This statement was quite true and will be borne out by later events. It no doubt had a great deal of weight in persuading many Italians to accept this proposal.

[92] The added post-script verifies the fact that the Emperor saw the note because it is written in almost the exact words of his covering note of approval. It is evident that the note was not rewritten but that the very document sent to Cavour was read by the Emperor.

[93] Prince Napoleon to Cavour, Paris, 13 April 1861. The complete document with the post-script is found translated into Italian in Chiala, *Cavour lettere,* IV, 211-214. The original French version without the post-script is found in Comandini, *op. cit.,* pp. 216-218. Mr. D'Hauterive, one of the very few who have been allowed to consult the Prince's papers, affirms the existence of a later marginal note by the Prince to this effect: "Premier projet de la Convention du 15 septembre entre la France et l'Italie."

Vimercati delivered this long letter to Cavour on the 15th.[94] Cavour was at first frightened (*effrayé*) at the conditions which it contained, but the longer he considered it, the more convinced he became that it should be accepted. Before arriving at a definite decision, however, he felt he should consult the leaders of Parliament as well as the King to ascertain the general Italian sentiment and discover whether others would foresee important obstacles.

He first spoke to Minghetti who tells us that Cavour was jubilant without however closing his eyes to the dangers involved. "We read, reread, and discussed together every part and became more and more convinced that it was necessary to accept it." Then Ricasoli's opinion was next thought necessary and he was called into consultation at the Ministry of Foreign Affairs. He gives his account of this interview in which he mentioned that Prince Napoleon was the author and that it was understood that Italy could annex Rome after a revolt and plebescite by the Romans. He seemed to recollect that the protection of the Pope's territory was only to be promised on the land side.[95] Ricasoli declared: "I approved this design with full satisfaction, and expressed the hope that it might be accepted because it appeared to me to have the characteristics of the combination which should bring us to Rome, that is by the act of the Romans themselves. . . . No obligation was undertaken by the Government contrary to the rights of the Nation."

Cavour, having obtained the approbation of the two most important leaders in the Chamber, then took the proposal to the King.[96] After Cavour saw Minghetti and Ricasoli, Minghetti tells us,

---

D'Hauterive to the author, Boissey-le-Châtel, 29 Sept. 1930. Other reproductions of this document can be found in Bollea, *Silloge,* pp. 443-445; Grabinski, *loc. cit.,* pp. 645-648.

[94] Masson, *loc. cit.,* pp. 388-390.

[95] Ricasoli's two accounts of these deliberations seem to confuse two different secret discussions of this project. The later consultation will be described in its place in the month of May.

[96] Cavour infers that he went to the King first but other accounts indicate that the King was consulted after the sense of the parliamentary leaders had been taken.

Then Cavour hastened to the King, who with his very rapid and sound intuition accepted the proposals immediately. To all others it remained a secret; and Cavour two days later, that is the 17th, sent Vimercati, who had been the bearer of the proposal, back to Paris with an affirmative reply. And this same Vimercati, who was informed of everything (*'era a giorno di tutto*), was instructed to carry the negotiations to their conclusion as quickly as possible.

Many of the facts in Minghetti's account were confirmed from other sources.[97]

The note which Vimercati carried from Cavour back to Prince Napoleon accepted the five points of the Prince's proposals and then went on with comments on what else might be added. The fourth point dealing with the Pope's army ought to be "drawn up so as to shock the national feeling the least possible." Cavour would leave most of the discussion to be carried on by Vimercati "to whom I have given long explanations" and who "is in a position to make me clear to Your Highness on all the points that it will be a question of determining." However, there were two observations which Cavour emphasized. First, France should recognize Italy at the time of the signing of the treaty. Secondly, France should promise her good offices in facilitating at least indirectly an accord between Italy and Rome on the bases of the Passaglia proposals. This would calm the Pope and make the Roman people more patient. The treaty should be concluded as quickly as possible and the negotiations should be kept closely secret both in Turin and Paris; Gramont especially should not be informed.[98]

The Prince informed the Emperor of Cavour's acceptance a day or so after he received this letter,[99] but a reply was not forthcoming for another ten days. During that time several incidents and developments took place. Not least among them was a leak of information on the negotiations. Three days after the

[97] For the various documentary accounts of the reception of these terms in Italy see the following: Minghetti, *Convenzione,* pp. 4-5; Masson, *loc. cit.,* pp. 388-390; *Carteggio Cavour-Nigra,* IV, 373-375; Ricasoli, *Lettere,* VII, 164-168, 236-239.

[98] Cavour to Prince Napoleon, Turin, 17 April 1861, *Carteggio Cavour-Nigra,* IV, 373-375; Comandini, *op. cit.,* pp. 219-221; Chiala, *Cavour lettere,* VI, 701-705.

[99] Thouvenel, *Pages d'histoire,* p. 312, note.

arrival in Paris of Cavour's reply Cowley knew of the general outlines of the proposed negotiation.[100] By 27 April Hudson also knew of it in Turin.[101] The newspapers of both countries began to make conjectures on the plausibility of the various rumors.[102]

One of the principal betrayers of the secret was Thouvenel himself. He was in the habit of seeking advice from Gramont at Rome and, feeling the need of advice from that source, he proceeded to reveal the plan in an indirect way to the very one whom Cavour most especially wished to be kept in the dark. Gramont had written Thouvenel at the end of March that it would be up to France to compel a solution of the Roman question. "A *contented* Pope is not necessary, what we must have is a free Pope." "What is most important in my [Gramont's] opinion is that France should do it in such a way that without abdicating [her position] she should not be the executor of the great works of destiny." Gramont minimized the political interest and activities of the Romans.[103] On the day after the dispatch of Prince Napoleon's proposal to Cavour, Thouvenel promised Gramont that he would soon tell him "how *I* (Thouvenel) understand the [provisional] solution of the Roman question . . . nearly on the bases that you indicate."[104] About two days after Cavour's favorable reply to France Thouvenel sent his promised plan to Gramont which was a description of the proposals sent to Turin on the 13th. Thouvenel did not mention that it had been proposed already to Turin or that the Emperor or the Prince had been involved in it. He only suggested it as one of his own possible proposals. "Putting your ideas together with mine, here is how I (Thouvenel) conceive the matter." The only variation of this reported plan from the Prince's proposal to Turin was that he would make an at-

[100] Cowley to Russell, Paris, 23 April 1861, *R.P.*, LVI.

[101] Hudson to Russell, Turin, 27 April 1861, *R.P.*, LXVIII.

[102] Thouvenel to Gramont, Paris, 28 April 1861, Thouvenel, *Secret,* II, 84-86.

[103] Gramont to Thouvenel, Rome, 30 March 1861, *ibid.*, pp. 22-28.

[104] Paris, 14 April 1861, *ibid.*, pp. 57-58. This is evidence that Thouvenel was *au courant* and that he considered the plan as *his own.*

tack on the present Pope's territory a *casus belli.* He did not mention Prince Napoleon in connection with this plan. If Gramont disagreed with the project, he was to wire, "I have received your letter and am going to answer."[105]

Gramont wired the agreed message of disapproval immediately,[106] and then he sent a long note in which he argued against a treaty. France could not recognize the Italian possession of so much Church territory. He saw the necessity for evacuation but felt that the Emperor should make an independent declaration stating that he was going to arrange with the Pope for the strengthening of the Papal army, then the French would leave Rome. Any attack on the Pope, however, would be considered a *casus belli* by France. French Catholics would not then oppose it since no territorial loss was recognized by France. This would also save Italy from making promises which she could not fulfill. France could carry on regular relations from then on with Italy without officially recognizing the territorial extent of the new Kingdom.[107]

During these days reports had come to Paris from various observers as to the stability of the new Italian Kingdom. Many believed that it was there to stay while a few felt that it would soon break down and therefore France could afford to ignore it. Thouvenel confessed to Gramont:

> Between these divergent appreciations the Emperor hesitates, and I, myself, do not feel well enough informed to advise him resolutely on this or that decision. I am therefore awaiting with impatience the letter you promised me by telegraph.[108]

During this same period of hesitation Cavour was having continued difficulties with Garibaldi. In the debates on the army bill Garibaldi had insulted the Ministry and Parliament. This had caused hard feelings and scandals which required in the end half-hearted reconciliations to save the prestige of the Government in its diplomatic and financial policies. When Garibaldi

[105] 21 April 1861, Thouvenel, *Secret,* II, 68-70.
[106] Rome, 24 April 1861, *ibid.,* p. 75.
[107] Rome, 27 April 1861, *ibid.,* pp. 75-83.
[108] 28 April 1861, *ibid.,* pp. 84-86.

visited Cavour, the latter took that opportunity to try to persuade the hero of Caprera to keep quiet during the negotiations with France. According to Cavour "he (Garibaldi) declared that he accepted that program and that he was ready to promise not to embarrass the course of the Government."[109] This is confirmed by Garibaldi himself who stated:

> I did not take Cavour's hand nor was it I who sought a reconciliation. I did consent, however, to an interview, the results of which for me are: equipment and justice for the Army of the South. If I thus succeed, I shall offer my small assistance to the Count's work. Otherwise I shall follow the path that has been marked out for us for a long time. . . .[110]

Garibaldi was no diplomat but he was interested to the extent of not wanting Italy to appear to be under French tutelage. With this fear in mind he ventured to write Cavour once a little later:

> I am all with you in caressing the French alliance, but, my dear Count, you ought to be the arbiter of Europe (as leader of the cause of liberty) and negotiate at least on terms of equality with one who wishes to seem the master.[111]

In the midst of all these events and revelations it is not surprising that the customarily uncertain Emperor should hesitate. His delayed reply to the Prince contained these words:

> Although it is urgent to make a decision in regard to Rome, I still hesitate to enter into definite relations with a Government which is at the mercy of Garibaldi's sulking, which can not organize anything at Naples, and finally which can not keep any negotiation secret for fifteen days.[112]

Napoleon's usual hesitations and delays had the one advantage of often making those with whom he was treating uneasy. If their position was clearly dependent on his policy, it would often make them more pliant. Cavour became quite concerned over the silence of the Tuileries. By the last of April

[109] Cavour to Vimercati, Turin, 27 April 1861, Chiala, *Cavour lettere,* IV, 223-224.

[110] To Guerzoni, Majatico, 29 April 1861, Chiala, *Cavour lettere,* VI, 706.

[111] Caprera, 18 May 1861, Chiala, *Cavour lettere,* VII, 711.

[112] 30 April 1861, D'Hauterive, *op. cit.,* p. 217.

when no response seemed forthcoming from France, Cavour wrote Vimercati a letter which began as follows:

> I was hoping that on your return to Paris you would announce that Mr. Thouvenel was ready to formulate the project of which he is the real author. I can not understand what stops him from beginning serious negotiations.

He instructed this representative to urge an early consideration of the matter. He feared he could not hold Garibaldi and the Romans under his control very much longer.[113]

On receipt of this note Vimercati tried to gain something of a definite nature from the hesitating French. In this he succeeded and he wired Cavour on 2 May that the Emperor had consented to have Thouvenel formulate the project. He wanted 6,000 of the troops to remain in Rome, however, and be withdrawn only gradually. Cavour replied that he wanted all troops to leave together and a definite time settled on for evacuation. He preferred to delay the evacuation if it could be made immediate and total when it took effect.[114]

Thouvenel in replying to Gramont's objections indicated his ideas right at this stage of the negotiations. He said he quite agreed with Gramont's suggestions, then inserting the characteristically diplomatic word "but," he went on to defend the plan of putting it in the form of a treaty. "It would compel [Victor-Emmanuel] to accept . . . the responsibility which I wish to impose on him." He intended to avoid an open recognition of the annexation of the Papal territory by inserting a preamble conceived in the following words:

> His Majesty the Emperor of the French does not mean to weaken in any sense the force of the reserves and protests formulated by the Papal Government.

Thouvenel would also reserve the right to arrange the definite date of evacuation with the Pope. But he thought that a solu-

[113] This letter from Cavour seems to confirm the conclusion that Thouvenel was the real author of the plan. 27 April 1861, Chiala, *Cavour lettere,* IV, 223-224; *Ques. romana,* II, 157-159.

[114] Cavour to Vimercati, Turin, 2 May 1861, Chiala, *Cavour lettere,* IV, 225-226; *Ques. romana,* II, 169-170.

tion was "indispensable" and a delay would only increase France's adversaries on all sides.[115]

Cavour conceived the idea of sending Pantaleoni to Paris at this juncture to help to overcome the hesitancies of the Imperial Government. Pantaleoni was not only going to press the Italian point of view against the modified French position, but he was also to inform Thouvenel of the situation in Rome. The information on Rome would include a first-hand account of the unsuccessful negotiations, a description of the uneasiness of the Roman populace, and a discussion of the favorable cardinals in the case of a future papal election. Pantaleoni's earliest reports were similar to those of Vimercati stating the difficulties which seemed to be developing in Paris. Pantaleoni drew up a memorandum for Thouvenel and saw Prince Napoleon infrequently. He gained the impression that the Prince had very little influence in governmental circles. Pantaleoni admitted in a letter to Hudson that he had been able to accomplish little more than keep Thouvenel informed on conditions in Rome. During one of his conversations with Thouvenel, Pantaleoni claimed that the Foreign Minister revealed his thoughts sufficiently to declare:

> How you other Italians are going to be able to come to an understanding with the Roman Curia and the Pope and at the same time plan to stay in Rome together is quite beyond my comprehension. But as long as we can leave there with honor, the rest is your affair.[116]

Toward the end of Pantaleoni's stay there is a suggestion that the possibility of making some territorial exchange in regard to Venice and the Balkans was discussed. Cavour remarked that "it appears . . . a little premature to deliberate on what part we should expect from the division of the spoils of the Turk." Cavour soon after this instructed Pantaleoni to return home instead of continuing on to London. This mission had very little effect other than to furnish Thouvenel with informa-

[115] 4 May 1861, Thouvenel, *Secret,* II, 90-92.
[116] Pantaleoni, *op. cit.,* p. 99.

tion on Rome, differing considerably from that frequently sent by Gramont.[117]

Hudson, the British Minister in Turin, seemed to be kept well posted on every stage of the negotiations. He reported that on 8 May Cavour received word from Paris that the Emperor wanted to leave Rome but was puzzled on what was a convenient time. He preferred not to make any arrangement with the Pope, and he hoped that Italy would guarantee the present territory and that the Romans would remain quiet if they were assured of the early departure of the French.[118]

The Emperor and Vimercati actually agreed on a plan of action on 10 May. Vimercati informed Castelli in the 10th that

> after a thousand disputes we have come to the following decisions: the recognition of the Kingdom of Italy will be an accomplished fact by the 20th of the month, and the withdrawal of the troops from Rome will already have begun. I charge you to keep this most secret: The Emperor wants it believed that I have utterly failed (*che io ho fatto fiasco*) in order to avoid interpellations in the Chamber and in the French Senate. Nothing must happen before June 10th when deputies and senators will all have been sent on their way (*saranno iti a spasso*).[119]

Cavour warned Paris that leaks of information seemed as likely there as in Turin. "I can understand how the Emperor might want the treaty to remain unknown until after 11 June, but to obtain that, Paris, instead of accusing us of indiscretions, should keep secrets a little better than it has."[120]

It had been agreed that Victor-Emmanuel should personally write to Napoleon III requesting recognition. Napoleon was to accede in a reply which would contain reservations denying any

[117] Documentary information on Pantaleoni's mission is found in Hudson to Russell, Turin, 27 April, 9 May, 1, 13 June 1861; Pantaleoni to Hudson, Paris, 21 May 1861; *R.P.*, LXVIII. Grabinski, *loc. cit.*, pp. 649-650. Cavour to Vimercati, Turin, 2 May 1861; Cavour to Pantaleoni, 21, 23, 27 May 1861, Chiala, *Cavour lettere,* IV, 225-226, 232-233; *Ques. romana,* II, 193-232, *passim.*

[118] Hudson to Russell, Turin, 9 May 1861, *R.P.*, LXVIII.

[119] Paris, 10 May 1861, Chiala, *Cavour lettere,* VI, 708. Vimercati also informed Cavour that it had been decided to accomplish the recognition by an exchange of letters between sovereigns in which both will define their respective policies. "Ceci n'est qu'une forme . . . de petite comédie." Paris, 11 May 1861, *Ques. romana,* II, 188-191.

[120] To Vimercati, Turin, 15 May 1861, Chiala, *Cavour lettere,* IV, 231. *Ques. romana,* II, 200-201.

responsibility for, or approval of, the Italian annexations of Papal territory. This reservation perturbed the Italians who demanded to see the reply before they sent their definitive request. On 15 May Cavour sent Victor-Emmanuel's draft request which was satisfactory to the French and thereupon Thouvenel and the Emperor began to compose the tentative reply.

(Vimercati to Castelli) You will see the projected reply of the Emperor and I think you will be satisfied with it. The most serious matter will be the formulation of the treaty,[121] but this will not be very bad either, even taking into account the grave difficulties which exist here and the various opposing influences which surround the Emperor.[122]

In the meantime there were grave deliberations going on in Turin. Hudson, who obtained detailed information of them, reported it all confidentially to Lord John Russell in the following significant note:[123]

There was a meeting at Cavour's house on the evening of the twenty-second to consider what is best to be done on the Roman question.

The persons present were Cavour, Minghetti, Ricasoli, and Silvestrelli.

The question was put by Cavour: what are the best means to pursue to come to a settlement of the Roman question. He set forth the difficulties which lie in the Emperor's way and in that of the Italian Government. The Emperor desires to withdraw his troops but expects Italy to guarantee the integrity of the Comarca of Roma and prevent internal disturbances. Italy can do no more than guarantee that no attack[124] shall be made on the Pope's states from the land side. Cannot guarantee the coast because the Pope may increase his army by foreign enlistment and therefore can exercise no surveillance on the ships under foreign flags bound for Civita-Vecchia. At the same time the question presses and by delay becomes more difficult for all parties. Cavour therefore asked Silvestrelli (the Roman) whether he thought the Romans would remain quiet after the withdrawal of the French troops. Silvestrelli said that it would be hard to hold down the Romans at all, that if Garibaldi would

[121] The treaty, therefore, had not been completed by 23 May.

[122] Paris, 23 May 1861, Chiala, *Cavour lettere,* VI, 712.

[123] Turin, 24 May 1861, *R.P.*, LXVIII.

[124] The Italians always stressed that they should not guarantee the 'integrity of the territory.' This would compromise their claim to the right to have Rome. They were willing, however, to guarantee it against *attack* which would not go counter to the national aspirations.

promise to be against an uprising, they might hold the Romans down for a short period.

Cavour replied that the term required by the Emperor for the maintenance of tranquility is six months.[125]

Silvestrelli did not believe it to be possible to maintain it for so long a period.[126]

Cavour asked could it be preserved for three months. Silvestrelli thought it might.

It was then decided that Cavour should send an agent to Garibaldi explaining the posture of affairs and requesting his concurrence in attempting to induce the Romans to listen to reason and not disturb the peace for three months after the withdrawal of the French.

In this course Ricasoli and Minghetti concurred and I understand that Cavour has written to Garibaldi and has sent his letter by a confidential agent.[127]

Cavour spoke vigorously as if excited by the presence of Ricasoli, his rival. Cavour is accused of wanting to stay in Turin and therefore to want to shelve the Roman question.[128] Therefore he wants to take some step to quiet this alarm about himself.[129]

[125] The fact that this declaration of the Emperor's attitude was made in a secret meeting and not for public justification or consumption would seem to confirm that that position was taken by Napoleon.

[126] We can be quite sure that Silvestrelli wanted to impress Cavour with the pro-Italian feeling of the Romans. No doubt Cavour made some allowances for his statements and concluded that if a promise of three months' quiet would satisfy Silvestrelli, it would really mean as much as six months. Gramont, looking at Rome from the opposite angle from that of Silvestrelli, reported home that Rome generally was for the rule of the Pope. The nobility, clergy, merchants, hotel-keepers, souvenir vendors, their employees and all those who benefited by the presence of the Pope feared that if Victor-Emmanuel came, Pius IX would go. Therefore only a few of the ignorant classes led by dissatisfied lawyers who could not hold any office under the existing form of priestly government threatened to disturb the peace. If Thouvenel took Gramont's report *cum grano salis,* still he would be satisfied with the 6- or 3-month promise on the basis of this reassuring account. See Gramont to Thouvenel, Rome, 6 April 1861, Thouvenel, *Secret,* II, 40-43.

[127] It is quite likely that this confidential agent was Senator Augusto Lorenzini, and he no doubt gained Garibaldi's consent. De Cesare recounts that Lorenzini went to Rome in May 1861 disguised as a herdsman and obtained the promise of the two revolutionary committees to desist from their activities "on the eve of, and the day succeeding, the departure of the French." This according to Lorenzini was all that Cavour and Napoleon wanted. It is quite certain that both Cavour and Napoleon demanded more than two days of quiet, so that if there is any truth to this account, either Lorenzini failed to recollect the details of his mission correctly, or else he was either misinforming his confident or was only able to obtain that negligible promise. See De Cesare, *Last Days of Papal Rome,* pp. 307-309.

[128] Massimo D'Azeglio expressed his conviction in a letter to Rendu that Cavour really did not want to go to Rome. He thought this was proven by the impossible conditions Cavour attached to the annexation of Rome. 1 April 1861, Eugène Rendu, *L'Italie de 1847-1865. Correspondance politique*

On the same day when the above conference was taking place in Turin, Thouvenel obtained from the Emperor the proposed response which would be eventually sent to Victor-Emmanuel. In the French Foreign Office Archives there are no documents or memoranda on this negotiation with Cavour. Those who collected and arranged the files of those Archives inserted this note in this gap:

> The project of a convention whose basis had been arranged at the suggestion of Mr. Cavour between that minister and Mr. Thouvenel in April and May, 1861 does not exist in the *cartons* of the *division politique*. Nor is there any trace of it in the official correspondence.[130]

However, in the Italian documents the Emperor's draft reply is found. The Emperor explained that he had broken his relations with Victor-Emmanuel because he did not wish to share in the responsibility for the policy of Victor-Emmanuel's Government and because he considered that policy ruinous to the Italian cause and to the peace of Europe. But material and political interests were being harmed by the lack of normal relations between France and Italy and Napoleon would be willing to renew these relations if he could receive *sincere* guaranties for the Pope and his present territory.

> It will therefore be impossible for me to recognize the new Kingdom of Italy as long as Your Majesty is not reconciled to the Pope, or as long as the Holy Father is threatened by an invasion of his remaining states by a regular or irregular force.[131]

Vimercati accompanied this projected Imperial reply with the following significant remarks:

> Pantachané (misspelling of Pantaleoni) continues to work on a sketch (of the cardinals) for Mr. Thouvenel. I must see him this morning to ask him to keep a reassuring tone in talking with the Minister and with all those whom he sees in regard to the preserva-

de Massimo D'Azeglio (Paris, 1867), pp. 184-185. Lord Cowley also ventured the opinion that that impression was entertained by many important French including Mr. Thouvenel. To Russell, Paris, 30 March 1861, *F.O., France,* 1389: no. 489.

[129] From internal evidence of other parts of this same letter it would appear that Silvestrelli himself was Hudson's informant.

[130] *Aff. Etr., M.D., Italie,* 37: p. 174.

[131] *Ques. romana,* II, 236-237.

tion of order in Rome after the departure of the French troops. The unitary tendency of the project must even be put in doubt. If they foresaw movements after the evacuation, it would prevent the conclusion of the treaty. Whatever happens afterwards Mr. Nigra will know how to get out of it by relating some shilly-shallying (*baringanles*)[132] to the Emperor and his Ministers, [133] while I am here all alone having no other active aid but that of poor Conneau and a little sympathy from the Emperor for some reason or other.

(Two o'clock) Mr. Thouvenel has just given me back the letter. The sentence has been struck out as I requested.[134] I send it to you this evening by Armillet. The important passage is: 'or that the Holy Father shall be threatened by the invasion of his remaining States by a regular or irregular force, or that the first hypothesis is not ready to be realized.'[134]

Mr. Thouvenel begs Your Excellency to send the King's autographed letter as soon as possible so that he may send you the emperor's reply without loss of time, and so that he can have something to hold His Imperial Majesty to his word. Of course, I repeat, you still have a chance to make any changes you deem necessary in the Emperor's letter. It would do no more than delay matters.

It is also understood with the Minister that in handing the official note to the Emperor, I shall ask for the copy of the treaty and of the separate protocol where all the questions will be regulated, and I shall bring it to you in Turin.

The Empress is still working against us. In spite of that, Thouvenel is satisfied because the Emperor has very definitely made up his mind. Conneau is of the same opinion. . . .

The French chambers will again have their sessions prolonged for a fortnight which will make it June 20th. This very unfortunate delay is due to the Minister of Finance who only today submitted his report on the budget to the committee. We cannot then expect to be recognized before the first days of July.[135]

One is able to infer from the contents of this note that there was to be an exchange of letters, a treaty, and a secret protocol. The treaty itself had evidently not yet been drawn up. It is also clear that Italy was consciously deceiving France on the possi-

[132] *Baringanles* is probably Vimercati's misspelling of *barguignage* (shilly-shallying) as the former word does not seem to exist.

[133] This reflects somewhat adversely on the sincerity of the Italian policy, at least as represented by Vimercati.

[134] The omitted sentence refers to one expressing the Emperor's regret for the annexations of 1861. The "first hypothesis" refers to the reconciliation with the Pope.

[135] Vimercati to Cavour, Paris, 23 May 1861, E. Artom, *L'Opera politica del senatore I. Artom nel risorgimento italiano* (Bologna, 1906), pp. 191-196. *Ques. romana,* II, 220-223.

bilities of a Roman revolt, while the Emperor was trying to negotiate without the knowledge of the French legislature.

Cavour replied to this note on 27 May sending the King's autographed letter requesting recognition. Cavour said the King wished only two slight modifications in the Emperor's proposed reply. Where the Emperor declared that he could not leave Rome "without sincere guaranties," he wished it to be changed to "without stipulating anything in favor of the Holy See," or "without serious guaranties," or just "without guaranties." Other than changing the tense of a verb to make it fit the rest of the passage, there were no other alterations. It was only because Cavour's opponents might hang on every word and quibble at every expression that he suggested these minor changes.

> I (Cavour) think it useful to obtain a formal promise from the Emperor. But once the engagement is made, I think it is not necessary to hasten the conclusion of the treaty if it can not be published right away.[136]

Victor-Emmanuel's letter was delivered to the Emperor. In it he said that he had not asked Napoleon sooner for recognition because he realized the Emperor's difficulties at home. He admitted frankly that Italy's conduct had been irregular, but national necessity compelled this policy and it had not caused a great disorder.

> Nevertheless, a feeling of uneasiness and regret exists in the nation's heart. It is due to the state of our relations with France (lack of recognition). The Italians can not accustom themselves to any other idea than that Your Majesty, who has played such a large part in their regeneration, is their best support, and they can but consider the French as brothers with whom they have been called to coöperate in the development of the great principles of modern civilization. Your Majesty can cause this distressing situation to cease. It is to this end that I appeal once again to the high and generous favor of Your Majesty.[137]

[136] 27 May 1861, Chiala, *Cavour lettere,* IV, 234. *Ques. romana,* II, 232-234.

[137] 27 May 1861, *Aff. Etr., C.P., Italie,* 351: pp. 300-302. This is the only important document in the French Foreign Office Archives bearing on this negotiation. It is in the handwriting, and bears the signature, of Victor-Emmanuel himself. *Ques. romana,* II, 234-235.

The recognition of Italy was imminent and Thouvenel felt obliged to prepare the other foreign powers, especially Prussia and Russia, for the step. On 29 May he sent a circular to his representatives in Berlin, St. Petersburg, and London to the effect that France had not changed her opinions of Italy resulting from the events of 1860. Nevertheless, France had to consider her proximity to Italy and the fact that several other countries had recognized her. It was being claimed that disorders were prolonged in South Italy because France neglected to recognize the Kingdom. As long as France refrained from recognition, the Italian Kingdom could not successfully float loans and France could not effectively restrain the dangerous movements which were likely to arise there. Moderate men were in power and if properly encouraged and advised might help to preserve the peace in the Peninsula.

Whatever may be the force of these considerations, the concern that the Emperor feels for the Holy See has stopped us up to this time from making any decision. To the reiterated demands of the Turin Cabinet we have always replied that nothing was possible if they did not in the meantime become reconciled with the Pope or if they did not offer guarantees of a nature to assure to the Sovereign Pontiff respect for his remaining territory, without prejudicing, besides, the value of his former protests concerning the provinces which he has lost. If we were able to obtain these guarantees, we would no longer have any fundamental objection to reestablishing our diplomatic relation with the Government of King Victor-Emmanuel. It is well understood also, as I have had the occasion to say before, that recognition does not imply our approval of the events which led to the present situation in the Peninsula nor does it imply any obligation to maintain it. We do not wish to consider whether it possesses durability and whether the unity is the definitive form under which Italy will be constituted. In coming to a decision we shall be guided then, ignoring these questions, by the sole consideration of our interests and of the impossibility in which we find ourselves of remaining to the detriment of our legitimate influence indifferent to the destinies of a country which is attached to France by so many bonds.[138]

The French Government also had the task of preparing its own public opinion for the move of evacuation. A fortunate

[138] Thouvenel to De la Tour d'Auvergne, Paris, 29 May 1861, *Aff. Etr., C.P., Prusse,* 339: pp. 265-267.

event in Rome gave it the occasion for indicating a justification of withdrawal in the *Journal des Débats*. On 4 June this paper noted that the Pope had been enthusiastically hailed by the Romans on his public appearance. The Clerical papers in France had stressed and elaborated on the Pope's popularity. Taking up the gauntlet which these Clerical papers threw down, the *Journal des Débats* inquired why the Clericals should oppose the withdrawal of French troops if the Pope was so popular.

> The question which has embarrassed the French Government for so long, and which has occupied the public mind to so great an extent no longer exists. There is no longer any reason why our troops should not be recalled from Rome. The time has come to assign the guarding and protection of the Holy Father to the love and fidelity of his own people.[139]

Cowley considered that this article reflected the policy of the French Government which would be carried out as soon as Parliament adjourned.[140] Claremont, the British military attaché in Paris, reported that at a dinner at the Palais-Royal Prince Napoleon had stated confidentially that France would recognize Italy as soon as the Chambers departed.[141]

But just when French recognition became quite certain and the Italians were only awaiting the prearranged reply to Victor-Emmanuel's request to the Emperor, Cavour became seriously ill. Ever since the violence of the debates with Garibaldi in April Cavour had appeared more excitable and irritable. At times observers thought he appeared flushed, at other times his features seemed drawn and pale. The tasks of internal reorganization and external negotiation in addition to the many petty difficulties coming in their wake were proving too much for Cavour's mental and physical constitutions. His excitability had appeared in the conference which he had on 22 May, and perhaps Ricasoli's presence should not be considered the only cause for it. On the evening of 29 May after a strenuous day of parliamentary debate he was taken violently by chills and showed some symptoms of apoplexy.

[139] *Journal des Débats*, 4 June 1861.
[140] Cowley to Russell, Paris, 4 June 1861, *F.O., France,* 1392: no. 65.
[141] Claremont to Cowley, Paris, 1 June 1861, *R.P.,* LVI.

News of his condition very soon reached Paris where the situation was not considered extremely serious. Vimercati sent the following interesting communication to the Count on 3 June:

> The Emperor had me summoned and I spent yesterday at Fontainebleau. He conversed with me a long time on our affairs, and on the way to proceed for the withdrawal of the troops from Rome, which will be done gradually and after a rather long delay. Exchange of letters and of the treaty should take place about the 20th. The Emperor has authorized me to go and see him at the Château whenever I deem it necessary, and urged me to tell you to take good care of yourself and get a little rest. His Majesty said: 'If Count Cavour was obliged to leave the Ministry on account of his health, I would do nothing about recognition.'[142]

By the fourth of June all those in close contact with Cavour realized that he was in a critical condition. Cavour, himself, fearing that this illness might be fatal, gave instructions to have Fra Giacomo, a parish curate, with him if he should be judged near death. Farini and Castelli, his close political associates, were constantly at his side. Often he was unable to converse with them, but seemed to have the Roman question on his mind. Minghetti and Farini could not have shown him Vimercati's last telegram because he was constantly asking whether word had come from Vimercati. He seemed to be expecting news of the Emperor's reply at any moment. On 5 June Cavour was obviously sinking. Fra Giacomo had administered the extreme unction in the afternoon and at nine in the evening the King himself came to the bedside. Cavour rallied on sight of the King and seemed to come out of his delirium enough to talk incoherently on political questions, confining his attention almost entirely to Rome. "Hasn't Your Majesty received the letter he expected from Paris? . . . I have so many things to communicate to you, a whole lot of papers to show you, but I am too sick, it will be impossible for me to go to see you; I shall send Farini to you tomorrow; he will tell you everything." The King left a little later visibly affected by the scene. After his departure Cavour continued his audible remarks: "Garibaldi is a fine man (*galant homme*); I certainly do not wish him ill. He

[142] 3 June 1861, Minghetti, *Convenzione,* p. 6. *Ques. romana,* II, 242.

wants to go to Rome and Venice, and so do I; no one is more impatient than we. As to Istria and the Tyrol, that's another matter. They will be for another generation."[143]

In his delirium he revealed no state secrets unless his mention of a letter from Paris might be considered as a revelation. However, even these remarks were always addressed to proper persons. The next morning at seven the stricken Count expired.[144] Almost his last thoughts on political questions had been on France and Rome. The keystone of the delicate arch, which had been under construction since Prince Napoleon's proposal of 13 April, had fallen. The fate of the arch itself can be briefly told.

Fifty minutes after the death of Cavour, Rayneval had dispatched a telegram to Paris with the tragic news.[145] Consternation prevailed in both capitals. Grey, the British chargé in Paris, heard expressed in every quarter the opinion that Cavour's death would retard recognition and evacuation.[146] The opinion of the postponement of evacuation at least seemed confirmed by Thouvenel's note to Gramont three days after the event:

> Everything disappears today before the great and sad event in Turin. Cavour's death profoundly modifies our situation and that of Italy, and to speak only of Rome, I renounce completely the idea of a treaty which did not have your approval. . . . My opinion is to resume our official relations with Turin . . . but [to declare] also in the most emphatic manner our intention not to leave Rome under present circumstances.[147]

In mid-June France recognized Italy, a step which will be described in more detail in the next chapter, but on that occasion she made it clear beyond all doubt that Rome would not be evacuated until the Pope's safety was assured. In a letter to Victor-Emmanuel the Emperor declared:

[143] Matter, *Cavour et l'unité*, III, 459-464.

[144] An interesting account of Cavour's illness and death is given in William Roscoe Thayer's *Life and Times of Cavour* (2 vols., N.Y., 1914), II, ch. xxxvi.

[145] 6 June 1861, 7:50 A.M., *Aff. Etr., C.P., Italie,* 351: p. 328.

[146] Grey to Russell, Paris, 7 June 1861, *F.O., France,* 1392: no. 77.

[147] 9 June 1861, Thouvenel, *Secret,* II, 133-135.

> While recognizing the new Kingdom of Italy, I shall leave my troops in Rome, so long as it is not reconciled with the Pope, or so long as the Holy Father may be threatened by the invasion of his remaining states by a regular or irregular force.[148]

These words, which were intended in the draft note to be a mere preliminary to the beginning of negotiations for evacuation, became in its official form, under different circumstances, the expression of the intention to defer indefinitely the discussions on evacuation.

By the death of a man the whole question of Rome and its evacuation was left suspended. What appeared to be only the negotiation of a few months was to be prolonged into a negotiation of years. As was feared by the statesmen of that day, the persistence of the Roman question became a source of great irritation between France and Italy in many other diplomatic questions of the future. Before the bases of the project conceived by Thouvenel could be actually included in a definitive agreement, many delays and vain efforts were to intervene. The years 1862 and 1863, while barren of any definite steps toward the evacuation of Rome, still are crowded with trials and errors, and shifting men and measures, all bound for the unattained goal. A knowledge of the events of these two years are necessary not only to show the continuance of the Roman question as the principal topic of French-Italian relations, but also to show clearly the difficulties which had to be overcome before a successful solution of the Roman question could be obtained.

Cavour had been the indispensable factor in 1861 for a successful solution. Of all the Italian politicians he had been the only one whom the Emperor had known and trusted. He had been the only man who could have been reasonably sure of continuing in power long enough to fulfill long-time promises. Finally he had been the one who could have extracted the maximum of promises from the extreme radicals and have transferred them with a degree of earnestness to responsible men of other states. With Cavour gone his successors became unknown quantities in

[148] Vichy, 12 July 1861, *Aff. Etr., C.P., Italie,* 351: p. 453. *Ques. romana,* II, 251.

diplomacy and the fate of the Italian state itself hung in the balance.

In this early phase of the Roman question the French situation is understood with considerable clarity. The veiled assistance and the feigned opposition of the Emperor to the Italian movement for unity in 1860 and 1861 is revealed, and his anxiety for the successful issue of the Pantaleoni and Passaglia negotiations is apparent. When this enterprise failed, the combined forces of Papal ingratitude, English pressure, Italian overtures, and a milder public opinion led the Emperor to treat seriously and exclusively on the basis of Thouvenel's proposal of evacuation without Italian annexation. This was to have left the Pope only in the face of a danger from the Roman populace which, it was believed, could be kept in order by a stronger Papal force and its own inertia. This attempt having also failed, the questions of the evacuation and disposition of Rome were still left to baffle all of Europe.

PART II

THE INTERREGNUM, 1861-1864

CHAPTER IV

RICASOLI AND THE ROMAN QUESTION

EVEN before the death of Cavour and at the very moment when the negotiations between France and Italy were most serious, other influences were being brought to bear on the Imperial Government to discourage a Franco-Italian settlement of the Roman question. These influences came from the directions of Austria and Spain.

As early as September 1860 Spain had proposed to France and Austria a congress of the Catholic Powers "to take into [immediate] consideration the position of the states of the Pope with a view of protecting His Holiness in his territories."

> Mr. Thouvenel . . . replied . . . that the Roman Catholic Powers were not alone entitled to decide upon questions affecting the Pope's temporal power, His Holiness holding his tenure of it by the same treaties as any other temporal sovereigns and those treaties not having been signed by the Roman Catholic Powers only, but together with others as well.

Thouvenel also declared that if such small Catholic Powers as Belgium and Bavaria were to be invited, England and Prussia should also have representation since they have more Catholic subjects than those two smaller states.[1]

In the first part of 1861 when France was gradually coming to a decision to evacuate Gaëta, Austria along with Russia and Prussia had objected to such a move.[2] After France had definitely decided to withdraw her fleet, she had received a suggestion, presumably from Russia, Austria, and Spain, to the effect of organizing a mixed squadron at Gaëta. Thouvenel declared this proposition had come too late.[3] It will be recalled that at this same time the representatives of Austria, Prussia, Russia, and Spain had tried to persuade Francis II not to evacuate his position. The Spanish minister did not press such advice, however, after he heard of the French determination to withdraw.[4]

[1] Cowley to Russell, Paris, 2 Oct. 1860, *F.O., France,* 1346: no. 1282.
[2] Same to same, Paris, 20, 24 Dec. 1860, *ibid.,* 1351: nos. 1638, 1673.
[3] Same to same, Paris, 21 Jan. 1861, *ibid.,* 1384: no. 106.
[4] Same to same, Paris, 21 Jan. 1861, *ibid.,* 1384: no. 108.

At the time that the Pope gave out his consistorial allocution insisting on a flat refusal to negotiate with Italy, it was known at the Vatican that Spain was about to sound out the Catholic Powers on the question of joint action in favor of the Pope. Early in April Cardinal Antonelli himself indicated that the prospect of Spain's aid caused the Vatican to decline negotiations with Italy.[5] This seems to be confirmed by the fact that at this time Antonelli boasted to Odo Russell that Spain was about to call a congress of the Catholic Powers which would endeavor to regain for the Holy See the possession of its lost territory. He declared further that Spain would occupy Rome if the French left.[6]

It was not until the end of May, however, that Spain approached France on the matter. The delay was no doubt caused by the attempt to enlist Austria's coöperation in the project. When the rumors of a French-Italian negotiation began to spread abroad, they spurred both Austria and Spain to engage France in a pan-Catholic program. On 28 May both Austria and Spain requested France to join with them in calling a congress of the Catholic Powers in order to prevent "the realization of the views expressed by Cavour."[7] It will be recalled that it was just during the last days of May that the Emperor had finally decided on the terms of a treaty with Italy. Thouvenel from the first was unfavorably impressed by the Austro-Spanish proposals, and, although he had not drawn up a reply by 2 June, he was determined that Austria and Spain should give assurances that their concern for the Holy See should not be complicated by territorial or dynastic interests of their own.[8] On the very day of Cavour's death the French Minister of Foreign Affairs drew up identical replies to Austria and Spain. He declared that France was as interested as any Catholic Power in

[5] Arbib, *loc. cit.*, p. 675. Passaglia to Cavour, Rome, 6 April 1861, *Ques. romana,* II, 117.

[6] Odo Russell to Russell, Rome, 9 April 1861, *R.P.*, LXXV.

[7] Metternich (Austrian Ambassador to Paris) to Thouvenel, Paris, 28 May 1861, *Aff. Etr., C.P., Autriche,* 479: pp. 341-348. *Livre Jaune,* (1861), pp. 26-28.

[8] Thouvenel to Gramont, Paris, 2 June 1861, Thouvenel, *Secret,* II, 128-129.

the protection of the Pope's person and in the maintenance of his spiritual power. However, France did not agree with the theory of mortmain in respect to the lost Church territories. In Italy France's only interest was in Rome but Spain and Austria had other interests in the Peninsula. For that reason they must limit themselves solely to the Roman question if they expected France's coöperation. Thouvenel assured them that France would enter no agreement which would sanction the loss to the Pope of Rome or his temporal power. In further contradiction of the mortmain doctrine Thouvenel insisted:

> The most ancient as well as the most recent historical traditions do not appear to sanction that doctrine, and . . . England, Prussia, Russia, and Sweden, powers outside the Church signed at Vienna with equal right as did France, Austria, Spain, and Portugal the treaties which restored to the Pope the possessions he had lost.[9]

This reply, which indicated that France would not join any movement directed against Italy as she was at present constituted and which in addition seemed to abandon the Pope's claims to his lost territory and to plead the cause of popular determination, certainly evinced a decidedly pro-Italian sympathy. Thouvenel himself pointed out to Gramont this tendency on the part of the Emperor:

> Perhaps you will see, as I do, an indication of His Majesty's dispositions in the fact that he insisted that I address without alteration my reply to the Ambassadors of Austria and Spain on the very day when we learned of Cavour's death.[10]

The Emperor may have been frightened by the loss of Cavour into discontinuing his negotiations on the Roman question, but his concern for the Pope was not greatly increased nor his sympathy for Italy diminished. Thouvenel informed England of the Spanish-Austrian proposal and declared that France would make no joint arrangement without the participation of all the Powers including Italy and without an adherence to the policy of non-intervention.[11]

[9] Paris, 6 June 1861, *Aff. Etr., C.P., Autriche,* 479: pp. 363-365. *Livre Jaune,* (1861), pp. 29-30.

[10] 9 June 1861, Thouvenel, *Secret,* II, 133-135.

[11] Paris, 10 June 1861, *Aff. Etr., C.P., Angleterre,* 720: pp. 23-24.

It might be of interest at this point to recount briefly the fact that the Papal nuncio at the court of Spain declared to the Spanish Minister of Foreign Affairs soon after Cavour's death that the Pope would be willing to accept a Catholic guarantee of the territory then in his possession. The Pope did not mean by this acquiescence to weaken the force of his former protests in regard to his lost territory. Spain, therefore, continued to push a joint agreement for the benefit of the Pope even if it were arrived at without a congress.[12] When Gramont tried to verify this new attitude of the Vatican, he received an emphatic denial. Antonelli declared that Pius IX would be compelled to ignore any Catholic agreement which made a distinction between his former and present territories.[13]

Before Cavour's death, as will be recalled, Thouvenel had written Prussia, Russia, and England detailing to them the necessity and justification of an early French recognition of Italy. In the light of the arguments used—the preservation of order in Italy and peace in Europe—recognition was more imperative now than before. This was Thouvenel's conviction as expressed to Gramont.[14] The Emperor evidently knew Thouvenel's opinion and agreed with it because he requested Thouvenel to draw up a memorandum on the recognition of Italy to present to the Council. Thouvenel sent the memorandum to the Emperor on the evening of June 9th.[15] In addition to the previous arguments for Italian order and European peace this memorandum expressed the fear that France might lose both Italy and England as allies. Furthermore, the memorandum contended that as a result of non-recognition the Northern Powers might be emboldened by Cavour's death to take some action to the disadvantage and embarrassment of France.[16]

The Emperor was at Fontainebleau and had as his guests

[12] Barrot to Thouvenel, Madrid, 12 June 1861, Thouvenel, *Secret,* II, 145-147.

[13] Gramont to Thouvenel, Rome, 25 June 1861, *Aff. Etr., C.P., Rome,* 1017: pp. 364-367.

[14] Thouvenel to Gramont, Paris, 9 June 1861, Thouvenel, *Secret,* II, 133-135.

[15] *Ibid.*

[16] Cowley to Russell, Paris, 28 June 1861, *R.P.,* LVI.

Walewski and Metternich, the Austrian Ambassador. Napoleon kept the memorandum for several days before he intimated his opinion. This delay made Thouvenel fear that the guests, who were averse to the recognition of Italy, might be influencing the Emperor against such a step. In such a case Thouvenel had decided to resign. Finally about 12 June the Emperor informed Thouvenel of his approval of the memorandum. He intimated that it would be presented at the next Council meeting at which time the Emperor would uphold the policy of recognition.

Tuesday, 14 June, was the day of the next Council meeting which would convene at Fontainebleau. During the discussions the Emperor turned to Thouvenel and asked him to inform the Council on the state of France's relations with Italy. The Foreign Minister drew the memorandum from his portfolio and proceeded to read and expound it to the Council.

> While he was in the midst of reading it, Her Majesty (who habitually attended the Councils) arose abruptly with the most violent signs of agitation. Then she bruskly left the room, her eyes filling with tears, while the ministers sat stupefied. The Emperor, after a rather long and embarrassing silence, finally in his usual calm way said to Marshal Vaillant, Minister of the Household, 'My dear Marshal, please follow and attend Her Majesty.'[17] Then the Council went on with its work.

The Empress did not confine herself to silent resentment for Thouvenel told Cowley that "nothing could surpass the bitter language of the Empress or the violence of Baroche. Walewski was much more moderate."[18]

The result of the deliberations was the decision to recognize Italy. Thouvenel disclaimed responsibility for the Emperor's earlier policy of aiding Italy in 1859, but he emphatically in-

[17] Grey (British chargé at Paris) heard indirectly through Morny that the Empress was in an especially agitated state of mind during these days because she recently had discovered that she could no longer bear children. At this period of life her physical condition and the mental apprehension that she would lose influence thereafter caused her to resent more violently any apparent disagreement with her views. Grey to Russell, Paris, 25 June 1861, *R.P.*, LVI.

[18] For documentary accounts of the Council meeting the reader is referred to the following sources: Thouvenel, *Secret,* II, 138-139. Grey to Russell, Paris, 25 June 1861; Cowley to Russell, Paris, 28 June 1861. *R.P.*, LVI. Grey to Russell, Paris, 14 June 1861, *F.O., France,* 1392: no. 128.

sisted that once that policy had been executed, France must keep Italy's favor or suffer the disadvantages of being entirely isolated. Much comment was occasioned by the fact that the Austrian Ambassador was still the Imperial guest at Fontainebleau when the decision for recognition was made.[19]

Thouvenel immediately informed Italy through the French chargé, Rayneval, of the French recognition. He stated that after considering Victor-Emmanuel's letter, the Emperor had arrived at this decision because the French policy toward Italy would otherwise be misjudged. On the other hand this recognition was not to imply French approval of the past Italian conduct nor was it to be interpreted as an encouragement to a future aggressive policy. France stood by her Warsaw declarations.[20]

> In renewing our official connections with the Italian Government we mean in no way to weaken the value of the protests formulated by the Roman Court against the invasion of several provinces of the Papal States.

France was also to continue to occupy Rome until a reconciliation or guaranties were assured.[21]

In his note to Rome Thouvenel was a little more definite in giving reasons for France's recognition because, of course, it was there that he would have the greatest difficulty in defending such a step:

> The government of the Emperor up until now had refused to recognize Victor-Emmanuel as King of Italy. . . . The death of Cavour had modified this situation. By depriving the cause of order and moderation in Italy of the statesman who rightly was considered

[19] Grey to Russell, Paris, 20 June 1861, *R.P.*, LVI.

[20] See above p. 24.

[21] 15 June 1861, *Aff. Etr., C.P., Italie,* 351: pp. 358-363. *Livre Jaune,* (1861), pp. 3-4. Before the Council meeting Persigny and Rouher as well as Thouvenel had pressed the Emperor to recognize Italy immediately and delay the Roman question for a time. When Ricasoli's consent to the division of the two questions was asked, Minghetti replied: "I have just seen Ricasoli. He accepts the separation of the two questions. Immediate recognition is the big question. . . . The Roman question can be put aside for the moment. . . ." Ricasoli soon regretted this backward step in the Roman question and he later made it the center of his policy to insist on its immediate solution. Vimercati to Minghetti, Paris, 10 June 1861; Minghetti to Vimercati, Turin, 11 June 1861; *Ques. romana,* II, 248-249.

its firm defender, this event revived the hopes of the most radical partisans of Italian unity and the spirit of adventure threatened to try again enterprises long thought to have been abandoned. Under such circumstances would it not have been feared that any longer abstention on our part . . . might become . . . a motive . . . for arousing the revolutionary party whose passions Mazzini is trying to excite at this very moment?[22]

Just as Thouvenel needed to take great pains to explain to Rome why France was recognizing Victor-Emmanuel, so the French Minister saw the necessity of carefully explaining to England why France could not evacuate Rome at that time. Here we see in documentary form the importance of Cavour as a factor in the earlier scheme.

The Emperor's Government at the same time was considering connecting the establishment of normal relations with the Italian Government with an arrangement of a nature to permit us to retire our troops from Rome at a more or less early date without having to fear new disorders and we were on the point of beginning conversations with Turin on this subject. We planned to have the decision of the Government of the Emperor as to recognition of Italy depend on the guaranties of security which we would be offered for the territories left to the Holy See.

Cavour's death has created difficulties whose range and extent have been accurately estimated by public opinion in all Europe and which can not be misconstrued on our part. The negotiations which we intended to complete in order to obtain from the Italian Government the promises necessary before we could proceed to the evacuation of Rome without prejudice to the independence of the Holy See might have caused delays and we had to calculate the effects of a further postponement on our part in the present circumstances. The ascendency possessed to so high a degree by Mr. Cavour was the assurance of the maintenance of internal order in the Peninsula and the guaranty of a peaceful foreign policy. Today when the extreme parties no longer have to take into account the energetic will which could restrain them, it is to be expected that they will redouble their efforts to assure the success of their views.

. . . We have [therefore] decided to separate the question of evacuation of Rome from that of the recognition of the Kingdom of Italy, so as to be able to reëstablish immediately our relations with the Turin Cabinet. . . . But at the same time I wish [England] to know that His Majesty's Government will continue to occupy Rome.[23]

[22] Paris, 15 June 1861, *Aff. Etr., C.P., Rome,* 1017: pp. 319-320.
[23] 17 June 1861, *Aff. Etr., C.P., Angleterre,* 720: pp. 30-34.

England was therefore actually informed of the negotiations with Cavour and was told that his death necessitated their discontinuance. This would silence English objections to the tabling of the Roman question. On the following day Thouvenel addressed a circular to all his foreign representatives containing a symposium of all his statements made to Turin, Rome, and London.[24]

It will be recalled that in the note to Turin three reservations were made to recognition: France still objected to the taking of Umbria and the Marches; she upheld the Pope in his protests; and she held to her Warsaw position as a check on an Italian aggressive policy. The force of the reserves was somewhat broken by a follow-up letter from Persigny to Ricasoli, Cavour's successor. It seemed that Ricasoli had written Persigny about the evacuation of Rome, and Persigny, an advocate of Italian unity, replied in the following tone:

> I urge you . . . to never attach more than a conventional importance to the forms, reserves, or formulæ which were intended to quiet the divided opinion in this great debate.[25]

It may be that the Emperor never authorized those remarks, but the fact that Persigny was the Minister of Interior in the Emperor's Cabinet and that he was thoroughly acquainted with the Emperor's attitude toward this question, would make such a statement significant and impress the Italians to no small degree.[26]

On the other hand, when Metternich, the Austrian Ambassador, expostulated with the Emperor about the embarrassing situation created for him by the recognition of Italy during his sojourn at Fontainebleau, and when he asked for some reassurances on France's policy to counteract the bad impression at Vienna, the Emperor declared it his belief that Italian unity would not last. The Emperor stated further that he preferred

[24] 18 June 1861, *Livre Jaune,* (1861), pp. 4-6.

[25] Paris, 17 June 1861, *Ricasoli lettere,* VI, 19-21.

[26] Persigny as Minister of Interior had charge of the press bureau. From his office usually went forth the official expressions of Imperial opinion, and it was one of his subordinates, La Guéronnière, who issued pamphlets from time to time on the Roman question at the instigation of the Emperor. See also below pp. 113-114.

three states in Italy: North, Papal, and South. He thought that Venice and the Legations would have to go with North Italy and the Marches and Umbria to the Pope. But France would never use military or diplomatic pressure on Austria in respect to Venice.[27]

While France was deliberating on recognition after the death of Cavour, what was taking place in Italy? There they had the problems of finding Cavour's successor, of holding down the revolutionists, and of continuing the negotiations for recognition and Rome. It was not as difficult to find the Great Minister's successor as one would be led to think. In fact Cavour had found his successor before his illness. Bettino Ricasoli, the leader of the Italian regeneration in Tuscany, one of the most outstanding citizens of Florence, had risen in the Italian Parliament during the dispute with Garibaldi and had roundly denounced the latter's attitude. He had practically issued from seclusion to defend the majesty of the Crown and Cavour's Government. Immediately after this notable speech, Cavour hurried to him exclaiming that if he, Cavour, should leave office that day, his successor was found. Ricasoli and Garibaldi were two of the strongest advocates of Rome as capital. Therefore, Ricasoli's reprimand was all the more forceful. It was only the matter of a month or so when Cavour's place became vacant. The country needed a strong man, favoring the ideals of the nation, but firm enough to restrain the extremists. It was a foregone conclusion that Ricasoli, who had recently been considered Cavour's competitor, would be selected by the King to head the Government.

The King summoned Ricasoli on 8 June and the interview resulting from this summons furnished a significant incident in France's relations with Italy. Hudson reported home that as soon as Victor-Emmanuel was assured of Ricasoli's acceptance, the Monarch handed the Tuscan a sealed letter.

Ricasoli looked at the address and seeing that it was to His Majesty, with 'Persigny' in the corner, gave it back to him. 'No,'

[27] Cowley heard this news and reported it to Russell, 4 July 1861, *R.P.*, LVI.

said the King, 'it is your constitutional duty to open and answer it.' Upon this the Baron opened it and read it to His Majesty. It was a letter from Count Persigny, written in the name of the Emperor to King Victor-Emmanuel.

It consisted of four sheets of good advice, but the gist of the letter seemed to lie in the last paragraph, where it sketched Ricasoli's character and says that although he is no friend of France, yet that the Emperor is satisfied he is the proper person to take up the reins which have fallen from the hand of Cavour.

The King instructed the Baron to thank the Emperor for his good advice and to say that he had followed it.[28]

Hudson was in the close confidence of Ricasoli and hence this information probably came rather directly to him. It is quite certain that the Emperor's advice was not needed by the King in his selection, so that the possibility that the letter was opened before Ricasoli's arrival does not necessarily prove that the Emperor influenced the choosing of the Italian prime minister. Certainly Ricasoli would prefer that the English Minister should think that the letter was "sealed" and that the King had decided on the appointment independently. What is more interesting from the historical point of view is that the Emperor used Persigny to convey his ideas. Ricasoli's reply to Persigny was undoubtedly the letter pleading Italy's cause to which Persigny referred in his letter to the Baron of the 17th. Since Ricasoli's reply was indirectly intended for the Emperor, Persigny must have seen the Emperor before communicating again with the Baron. Therefore, the circumstances of Persigny's intimacy with the Emperor would heighten the importance of his minimizing the reservations in his next letter to Ricasoli.[29]

The new minister immediately informed Hudson of his appointment: "I have just come from the King, and I have accepted. Now we shall think of doing the best possible."[30] His new cabinet, which was announced in Parliament on 11 June, included Minghetti, Peruzzi, and Menabrea. Ricasoli himself

[28] Hudson to Russell, Turin, 10 June 1861, *F.O., Italy,* 7: no. 274.
[29] See p. 112.
[30] 8 June 1861, *R.P.,* LXVIII.

kept the portfolio of foreign affairs.[31] He soon drew up a note to France in which he assured her that he had no intentions of inaugurating an aggressive foreign policy. He would follow Cavour's plan of action and hoped that the Emperor would soon find it possible to evacuate Rome and mediate between the Pope and Italy for a final solution of their disputes.[32]

A few days later, on 25 June, the Italian Prime Minister made a speech to the Chamber which began with a formal announcement of French recognition. This recognition, he continued, had not required the least sacrifice of Italian rights or interests. Musolino, one of the extremists, immediately formulated a set of questions which he asked the Minister to answer: What had become of those rumored negotiations on the evacuation of Rome? When would the Italians have Rome as their capital and how did the Minister intend to obtain it?

Ricasoli replied with caution:

> As to Rome I can assure the Chamber that the Government has no intention of allowing the question to sleep. . . . But, the Chamber will understand that it is a rather serious matter which must be settled with all its difficulties only by means of negotiations. Our communications with His Majesty the Emperor of the French are continuous and I hope that in a time, which certainly I could not yet designate, this result may be brought about. . . . In the meantime I can assure you that the recognition of the Italian Kingdom includes no condition, and no offense to our national rights.[33]

From this declaration it would appear that this Tuscan enthusiast for the annexation of Rome was beginning with a very moderate policy in that respect. The Emperor was pleased with a speech which emphasized a solution only by means of negotiation and which refused to promise any definite date of accomplishment.[34]

Although the Italian Parliament seemed to approve Rica-

[31] Rayneval to Thouvenel, Turin, 11 June 1861, *Aff. Etr., C.P., Italie,* 351: p. 341.

[32] Turin, 21 June 1861, *Aff. Etr., C.P., Italie,* 351: pp. 394-398. *Livre Jaune,* (1861), pp. 6-8. *Libro verde,* (21 June 1861), pp. 3-5.

[33] *Atti ufficiali, Chamber,* 25 June 1861, pp. 834-835.

[34] "L'Empereur en était très satisfait." Vimercati to Ricasoli, Paris, 27 June 1861, *Ricasoli lettere,* VI, 32.

soli's moderate policy, the Premier began to interpret the expressions of public opinion in the press as most insistent on an early annexation of Rome. Mr. Chiala, who made a careful study of press opinion of this time in Italy in his *Pagine di storia contemporanea,* declared that after Cavour's death "at Milan, Florence, Naples, Palermo, Bologna, and elsewhere there was raised a general outcry to the effect that it was impossible to govern Italy from Turin, and that every effort should be made to possess Rome at any cost."[35] Ricasoli's sympathies tended to make him magnify the importance of the public pressure. To D'Azeglio in London he wrote:

> It is indeed certain that while the Emperor of the French persists in the shackles in which he detains the Roman affair, this [question] is becoming every day more exasperating and odious; and Italy, who only today shows good sense, must soon lose patience in trying not to be offended by the results.[36]

Therefore Ricasoli felt himself called upon to make the Roman question the leading problem on his program. When he dispatched a special minister to France to receive the recognition of the Emperor, he hoped to give this mission an additional task of reopening negotiations for evacuation.

The selection of the proper person for this mission was a matter of supreme importance. Hence it was that the choice fell on Count Arese of Milan. Arese had been a leader against Austria in Lombardy before 1859, and therefore his Italian loyalty could not be questioned. But more important than all else, he was one of Napoleon's closest friends. With Cavour gone, probably no other Italian possessed as much of the Emperor's confidence as did Arese. This count was perhaps more conservative and less adventurous than Cavour. He had been almost a brother to Louis Napoleon during his youthful years of exile. When the future Emperor had fled to the United States, Arese had followed him at Hortense's request and had remained with him during his entire stay in North America. Firmly established on the French throne, Napoleon III had not for-

[35] Chiala, *Pagine di storia,* I, 19.
[36] 24 June 1861, *Ricasoli lettere,* VI, 25-27.

gotten his friend and his door was always open to this distinguished Milanese.

While Arese was debating whether to accept the appointment, he wrote to Conneau in Paris for advice. That physician, another of Napoleon's lifelong companions, replied immediately in terms which show other reasons to justify the selection of Arese.

Your trip to Paris is not only useful but necessary. No one but yourself can have the recognition of Italy accepted by a person[37] whom I shall not name, but who is not the Emperor. . . . I assure you that you are the only one who can do some good. Be convinced that you will be personally well received and that you will be able to say many things which would be neither fitting (*loisible*) nor permissible in another. You are loved by one[37] who detests us.[38]

After receiving this advice, Arese accepted the mission. In his credentials for the Emperor which authorized him in the name of the King to officially notify France of the formation of the New Italian Kingdom, there was a phrase which was intended to open discussions on other matters.

I (Victor-Emmanuel) beg therefore that Your Majesty give entire faith to all that Count Arese may have to say to you for me. . . .[39]

Arese was furnished with definite instructions by Ricasoli to guide him in the negotiations he was about to open. He was to show the need "of at least one step" in the solution of the Roman question. If the present Pope continues to live, France should aid Italy in opening negotiations with the Vatican.

The Government of the King is disposed to accept the plan of a treaty proposed by Prince Napoleon and formulated under five heads in his letter dated 13 April 1861, which was approved by the Emperor.

[37] It is quite evident from the context that Conneau meant the Empress.

[38] Paris, 24 June 1861, R. Bonfadini, *Vita di Francesco Arese* (Turin, 1894), p. 374. Comte Joseph Grabinski, *Un ami de Napoléon III. Le comte Arese et la politique italienne sous le Second Empire* (Paris, 1897), pp. 191-192.

[39] 27 June 1861, Bonfadini, *Arese*, pp. 272-273. *Ques. romana*, II, 250-251.

If this was not acceptable to France, Ricasoli was willing to have Arese propose that the French troops be substituted by either Italian troops or by a mixed garrison of French and Italian or Italian and Papal troops. In direct negotiations with the Vatican Italy would stand on the basis of Passaglia's proposal and the "free Church in a free State." If France should decline these suggestions Ricasoli offered to consider the Vatican City plan. In case Pius IX should die France and Italy should agree on common action to influence a favorable choice of a successor by the Council of Cardinals. Arese was to suggest working through Cardinals Di Pietro and De Silvestri for the selection of Santucci or Bofondi. The Roman populace before the selection of the new Pope would have a right to renounce their loyalty and vote on what they should like to do. France and Italy should not let the Cardinals choose a new Pope before Pius IX's death became known. The French troops could guarantee the legality of the plebiscite if the Romans chose to join Italy. France and Italy should refuse to recognize a pope if he were elected outside of Rome, particularly in Austria.[40]

Arese arrived in Paris on 30 June and went to see Thouvenel at two in the afternoon. Thouvenel thought Ricasoli was in too much of a hurry and indicated that he could do nothing on the Roman question right then. Arese pressed all the arguments in favor of the need of some step, but Thouvenel could see no way to take any step during the lifetime of Pius IX. The Emperor was bound by honor to protect that Pope, and the French Council, Senate, and Legislative Body were already criticizing even the recognition of Italy. Arese countered by claiming that if a new Pope still found himself protected by French troops, it would be just as difficult for the French to retire as it was before. Thouvenel replied:

> Once the Pope is changed, the recall of the troops will become easier. Either one of two things will happen: the Pope will come to an agreement with you and we shall retire with honor; or he will continue in his obstinacy and we will leave him to his fate by making him responsible for his conduct.

[40] Ricasoli memorandum for Arese, Turin, 30 June 1861, Bonfadini, *Arese,* pp. 276-278.

This statement did not satisfy Arese who offered to negotiate immediately on the Passaglia basis. He also showed the danger of waiting for the death of the Pope. Thouvenel thought the death of His Holiness was very imminent, and French troops in Rome would be handy in influencing the choice of his successor. They were agreed on Santucci. Thouvenel felt that a plebiscite during the vacancy would appear too much like a "finesse" (*tour de passe*). He could not see how Victor-Emmanuel and Pius IX could rule together in Rome. It would mean the eventual flight of the Pope. Nothing more was discussed or accomplished at this interview.[41]

That evening Arese received an invitation from the Emperor to come to Fontainebleau for dinner the next day and to stay overnight. They had a conference during most of 2 July. Arese reported that the Emperor "confirmed what Thouvenel said and is in complete accord with him."[42] On the next day Arese wrote a more detailed account to Ricasoli:

> The Emperor repeated that he would be very glad to be able to recall his troops. 'Find some honorable way for me to leave, *and I will leave you free to act on your own responsibility according to your interests.* But I can not recall my troops without guaranteeing the security of the Pope, and hence, unless you have come to an agreement with the Court of Rome. But while the present Pope lives all hope of even opening negotiations is vain.'

The Emperor was agreed on Santucci but feared that even he would not accept the Passaglia proposals. "If the new Pope was absolutely reactionary," declared the Emperor, "not being connected with him by so many ties of deference I would recall my troops."

> On my proposing to resume the negotiation on the five points proposed by Prince Napoleon, the Emperor replied that he had recently become convinced of the impossibility of executing that plan at present.

Napoleon thought that the Vatican City plan was impossible because it involved negotiations with the Pope which the latter

[41] Arese to Ricasoli, Paris, 1 July 1861, *Ricasoli lettere,* VI, 36-39. Bonfadini, *Arese,* pp. 279-282.

[42] 2 July 1861, Bonfadini, *Arese,* p. 185.

always declined. The Emperor saw more chance of success in something like the Vicariat plan.[43]

In the meantime on 1 July Ricasoli had delivered a speech in Parliament in favor of floating a loan. This involved foreign relations and since Ricasoli was also the foreign minister, it is not surprising that the Baron included some remarks on foreign policy in his discourse. However, these words were uttered in a less cautious and more extreme a manner:

> The Government realizes the grave task expected of it; it is resolved to perform it; and, with God's aid, it shall. The opportunity which is bound to come in time, will open the way to Venice.
>
> In the meantime let us think of Rome.
>
> Yes, we want to go to Rome. (*Movement of attention.*) Rome politically separated from the rest of Italy will always be a center of intrigues and conspiracies, a permanent menace to public order. For the Italians, therefore, to go to Rome is not only a right but an inexorable necessity. (*Good.*) But how should we go there? The Government of the King . . . will be open and precise on that point. (*Profound silence.*) We do not want to go to Rome by insurrectionary, violent, rash, and ill-advised disorders which might endanger our acquisitions already made and compromise the work of nationalization.
>
> We wish to go to Rome in accord with France. You, Gentlemen, have declared it in your memorable session of 27 March. The Government can not separate itself from the decision of Parliament.[44]

These comments on Rome were still moderate but to the French it seemed rather useless and dangerous to dwell on a question which could not be immediately decided. However, the slight suggestion of claims to Venice caused still more alarm. Was Ricasoli weakening under pressure from the Italian extremists to the extent of entertaining aggressive designs on Venice? Arese added at the end of his report on his conference with Napoleon that "the Emperor did not conceal the fact that your latest speech makes a bad impression on him, and certainly it does not make a bed of roses for me." On the following day Arese wired Ricasoli:

[43] Arese to Ricasoli, Paris, 3 July 1861, Bonfadini, *Arese,* p. 282. Grabinski, *Arese,* pp. 193-195.

[44] Arbib, *loc. cit.,* pp. 683-684. *Ricasoli lettere,* VI, 439-440. *Aff. Etr., C.P., Italie,* 351: pp. 433-434.

Your speech on the loan is very badly interpreted here. Have *l'Opinione* declare in an article that in speaking of a favorable occasion (for Venice) you were alluding to the Eastern question.[45]

France's uneasiness over the speech was made more acute by the alarm caused in Austria. Rechberg told Moustier, the French Ambassador, that it was an evidence of Italy's aggressive policy toward Venice. Moustier said that France greatly regretted the speech but felt assured that it was only a parliamentary manoeuvre to check the radicals. Rechberg also wrote to Paris in the same vein. In this last communication the Austrian Minister showed great concern for the Roman question. When the Kingdom of Italy eventually fell from its own weakness, Austria wanted to coöperate with France in making a permanent arrangement in the Peninsula on the basis of the maintenance of the temporal power.[46] On the other hand England tried to reassure France that Ricasoli's speech did not change (England's) conviction that Ricasoli intended a peaceful policy.[47]

The Italian Minister was indeed irritated by the reports of the French *non-possumus*.

Thouvenel says that I am in a hurry. I have reason to be. In my private letter I used language as simple as truth itself, without oratorical figures of speech. I conceived matters from the real point of view of French and Italian interests. I fulfilled my duty.[48]

Ricasoli held to the advisibility of his words spoken in the Chamber, but consented to have the *Opinione* interpret his words as referring to the Eastern question.

I am satisfied that I can declare . . . that my words on the occasion of the loan question were very favorably received by the Italians. I can not conceive of either a weak or a hot-headed government. I *can* conceive of a government which knows exactly what it wants and which ought to have spirit enough to be able to tell it to

[45] 3 July 1861, Bonfadini, *Arese,* p. 278.

[46] Moustier to Thouvenel, Vienna, 14 July 1861, *Aff. Etr., C.P., Autriche,* 480: pp. 80-83. Rechberg to Metternich, Vienna, 28 July 1861, *ibid.,* pp. 95-103.

[47] Flahault to Thouvenel, London, 9 July 1861, *Aff. Etr., C.P., Angleterre,* 720: p. 78.

[48] Ricasoli to Arese, Turin, 3 July 1861, Bonfadini, *Arese,* p. 286.

the Nation and at the same time be able to declare what means it will use to attain its predetermined goal.

Such an attitude, he believed, would strengthen the Government, assure the existence of the united nation, prevent the radicals from independent action, and avoid the disturbance of European peace.[49]

It was quite evident that nothing could be accomplished by Arese when France was so cautiously retreating into her shell at the same time that Ricasoli was so boldly declaring Italy's intentions. Furthermore, Gramont was in Paris at this time deriding the Italian attempt at union, and showing how powerless the Kingdom was in attempting to restore order in Naples. His presence no doubt tended to make the French Government more cautious toward Arese.[50] The Milanese count saw the Emperor again on the third and found the latter had not changed his mind. Arese began his round of visits of courtesy. He saw Thouvenel and conferred on him the Grand Cross of St. Maurizio and Thouvenel had conferred on Arese the Grand Cross of the Legion of Honor. Thouvenel gave Italy a last warning not to provoke Austria since that country was now stronger by having come to an agreement with Hungary.[51]

Arese was compelled to leave Paris without having accomplished more than to be received as an envoy, the formal act of recognition of the united Italian Kingdom. He showed his bitterness toward the Emperor and his lack of sympathy for Ricasoli in a few remarks he made to Baron D'Ambès:

> Napoleon has not consented to accept Ricasoli's program. I thought as much. Our old friendship did not suffice to induce him. I consider it absurd to have appointed him (Ricasoli) President of the Council. He is too hasty in all the decisions he comes to. He has no dexterity. He will tie the knots again that we have been at such pains to untie.[52]

[49] Ricasoli to Arese, Turin, 3, 5, 6 July 1861, Bonfadini, *Arese,* pp. 287-289.

[50] Cowley to Russell, Paris, 5 July 1861, *R.P.*, LVI.

[51] Arese to Ricasoli, Paris, 5, 6 July 1861, Bonfadini, *Arese,* pp. 288, 291-292.

[52] Baron D'Ambès, *Intimate Memoirs of Napoleon III.* Edited and translated by A. R. Allison. (2 v. Boston, 1912), II, 245.

Cowley wrote home that "Arese went away very much disgusted and disappointed with his reception here, and the non-result attending his mission."[53]

It is evident that Arese was not sympathetic with Ricasoli's extreme position. He resented having his friendship minimized with the Emperor in the name of impossible demands. He was also chagrined that his influence with the Emperor was of so little avail in furthering the Italian cause. The Emperor's caution and Ricasoli's rashness when combined were bound to result in a stalemate.

Thouvenel took upon himself the task of closing this phase of the negotiations by writing a frank and straight-forward note directly to Ricasoli. He showed it first to the Emperor who "very strongly approved of it."[54] Thouvenel declared that although France recognized Italy and was willing to let her try a system of centralized unification, yet there were "two subjects," Rome and Venice, "which we do not regard in the same light as does the Turin Cabinet." The Catholics of France and Europe seem convinced of the Pope's need of temporal power.

> It is that interest which circumstances have placed in our keeping. Neither our honor nor our conscience permits us to recall our troops as long as an accord shall not be established between the Holy See and the King of Italy—an accord very difficult not only to conclude today but even to negotiate. The Emperor informed Count Arese of his full opinion in this respect and it corresponds exactly to what I am saying here. . . . Let this burning question be adjourned to times more calm and propitious.

The writer also begged the Baron to desist his agitation on the Venetian question. Austria had just strengthened herself by an agreement with Hungary; she had become alarmed by Ricasoli's veiled statements, and might wish to take this occasion to prevent a successful Italian attack by crippling Italy before she was too strong.[55]

On the heels of Arese's mission came the provincial reports of public opinion. A great deal has happened since April: es-

[53] 15 July 1861, *R.P.*, LVI.
[54] Thouvenel to Flahault, Paris, 9 July 1861, Thouvenel, *Secret*, II, 154.
[55] 8 July 1861, *Aff. Etr., C.P., Italie,* 351: pp. 443-445.

pecially the death of Cavour and the recognition of Italy. It was no doubt with great interest then that Napoleon turned to these indicative straws before he took any very decided steps. With the mildly favorable reports of April in mind he had made the recognition a *fait accompli.* The July reports would reveal the public reaction to the measure. As a matter of fact the sentiment seemed slightly less favorable to Italy than before. In the Besançon district they were pleased with the reserves in the recognition but the Clericals were actively hostile to that step. In Bourges the people were very much opposed to the recognition. They felt it an encouragement to unification which they disapproved, and they desired that the Government should assure the continued protection of Rome. In August a notice was sent to all the bishops to recommend celebrations on the Emperor's birthday. This note stressed the services of France in advancing the Church's missionary work in the Far East and in Syria. But the report of the celebration in Besançon was disconcerting. "The abstention [of] the rich and especially [of] the Legitimist nobles was almost absolute. The attitude of the clergy was very cold." In and around Agens there was little interest in foreign affairs and no enthusiasm for Italian unity. The people of Aix regretted the loss of Cavour and the Clericals had tired of their agitation. In Brittany there was very little excitement over a recognition with reserves. The Clericals were embarrassed because they could not accuse the Government of abandoning the Pope. In spite of the positive opinions for the Church and those of a more neutral color, there were some sections which remained decidedly pro-Italian. Normandy was still unsympathetic toward the Papal cause. There was a general marked satisfaction over recognition and a common expression of regret over the loss of Cavour. "On this occasion the religious question was not evoked; minds are calm, the clergy reserved and prudent, the masses indifferent." In Picardy the recognition *with the reserves* had no bad effect. The clergy was so concerned over the health of the Pope that it had not showed any signs of criticizing the foreign policy. In Bordeaux they had expected an early recognition and those who might have opposed it, had become wearied of disputing. Likewise at Lyons they had foreseen France's recognition of Italy and were further reassured by the wise conditions attached to it.[56] It was apparent that whatever the varying shades of opinion were, there was very little direct enthusiasm for Italy. Wherever there had been an approval of recognition it had been in the light of the reserves. If the reserves had been made for public consumption, as Persigny claimed, they had not been in vain. Certainly the Government found little encouragement to follow a more pro-Italian course in the future.

After Arese's mission of courtesy it then became incumbent on France to return it. This gave the Emperor the opportunity of replying to Victor-Emmanuel's personal letter. On 9 July Thouvenel informed Rayneval that General Fleury had been chosen for this mission.[57] General Fleury would be very acceptable to Italy because he recalled the days when the French army had coöperated with the Italians against the Austrians in 1859. Furthermore, Victor-Emmanuel's sympathies would be touched because he always appreciated a military man more than a civilian. The letter which Fleury bore was given him by the Emperor at Vichy. At the outset it struck a sympathetic note for the Italians. The Emperor inferred that he recognized Italy in order to comfort it in its grief over the death of Cavour. "By it (recognition) I wished to give a new proof of my sympathy for a cause for which we have fought together." He mentioned again the reserves and the necessity of remaining in Rome for a while. The Emperor's ending was as judicious as the beginning:

> Unity must follow and not precede the Union. (This referred to the need of Italy to be patient and organize what she already had.)

[56] *Rapports des procureurs,* Besançon, 4 July 1861, 373: v. 5; Bourges, 2 July 1861, 374: v. 3; Agens, 6 July 1861, 370; v. 4; Aix, 8 July 1861, 370: v. 4; Rennes, 12 July 1861, 386: v. 4; Amiens, 2 July 1861, 371: no. 2176; Bordeaux, 7 July 1861, 374: v. 3; Caen, 11 July 1861, 375: v. 4, Minister of Public Instruction and Worship to bishops, Paris, 3 August 1861: procureur-général to Minister of Justice, Besançon, 17 August 1861, *Archives nationales,* BB[18], 1636: A[3] 5379.

[57] Paris, 9 July 1861, *Aff. Etr., C.P., Italie,* 351: p. 445.

But this conviction of mine shall in no way influence my conduct. The Italians are the best judges of what is best for themselves, and it is not for me, who am founded on a popular election, to pretend to influence the decisions of a free people.[58]

Cowley was very much disappointed with the letter, when he learned of it later, because he saw in it the possibility of a prolonged occupation in Rome. Arese's failure was only too surely confirmed.[59]

Fleury left Vichy on the 13th, stopped at Lyons for a day, and proceeding to Turin, arrived there on the 16th. He received a very enthusiastic welcome from the Turinese. On the 18th he saw the King who arranged a great royal banquet in his honor. The fact that the King usually disliked these formal banquets is an evidence of the pleasure caused him by Fleury's mission. Certainly it differed greatly from Napoleon's welcome of his personal friend which occurred in the bustle and confusion of preparations for the summer vacation at Vichy.

Fleury quite succumbed to the Italian hospitality although its sincerity was not entirely unmixed. The Italians filled his ear with the inevitability of the Italian union and of the certainty of victory over the disorders in Naples. By the 19th Fleury was telegraphing Thouvenel that there was a great *conspiracy* afoot in Naples. Francis II was actively helping the insurgents. Armies enrolled in Rome were proceeding to the border. "The last stand of reaction." Later in the same day he wired again:

The King gave a very fine reception to the letter as well as to the commentaries with which I was authorized to accompany it. The King and his Prime Minister have the wisest of intentions and are determined to follow the Emperor's counsels.

Now as to Rome. . . . Promise of the status quo.

He goes on to say that he was received as an *ambassador*. The Government was confident of putting down the troubles in Naples. On his return he told Claremont, the British military attaché, that he was extremely pleased with his reception. He affirmed that

[58] Napoleon III to Victor Emmanuel II, Vichy, 12 July 1861, *Aff. Etr., C.P., Italie,* 351: p. 453.

[59] Cowley to Russell, Paris, 17 March 1862, *R.P.*, LVII.

the old order could not be restored. Claremont remarked in a letter to Cowley that people began to fear that Fleury had been too Italian during his mission.

Fleury was certainly more of a soldier than a diplomat. He interpreted the attentions as a personal tribute to himself rather than as the customary forms due to a representative of a leading state of Europe. His sincere nature, quickened by the partisan accounts of the Italians, failed to grasp the intentions beneath the surface. But no harm was done by his capture because the French Foreign Office knew Fleury as well as they did the Italians. They may have even foreseen his captivation because the Emperor told him that he need not bother to send in detailed accounts of his mission.[60]

Having gone through the courteous formalities of recognition through the medium of special envoys, it then became necessary for Italy and France to assign regular ministers to their respective legations in Paris and Rome. When France had withdrawn Talleyrand from Turin in protest against the Sardinian invasion of Umbria and the Marches, Cavour had been compelled to recall Nigra from Paris. Nigra was well known and well liked in Paris. He was a loyal Italian patriot but with conservative and sensible views. Cavour realized his value as the Italian minister in Paris but he had to give him other employment until relations were renewed with France. He therefore sent Nigra to Naples to help reorganize that distracted country, "Paris still remaining his eventual destination."[61] Although Cavour did not live to carry out Nigra's "eventual destination," Ricasoli, impressed by Nigra's fitness and perhaps influenced by Cavour's expression of intention, began to consider Nigra's appointment. On 17 July he asked Gropello, the Italian

[60] The following are the documentary references bearing on the Fleury mission: Rayneval to Thouvenel, Thouvenel to Rayneval, same to same, 13 July 1861, telegrams; Rayneval to Thouvenel, 16 July 1861; Ricasoli to Gropello, 17 July 1861; Fleury to Thouvenel, same to same, 19 July 1861; *Aff. Etr., C.P., Italie,* 351: pp. 456-458, 464-465, 468-470. Claremont to Cowley, Vichy, 27 July 1861; same to same, Paris, 31 July 1861, *R.P.,* LVI.

[61] Cavour to Vimercati, Turin, 4 Jan. 1861, Chiala, *Cavour lettere,* p. 666.

chargé, to ascertain whether Nigra's appointment would be acceptable to France.[62]

There being no opposition to Nigra's appointment, he was sent to Paris on the very last of July. Ricasoli gave him certain instructions as to the attitude to assume on again taking up his duties. Regard should be had to the difficulties which France faced. Nevertheless Nigra was to object to the publication of reports of atrocities committed by Italian soldiers on the border. He was to complain that Goyon, the general of the French army in Rome, allowed the furnishing of arms to the brigands by Rome. These events raised the question of the evacuation of Rome.

> Let us take heed that that question does not separate us (France and Italy), but it is for France to take care that she does not compel Italy to abandon the course of prudence and sane principles indicated up to the present time. . . .[63]

On the same date Ricasoli sent a circular to all Italian representatives abroad laying eventual claim to Italian territories now withheld from Italy by foreign powers. He inferred that Italy would now strive to make herself "well organized, well armed, and strong" and then all Europe would see the advisability, for the sake of the peace of the Continent, of giving Italy what justly belonged to her.[64] On 2 August he sent another note to Nigra similar to the first one adding that since the Pope's death did not seem near, a postponement of the solution until that time might seriously impair the relations between France and Italy.[65]

Nigra, soon after his arrival in Paris, sent out a call to Prince Napoleon for aid. He asked the Prince to hurry back to Paris so that both of them might approach the Emperor about Rome. Nigra inferred that the Emperor's ministers suggested that His Majesty was angry with Mérode, the Papal

[62] 17 July 1861, *Aff. Etr., C.P., Italie,* 351: pp. 468-470.
[63] Ricasoli to Nigra, Turin, 31 July 1861, *Ricasoli lettere,* VI, 73-77.
[64] 31 July 1861, *ibid.,* p. 445.
[65] 2 Aug. 1861, *ibid.,* pp. 77-83.

minister of war, and therefore would be in a good mood for a proposal.[66]

When Rayneval called on Ricasoli in Turin and informed him of substantiated denials of aid to the brigands from Rome, Ricasoli still insisted on his charges and warned Rayneval that something would soon have to be done on the Roman question.[67] At the same time Ricasoli was trying to keep down the agitation of the extremists by demonstrating the activities of the Government on the Roman question. He asked Silvestrelli and his friends to help strengthen the present Italy and wait for the Government to act.[68]

On 7 August Nigra was able to have an interview with Thouvenel in which he stressed the need of some action on Rome. Thouvenel replied that the Emperor really desired to withdraw from Rome but public opinion as shown by the attitude of the Senate and Legislative Body hampered him.[69] He assured Nigra that France was endeavoring to have Francis II leave Rome. Nigra reported home:

> I gather from all that Thouvenel had to say that there may be at this time developing in the Emperor's mind a more or less complete solution of the Roman question but that this project depends again on some reply which he is awaiting from Rome and from eventualities awaited elsewhere.[70]

On the following day Nigra wrote another more discouraging dispatch. Although Benedetti, director of the political division of the French Foreign Office, thought that France might be inclined to resume negotiations on the treaty, still a condition of stalemate seemed to be approaching. The Emperor, according to Nigra, was touring around from Châlons, Biarritz, and Compiègne, and Thouvenel was in the country. There would be a delay of at least two months.[71]

[66] Paris, 2 Aug. 1861, Comandini, *op. cit.,* pp. 222-223.

[67] Rayneval to Thouvenel, Turin, 3 Aug. 1861, *Aff. Etr., C.P., Italie,* 352: pp. 7-8.

[68] Ricasoli to Silvestrelli, Turin, 7 Aug. 1861, *Ricasoli lettere,* VI, 84-85.

[69] It is more than likely that the July reports of the *procureurs-généraux* had considerable influence in determining Thouvenel's estimation of public opinion.

[70] *Ibid.,* pp. 85-88.

[71] *Ibid.,* pp. 88-89.

One hopeful sign at this time for the Italians was the success of their loan. By 8 August it was oversubscribed. In Italy 46,000,000 lire had been taken. One French banker alone took 60,000,000 lire and there were many other small and large subscribers. This popular acceptance of Italian securities in France was interpreted not only as an evidence of the faith in the success of the Italian union in France but also of French approval of that union.[72]

In spite of this encouraging sign the conviction was gradually pressed upon the Italians that France would not take up the Roman question at that time. Persigny insisted that Italy should become resigned to the status quo for the present and turn her attention to internal organization.[73] Nigra told Ricasoli that Rouher and Thouvenel shared Persigny's opinion.[74] Vimercati wrote Arese from Paris that opinion there could be summed up in the admonition:

> Organize what you have, prove that Italian unity is possible, and then we shall see what we can do for Rome. We do not wish to sacrifice the temporal power for an ideal which can not possibly be realized.[75]

When a delegation of Romans led by Prince Piombino petitioned the French Government to evacuate Rome, Thouvenel refused to see them or accept the petition for reasons of propriety (*convenienza*).[76] When Cowley inquired of Thouvenel in regard to the Emperor's future Roman policy, he received the reply that

> it was out of the question that the French troops should leave Rome at present, that the outcry in France would be so great that no ministry would be found to countersign the Emperor's decree.[77]

In spite of the embarrassment caused to France by the unending Italian insistence on a solution of the Roman question, Thouvenel had to open up a new channel for the conveyance

[72] Rayneval to Thouvenel, Turin, 8 Aug. 1861, *Aff. Etr., C.P., Italie,* 352: pp. 13-16.

[73] Persigny to Ricasoli, Paris, 9 Aug. 1861, *Ricasoli lettere,* VI, 91-92.

[74] 16 Aug. 1861, *ibid.,* pp. 97-98.

[75] 25 Aug. 1861, Bonfadini, *Arese,* pp. 298-299.

[76] Nigra to Ricasoli, Paris, 22 and 24 Aug. 1861, *Ricasoli lettere,* VI, 101-102, 120-121.

[77] Cowley to Russell, Chantilly, 29 Aug. 1861, *R.P.,* LVI.

of these unwelcome demands by appointing a minister to Turin. At the time of Arese's mission there had been some discussion of raising France's legation at Turin to the grade of an embassy. This was not done, however, during the Second Empire and the grade of legation remained to hamper friendly relations with Italy during the early years of the Third French Republic. Arese claimed that he would try to get either La Valette or Benedetti appointed. La Tour d'Auvergne was thought to be another possibility, while Talleyrand was eliminated by his appointment to Belgium.[78] Four days later (5 July) Arese had the assurance that Benedetti would be the choice,[79] but it was not until over a month later (12 August 1861) that Thouvenel asked Italy for her approval of this appointment. This approbation was duly given, and Benedetti was sent to his post on August 26th.[80] Although Italy may have been disappointed that France sent only a minister, she could be somewhat consoled by the fact that Benedetti had previously held the important position of director of the political division in the Foreign Office. When there seemed to be no hope of negotiating in Paris, Nigra had suggested that Ricasoli try to open negotiations through Benedetti. Hence it is this channel of communication which furnished the next step in the Italian-French negotiations.

On the day Benedetti left for Turin (26 August 1861) Ricasoli sent a note to Nigra which might be considered the opening move in the attempted mediation plan. The Italian Prime Minister explained the critical political situation in Italy: the gradual division which the question was making in Italy both morally and geographically. In the light of this danger Ricasoli revealed a positive plan of action. He would propose reconciliation to the Pope on terms similar to those of Passaglia. He would draw up the plan and write a letter to the Pope. He would ask France to transmit these to Rome and facilitate the negotiation toward a successful conclusion. The plan, Ricasoli thought, would have the double advantage, if it failed, of show-

[78] Arese to Ricasoli, Paris, 1 July 1861, Bonfadini, *Arese,* pp. 279-282.
[79] *Ibid.,* p. 288.
[80] *Aff. Etr., C.P., Italie,* 352: pp. 22-23.

ing up the obstinacy of the Papacy and linking France with the rejection of the offer. Thus France in her pique might be led to evacuate anyway.[81]

In his first interview with Benedetti, Ricasoli suggested vaguely a possible move in the direction of pourparlers with Rome. He did not suggest at that time that France would be implicated and he did not indicate what would be the terms except that it was not his intention to bring up the question of the temporal power at first. Benedetti hinted that Ricasoli's earlier aggressive attitude might make any attempt at conciliation abortive. Shortly after this Benedetti had an audience with the King. The King mentioned the fact that Ricasoli was meditating a plan of conciliation and he went as far as to suggest the advisability of French mediation.[82]

Just at this juncture Ricasoli sent out a circular note denying that the trouble in Naples were caused by the weakness of Italy and the dislike of the union by the Neapolitans. He countered by accusing the Pope and Francis II of abetting these revolts. Benedetti pointed out that such a tone would hardly encourage a conciliatory attitude in Rome, but Ricasoli insisted that he must forcefully deny false accusations.[83] Thouvenel approved of Benedetti's language in this matter and he reserved comment on the suggestion of mediation until he knew of the terms of the Italian proposals.[84]

By 3 September Ricasoli had drawn up his proposals and sent them to the King for the latter's approval.[85] On 10 September he delivered them to Benedetti who took them personally to Paris.[86] The proposals consisted of a memorandum of twelve articles and two letters directed to Antonelli and Pius IX respectively. The twelve articles consisted of concessions which Italy was willing to make: 1) There would be preserved for the

[81] Ricasoli to Nigra, Turin, 26 Aug. 1861, *Ricasoli lettere,* VI, 103-107.
[82] Benedetti to Thouvenel, Turin, 30 Aug. 1861, 1 Sept. 1861, *Aff. Etr., C.P., Italie,* 352: 38-51.
[83] Same to same, Turin, 1 Sept. 1861, *ibid.,* pp. 52-59.
[84] Thouvenel to Benedetti, Paris, 2 Sept. 1861, *ibid.,* pp. 61-63.
[85] Benedetti to Thouvenel, Turin, 3 Sept. 1861, *ibid.,* pp. 67-70.
[86] Benedetti to Thouvenel, Turin, 8 Sept. 1861, *ibid.,* pp. 78-81.

Pope "dignity," "inviolability," and "all the other prerogatives of sovereignty" customary for sovereigns; for the cardinals, their princely titles. 2) Italy would not interfere with the execution of any spiritual acts of the Pope. 3) The nuncios could go and come freely. 4) The Pope could freely communicate with the bishops, and he could hold councils and synods when and where he pleased. 5) The Government would not interfere with the spiritual ministry of the Italian bishops. 6) The bishops were to be held responsible to the Italian Government, however, in case of crimes or infractions against the laws of the State. 7) The King of Italy would renounce all ownership of ecclesiastical property. 8) The Italian Government would renounce all influence in the selection of bishops. 9) Italy would furnish the Pope with a fixed income. 10) Italy would coöperate with the other Catholic Powers in determining her quota for a sufficient income for the Papal Court. 11) Italy would give guaranties for the execution of the above points. 12) For the above concessions the Pope was to agree to negotiate.[87] It will be noticed that the sacrifices which the Pope would have to make were not mentioned and there was hardly even a vague suggestion of the loss of temporal power. The letter to the Pope was a little less diplomatic. It recounted first the disappointment the Pope had caused by abandoning the cause of Italy in 1849, continued by showing how his present attitude was tending to divide both Italy and the Church, and concluded with a plea for negotiations. That addressed to Antonelli was just a request to transmit the plan to the Pope and to give it very serious consideration.[88] To complete the proposals Ricasoli sent Nigra a request for French mediation. He was to explain to France that since Italy had no relations with Rome and since the former direct proposals had been rejected by the Pope, Italy must rely on France to transmit this project and use her influence to

[87] Ricasoli memorandum, 10 Sept. 1861, *Libro verde,* (20 Nov. 1861), pp. 6-7. *R.P.*, LXVIII. *Ricasoli lettere*, VI, 158-160.

[88] 10 Sept. 1861, *Libro verde,* (20 Nov. 1861), pp. 1-8. *Aff. Etr., M.D., Rome*, 124: (10 Sept. 1861). *R.P.*, LXVIII, (10 Sept. 1861). *Ricasoli lettere* VI, 149-158.

open negotiations directly between the Governments of the Pope and the King.[89]

After Benedetti delivered the notes to Thouvenel, the latter informed Nigra that before anything should be done, both he and the Emperor would have to study them and await La Valette's arrival in Rome.[90] In passing this news on to Ricasoli, Nigra revealed more clearly the Italian intentions:

> The Pope will not reply or will reply in the negative. To associate France with this refusal seems to me highly politic.[91]

Hoping no doubt that the word would eventually reach Thouvenel, Nigra confided to Cowley that if France failed Italy at this point, Ricasoli's disappointment would be so great that he would have to take the question into his own hands.[92] Cowley, obedient to the laws of human nature, saw Thouvenel the next day and engaged him in conversation on the Italian proposals. Thouvenel gave him the impression that he was opposed to Ricasoli's plan of action and preferred to postpone the question to a more favorable time.[93]

Thouvenel was quite reticent to Nigra on his return (17 September). He said that the Emperor would have to consider the correspondence until the 25th. Furthermore, it might be necessary to wait until La Valette had gone to Rome and sounded them out. Nigra was greatly alarmed by the delay and especially by the suggestion that Rome would be *sounded out* before France forwarded the proposals. This sounding out might reveal the Pope's intention to refuse and prevent France from being rebuffed. Nigra tried to impress on Thouvenel the necessity of haste in the matter before the Italian public got out of hand. But Thouvenel always replied by advising Italy to be patient.[94]

[89] 10 Sept. 1861, *Libro verde,* (10 Nov. 1861), pp. 8-11. *Aff. Etr., M.D., Rome,* 124: (10 Sept. 1861). *Ricasoli lettere,* VI, 145-149.

[90] Thouvenel to Nigra, Paris, 12 Sept. 1861, *Ricasoli lettere,* VI, 160-161, note. Gramont had been transferred from Rome to Vienna and La Valette was appointed to take his place. Thouvenel to Gramont, Paris, 29 Aug. 1861, Thouvenel, *Secret,* II, 163-164.

[91] Paris, 13 Sept. 1861, *Ricasoli lettere,* VI, 160-163.

[92] Cowley to Russell, Paris, 16 Sept. 1861, *R.P.,* LVI.

[93] Same to same, Paris, 17 Sept. 1861, *F.O., France,* 1396: no. 1127.

[94] Nigra to Ricasoli, Paris, 17 Sept. 1861, *Ricasoli lettere,* VI, 165-166.

The situation, concluded Ricasoli, would certainly have to be explained to Parliament by November.[98]

Having noticed Nigra's mention of the Prince's probable return during the middle of October, Ricasoli wrote Jerome Napoleon a note on the 14th of that month. He declared that the Roman question was the root of all of Italy's difficulties and besought the Prince to persuade the Emperor to undertake its immediate solution.[99] He also had the King write him, and Rattazzi, who undertook a personal mission to France,[100] called on the Prince with the same request. On receiving Ricasoli's letter the Prince immediately wrote to the Emperor, told him of the three approaches made to him, and then asked whether the Emperor would permit him any share in these deliberations. Would the Emperor allow his position as cousin of the ruler of France and son-in-law of the ruler of Italy to be used as an semi-official (*officieuse*) channel for negotiations? Shall I tell them politely, "Leave me alone!" or "This is what I can do for France and Italy"?[101] The Emperor replied almost a week later that he "asked for nothing better than that you should be the intermediary of the requests and desires of your father-in-law."[102] It will be noted that the Prince was not asked to be the intermediary for Emperor Napoleon. No steps were taken through Prince Napoleon at this time, however. He wrote back in a very discouraging tone to Ricasoli that the Emperor seemed to be the only one in the Government who wanted a solution. He suggested that Ricasoli should take up the treaty begun with Cavour, adding that this was a very weak suggestion, but "it is not my job to change this situation."[103]

Rattazzi's visit to Paris is an event of considerable significance in other ways than in what it actually accomplished on the Roman question. It also revealed the political divisions which

[98] Turin, 8 Oct. 1861, *Ricasoli lettere,* VI, 190-194.
[99] *Ibid.*, pp. 201-202.
[100] This mission is treated separately below.
[101] 16 Oct. 1861, D'Hauterive, *op. cit.*, pp. 223-226.
[102] 22 Oct. 1861, *ibid.*, pp. 226-227. Comandini, *op. cit.*, pp. 223-224.
[103] "Elle ne dépend pas de moi de *changer* cette situation." 31 Oct. 1861, *Ricasoli lettere,* VI, 219-221.

were gradually growing up in Italy. Rattazzi had been unfriendly to Cavour but he was still more so to Ricasoli. He had been elected to the first Chamber in the Parliament of united Italy and while in that office he had not restrained Garibaldi's attacks on the Chamber and the Minister sufficiently to suit either Cavour or Ricasoli. Therefore when Ricasoli formed his cabinet, he neglected to include Rattazzi. Later Minghetti, who was Minister of Interior, proposed the organization of Italy into regions along the lines of the former states. This was opposed by nationalist majorities which wanted all provincialism to be sacrificed for the cause of the nation. About the time that Ricasoli proposed his mediation plan to France, Minghetti was forced to resign because of lack of support for his scheme in the Cabinet.[104] Everybody thought Ricasoli would then be forced to include Rattazzi in the Cabinet. Ricasoli, however, still did not seem inclined to appoint him. Even when he could not find anyone else to fill the vacancy, he assumed the duties of heading both the foreign and interior ministries rather than arrange with Rattazzi.[105] From then on there seemed to be rumors of intrigues to put Ricasoli out and allow Rattazzi to replace him.

About the middle of October Rattazzi, as President of the Chamber, decided to visit France. He told Hudson that he wanted to avoid the intrigues which were working to have him replace Ricasoli. He claimed that he was not against the Ricasoli Government and would support it.[106] Nevertheless, since Rattazzi spent most of his time in trying to further the Roman question, and since he did all his reporting to the King and spoke to the Emperor in the name of the King, it is quite likely that he had a mission directly from Victor-Emmanuel to push French evacuation and perhaps the Venetian question. He arrived in Paris at about the same time as the Prince, and he immediately besought His Highness to do something for Italy. Then he saw Thouvenel in preparation for an audience with the Emperor. Thouvenel

[104] Minghetti, *Convenzione,* pp. 7-8.

[105] Benedetti to Thouvenel, Turin, 30 Aug., 1 Sept. 1861, *Aff. Etr., C.P., Italie,* 352: pp. 38-47, 52-59.

[106] Hudson to Russell, Turin, 20 Oct. 1861, *R.P.,* LXVIII.

gathered from their conversation that Rattazzi was willing to forego Rome as capital for the time being if Italy could only annex it. Rattazzi also suggested that they return to the arrangement begun with Cavour.[107] Nigra, who accompanied Rattazzi on his visit to Thouvenel, reported that Thouvenel held to his previous position. But Nigra noted two significant statements made by the French Foreign Minister: 1) "that the Italian unity was an accomplished fact . . .", 2) "that the temporal power is a dead corpse (*cadavere morto mortissimo*) but that it can not be buried until the conviction of its death has penetrated into the minds of the people." Rattazzi also saw Persigny and Gramont. The former proposed the vicariat plan, the latter the Cavour arrangement by declaration instead of by treaty.[108]

Rattazzi saw the Emperor on the morning of 22 October. In the meantime he had been able to see Conneau, Princess Clothilda, and La Valette, besides the others already mentioned. He spent an hour and a half with the Emperor. Rattazzi's own story of the conference told to the King will give a clearer idea of the interview.

> Before I had a chance to give him a survey (of the Roman question) or to speak of other things, he declared to me in the most precise terms that he desired as much as anyone else to solve it quickly . . . but he could not see a possibility right now unless they could find some correct way for him to withdraw his troops from Rome.
>
> . . . If all I had to do was to cut off my finger to find a way to leave Rome in a suitable manner and end the whole question satisfactorily, I would do it immediately.

When Rattazzi asked just what he might report to Victor-Emmanuel, the Emperor replied that Italy should wait in an expectant mood (*au jour le jour*) for the proper occasion to arise which might be the death of the present Pope.

> None of the projects made up to now appeared to him (the Emperor) satisfactory. He would study incessantly to find a way to arrive at that goal, and when he had, he would not delay to take

[107] The Cavour arrangement, which was eventually with some modification made the basis of the September 1864 Convention, was time and again suggested in the meantime. Thus there seemed to be almost a chain of occasions which kept the provisions of 1861 and 1864 linked together. Thouvenel to Emperor, Paris, 19 Oct. 1861, *Aff. Etr., C.P., Italie,* 352: p. 153.

[108] Nigra to Ricasoli, Paris, 21 Oct. 1861. *Ricasoli lettere,* VI, 214.

advantage of it. In the meantime it would be good for us (Italians) to devote ourselves to the continuous and undivided task of establishing ourselves internally and organizing our army well.

Rattazzi concluded that Italy must give up the idea of going to Rome immediately.[109]

Nevertheless, this special envoy returned to the charge once more before leaving Paris. He addressed a long note to the Emperor in which he explained the views of Victor-Emmanuel.[110] The King was willing to drop temporarily the question of making Rome the Italian capital, but he felt that some step would have to be taken to satisfy Italian radical opinion. This step, he believed, should be the substitution of an Italian garrison for the French in the remaining Papal States. The Emperor was requested to have the proposed change accepted by the Pope. It was thought that the Pope would refuse, but the refusal in addition to the Italian proposal and the French mediation would reveal the favorable dispositions of France and Italy in contrast to the Pope's stubbornness. This would at least relieve the situation temporarily as regards the extreme opinion in Italy.[111] Victor-Emmanuel II had expressed the same opinion to Benedetti in Turin. Hence it is clear that he and Rattazzi were in accord.[112] Both the King and Rattazzi were careful not to appear opposed to Ricasoli in the eyes of France. Nevertheless, their separate approaches to France were interpreted by Ricasoli as evidence of a lack of harmony between himself and the King.[113]

[109] 23 Oct. 1861, *Aff. Etr., M.D., Rome,* 124: (23 Oct. 1861). Napoleon III to Prince Napoleon, Paris, 22 Oct. 1861, D'Hauterive, *op. cit.,* pp. 226-227. Comandini, *op. cit.,* pp. 223-224. Nigra to Ricasoli, Paris, 24 Oct. 1861, *Ricasoli lettere,* VI, 215.

[110] "Le roi me chargeait de soumettre à Votre Majesté, etc. . . ." This statement and the plan which he offered shows that Rattazzi was representing the King in a policy not in entire harmony with that of Ricasoli.

[111] Rattazzi to Napoleon III, Paris, 31 Oct. 1861, Thouvenel, *Pages d'histoire,* pp. 310-314.

[112] Benedetti to Thouvenel, Turin, 24 Oct. 1861, *Aff. Etr., C.P., Italie,* 352: pp. 174-182.

[113] Ricasoli to Nigra, Turin, 12 Jan. 1862; Nigra to Ricasoli, Paris, 16 Jan. 1862; *Ricasoli lettere,* VI, 292-298, 301-306. Ricasoli declared to Nigra that if the King is intriguing, "I will leave the ministry only when I am so inclined (*quando lo vorrò*), and I shall be so inclined only when I can tell the nation why I leave." Turin, 18 Jan. 1862, *Ricasoli lettere,* VI, 318-320.

The Emperor replied to Rattazzi by saying that although he wanted very much to leave Rome, he could not immediately take such a step. There was no mention of approval or disapproval of the suggestions made in Rattazzi's note.[114]

It was again made evident that France could not be persuaded to take any definite action in regard to Rome at this time. France had hesitated when Cavour was alive. With an Italian Government of questionable strength and with the disagreements existing between Italy's most important leaders, certainly France could find no effective guaranties for the Pope from any assurances given by Turin. Thouvenel declared that "Mr. Rattazzi's voyage had not advanced the Roman question and the Emperor seems decided to continue the status quo."[115] Rattazzi himself was reported to have told Mr. Borten, the proprietor of the *Journal des Débats*, that he "had failed to obtain any immediate steps towards a solution of the Roman question."[116]

After the death of Cavour England had been moderately gratified to learn of the French recognition of united Italy. But this satisfaction had been largely counteracted by the news of the continuance of the French occupation of Rome. Russell and Palmerston were kept informed of Ricasoli's mediation plan and its reception in France, and they refrained from any interference in the matter until they could see what action might be taken. "We must wait for the Emperor and Ricasoli to make the first move," were the words of Russell to Cowley.[117]

When France appeared to shelve the Ricasoli proposal, however, and when Hudson continued to beg that England press France to some action in regard to Rome,[118] Russell began to bestir himself. He wrote a private letter to Cowley complaining of the postponement of French evacuation and inquiring about

[114] Compiègne, 2 Nov. 1861, Thouvenel, *Pages d'histoire,* pp. 314-315.

[115] Thouvenel to Benedetti, Paris, 26 Oct. 1861, Thouvenel, *Pages d'histoire,* pp. 307-309.

[116] Cowley to Russell, Paris, 12 Nov. 1861, *R.P.,* LVI.

[117] Abergeldie, 9 Sept. 1861, *ibid.,* CIV.

[118] Hudson to Russell, Turin, 23 Aug. 1861, *F.O., Italy,* 8: no. 355.

the advisability of a note to France.[119] Cowley replied that he feared such an action would only prolong the present situation because France always resented any semblance of foreign dictation.[120] A week later in an interview Cowley learned from Thouvenel that France was not going to deliver the Ricasoli proposals until La Valette had been to Rome a short time. Thouvenel insisted that Rome was not a purely Italian question but one for all the Powers.[121] This provoked Russell still more and made him warn France that she was endangering her entente with England. He hinted that she might soon find herself without allies.[122]

Russell soon became convinced that more pressure was necessary from England. British influence had seemed to accelerate the negotiations with Cavour; the lack of British interest now seemed to be slowing up the solution of the matter. A note was soon drafted and sent to Paris with the approval of the Queen and Palmerston in which the rights of the Italians were defended and the positions of the Pope and France were roundly criticized. The fate of the temporal power, according to Russell, was "a matter which concerns the Italian people alone, and in no respects . . . concerns the Catholics in other parts of the world." "The . . . temporal condition of the Pope is anything but independent for he is maintained . . . solely by the bayonets of 25,000 French troops." France was blamed for encouraging brigandage in Italy by the presence of her troops in Rome. "The Emperor would hardly permit a prince to reside [in Avignon] under the title of Henry V;[123] still less allow him to pay and arm bands of Legitimate guerrillas to disturb the peace of South France." While Cowley was not to deliver the note to France, he was to ask the Emperor for reports of progress on the Roman question and conform his own language to the tenor of the above dispatch.[124]

[119] Abergeldie, 4 Sept. 1861, *R.P.*, CIV.

[120] Paris, 12 Sept. 1861, *ibid.*, LVI.

[121] Cowley to Russell, Paris, 17 Sept. 1861, *F.O., France,* 1396: no. 1127.

[122] Russell to Cowley, Abergeldie, 29 Sept. 1861, *R.P.*, CIV.

[123] Henry V was the title which the Bourbon pretender to the French throne would have taken at that time.

[124] Russell to Cowley, London, 4 Oct. 1861, *F.O., France,* 1380: no. 1046.

It was not until the latter part of the month of October that Cowley saw the Emperor. "There was little novelty in what [the Emperor] said": regret . . . his honor . . . no apparent solution. He would welcome any suggestion of a solution, however, "which he could accept with consistency and which must not savour of *foreign dictation.*" Cowley suggested that since the Emperor saw no way to leave Rome during the lifetime of the present Pope, he should inform Rome of France's intention of withdrawing immediately on his death. Such a declaration would make Rome more conciliatory, prepare French opinion, and reassure Italy and England.[125]

The above suggestion by Cowley had not been in his instructions but Russell was favorable to the idea and wrote a sketch of it to Hudson to enable him to sound out Ricasoli on the matter.[126] Palmerston was not favorable to Cowley's suggestion and objected that the Pope might live for fifteen years longer. Ricasoli was very much opposed and charged Cowley with entertaining anti-Italian sentiments. In a letter to D'Azeglio the Italian Prime Minister begged him to have England remonstrate to France.[127]

Just at this time Odo Russell was returning from Rome and had had an interview with the Emperor on his way through Paris. Several times during their conversation according to Odo Russell, the Emperor had asked him to suggest a way by which France might withdraw from Rome. However, Russell repeatedly avoided committing himself to any program of a solution. Finally, when he was about to leave, the Emperor again asked Odo Russell to write him whenever he thought of a plan.[128]

Although Cowley, who was present at the interview, claimed that Napoleon's request was only in the nature of a polite fare-

[125] Cowley to Russell, Paris, 22, 23 Oct. 1861, *F.O., France,* 1398: nos. 1253, 1255.

[126] Russell to Cowley, Pembroke Lodge, 24 Oct. 1861; London, 28 Oct. 1861; *R.P.*, CIV.

[127] 27 Nov. 1861, *Ricasoli lettere,* VI, 242-244. Cowley to Russell, Chantilly, 18 Nov. 1861, *R.P.*, LVI.

[128] O. Russell to Russell, Paris, 15 Oct. 1861, *R.P.*, LXXV. Cowley to Russell, Paris, 5 Nov. 1861, *ibid.*, LVI.

well remark, both of the Russells took the Emperor's request more seriously. As a result of Ricasoli's request and the Emperor's encouragement the elder Russell began to think of writing a note to France with a definite proposal. But Cowley was of the opinion that the moment was not well chosen for such a step since even Nigra was favorable to a temporary postponement of the question.[129]

One other factor tended to delay the British proposal. The English had suddenly become involved in the *Trent* affair with the United States and they needed the coöperation of France in opposing the American violation of international law. "This American business has made us lose sight of Rome and everything else," Russell wrote Hudson.[130] Two days later he said to Cowley that because of the fine attitude assumed by France in the *Trent* affair he felt that "no dispatch (on the Roman question) need be written now. I have no pressure for it except from Turin and that I may disregard."[131] Thus the action of an American officer in West Indian waters unwittingly aided in postponing for over a month a further British intervention in favor of the Italian cause in Rome.

When Ricasoli became convinced of the failure of his mediation proposal and Rattazzi's mission, he realized that some other step would have to be taken before Parliament met on 20 November. As a last hope he proposed through Benedetti that France allow a mixed French and Italian garrison in the important towns outside of Rome and Cività-Vecchia. This would aid in stopping brigandage and at the same time reassure Italian public opinion with at least a slight advance in the direction of Rome.[132] Thouvenel's attitude was quite indefinite, however. Ricasoli's suggestion could not be considered immediately and in the meantime Thouvenel hoped that the Italian Govern-

[129] Cowley to Russell, Paris, 5, 18 Nov. 1861, 5 Dec. 1861, *ibid.*, LVI.
[130] London, 9 Dec. 1861, *ibid.*, CIV.
[131] Pembroke Lodge, 11 Dec. 1861, *ibid.*, CIV.
[132] Turin, 5 Nov. 1861; Benedetti to Thouvenel, Turin, 5, 6 Nov. 1861; *Aff. Etr., C.P., Italie,* 352: pp. 230-231, 208-216, 219-229. Ricasoli to Nigra, Turin, 6 Nov. 1861, *Ricasoli lettere,* VI, 227-230.

ment, neglecting Rome and Venice, would turn its attention to the internal organization of the country.[133]

Thus Ricasoli's last minute hopes began to fade. With the assembling of Parliament only a week away he had to determine just how he would explain the failure to advance the Roman question. Nothing remained but to reveal to the Chamber the mediation plan and how France had refused to forward the notes to Rome. The knowledge that Ricasoli had made a serious attempt to solve the Roman question would silence much criticism.

But how could the revelations be made so as not to embarrass France? Foreseeing this difficulty Ricasoli had asked Russell's advice and had sent him copies of the notes included in the offer to Rome. Ricasoli thought that the presentation of such diplomatic documents to the Parliament would set a precedent under the new Italian constitution. Since that constitution was modeled after that of Great Britain, the Italian Minister wished to draw on the experience of the *mother* government. Russell advised that the King should mention the documents in his speech and then they should be published in a blue book. He strongly favored their publication but warned Italy to publish no document involving France's attitude without previous consent from Paris.[134]

On the eve of the opening of Parliament, Ricasoli informed Benedetti of his decision to present to the Chamber the documents which France had been asked to forward to Rome. At Benedetti's request Ricasoli promised that no blame would be attached to France for not transmitting them.[135] On being informed by Benedetti, Thouvenel replied that he knew of no objection to Ricasoli's revelations to the Chambers.[136]

Since this session was not the first of the existing Chamber,

[133] Thouvenel to Benedetti, 11 Nov. 1861, *Aff. Etr., C.P., Italie,* 352: pp. 238-239.

[134] Hudson to Russell, Turin, 20 Oct., 3 Nov. 1861, *R.P.,* LXVIII. Russell to D'Azeglio, London, 3 Nov. 1861, *Ricasoli lettere,* VI, 223.

[135] Benedetti to Thouvenel, Turin, 19 Nov. 1861, *Aff. Etr., C.P., Italie,* 352: pp. 276-284.

[136] Thouvenel to Benedetti, Paris, 19 Nov. 1861, *ibid.,* p. 272.

the Italian King would not make a speech. Hence Ricasoli had a colleague interpellate him on the Roman question in order that he might have an occasion to explain his endeavors during the preceding months and have a pretext for presenting the documents. The preliminaries having been carried out, Ricasoli addressed the Chamber on the twentieth. He reiterated his determination to go to Rome only by orderly and peaceful means and in accord with France.

> The Royal Government was therefore consistent with its declarations. . . when it endeavored to solve the Roman question by means of agreements with the Holy Father, on the bases of the respective liberty of Church and State, and when it turned to the Imperial Government of France to be the mediator of its sentiments and proposals at the Holy See.
>
> At that time unfortunately it did not seem that the Holy Father was disposed to lend an ear to any proposals whatever; and the Imperial Government in its wisdom judged that in such a state of things it would not be opportune to undertake the presentation of the project which the King's Government, in the rectitude of its intentions toward the Church, had compiled with such care.[137]

Ricasoli's revelation of the mediation project definitely brought that enterprise to an end. While Thouvenel had not objected to its publication, he declared that Rome and Turin were so diametrically opposed to each other on the Roman question that Ricasoli's proposals would never have satisfied the Holy See. France had therefore declined to forward them in the capacity of mediator.[138]

The effect of the publication of the mediation project on public opinion was not as favorable as Ricasoli might have hoped. Hudson declared that "by the opinion I hear at this place (Turin) I should say that the terms offered to the Pope are considered not sufficiently stringent."[139] Thouvenel observed to Benedetti that "Ricasoli's documents have resulted in nothing more than a complete *fiasco* in France at least, . . . among

[137] *Ricasoli lettere,* VI, 447-448.

[138] Thouvenel to Benedetti, Paris, 26 Nov. 1861, *Aff. Etr., C.P., Italie,* 352: pp. 313-315. An incomplete and censored copy of this note appears in *Livre Jaune,* (1861), pp. 11-12.

[139] 26 Nov. 1861, *F.O., Italy,* 9: no. 416.

the friends as well as among the adversaries of the Italian cause."[140] Benedetti was quite concerned over Ricasoli's failure to gain the approval of Italian public opinion for his past measures. Benedetti saw that Ricasoli had in effect accepted the policy of forgetting Rome while he strengthened the interior. But Italians thought that the presence of Francis II and the French in Rome was the principal cause of the Italian internal disorder. Hence Benedetti felt obliged to suggest to Paris that they do all they could to remove Francis II. This act would aid Ricasoli in his new endeavor and create a better feeling toward France.[141]

For a better understanding of the general sentiment of the French people at the time of the debates in the Italian Parliament an examination of the October reports of the *procureurs* is again very helpful. The predominant attitude was that of indifference. But where there was a definite appearance of opinion, it seemed more often pro-Italian. The indifference itself seemed to indicate less interest in the welfare of the Holy Father.

Among the regions most loyal to the cause of the Church was Montpellier where the only question of foreign relations which interested the people was the maintenance of the French troops in Rome. Not long ago there had been an enthusiastic demonstration in that town in favor of the "Pope-King." In Besançon public attention was still given to the affairs in Italy. The upper classes with more political influence seemed concerned for the Pope's welfare; the inarticulate masses were indifferent. Likewise in the departments of Marne and Seine-et-Oise public concern was for the temporal power of the Pope but the masses showed little interest for either side.

There were a larger number of districts which showed more indifference toward the Roman question. From Picardy came the report that

> the Roman question reduced to more just proportions has lost much of its earlier passion. . . . Opinion in Picardy leaves the arrange-

[140] Paris, 26 Nov. 1861, (official), *Aff. Etr., C.P., Italie,* 352: pp. 313-315; (private) Thouvenel, *Pages d'histoire,* pp. 319-320.

[141] Benedetti to Thouvenel, Turin, 25, 26 Nov. 1861, *Aff. Etr., C.P., Italie,* 352: pp. 296-302, 319-329.

ment of Italian affairs entirely with the Emperor and would show no more impatience with the status quo than it would excitement over a solution concurred in by His Majesty.

In Normandy minds were less preoccupied by the Roman question and the clergy was calm. An identical report came from Brittany. At Lyons opinion, less interested in Rome, was willing to let the Emperor handle the matter according to his own judgment. In the Haute Saône, while there was an interest in the Roman question, yet there were apparent a desire for a solution and a concern for the disorder in South Italy. In Agens the opposition to the Government diminished the longer the Roman question remained unsolved.

In addition to a few instances of clerical sympathy and many more of benevolent indifference to the French policy in Rome there were several expressions of sentiment showing a growing favor toward Italy. At Bordeaux opinion was alienated from the cause of the temporal power because of the Pope's uncompromising attitude and because of his Minister of War's anti-French actions. At Marseilles the merchant class was alarmed by the Pope's refusal to negotiate. A prolongation of the uncertainty in Italy was seriously hampering the commerce of that port.[142]

But further inquiry was made by the French Government into the opinion of these indifferent districts in an endeavor to ascertain whether this indifference indicated a pro-Vatican or pro-Italian trend. The prefects were asked to report on the principles held by the newly elected deputies in their respective departments. In their replies further light is thrown on the shades of doubtful opinion. Cowley reported as follows to London:

> I have myself reason to know that inquiries have been made of the *Préfets* of the different departments as to the probable results of the new elections for the legislative body, and that the replies have been in general favorable to the Italian cause.[143]

[142] *Rapports des procureurs:* Montpellier, 10 Oct. 1861, 380: V. 4; Besançon, 22 Oct. 1861, 373: V. 5; Paris, 26 Nov. 1861, 384: V. 8; Amiens, 12 Oct. 1861, 371: V. 4; Caen, 10 Oct. 1861, 375: V. 4; Lyon, 8 Oct. 1861, 379: V. 5; Rennes, 17 Oct. 1861, 386: V. 4; Agens, 3 Oct. 1861, 370: V. 4; Bordeaux, 12 Oct. 1861, 374; V. 3; Marseille, 5 Oct. 1861, Aix, 7 Oct. 1861, 370: V. 4.

[143] 3 Sept. 1861, *F.O., France,* 1396: no. 1088.

The impression given by the reports of the prefects was borne out by the ensuing session of the French legislature.

Again it seemed that the Emperor was being influenced by various forces from different quarters to seek a way out of his unpleasant position in Rome. English pressure had begun to reappear and Italian opinion was becoming restive as a result of the disorders in South Italy and the Minister's lack of accomplishment. On the other hand French opinion seemed less alarmed over the Pope's position and more willing to trust to the Emperor to find a solution. As Ricasoli himself began to lessen his importunities and turn his attention to Parliament and domestic matters, Napoleon began to concern himself seriously with the problem of Italy and Rome. As early as November 19th Cowley reported that the Emperor had said "he was seriously occupied in examining how the French occupation might be brought to an end."[144] This was not just a statement to quiet English apprehension for Thouvenel himself told Benedetti on the 26th that "the Emperor has said a few words to me about his [plan], which is not yet fully developed."[145]

By the last of December the Emperor had drawn up his plan of a French-Italian accord which consisted of the following ideas: 1) Italian recognition of the Pope's temporal power where it still existed, 2) Italian promise not to allow an act of aggression against this territory, 3) Italian guaranty of free communication and commerce between Italy and the Papal territory, 4) Papal subjects to have Italian citizenship when in Italy, 5) Italy to take her proportional share of the public debts of the annexed Papal States, 6) Italy to agree to send troops to keep order in the Papal States on the application of the Pope, 7) Victor-Emmanuel to accept the title of Vicar of the Holy See (no definite territory indicated), 8) France to present Italy's declarations to the Pope, and persuade him to liberalize his government, 9) France to evacuate almost all of the Pope's territories immediately after the ratification of a Franco-Italian

[144] 19 Nov. 1861, *F.O., France,* 1399: no. 1346.
[145] 26 Nov. 1861, Thouvenel, *Pages d'histoire,* pp. 319-320.

convention along the lines indicated above. Thouvenel sent this proposal to Benedetti with instructions not to present them to Italy but to hold them for perusal and future use.[146]

Thouvenel explained the substance of the Emperor's plan, however, to Nigra and the latter wrote immediately to Ricasoli advising him to give it favorable consideration. Nigra thought it would be necessary to get the French out first and take possession of Rome later as a second step. "This is the only solution which has the chance of being considered here." After all, France, according to Nigra, was Italy's friend and Italy should give as favorable consideration as possible to proposals from Paris.[147]

Nevertheless, Ricasoli rashly persisted in an extreme view of the matter. It is strange that a Minister whose position was every day becoming weaker at home, who time and time again had begged for "just one step" toward a solution, and who had tried in vain before to move France to any action in the matter, should reject abruptly the first offer made to him from Paris. In a conversation with Benedetti he "did not conceal the fact that it would be impossible to support an accord based on the maintenance of the temporal power." "I (Benedetti) tried . . . to bring Mr. Ricasoli back to earth (*à la réalité*) . . ., but the President of the Council persisted in his opinions; faith with him . . . takes the place of reason and he has complete faith in the success of his own program."[148]

In a very interesting Council meeting of 2 January it would seem that Napoleon himself did not wish to proceed with the arranging of the Roman question. Fould had reported a financial disturbance caused by the decline of the Italian bonds. He said that this situation could only be remedied by "raising the political position of Italy." " 'But how,' rejoined the Emperor." Fould said it was not his work to find a remedy. He was indicating only the financial consequences. Persigny immediately

[146] Last of Dec. 1861, Thouvenel, *Pages d'histoire,* pp. 323-325.

[147] 29 Dec. 1861, *Ricasoli lettere,* VI, 262-268.

[148] Benedetti to Thouvenel, Turin, 16 Jan. 1862, *Aff. Etr., C.P., Italie,* 353: pp. 55-60.

observed that the remedy laid in "working for the unification of Italy."

> He was beginning to touch upon the evacuation of Rome when he was stopped by the Emperor who said to him, 'There you are again with your hobby-horse (*marotte*),' and immediately turned the attention of the Council to other subjects.[149]

But this change of subject on the part of the Emperor does not necessarily indicate the abandonment of his earlier scheme. He was evidently developing this project, as he often did, without the knowledge of the Council. He certainly would not acquaint them with a scheme before he had heard from Italy. Besides the presence of some Clerical members or the Empress[150] would also incline him to avoid the subject in order to prevent a crisis which some members were not unwilling to create.

Nothing more was done about this particular proposal after news of its unwelcome reception in Italy. The meeting of the French Parliament was approaching anyway and it seemed advisable to await its discussions to determine more exactly the state of opinion in the country.

The Imperial Government realized that the Italian situation would be the most important item of foreign affairs to be considered by the new Parliament.[151] It would be necessary, therefore, for the French Government to explain and defend its position of no progress which it would have to report. Thouvenel, who was becoming more and more pro-Italian, felt that it was the Pope's uncompromising position which was responsible for the absence of a solution, but he had no document to offer as satisfactory proof of his conviction. Lord Cowley's report to London describes vividly the method used by Thouvenel to remedy this deficiency:

[149] Cowley to Russell, Paris, 2 Jan. 1862, *F.O., France,* 1431: no. 6.

[150] It is not certain that the Empress was present at this particular meeting but she generally attended sessions of the Council. Certainly some of the members with Clerical leanings were there.

[151] This realization was confirmed by the succeeding events. Lord Cowley reported later to Russell that in the French Parliament "the bulk of the discussion on foreign matters turned this year, as last, upon Rome and Italy." Paris, 25 March 1862, *F.O., France,* 1436: no. 398.

As the moment approached for the annual meeting of the French Chambers, and for the compilation of the French Blue Book,[152] it was found that the correspondence with Rome during the past year had been of so meagre a nature that little could be extracted from it to throw any light upon the Roman question. It was therefore determined that Mr. Thouvenel should address a dispatch to the Marquis de La Valette urging the Papal Government to come to some definite arrangement with the King of Italy.[153]

It was thought that the Pope would refuse and then the request and refusal would furnish the necessary documentary material for a governmental defense and, as Nigra hoped, for a beginning of a real solution.[154]

The note in question, which was sent on 11 January, is so much more positive than most other notes to Rome that it is worth while to quote it at length to show what Thouvenel and the Emperor were willing to present to Rome and the French Parliament.

> . . . The moment has come to indicate to you (La Valette) the ideas of the Emperor's Government as a whole on the respective situations of the Holy See and Italy. France's position is found to be too profoundly affected by the antagonism of the two causes for which her political and religious traditions command equally her sympathy, so that she can accept indefinitely the responsibility of a *status quo* as harmful for one as for the other, and to give up hope of opening the way for an arrangement.
>
> The Emperor's Government does not need to express again its regrets for the events which happened in Italy during the course of the year 1860, and which must cause the Holy See acute and legitimate pain. The natural run of human events, however, leads them sooner or later to leave the paths of ordered reason (*à passer de l'ordre de la raison*), and it is under this last aspect that policy in the end is forced to consider them. The question of the day, then, is to know whether the Pontifical Government still intends to employ for the conduct of its relations with the newly established order in the Peninsula the inflexibility which is the first of its duties and incontestable rights in matters of dogma, or whether, whatever may be indeed its judgment on the transformation brought about in Italy, it may decide to accept the necessities which grow out of this obvious fact.

[152] The English called such a compilation a *Blue Book,* but in France they came to call it a *Livre Jaune* or *Yellow Book.*

[153] 24 Jan. 1862, *F.O., France,* 1431: no. 80.

[154] Nigra to Ricasoli, Paris, 16 Jan. 1862, *Ricasoli lettere,* VI, 299-301.

By recognizing the Kingdom of Italy the Government of the Emperor acted on the conviction that the hypothesis of a restoration of the past was not realizable, and, without mentioning the [non-Catholic Powers], the successive decisions of Portugal, Belgium, and Brazil have certainly the same meaning. Among the Catholic monarchies there are thus only three which have refrained from establishing official relations with the Turin Court: these are Austria, Spain, and Bavaria, and it is permissible to suppose that the peculiar position of these Powers in regard to the dispossessed sovereigns of Naples, Parma, Tuscany, and Modena has not been without some influence on their line of conduct. Besides, no cabinet thinks of reacting by force against the present order in the Peninsula. Openly proclaimed or tacitly admitted, the principle of non-intervention has become the safeguard of European peace, and the Court of Rome certainly does not intend that foreign aid shall be the means for reconquering provinces which it has lost. I go further: I refuse to believe that it would ever consent, itself, to provoke, in the interest of a very doubtful success, one of the most fearful conflagrations that history might have yet recorded. The lessons of experience as well as considerations most likely to affect the Holy See, do they all not recommend it to resign itself, without giving up its rights, to the accomplished facts, which would restore calm in the minds of the Catholic world, would reëstablish the traditions of the Papacy, which has for so long covered Italy with its protection, and would attach to itself again the new destinies of a nation which has undergone so much and after so many centuries has been delivered to herself? . . . This order of ideas once admitted, we would employ our most sincere and energetic efforts to have Turin accept [a] plan of conciliation the bases of which we would have drawn up with the Government of His Holiness. Italy and the Papacy would cease then to be in opposite camps; they both would soon resume their natural relations, and thanks to the obligations of honor guaranteed by the word of France, Rome would find in need a support from the very quarter from which the danger seems to threaten her today.[155]

La Valette read this note to Antonelli on 17 January and asked for a favorable reply from the Vatican. But the Cardinal Secretary of State seemed ready to refuse to negotiate without any further consideration.

No agreement is possible between the Holy See and those who have despoiled her. . . . We will *never* negotiate with our despoilers, I can only repeat that all agreement on that subject is impossible. . . . The Sovereign Pontiff, before his election, as well as the Car-

[155] Thouvenel to La Valette, Paris, 11 Jan. 1862, *Aff. Etr., C.P., Rome,* 1019: pp. 23-26. This was printed in 1862 in the *Livre Jaune,* (1861), pp. 33-35.

dinals at the time of their appointment took the oath never to cede Church territory. The Holy Father, therefore, will not make a concession of such a nature; a Conclave would not have the right to do it; a new Pope could not do it; his successors for the centuries to come would be no freer to do it.[156]

La Valette hoped that Antonelli's answer was not final and persuaded the Cardinal to consult the Pope before declaring such a reply to be definitive. But the Pope's attitude only confirmed that of Antonelli, and Antonelli informed La Valette that he had nothing to add to, or detract from, his reply.[157]

Cowley observed that

Mr. Thouvenel is rather satisfied than otherwise with this reply. . . . He hopes that it may open the eyes of France to the impossibility of arriving at a transaction with the Pope and so induce her to become impatient of the expense caused by the prolonged occupation of Rome.[158]

Thouvenel informed Italy that he regretted that both Rome and Turin had rejected offers of a solution. And such was the case. Both governments had been asked by France to negotiate and both had refused. But a distinction should be made between the two refusals. Italy had refused an offer because of certain undesirable clauses while the Vatican had refused to negotiate under any circumstances.

The Emperor's speech at the opening of Parliament on 27 January declared that the reason for the French recognition of Italy was to facilitate a reconciliation between two antagonistic causes. No mention was made of the Pope nor the French occupation of Rome.[159] The effects of this speech as well as the publication of the Thouvenel-La Valette notes, according to Deputy Königswarter, "calmed, at least in appearance, the warlike attitude of the Clerical majority of the Senate."[160] An in-

[156] La Valette to Thouvenel, Rome, 18 Jan. 1862, *Aff. Etr., C.P., Rome,* 1019: pp. 31-39. Published later in the *Livre Jaune,* (1861), pp. 35-37.

[157] Antonelli to La Valette, Rome 18 Jan. 1862, *Aff. Etr., C.P., Rome,* 1019: p. 40. *Livre Jaune,* (1861), p. 38.

[158] See note no. 153. Thouvenel told Nigra that the Pope's refusal was more to Italy's advantage than disadvantage. *Ricasoli lettere,* VI, 344-345.

[159] *Annales du Sénat et du Corps législatif,* (session of 1862), 27 Jan. 1862, p. 6.

[160] Königswarter to Ricasoli, Paris, 3 Feb. 1862, *Ricasoli lettere,* VI, 347-351.

dication that the French Government favored Italy might be found in the fact that Italy's refusal was not published while that of the Vatican was. Thouvenel began immediately to take advantage of the embarrassment of the Clericals by requesting a clause in the Parliament's reply to the Emperor's address which would express "regret that the Court of Rome had replied with so much inflexibility to the benevolent proposals of conciliation made by the Emperor." The clause was proposed in the Senate committee where there was a majority of seven out of ten favorable to Italy. On 17 February the reply to the address was reported to the Senate by the committee. It contained the famous regret clause which was worded in part as follows:

> No doubt, Sire, you feel the regret which we also feel very deeply, in finding on the one hand impulsiveness and immoderate demands, and on the other hand resistance and immovableness. But your counsels are those of wisdom, and it is unnecessary to say . . ., here, that the greatest accomplishments must have calmness and moderation in order to be established; there, that the most righteous causes may be diverted by extreme refusals, incompatible with the good conduct of human affairs.[161]

Since the Senate contained a slight Clerical majority, it is not surprising that a great deal of opposition was offered to this clause. On 20 February Ségur-d'Aguesseau, a Clerical, launched into a very violent speech in which he insulted Persigny, who was less anti-Clerical at this moment. Thouvenel, Baroche, and Bourcoing, all members of the Government, were compelled to oppose him in the debate. The Prince was present but remained silent. He had decided to let the ministry oppose the Clericals, which would put the latter in a bad light and at the same time force the former to become a public champion of the Italian cause.

By the 22nd Prince Napoleon could refrain no longer. He had been preparing a long speech before the opening of Parliament. The Emperor had encouraged him to speak and had furnished him with official documents. The Prince had also cor-

[161] *Annales du Sénat,* (session of 1862), 17 Feb. 1862, p. 146.

responded with La Valette on the possibilities of a solution on the death of the present Pope. La Valette's reply had been in the negative. Now the Prince stood and violently attacked both Austria and the Papal Government. Austria was harboring aggressive intentions against Italy and indirectly against France. He attempted to show conclusively that the Pope had always been ungrateful to France for her help whether it came from Bourbons, Orleanists, or Bonapartes. On 1 March he continued by declaring that France's policy should be to withdraw her troops immediately from Rome. The Pope, he declared, was only waiting for Austria to move against Italy and France. The Pope should not be allowed the temporal power. Rome should be left to the Romans. They alone should decide whether they want the Pope or Victor-Emmanuel as their sovereign.

Again the Prince's speeches made a great sensation. Austria immediately objected officially to the Prince's language and demanded that the Ministry reply to the Prince in the Parliament so as to publicly decline governmental responsibility for his declarations. Thouvenel not only refused to reply but he refused to receive the Austrian note as an official communication. He stood by the right of members of Parliament to speak freely, and denied that anything which the Prince said was official. Public and parliamentary opinion was also greatly aroused: the upper classes with intense indignation, the lower classes with unbounded enthusiasm. Nigra felt that all this agitation would at least strengthen the conviction that a solution was absolutely necessary.

On 3 March toward the end of the heated discussion on the regret clause Mr. Billault, the Government's spokesman in the Senate, rose and gave a very moderate speech. He said that Ricasoli's proposal for French mediation had not been accepted because the offer made to the Pope by Italy was obviously inacceptable. But Italy was willing to settle the Roman question while the Vatican had always refused. Three times the Pope has been made an offer which would preserve his temporal power: one by a confederation, again by a vicariat proposal for all his former territories, and lastly the full temporal power in his present territories. All these offers had been met by an absolute refusal. Billault felt that the oath taken by the Pope and Cardinals was aimed at the medieval tendency of nepotism and did not concern the present question. In fact, Popes had surrendered their temporal rights to France in Avignon and Venaissin, and to Austria on the left bank of the Po without any qualms. It seemed unreasonable that the Pope could not negotiate in a like manner with Italy. He asked the Senate to add its approval to the firm request of France for reconciliation by approving the regret clause. At the end of his speech the Senate voted the regret clause by acclamation. By 20 March both houses had approved the regret clause and a definite victory had been won by the anti-Clericals.[162]

The importance of the new attitude assumed by the French Parliament will be seen later in the influence it had on the Imperial Council. For the moment it alarmed the Pope who said he would not refuse to *consider* a French proposal but he would refuse to accept it if it meant a reconciliation with Italy.[163] La Valette, who threatened to resign if the regret clause were defeated, could then continue his duties with a certain satisfaction.[164]

Unfortunately for Ricasoli, however, these votes by the French chambers did not come in time to save him from resignation. Up to this time he had been unable to make any progress toward a solution of the Roman question. This failure had led to his downfall before the results of the discussions in the French chambers could be known. His last desperate attempts to obtain

[162] The source references to the debates on the regret clause will be found in part in the following more important collections: *Annales du Sénat, etc. . . .*, (session of 1862), Senate, 2 Feb., 1, 3 March 1862, pp. 170-180, 358-377, 379-399. *Aff. Etr., C.P., Italie,* 353: pp. 133-140; *Autriche,* 481: pp. 74-77, 78-81. *Ricasoli lettere,* VI, 344-345, 347-351, 355-357, 364-366, 375-377, 390-392, 403-405. *F.O., France,* 1436: no. 398. Comandini, *op. cit.,* pp. 225-226.

[163] La Valette to Thouvenel, Rome, 11 March 1862, *Aff. Etr., C.P., Rome,* 1019: pp. 200-202.

[164] La Valette to Prince Napoleon, Rome, 18 Feb. 1862, Comandini, *op. cit.,* pp. 225-226. Tissot, La Valette's Secretary, to his father, Rome, 13 Feb. 1862, published in the *République française,* 10 Sept. 1892.

the French evacuation of Rome and the events surrounding his sudden resignation go to make up the last phase of the Ricasoli period of negotiation.

Ricasoli had refused the French offer of a settlement by a reciprocal recognition of the *status quo* on the part of Rome and Turin, an offer which gave several eventual advantages to Italy. He had done this because it did not recognize nor advance the right of Italy to make Rome its capital. Then within one week thereafter he began to propose the old Cavour plan to France which advanced the *Roma capitale* cause no more than the plan which he had refused.[165]

Thouvenel in his turn declined to undertake negotiations at that moment on such a basis. Nigra reported that "any decision as well as any action relative to this question is at this time subordinated to the results of the discussion on the address in the French chambers."[166] Thouvenel declared that during the time of Ricasoli's government the latter had allowed and encouraged agitation for Rome. Therefore, under those circumstances the French government could not consider guaranties of the Pope's territory as sufficient. "It is not, besides, when cries of 'Down with the Pope-King' are resounding throughout the Peninsula that I would advise the Emperor to make a decision."[167]

Not at all deterred by these evident refusals of sympathetic Thouvenel to consider solutions during the time of the heated discussions in the Parliament, Ricasoli hastened to offer another plan and to press it with an apparent abandon of all consideration for the French position. The Emperor should declare "resolutely" to the Pope his determination to withdraw in two months. Italy would give the necessary guaranties.[168]

Such rash, hot-headed insistence was beginning to weaken Ricasoli's position in all quarters. He had lately berated Eng-

[165] Ricasoli to Nigra, Turin, 28 Jan. 1862. *Ricasoli lettere,* VI, 343.

[166] Nigra to Ricasoli, Paris, 30 Jan. 1862, *ibid.,* pp. 344-345.

[167] Thouvenel to Benedetti, Paris, 11 Feb. 1862, Thouvenel, *Pages d'histoire,* pp. 352-355. See also Cowley to Russell, Paris, 26 Sept. 1862, *F.O., France,* 1445: no. 1135.

[168] Ricasoli to Nigra, Turin, 23 Feb. 1862, *Ricasoli lettere,* VI, 401-403.

land for seeming to abandon Italy for the interests of Austria. D'Azeglio had had to soften the dispatch in conferring with Lord Palmerston, and the latter wished to have Ricasoli reminded that England was the best friend he had. Before the latest proposal to France, Ricasoli had goaded her with similar virulent communications. France was to be blamed for brigandage; he did not care if France did divide the Roman question into two parts, Italy must have Rome; he had been waiting three months for a French proposal, etc. France might have been instrumental in strengthening the brigands and Italy may have deserved Rome, but certainly Ricasoli did not contain himself nor handle the matters in the diplomatic spirit which they required. His flat refusal to consider the eventual French offer was only the climax of a long series of blunders. It was not surprising that Thouvenel should reply by advising Ricasoli to forget Rome, turn to the task of organizing Italy, and reconcile hostile factions for the greater strengthening of the Italian Government.[169]

This reply was particularly bitter since it arrived in the midst of the contest between Ricasoli and the King over the very question of those hostile factions. This internal quarrel led in a few days to Ricasoli's resignation.

In December during further Parliamentary debates on the Roman question Ricasoli had continued to demand Rome as Italy's capital but had adhered to the Cavour program of no forceful means and an accord with France. Although he had met strong opposition, he was able to carry a vote of confidence in the Chamber which reasserted the order of the day voted on 27 March 1861.[170]

In spite of this apparent confidence the Chamber was divided on the question of Rattazzi. Rattazzi had been against Cavour and Ricasoli at an earlier time,[171] and the antagonism had not ceased when Ricasoli formed his government. The same Chamber which approved Ricasoli's first cabinet also continued Rat-

[169] *Ricasoli lettere,* VI, 254-256, 280-292, 338-341, 401-403. Thouvenel to Benedetti, Paris, 26 Feb. 1862, *Aff. Etr., C.P., Italie,* 353: p. 183. On the adjournment of the Roman question see Maurain, pp. 506-515.

[170] Arbib, *loc. cit.,* pp. 687-689. *Aff. Etr., C.P., Italie,* 352: p. 381.

[171] Vimercati to Castelli, Paris, 2 Feb. 1861, Chiala, *Cavour lettere,* VI, 679.

tazzi as its president. When Rattazzi had gone to Paris, Ricasoli had suspected him of intriguing with France for the downfall of the Italian Ministry. This suspicion was encouraged by the fact that the French press began to criticize Ricasoli severely and compliment Rattazzi. Furthermore, Pepoli, an Italian relative of Emperor Napoleon, joined the group supporting Rattazzi against Ricasoli. La Guéronnière, Napoleon's pamphleteer, even wrote an article in *La Patrie* hostile to Ricasoli and his policy.

These signs alone would have been sufficient to antagonize Ricasoli both toward France and Rattazzi, but when Benedetti began openly to work in the interest of Rattazzi's appointment as a member of Ricasoli's cabinet, Ricasoli's uncompromising tendencies showed more than ever. Benedetti claimed to Ricasoli that he was making the suggestion for the purpose of harmony in order to strengthen the Government, but when Ricasoli refused the advice, Benedetti said he had to abstain "from insisting for fear he might see in my language some proof of the intentions with which they are pleased to impute us."

Rattazzi, wishing to avoid any semblance of ambition, offered to coöperate with Ricasoli either in the Chamber or in the Cabinet. Ricasoli thanked him but gave him no cabinet position. The Prime Minister claimed that he had no confidence in Rattazzi who, as President of the Chamber, had allowed Garibaldi to insult the Chamber, the King, and the Ministry. Besides, by his friendliness with the extreme Left, Rattazzi seemed to be the tool of France. Ricasoli put these considerations directly before the King and said if the King was not satisfied, he would willingly resign. The King supported Ricasoli at this time in order not to disturb the political situation. Ricasoli, therefore, held both portfolios of Foreign Affairs and Interior for want of any one who would consent to hold a position obviously destined for Rattazzi.[172]

[172] References on the Ricasoli-Rattazzi feud may be found among the following documents: *R.P.*, LVI, 5 Nov., 3 Dec. 1861; LXVIII, 3, 27 Nov., 12 Dec. 1861; CIV, 2 Nov. 1861; CIX, 9 Dec. 1861. *Aff. Etr., C.P., Italie,* 350: pp. 219-229, 251-259, 386. Thouvenel, *Secret,* II, 194. *La Patrie,* 20 Feb. 1862. *Ricasoli lettere,* VI, 240-242, 247-252.

The situation was aggravated by the fact that Victor-Emmanuel and Ricasoli pursued opposite policies. The King preferred to let the Roman question rest while he took up the Venetian question by encouraging revolts in the Balkans. Thus the alliance proposal which Rattazzi carried to France looked more toward eventualities in the East. When Ricasoli was pushing the Roman question, the King would show no haste in the matter to the French Minister. It became the constant charge of Hudson, the British Minister at Turin, that the King was under the influence of France and Rattazzi and that he was trying to thwart the plans of the Ricasoli government.[173]

Ricasoli's heedless methods of diplomacy were likewise alienating the sympathy of his two most important ministers abroad. It has already been seen how D'Azeglio in London tried to soften the harsh words of his superior which were directed to that quarter. Similarly Nigra, who had been Cavour's favorite for the Paris post, could not but mark the difference in manner between Ricasoli and his predecessor. On one occasion when Ricasoli was breathlessly imploring France to make some kind of immediate agreement in regard to Rome, Nigra boldly replied with the suggestion that to delay a solution would be to Italy's advantage. The Italian Minister at Paris reasoned that the permanency of Italy's position would become more assured with time and therefore she would have to make less concessions for Rome later than at that moment.[174] This difference of opinion between Nigra and Ricasoli became so noticeable that even Cowley remarked about it to Russell.[175] When Napoleon offered a solution, Nigra advised acceptance because he was sure Rome would refuse, but, as has already been shown, Ricasoli rejected it. Nigra did not coöperate more than perfunctorily with Rattazzi during his September mission, but because of his known views of the situation, many at home charged that Nigra was numbered among Ricasoli's political opponents. These charges angered

[173] *Aff. Etr., C.P., Italie,* 352: pp. 174-182, 219-229; *M.D., Italie,* 37: pp. 162-168. *R.P.,* LXIX, 26 Jan. 1862.
[174] 27 Sept. 1861, *Ricasoli lettere,* VI, 180-181.
[175] Cowley to Russell, Paris, 5 Nov. 1861, *R.P.,* LVI.

Nigra, who at the first favorable moment wrote directly to Ricasoli, showed him how from the moment of Italy's unity he had been abroad and had formed no party affiliations, advised Ricasoli not to break with the King, and finally asked to be relieved of his post. "Find someone who has 50,000 francs to spend besides his salary. Believe in him and support him."[176] Then it was that Ricasoli declared in reply that he had complete confidence in Nigra, that he knew of no one better fitted for the Paris post, and that he (Ricasoli) would only resign, himself, "when he was so inclined."[177]

It was just before the arrival of the last French refusal of Ricasoli's most recent fantastic proposal that events began to develop which were to make Ricasoli "so inclined." On 25 February there appeared a split in the majority which was supporting Ricasoli in the Parliament. The Piedmontese, including some of Cavour's relatives, showed a sullen dislike for Ricasoli. It was charged that they were jealous of a Tuscan at the head of affairs. With this extreme right group joined to the Rattazzi Left Center, Ricasoli's position became precarious. At the Council of Ministers on the 26th the reorganization of the Cabinet was suggested. This was aimed at Cordova, the Minister of Agriculture, who had shown pro-Rattazzi sympathies. The next day the Ministers waited upon the King for the regular Council meeting. But the King sent down word that he was indisposed. The messenger also let the ministers know that His Majesty had not been so indisposed that he had not been able to have an hour's conversation with Cordova just a short time before. It was surmised that Cordova had been able to precede the Cabinet and explain his side of the case to the King before the meeting.

After Ricasoli returned to the Foreign Office, he received the following flippant note from the King:

Dear Baron. It seems to me that difficulties are ever increasing, and that all is not going smoothly. I wish I could have your liver,[178]

[176] Paris, 16 Jan. 1862, 26 Jan. 1862, *Ricasoli lettere,* VI, 301-306, 332-336.

[177] Turin, 18 Jan. 1862, *ibid.,* pp. 312-320.

[178] *Liver* is a favorite Italian expression for courage.

my dear Baron, but God does not endow me with the prerogative of restraining human emotion. I hope you are more enlightened than I, and with that Victor-Emmanuel takes the hand of Bettino Ricasoli like a good and true friend.[179]

An analysis of this note sent under the existing circumstances will give some idea of the effect which it had on the austere Tuscan Prime Minister. Ricasoli took himself and his position quite seriously. He had always shown the utmost outward respect for the King. In serious matters of state such as the content of the above note he expected a similar respectful attitude on the part of the Sovereign. Instead, the King addressed him as *Baron* rather than as President of the Council, spoke of *liver*, and closed as man to man instead of as King to Prime Minister. The King may have sincerely intended the informal nature of the note to carry a tone of friendliness in a discussion of delicate subjects, but Ricasoli seemed to be in no mood to so interpret the King's method of approach. In the first sentence the King allowed himself the questionable constitutional privilege of expressing his lack of confidence in the Ministry before he had been so instructed by a vote of the Parliament. In the second sentence there appeared a veiled charge that Ricasoli ignored the feelings of the people. In the third he inferred that either Ricasoli might be poorly informed or that the latter had neglected his duty of keeping the King informed.

Ricasoli, never forgetting the respect due to the King, replied in a very formal style by tendering his resignation and that of the entire Cabinet.

To make the opinion of the Government efficacious for the good of the Crown and the nation it is essential to have *not only the support of Parliament* but also the full and certain confidence of the Sovereign.

The resigning Prime Minister concluded with "protests of sincere devotion to the *Constitutional* Monarchy."[180]

The King seemed to feel the reflection cast upon the constitutionality of his action, and in his reply, which revealed more

[179] Turin, 27 Feb. 1862, *Ricasoli lettere,* VI, 407-408.
[180] 28 Feb. 1862, *ibid.,* pp. 417-418.

openly the reasons for his opposition to Ricasoli, he attempted to take a more conventional stand.

> For some months I and a considerable (*rispettabile*) part of the Representatives of the Nation have deplored seeing the Ministry not constituted and completed as they would have liked it, we deplored seeing the course of public affairs neglected, those things left undone which ought to have been done. . . . In regard to the decision made by the Ministry, I, however, standing always first of all on the purity of the Constitutional Régime, desire to have it ascertained and be convinced myself that the Ministry enjoys the confidence of the *real* majority of the Chamber. It will be insufficient to convince me (of that confidence) if you should obtain a favorable vote by the support of the *extreme Left.*[181]

Again the King had tread on dangerous ground by indicating his hostility to a particular faction of the Chamber whose votes he would not recognize in the counting of a clear majority. He aroused conservative Ricasoli still more by insinuating that the latter depended on, and might receive, support from the extreme Left.

Ricasoli replied on the same day in the most formal way, beginning the letter with the exclamation, "Your Majesty!" He insisted on their resignations and added:

> I particularly must regret the idea . . . in Your Majesty's mind that I had sought support in the extreme Left of the Parliament.
>
> Your Majesty! I have not sought and will never seek other support than in the Constitution (*Statuto*) and the laws. . . .[182]

Victor-Emmanuel, not able to refuse the resignations a second time with dignity, consented to the Ministry's decision. After thanking them for their loyal service, he informed Ricasoli that he had requested "Rattazzi to form a new cabinet."[183]

Ricasoli, Hudson, and Russell all charged France with the responsibility for the downfall of the Ricasoli Government.[184]

[181] I March 1862, *Ricasoli lettere,* VI, 418-419.

[182] 1 March 1862, *ibid.,* pp. 420-421.

[183] 1 March 1862, *ibid.,* p. 421. For interesting contemporary accounts of the resignation read the following documents: *F.O., Italy,* 21: no. 37; 22: no. 91. *R.P.,* LXIX, 1 March 1862.

[184] Russell to Cowley, London, 5 March 1862; Hudson to Russell, Turin, 15 March 1862; *R.P.,* CV, CX, LXIX. Ricasoli to Pietri, Brolio, 30 July 1862. *Ricasoli lettere,* VII, 86-89.

Russell even heard that the Empress had exclaimed, on hearing of Ricasoli's fall, "Rome is saved forever!" Ricasoli, of course, would obviously desire to put the blame on someone else than himself for his downfall. The English, too, would like to embarrass both France and Rattazzi by such a charge. Hence such declarations should not be trusted too completely.

After more careful study it would seem that France herself can not be entirely blamed for the change of ministry in Italy. Instead it appeared that France wanted to keep Ricasoli at the head of the Government but have Rattazzi included as well. Napoleon wanted Italy strong enough to back guaranties so as to release him from the burdens of the occupation. The union of factions would lead to such an internal fortification. It is quite obvious that any man in Italy openly sponsored by France would be immediately defeated by a reaction of national pride. France's position would be weakened rather than strengthened. The Emperor declared to Cowley that "so far from wishing for Baron Ricasoli's retirement, he was sorry for it, for Italy wanted a strong government and he did not think the Cabinet of Mr. Rattazzi contained elements of such strength."[185] Thouvenel also sent several dispatches to London denying French pressure for the resignation. "Rather than Ricasoli's retirement I would have much preferred his union with Rattazzi."[186] London appeared, at least, to be convinced by the French protests of innocence. Flahault declared that he left Russell "convinced that the rumors of an intervention by the Government of the Emperor, in this circumstance, were entirely without foundation."[187]

It is more likely that Thouvenel's instructions to Benedetti to arrange a reconciliation between Ricasoli and Rattazzi were executed in a fashion hostile to Ricasoli. Ideville, who was one of the members of the French Legation at Turin, reported to

[185] Cowley to Russell, Paris, 10 March 1862, *F.O., France,* 1434: no. 298.

[186] Thouvenel to Flahault, Paris, 7 March 1862. Thouvenel, *Secret,* II, 241. Same to same, Paris, 18 March 1862, *Aff. Etr., C.P., Angleterre,* 721: pp. 92-93.

[187] Flahault to Thouvenel, London, 20 March 1862, *ibid.,* 721: p. 97.

the Quai d'Orsay Benedetti's dislike for Ricasoli and his preference for Rattazzi: "Ricasoli displeased Mr. Benedetti." Rather the French Minister "looked to Mr. Rattazzi . . . as his *frère d'âme*."[188] It is not surprising that since Benedetti's disinterestedness was questionable, Ricasoli should spurn his serious offers of reconciliation. Nor is it surprising that Benedetti, encountering the subbornness of the President of the Council, should follow his inclination by thereafter sponsoring Rattazzi's cause against Ricasoli. Hudson reported that at the Royal Ball at Milan the evening following Ricasoli's resignation Benedetti appeared so jubilant that Madame Benedetti was led to remark: "What is the matter with my husband? I haven't seen him dance so much since we were married."[189]

Ricasoli, the strongest man in Italy after Cavour's death, had Rome as his most vulnerable spot. France's satisfaction at his appointment was therefore considerably tempered by the realization that it was that very Roman question which affected France most in her dealings with Italy. Ricasoli, combining an ardor for Rome as capital with an unrelenting character, was the principal cause not only for the failure of the negotiations on the Roman question but also for his own downfall. Rattazzi, who assumed the direction of Italian affairs more because of the weakness of his predecessor than because of any particular strength of his own, would hardly inspire French confidence in the possibility of a stronger Italian state and of more sure guaranties for the safety of the temporal power in Rome.

[188] Ideville memorandum, *Aff. Etr., M.D., Italie,* 37: pp. 162-168. Ideville, *Journal,* I, 273-276.

[189] Hudson to Russell, Turin, 15 March 1862, *R.P.,* LXIX.

CHAPTER V

RATTAZZI'S MINISTRY AND ASPROMONTE

DURING the debates in the French Parliament and the ministerial crisis in Italy, England has been again exerting pressure on France for the evacuation of Rome. Therefore, before attention is turned to Rattazzi and his future policy, a careful consideration should be given to this intervening episode.

It will be recalled from the previous chapter that England with Italy's encouragement had thought seriously of again demanding of France her evacuation of the Papal States. Lord Russell had been deterred from taking this step by the *Trent* affair with the United States. Being in need of French coöperation in that question, the English statesman felt impelled not to make France feel uncomfortable in other matters.

Hardly a month had passed, however, when Russell began to think seriously of drawing up a stern note to France on the Roman question. On New Year's day of 1862 Russell announced to Cowley that he would soon send a dispatch on the Roman question.

> It is impossible the Emperor can occupy Frosinone with any view but to prevent the union of Italy. He might reduce his army at Rome to 10,000 men fully suff [icien]t.[1]

On the following day he wrote another private letter to Cowley which contains a statement which would seem to indicate that Russell was more favorable to Italy than to Austria in the Venetian question.

> The Roman despatch is gone down to Osborne for the Queen's approbation. It will not weigh for much one way or the other.
>
> I think of writing a dispatch dissuading French intervention in Italy in case Italy should attack Austria. But it will be only a despatch in reserve in case the question shall arise.[2]

Evidently from the beginning Russell had little faith in the efficacy of his remonstrances to France.

[1] London, 1 Jan. 1862, *R.P.*, CV.
[2] 2 Jan. 1862, *ibid.*

The note itself was dispatched on the fourth with the approval of both the Queen and Palmerston. It declared that since the Congress of Vienna there had been several foreign occupations in various parts of Europe. These had been justified on the ground of strengthening the occupied state so that it might keep order and reform its administration.

> On this point . . . the occupation of Rome by France has entirely failed. The government of the Pope has rejected every concession which prudence suggested, and is more detested and more helpless now than it was in 1848.

Again it had been contended that the occupation of Rome was peculiar in that it was to protect the spiritual freedom and sanctity of the Pope. This purpose, however, was being perverted by the Pope himself into an attempt to replace Francis II on the throne of Naples.

> The French Army therefore gives the Pope the advantage of a position under cover of which missiles may be discharged against the towns and villages of Southern Italy. Bandits are clothed, armed, and paid by the committees and emissaries of the Ultramontane Party, sitting in various towns of Europe and acting from the Roman territory. The district of Frosinone especially gives the armed bands of the Church the means of issuing to fight, murder, and plunder among the towns and villages of Southern Italy.
>
> Without diminishing the number of French troops in the Roman territory, they might be confined to the Comarca of Rome and the province of Civita-Vecchia.
>
> This would be practically an immense gain to Italy without any sacrifice of the protection given by the Emperor to the Holy Father.
>
> But in fact as the number of the French Corps of occupation was greatly increased in 1860 owing to temporary causes, there seems no reason why, those causes having ceased to operate, the French army in Rome should not be reduced to the force which for ten years has been deemed a sufficient garrison for Rome and Civita-Vecchia.[3]

Cowley's replies to this dispatch were hardly encouraging. He reported Thouvenel to have said that steps were being taken through the officers of the French and Italian armies to suppress brigandage. Indeed Cowley was sure that Thouvenel felt the same as Lord Russell in the matter, but the French Foreign

[3] London, 4 Jan. 1862, *F.O., France,* 1419: no. 11.

Minister did not agree with the British Foreign Minister on the remedy to be applied.

> Mr. Thouvenel states that the French Government has reason to know that were the step thus recommended to be taken, the Pope would leave Rome. . . .[4]

While England was thus firmly battling for the cause of the Italians in Rome, Ricasoli was ungratefully addressing reproaches to the British Foreign Office. He charged that England was allowing Cowley to remain in Paris when it was known that he harbored anti-Italian sentiments. He further complained that England was so selfishly safeguarding her own interests that she failed to induce France, Austria, Prussia, and Russia to do justice to Italy.

Russell defended Cowley, and when Cowley was informed of Ricasoli's accusation, he flatly denied that he was anti-Italian.

> I (Cowley) . . . asked Mr. Thouvenel categorically whether I had ever employed language in conversing with him which he could construe into an expression of condemnation of Italian unity. To this he could give but one answer—no.

Russell suggested that Ricasoli should guarantee the Vatican City to the Pope. This suggestion was in line with Napoleon's offer to Italy on 16 January. Palmerston, on the other hand, always averse to French suggestions, agreed with Ricasoli in refusing any concession to the temporal power. It was Palmerston, too, who defended England against Ricasoli's charges.

> When Ricasoli complains of our selfishness and our lack of accomplishment, he should remember that our influence with the Powers is limited by the fact that we only have peaceful and diplomatic means at our disposal. As to selfishness, any minister of a country is selfish in the sense that he must always shape the events according to the interests of his own country. But we have adopted [a policy] toward Italy which no one will deny to be highly conducive to her consolidation, and we are still disposed to work for it as we do now. But if our instances are coldly received in Berlin as in St. Petersburg and Vienna, why blame us? Does he think I am a magician, and can do everything he asks? He must confine himself to what is possible.

[4] Paris, 10, 12 Jan. 1862, *F.O., France,* 1431: nos. 26, 33.

The quick defense by the Englishmen as well as the weakening of his position at home caused Ricasoli to trim his angry sails in that quarter. D'Azeglio, with evident relief, was able to report that Ricasoli seemed "more calm . . . and more confident of the support England is able to give our cause."[5]

The French evacuation of Rome, however, was so much an English interest that none of Ricasoli's unfair charges deterred Russell from continuing his demands on France. On 5 February, while still desirous of a French evacuation of all except the Vatican City and Civita-Vecchia, Russell declared that he would feel some satisfaction if the French would only leave Frosinone and Velletri. An Italian occupation of these places would facilitate materially the war against the brigands.[6] On the 13th Russell suggested that the French retire enough to allow the Italians to occupy the mountainous regions on the frontier.[7]

Thouvenel's reply to Cowley's importunities was ever the same.

> Mr. Thouvenel declared it to be impossible to comply with Your Lordship's suggestion as such a compliance would, he asserts, place the Emperor in contradiction with the assurance which His Majesty had given to the Pope, that he would not permit the entry of any Italian troops upon any part of the territory now occupied by French troops.[8]

A few weeks after this Cowley had a chance to talk with the Emperor. At this time he asked Napoleon whether this insistence on maintaining the occupation was caused by a promise to remain in Rome as long as the present Pope should live. "The Emperor answered without hesitation that he had never given any promise of the kind and that it was perfectly well known at Rome that he had not done so."[9]

[5] Russell to D'Azeglio, Pembroke Lodge, 23 Jan. 1862, *R.P.*, CX; *Ricasoli lettere,* VI, 337, note. D'Azeglio to Ricasoli, Broadlands, 26, 26, 27 Jan. 1862, *Ricasoli lettere,* VI, 326-330, 336-341. Cowley to Russell, Paris, 28 Jan. 1862, *F.O., France,* 1432: no. 96. D'Azeglio to Russell, London, 30 Jan. 1862, *R.P.,* LXXI.

[6] 5 Feb. 1862, *F.O., France,* 1420: no. 125.

[7] 13 Feb. 1862, *ibid.,* no. 162.

[8] Paris, 18 Feb. 1862, *F.O., France,* 1433: no. 175.

[9] March 1862, *F.O., France,* 1434: no. 297.

It was right after the French Government's refusal of the English offer that the *Journal des Débats*, a paper moderately sympathetic with the Italian cause, offered a plan of solution. After charging that public enthusiasm in Rome for the Pope was aroused largely by mercenary methods, this journal proposed that all of the Pope's territory be occupied jointly by French and Italian troops. Then, when the Pope had become accustomed to the safety assured by the presence of the Italians, and when the passions of the Romans had subsided so that there would be no danger anyway, the French might withdraw altogether.[10]

Cowley's interest was greatly aroused by this suggestion. He immediately sent a copy to Russell and then interviewed Thouvenel on the matter. "But His Excellency showed no disposition to support it. He declared that France had had enough of mixed occupations."[11] But Russell, too, in reply to Cowley's report on the *Journal des Débats* plan, thought that "a mixed French and Italian garrison at Rome would not be convenient." He still adhered to his proposal of a French evacuation of the left bank of the Tiber. "If you see the Emperor, pray tell him my despatch contains the solution *for which he asked Odo*."[12]

When Cowley again approached Thouvenel in the interests of Russell's plan, Cowley reported,

Mr. Thouvenel said that he feared Your Lordship's plan would not be accepted by either party, the Pope declaring that he will listen to no arrangement which did not restore to him the possessions which he lost, and the Italian Government refusing to sanction any settlement which did not recognize Rome as the capital of Italy. Between the profession of two such extreme opinions no solution seemed possible, for France could not permit Italian troops to enter upon the territory occupied by her without the Pope's acquiescence. Besides, said Mr. Thouvenel, why are we asked to give up Rome and the Patrimony of St. Peter to the King of Italy? The utmost that can be expected of us would be the restoration of Rome to the Romans. I said that as far as Her Majesty's Government is concerned,

[10] *Journal des Débats*, 12 March 1862.

[11] Paris, 14 March 1862, *F.O., France,* 1435: no. 347. *Parl. Papers,* (1862), LXIII, 487.

[12] 17 March 1862, *ibid.*, pp. 487. 19 March, 1862, *R.P.*, CV.

I would answer for their being satisfied with such an arrangement, meaning, of course, that the Romans should be masters of their own destinies.

Cowley insisted that in that case the Pope's army would have to be made up of Romans and not of foreigners.[13] Thouvenel in commenting on Russell's plan to Flahault said, "That is not the solution."[14]

Russell was quick in replying to Thouvenel's objections. To Thouvenel's declaration that neither party would accept his proposal, Russell countered by stating, "I never imagined that the Pope would accept it." Neither would the Italians accept it, according to Russell, unless they knew it was to be temporary. The British Minister went on to say that it would be more dangerous to give Rome to the Romans than to the Italians because the former condition would mean revolution and bloodshed. The Pope had committed enough acts of hostility against Italy to justify her in attacking his territory. Only France's illegal occupation was preventing Italy from obtaining redress.[15]

In an ensuing interview with Thouvenel, Cowley was told that the Emperor heartily agreed with his Minister's refusal. Thouvenel then went on to deny that Italy had any claims according to international law for the possession of Venice or Rome. But Cowley considered this a weak argument since France had not insisted on international law in the cases of Umbria, Tuscany, and Naples.[16]

Russell thereupon dropped the controversy.

I wish to give expression to our views respecting Rome, and by no means to keep up a controversy with Thouvenel.

You (Cowley) will not therefore read my fresh despatch to Thouvenel.

All that I want is that when the Emperor speaks as he did to Metternich of disorder in the South of Italy, we may be able to reply that we have already pointed out to him the source of that

[13] 20 March 1862, *Parl. Papers,* (1862), LXIII, 487-488.

[14] 21 March 1862, Thouvenel, *Secret,* II, 260.

[15] 22 March 1862, *F.O., France,* 1421: no. 320. *Parl. Papers,* (1862), LXIII, 488-489.

[16] Cowley to Russell, Paris, 28 March 1862, *F.O., France,* 1436: no. 413. *Parl. Papers,* (1862), LXIII, 489.

disorder, and that if he will place the Pope and the ex-King of France at Avignon, he will have similar disorders in the South of France.[17]

Again in a later private letter to Cowley, Russell declared:

> I think the Roman affairs must now be left to the Emperor, the King, and the Pope-King to manage as they can. I have given my view of an honest compromise but if crooked ways suit the Emperor and Rattazzi better, it is no business of ours to meddle.[18]

Thus it seemed that Russell's own prediction that his remonstrances would be of no avail was fulfilled.

The French, however, experienced no great relief from the cessation of outbursts from London, for no sooner had Russell become silent than disturbing reports of English activity in Vienna began to come from Gramont. This French Ambassador had unearthed a secret memorandum of a Mr. Klindworth containing supposed instructions from Palmerston. Klindworth was to sound out Vienna about an Anglo-Austrian alliance. He was to frighten the Austrians by predicting the formation of an alliance of Italy, France, and Russia against Austrian interests in the Balkans. Austria would gain little sympathy from Prussia, and therefore Austria's only hope was to ally herself with Great Britain.[19] The fact that Palmerston was known to be Francophobe and that England had just ceased her pressure directly from London made France all the more suspicious. Perhaps, the French thought, Palmerston had allowed Russell to try his direct negotiation first and that failing, he would scheme something himself.

By May 1st France was more reassured about this secret mission. It was found that Klindworth had gone to observe Austria's internal situation. Furthermore Palmerston's declarations in Parliament, which were not entirely favorable to Austria, tended to lessen France's apprehension.[20] What is of particular interest, however, is the fact that during the month

[17] 29 March 1862, *R.P.*, CV. London, 2 April 1862, *F.O.*, *France*, 1422: no. 368. *Parl Papers*, (1862), LXIII, 489-490.

[18] London, 10 May 1862, *R.P.*, CV.

[19] Enclosure of Gramont to Thouvenel, 31 March 1862, *Aff. Etr.*, *C.P.*, *Autriche*, 481: pp. 203-206. Thouvenel, *Secret*, II, 284, note; 290-291.

[20] Gramont to Thouvenel, Vienna, 1, 2, 7 May 1862, *Aff. Etr.*, *C.P.*, *Autriche*, 481: pp. 200-202, 210, 234-236.

of April, while France was still fearful of the effects of the Klindworth mission, the French Ministry and the Emperor seriously occupied themselves with a search for a solution of the Roman question. This search will be discussed a little further on. In the meantime a few intervening matters must be considered.

In January and April more reports on French public opinion came in from the provinces. It offered an opportunity to study the effects of the Parliamentary debates on public opinion, and measure how much the Government would be supported by that opinion in the approaching efforts toward a solution. The January reports, while generally reflecting moderate or disinterested attitudes, gave a few examples of new sympathy for the Pope. In Lyons, where interest was waning, the only concern which persisted was for the temporal power of the Pope. This is surprising because Lyons had generally been opposed to the Pope. In Brittany, which had formerly been abandoning the Pope's cause, the Legitimists and Clericals were joining forces and becoming active. Reports from Normandy and the regions around Besançon all indicated a continued and increased indifference toward the Roman question.

The April reports, which came after the parliamentary debates, seemed decidedly more pro-Italian. No opinion seemed decidedly in favor of the Pope. Only signs of indifference and moderation and a few indications of sympathy for Italy seemed to be prevalent. In Picardy the economic question raised by the American Civil War had almost entirely dominated the thoughts of the people. From Besançon, which had previously been consistently Clerical in opinion, came the following report:

> Even within the clergy hardly more than the furious minded demand the restoration to the Holy Father of his former boundaries, and likewise only the few excited to the opposite stand think that Italy should be completed by giving Rome to Piedmont. It is between these two radical solutions that opinion tends more and more to settle.

The Roman question was no longer a topic of excitement at Bourges. Montpellier *procureurs* said that the excitement there over Rome and Italy had subsided. The people would be willing to see the Pope limited to his present possessions. Brittany again appeared to be losing interest in the question. From Aix came the report that the Prince's speech had so enthused the radical republicans that many had organized *cercles impériaux* or *cercles Napoléons*. From Bordeaux came reports of satisfaction over the attitude of Parliament on the Roman question.

Public opinion has shown itself very satisfied with the unanimous vote on the paragraph relative to Roman affairs (regret clause).

The Government's policy seems to have gained almost the unanimous approbation of opinion. . . . The solution proposed by the Government, although temporary in nature, has been generally approved.

The report from Normandy declared that "the votes of the Senate and Legislative Body on the Roman question. . . have satisfied the wise and prudent minds which are in a very great majority." Lyons seemed to revert to its usual position which was in favor of the regret clause but not favorable to Italy's extreme demands.[21] The favorable reaction of opinion to the regret clause could not but encourage the Government to find a solution.

Nevertheless, before any voluntary step was taken by France toward a solution, her statesmen would certainly examine the men and policies of the new ministry in Italy. The influence of personnel on events is very great, as Cavour's death had shown. Therefore a change from Ricasoli to Rattazzi would not be without considerable importance. His cabinet which was announced on 3 March contained Durando as Minister of Foreign Affairs, Cordova as Minister of Interior, Depretis as Minister of Public Works, and Pepoli as Minister of Commerce. The last two were numbered among those of the Left and Benedetti, who had worked so whole heartedly for Rattazzi, was forced to complain

[21] *Rapports des procureurs.* Lyons, 27 Dec. 1861, 1 April 1862, 379: v. 5; Caen, 13 Jan., 8 April 1862, 375: v. 4; Agens, 7 April 1862, 370: v. 4; Besançon, 29 Jan., 14 April 1862, 373: v. 6; Bordeaux, 30 Jan., 15 April 1862, 374: v. 3; Amiens, 31 March 1862, 371: v. 4; Aix, 9 April 1862, 370: v. 4; Bourges, 5 April 1862, 374: v. 3; Montpellier, 10 April 1862, 380: v. 4; Rennes, 9, 28 Jan. 1862, 7 April 1862, 386: v. 4.

that his protégé adhered to the Left and very little to the Right.[22] Pepoli, it may be of interest to note, was a distant relative of the Emperor.

Thus it was with even greater anxiety that Thouvenel and the Emperor awaited the first official declarations of policy. This came on the 7th when the new Prime Minister had occasion to sketch his policy before the Chamber. His first statement was destined to excite France in her most tender spot: Rattazzi hoped for an alliance with France and England, or at least with *one* of them. On the Roman question he declared that moral force had already advanced the Italian cause, as witnessed by the votes of the French Senate and Legislative Body. He too then promised to avail himself of the moral means of furthering Italy's Roman aspirations in the future.

> Besides moral means, Gentlemen, I also said that it was wise to resort to diplomatic means. And here also the Parliament has traced the way for us; and it is this that we are determined to follow. You proclaimed that we should go to Rome in accord with France. Fine, that is our motto. We intend to proceed in accord with France in the solution of such questions.

To abandon France, according to Rattazzi, would be more harmful to Italy than to France. But in addition to alliances, coöperation with France, and the Roman question Rattazzi would give careful attention to internal reforms.[23] They were rather all-embracing promises which this new leader was making. If his predecessor was unable to accomplish much in any of these projects, one would be led to doubt the wisdom of such an extravagant program.

It is interesting to observe the favorable receptions which Rattazzi's initial pronouncement obtained in Paris and London and yet, at the same time, to find on what opposite grounds each capital founded its favor. Thouvenel declared:

> We see with pleasure that [Rattazzi] looks at [Roman affairs] with calmness and announces the determination not to look for a solution of that question outside of the paths of conciliation and of understanding with the Government of the Emperor.

[22] 3 March 1862, *Aff. Etr., C.P., Italie,* 353: pp. 204-208.
[23] *Atti ufficiali,* Chamber, 7 March 1862, pp. 1981-1982.

The French Minister further denied that the presence of Pepoli in the Cabinet in any way could indicate French solidarity with the existing Italian Government.[24] Then came Russell's approbation a few days later:

> It is with much gratification that Her Majesty's Government learn that Mr. Rattazzi considers it his bounden duty to follow up that vote of the Italian Parliament which represents Rome as the capital of Italy, and that nothing should divert his attention from that cardinal point of Italian policy. Her Majesty's Government entirely concur in the opinion of the Prime Minister that Italy cannot be constituted without Rome.[25]

France and England were congratulating Rattazzi for quite opposite reasons. This may bear witness to the cleverness of Rattazzi's speech, but even more does it reflect the evident antagonism of both the English and French in Italy and their determination to guide the new minister into their own favorite "paths of righteousness."

Rattazzi's next move was to compose a circular to his representatives at the various capitals. This had a much more aggressive tone and certainly alarmed the French by the fact that it showed a tendency to follow England's advice rather than that of France. However, the encouragement for such a document came partly from a French source—none other than from Prince Napoleon himself. Rattazzi less than a week after his speech in the Chamber wrote to the Prince: "I shall not neglect to prepare a note in the sense that Your Highness has so opportunely suggested."[26] The circular dispatch sent out on 20 March soon caused a buzz of excitement in several foreign chanceries. The dispatch dwelt more at length on the same topics which the Prime Minister had previously discussed in the Chamber. But the tone was entirely changed. Rattazzi claimed both Rome and Venice for Italy. He said he would not disturb the Venetian question at that time but he recognized Venice as a sore spot which might break the bonds of patience of the Italian

[24] Thouvenel to Benedetti, Paris, 11 March 1862, *Aff. Etr., C.P., Italie,* 353: pp. 224-225.

[25] Russell to Hudson, London, 14 March 1862, *F.O., Italy,* 19: no. 44.

[26] Rattazzi to Prince Napoleon, Turin, 13 March 1862, Comandini, *op. cit.,* pp. 226-227.

Kingdom. Then in regard to Rome, after denouncing the temporal power and asserting Italy's claim to the city as its capital, he launched into a denunciation of the Pope and Francis II for the brigandage in South Italy. But Rattazzi went even further and suggested a French connivance for ulterior motives.

The resistance which Rome offers to the legitimate aspirations of Italy in the name of an interest which is neither comprised nor menaced results evidently, whatever may be the intentions of the authors of that resistance, less in alarming consciences against imaginary perils than in upholding the interest of parties uninterested (*étrangers*) in religion, and who are searching at that very court and through the influences at their disposal for a leverage which they lack in the political field.[27]

Although the statement might appear to refer to the Legitimists generally, at the same time it could be inferred to mean the French Government which was clearly the tool of Legitimist pressure at home.

It is not surprising then that France should react in a much more unfavorable manner to the circular dispatch than to Rattazzi's earlier speech. Thouvenel quickly replied through Benedetti who was instructed to protest to Rattazzi against his extreme claim to Rome as Italy's capital.

This new affirmation of a right whose legitimacy we do not recognize, obliges me to restate myself the reserves formulated by the Government of the Emperor at the time when he decided to recognize the Kingdom of Italy.

Furthermore Thouvenel regretted the alarm which Rattazzi's circular would cause in Austria because of the extreme declarations it contained in regard to Venice.[28] It will be remembered

[27] Rattazzi to Italian Representatives, Turin, 20 March 1862, *Libro verde,* (12 July 1862), pp. 1-6.

[28] 28 March 1862, *Aff. Etr., C.P., Italie,* 353: pp. 310-312. In a private letter to Benedetti Thouvenel declared: "I am telling you in an official dispatch what I think of Mr. Rattazzi's unfortunate circular. The Emperor read my dispatch and thought it was indispensable to write it in order to set us right with the Senate and Legislative Body. That is really its principal purpose, but if it can also serve to recall the Italian Government to a realization of the real situation, I shall not be sorry." Thouvenel, *Pages d'histoire,* p. 360. In regard to Austria's alarm see 20 April 1862, *Aff. Etr., C.P., Italie,* 353: p. 415. Cowley to Russell, Paris, 1 April 1862, *F.O., France,* 1436: no. 436.

that France's reservations also covered this point in reiterating her position assumed at the Warsaw Conference.

When Benedetti saw Rattazzi, he rebuked him also for the needlessness of the circular. If Rattazzi had remained silent, France could have remained silent. As it was, France was forced to proclaim again declarations which she would prefer to withhold. Rattazzi, however, still insisted on the necessity of the circular and declared that the internal order in Italy would be seriously endangered if the people began to think that France no longer seconded their national aspirations.[29]

Thus it would seem also that the eventual results were proving the non-existence of French influence in the change of the Italian ministry. Certainly Rattazzi was making it more uncomfortable for France and was emphasizing the Roman question even more than his predecessor. What was more disconcerting to the French, however, was the fact that this supposed francophile and anglophobe Rattazzi was opposing France and upholding England. It was just at this same time that Russell was pushing his proposal for the cession of the left bank of the Tiber to Italy. Rattazzi in a conversation with Hudson declared that he would support Russell's temporary plan but would never accede to Thouvenel's suggestion of the permanent independence of the city of Rome.[30]

Thus it came about that before the month of April various forces were at work to impel the French leaders on their own initiative to seriously search for a solution of the Roman question. Italian public opinion seemed to be increasingly insistent on a favorable solution of the Roman question. Each succeeding ministry, whether led by Cavour, Ricasoli, or Rattazzi, was compelled to stress the Roman question in order to keep itself in power. Ricasoli had obviously lost his hold on Italy because of the lack of any headway in the matter. This situation spelled nothing less than an eventual Italian estrangement with France. All France's advantage gained in Italy in 1859 would be irre-

[29] Benedetti to Thouvenel, Turin, 5 April 1862, *Aff. Etr., C.P., Italie,* 353: pp. 341-349.

[30] Hudson to Russell, Turin, 25 March 1862, *F.O., Italy,* 22: no. 80.

trievably lost. But this was not all. France's only other associate since the Crimean War, England, was now pressing her on the same subject. England, too, as France's only rival for influence in Italy was seemingly displacing the former French-Italian solidarity by a British-Italian community of interest. Worse still, there was some suspicion that England might draw Austria into an alliance against France. This would mean practically a French isolation in Europe and just as surely a weakening of the Empire at home. If French public opinion would allow it, something then had to be done in regard to Rome. Fortunately the January reports had indicated a general lack of interest in the Roman question in France, the parliamentary debates had ended in a regret clause aimed at the Pope, and the April reports showed a lessening of sympathy for the Vatican. The field seemed conveniently open for some action on the thorny subject of Rome. The resulting deliberations are consequently the next objects of our attention.

As far back as December 1861 Thouvenel had wanted to bring the Roman question squarely before the Emperor's divided Council and thrash out the subject decisively. Prince Napoleon, Fould, Persigny, and Rouher had also favored such a step.[31] It was thought that there was such a large majority of the Council in favor of an arrangement based on the *status quo* that Walewski and Randon, the only extreme supporters of the Pope, would have to withdraw their opposition or resign from the Council. But the January reports did not give a definite enough evidence of public support of the majority of the Council to strengthen their contentions and the Parliamentary sessions were near. Accordingly the important Council discussion was postponed.

But after the events already recounted had taken place and when both England and Italy were pressing for a temporary arrangement, Thouvenel began desperately to consider what might be done.

> This unfortunate question of Rome is weakening my health and exhausting my mind. . . . I am expecting [Mr. de La Valette] next

[31] Cowley to Russell, Paris, 18 Dec. 1861, *R.P.*, LVI.

week and we will see together what stand can be taken as a result of the double effect of the irritation and consternation which the debates on the address produced on the Pope's followers and on His Holiness himself.[32]

In fact the occasion of La Valette's return from Rome offered the opportunity for the French Government to undertake the solving of the perplexing and persisting Roman tangle. La Valette had drawn up his own plan which he proposed to the Emperor at their first conference. It consisted of the following provisions:

1. A treaty was to be offered to Italy containing the following provisions:
    a) Italy was to recognize the sovereignty of the Pope over the present territory which he possessed.
    b) Italy was to guarantee this territory from all regular or irregular attack.
    c) Italy was to assume its proportion of the Pontifical debts for the Church States annexed to Italy.
    d) France was to withdraw her troops from Italy in . . . (perhaps 12 or 15 months).
2. A proposal was to be offered to the Pope by which he was to acquiesce in, without recognizing, the territorial *status quo* providing the above treaty was signed.

As will be observed, this plan corresponded to Thouvenel's plan negotiated with Cavour in 1861 with the exceptions that the Pope would be included in the negotiations and Italy would recognize and not just acquiesce in the Pope's temporal sovereignty.

"His Majesty listened to his plan . . . and regarded it with favor." But La Valette continued by declaring that if that policy was accepted by the French Government, he would insist that all French officials who worked with him should be in sympathy with that line of action. This meant that he wanted Goyon to be replaced in Rome by some general less sympathetic with the reactionary party there.[33]

[32] Thouvenel to Gramont, Paris, 22 March 1862, Thouvenel, *Secret,* II, 262-264.

[33] Cowley to Russell, Paris, 4 April 1862, *F.O., France,* 1436: no. 445. In this letter Cowley stated that "in regard to the plan brought forward

The methods employed in this project were similar to the methods used by Cavour in his direct negotiations with Rome. It was an attempt to weaken the cause of the Pope by making him utter another refusal. Vimercati was again in Paris as a semi-official auxiliary to Nigra. In an audience which he had with the Emperor on 7 April the Emperor is reported to have declared:

> I have a new project which I have been studying for some time; I have still to set it down, in order to round it off in a practical way, although I am convinced in advance that it will not be accepted. . . . I shall let you know my ideas in a few days, which I may engage you to transmit to Turin in an entirely semi-official capacity and under the seal of the greatest secrecy.

Vimercati felt that if Italy could pretend to accept the plan, providing it did not demand too many sacrifices, he was sure the Pope would refuse. Thus Italy would gain favor and at the same time see the Pope lose much of the sympathy that he had thus far retained.

This project which the Emperor had been considering did not turn out to be La Valette's proposal at all. It was similar to the Vicariat plan but included the idea that Italy should recognize the Pope's sovereignty over the territory taken from him by Italy as far as the Apennines. Thouvenel told Vimercati the next day that he and La Valette were convinced "that the Emperor's project will be rejected by the Pope." After this refusal Thouvenel would propose his former plan which he negotiated with Cavour.[34] From the tone of a letter to Gramont it would appear that Thouvenel objected to the Emperor's plan even as a preliminary step.

---

by Mr. de La Valette, Mr. Thouvenel has, in the strictest confidence, given me an outline of it." This is the plan reproduced in the text. Russell's reply was as follows: "If this Italian scheme of Mr. La Valette's is proposed to the Government of Victor-Emmanuel, we shall take no part and give no advice. . . . I wash my hands and will have no concern in garroting the Pope." Russell to Cowley, London, 5 April 1862, *R.P.*, CV.

[34] Vimercati to Rattazzi, Paris, 7 April 1862, "Sulla via di Roma- da Aspromonte a Mentana," *Nuova Antologia,* Ser. IV, LXXXV, (1 Jan. 1900), 9-11.

As for me, my dear Duke, I think as do you, that nothing practical can be done outside of what was discussed before the death of Mr. Cavour.[35]

Thouvenel found himself in a difficult position. He had long been urging the Emperor to take some step in the matter of Rome. Now, although the Emperor was formulating a plan, Thouvenel found it inacceptable. How was he to avoid discouraging the activity of the Emperor and still humor him into a more feasible plan? "I have to do soldering more often than sapping[36] and I do believe that this work will have some results." Thouvenel told Benedetti that he had proposed the Cavour plan to the Emperor with a clause providing for a delay of the withdrawal until the Pope could provide for his protection. He claimed that Billault, Rouher, Fould, Baroche, and Troplong were in favor of his plan. "His Majesty . . . is working on a plan . . . which I regard as absolutely inacceptable, but which I am letting him finish before advocating mine more vigorously." Both were to be presented and discussed in the Council.[37] The difficulty of the situation was increased by the obvious embarrassment to the Ministers when they contemplated the necessity of criticizing the Emperor's own plan.

At one stage of the Emperor's formulation he seemed to have entertained the possibility of applying to Rome the home-rule plan of government of the city of London. Such a fantastic plan was abandoned when Flahault, La Valette, and the consular director, Mr. Herbet, advised against it. Thouvenel remarked that "St. Paul can not be used as an example for St. Peter."[38]

Two intervening events took place at this time which threw some light on the attitude of the French Government. Victor-Emmanuel had decided to visit Naples again in order to show his popularity in this troublesome area. The English fleet had decided to pay him a visit of courtesy at that place. This promp-

[35] Thouvenel to Gramont, Paris, 8 April 1862, Thouvenel, *Secret,* II, 272-273.

[36] "Il me faut me servir plus souvent de la soude que de la sape."

[37] Thouvenel to Benedetti, Paris, 12 April 1862, Thouvenel, *Pages d'histoire,* pp. 365-366.

[38] Thouvenel to Flahault, Paris, 14 April 1862, Thouvenel, *Secret,* II, 276-277.

ted the French to do the same. It would be seen as an act of sympathy for Italy without compromising their position in Rome. Furthermore the presence in Rome of a delegation of French bishops would arouse Italy unless something was done to counteract it. "We would have nothing to gain . . . by letting the English increase their influence in Italy at our expense," was Thouvenel's argument. Indeed this reveals quite strikingly the rivalry between France and England for Italian favor.

Italian public opinion responded very favorably to the friendly gesture by France. The extremists were quieted; the moderate patriots regained hope of help from France; and the statesmen were relieved of some of the public pressure for action which had caused them considerable alarm.[39]

The other intervening event was the recall of Goyon during the first week of May. He at first was only asked to come home for consultation. Only later did it appear that his recall was permanent. This recall was interpreted by many as the first step in the evacuation of Rome. It was rumored that Goyon was consulted on the question of reducing the force of occupation. Monsignor Berardi complained to the French chargé on behalf of the Vatican that the visit of the fleet and the recall of Goyon at the same time that Palmerston and Victor-Emmanuel were delivering speeches hostile to the Vatican were evidences of French abandonment of the Pope. Thouvenel, however, only denied in rather general terms Rome's charge of abandonment. Goyon's recall was shown to be permanent by the appointment of Montebello as his successor. But the gratification felt by the friends of Italy was checked on learning that Montebello's wife was very pro-Vatican and in close touch with the Empress.[40]

[39] On the French fleet to Naples see: Thouvenel to Gramont, Paris, 23 April 1862, Thouvenel, *Secret,* II, 282; Benedetti to Thouvenel, Turin, 25 April 1862, *Aff. Etr., C.P., Italie,* 353: pp. 394-395; Thouvenel to Belline, Paris, 3 May 1862, *Aff. Etr., C.P., Rome,* 1020: p. 3.

[40] Kisseleff to Rechberg, Paris, 8 May 1862; Thouvenel to Belline, Paris, 17 May 1862, *Aff. Etr., C.P., Autriche,* 481: pp. 225-228; Rome, 1020: pp. 33-34, 56. Cowley to Russell, Paris, 8, 29 May 1862, *F.O., France,* 1438: no. 596; 1439: no. 708. *Opinion nationale,* 9 May 1862.

Hopes or fears, however, were to be confirmed or disappointed by the events which were moving rapidly to a climax in the councils of the French Government.

On 20 May 1862 the Emperor addressed to Thouvenel a letter defining his position on the Roman question which was obviously intended for eventual publication. The Emperor declared that he refused to take an extreme stand on the Roman question. He opposed the Italian demand for the destruction of the temporal power just as he objected to the Pope's refusal to negotiate with a recognized Italian nation.

> [Reconciliation] might be obtained by a combination which, while maintaining the Pope master in his own house would lower the barriers which separate today his states from the rest of Italy.
>
> That he may be master in his own house, independence should be assured him and his power accepted freely by his subjects. It is to be hoped that it will be that way when, on the one hand, the Italian Government promises France to recognize the States of the Church and to accept an agreed boundary; and, on the other hand, when the government of the Holy See, going back to her old traditions, may consecrate municipal and provincial privileges in such a way that those communities may, as they say, be administered by themselves.[41]

It will be noticed that the note inferred self-determination and self-government by the people in the Pope's territory. On the other hand, it provided for Italian *recognition* of a Papal State and the temporal power.

The return of La Valette to Rome was seized upon by Thouvenel and others as the occasion for the crystallization of the Imperial Government's attitude and plan of a solution. The note to Thouvenel was to determine the attitude, and at about the same time the Emperor offered to Thouvenel and the Council his own plan of a solution. Cowley, as we have seen, was always quickly and well informed of developments. He reported:

> The plan as stated to me was as follows:
>
> Rome and the Patrimony of St. Peter to remain under immediate

[41] 20 May 1862, *Aff. Etr., C.P., Rome,* 1020: pp. 115-118; *Autriche,* 481: pp. 250-254. *Livre Jaune,* (1862), pp. 3-6. This note was later made public in the *Moniteur universel,* 25 Sept. 1862. The form of the note Thouvenel said "had been modified between the 20th and the 30th of May but . . . that it was published in the exact words in which it was transmitted to La Valette." Cowley to Russell, Paris, 26 Sept. 1862, *F.O., France,* 1445: no. 1136.

Government of the Pope, but with a *Conseil d'Etat*, the members of which were to be chosen under some form of popular election, with the power of determining the budget, local news, etc., the Pope to have a veto over the proceedings of this body.

The whole of the States which formerly belonged to the Pope to recognize His Holiness' nominal sovereignty. The States themselves to be divided into circles or departments over which lay governors are to be placed, having similar powers to those possessed by the Lord Lieutenant of Ireland. The Governor to be named by the Pope.

The Italian troops to have the right of garrison in all places except Rome and the Patrimony of St. Peter. The Pope, if he pleases, to have his own troops in Rome and the Patrimony.

The Roman States thus reconstituted to send deputies to the Italian Parliament, senators to the Italian Senate. The Pope to have a veto power over all laws passed by the Italian Parliament, in so far as they may affect Rome and the Patrimony.

All Roman citizens to be eligible to offices under the Italian Government.

The Pope to be represented at Foreign Courts.

The Pope to have uncontrolled power over the clergy, monastic orders, and churches in Italy.

The Papal arms to be placed in the center of the Italian flag. The Italian money to be struck with the Pope's effigy. Arrangement for the Pope's income.

Guarantee of the plan by the Roman Catholic Powers.[42]

Thouvenel declared that Persigny was the real author of the plan, but the Emperor had eagerly adopted the Minister of Interior's views as his own. Thouvenel, however, thought the plan "senseless." In the council Thouvenel drew up his objections to this plan: The King of Italy could not, and would not, agree to such a transfer. To give the Pope such ecclesiastical powers would not only be dangerous to Italy but would also set a bad precedent for France's ecclesiastical relations later.[43] Thouvenel insisted on the plan used in the negotiations with Cavour as the only acceptable one.[44]

[42] Cowley to Russell, Paris, 20 May 1862, *F.O., France,* 1439: (secret, no number, Cowley's own signature at the end). In this same note Cowley declared: "I ascertained that [the plan] existed in the Emperor's own handwriting"; and again, "Mr. Thouvenel . . . read me the Emperor's memorandum which . . . goes on to propose the measures which I have enumerated above. . . ."

[43] Thouvenel confided to Gramont that "the Emperor still dreams of his *impossible* marriage." Paris, 24 May 1862, Thouvenel, *Secret,* II, 303-304.

[44] See above note no. 42 for the source of this information. The reader will again note Thouvenel's advocacy of the plan used with Cavour. This is

Vimercati, who gained his information from Rouher, gave an account of the debates in the Council between the 23rd and the 28th. On the 23rd the Emperor modified his proposal so that it did not include any retrocession of territory by Italy. But after Rouher had fought energetically against it and when it appeared that Walewski was the only minister favoring it, the Emperor withdrew it altogether. On Sunday the 26th Thouvenel and Rouher had a private two-hour conference with Napoleon. They tried to win the Emperor to the earlier Cavour treaty but modified so as to provide for a gradual withdrawal over a period of three years. But the Emperor objected to the long period of time before complete evacuation would take place.

> I am quite willing to come over to your project, but I'd rather not have a definite period before evacuation. Three years is a long time, and yet I could not propose a shorter period.

Thouvenel and Rouher continued the argument until the Emperor finally accepted their point of view. He would discuss the plan before the Council on Wednesday, 28 May.

At the Council meeting Thouvenel presented and defended his plan of the Cavour treaty with a period of three years before evacuation. Rouher also discussed the project favorably at great length. The Minister of Marine did likewise. Only Magne, Walewski, and Persigny opposed it. Persigny, who had suggested the Vicariat part of the Emperor's plan, opposed the Thouvenel plan on the same grounds on which Thouvenel had opposed the Emperor's plan. He insisted that Victor-Emmanuel could not recognize nor acquiesce in the temporal power of the Pope. Since the Council appeared more divided on this plan than in its opposition to the Emperor's, the Emperor decided not to adopt either one for the present.

This, of course, did not please Persigny who did not want to see the matter dropped any more than did Thouvenel and Rouher. Feeling some responsibility for the failure of Thouvenel's more practicable plan, Persigny on the 29th succeeded in

just another indication which would confirm the conclusion of Thouvenel's authorship of the "Cavour plan."

arranging between the Emperor and his Minister of Foreign Affairs the adoption of a plan of action. This consisted of the dispatch of a note to the Vatican which would insist on an early solution of the Roman question and hint at the withdrawal of French troops at a not far-distant time.[45]

The note was drawn up for La Valette before he left for Rome and contained as an inclosure the Emperor's note of 20 May to Thouvenel. It declared that France would not recognize Italy's claim to Rome as her capital, nor Italy's right to possess the rest of the Pope's territory. On the other hand France would not support the Pope's claim for more than he now possesses. On the basis of a general acquiescence in the *status quo* France would be ready to arrange with the other Catholic powers, including Italy, a guaranty of the Pope's remaining territory, a civil list, and a proportional division of the Papal debt between Italy and the Government of the Holy See.

> In order that your (La Valette's) overtures may reflect the benevolent sentiment which animates the Emperor, they should contain no suggestion of severity or blame. You should, however, leave the impression (*laisser pressentir*), if they offer you as categorically as in the past the theory of inflexibility, that the Government of the Emperor will be unable to conform its conduct to it, and that, if it became unfortunately convinced that its efforts to persuade the Holy Father to accept a transaction had become henceforth useless, it would find it necessary, while safeguarding as much as possible the interests covered up now by its solicitude to see how it might by itself get out of a situation which misrepresents its policy by being prolonged beyond a certain period and which only serves to throw opinion in a greater disorder.[46]

La Valette left for Rome about 2 June and at that time the *Constitutionnel* published an article which was thought to express the Government's opinion. Those who thought that with

[45] The inside story of the Council meetings are found in the following accounts of Cowley and Vimercati who received their information probably from Thouvenel and Rouher themselves. Cowley to Russell, Paris, 29 May 1862, *F.O., France,* 1439: (secret). Vimercati to Rattazzi, Paris, 29 May, 2 June 1862. "Sulla via di Roma- da Aspromonte a Mentana," *Nuova Antologia,* Ser. IV, LXXXV, (1 Jan. 1900), pp. 13-14.

[46] Thouvenel to La Valette, Paris, 31 May 1862, *Aff. Etr., C.P., Rome,* 1020: pp. 120-122; *Autriche,* 481: pp. 281-289. *Livre Jaune,* (1862), pp. 7-9. Thouvenel, *Secret,* II, 408, note.

La Valette's departure the beginning of an early solution had begun would very likely be mistaken. Such a difficult problem needed time and patience. It was, however, hoped that the Pope would withdraw his *non-possumus* in favor of some conciliatory arrangement.[47]

While awaiting developments in Rome, France and Italy found plenty to occupy their attentions. Garibaldi had begun to plot an attack on the Trentino in May, and the Italian Government had been able to thwart his plans and send him home to Caprera. However, the unsuccessful attempt by Garibaldi had increased the impatience of the Italians and the Government felt more than ever in need of some positive step in regard to Rome. The note to Rome probably promised no definite action by France which would satisfy the Parliament. Furthermore, another regret clause after another Papal refusal would have little, if any, effect on the minds of the Italians. Consequently the Italian Government began to approach France with requests for some solution and particularly for the removal of Francis II from Rome. Rattazzi wrote a long Ricasoli-like letter to Prince Napoleon and also one to Thouvenel in which he pleaded that France come to a quick decision on the evacuation of Rome. Victor-Emmanuel also wrote one to the Emperor and to Prince Napoleon in which he stressed particularly the removal of Francis II from Rome.[48]

Although no reply seems to exist from the Prince or the Emperor, Thouvenel revealed his attitude at this time toward Italy in a conversation with Cowley.

> Mr. Thouvenel proceeded to say that there was one thing which the Italians must learn: namely, that the Emperor could never place Rome in the hands of the King of Italy. The Italians might render it possible for His Majesty to abandon Rome to the Romans. If the Italian Government would enter into engagements to respect, and cause to be respected, the territory still under the Pope's authority, the French troops might in a short time be withdrawn. It would then

[47] *Le Constitutionnel,* 2 June 1862, article by Paulin Limagrac.
[48] Rattazzi to Prince Napoleon, Turin, 2 June 1862, *Nuova Antologia,* Ser. IV, LXXXV, (Jan. 1900), pp. 15-17. Victor-Emmanuel II to Prince Napoleon, Turin, 2 June 1862, Comandini, *op. cit.,* pp. 229-230.

be seen whether the Pope could by salutary reforms continue to govern what remained to him. If Italy could be induced to give the Pontifical Government a fair chance of accommodating themselves to the necessities of the time, and failure was the consequence, it would be seen and felt that the fault rested with the Pope alone and it would be wise in the Italians to allow the Pope ample time to make the experiment and not in their impatience pluck the fruit before it could be ripe.

Mr. Thouvenel's language would appear to indicate that the present notion of the French Government is, if I may use the expression, to allow the Pope to cut his own throat—that is, they desire that His Holiness should have the certainty of two or three uninterrupted years of reign over the territory which he still possesses, unprotected by French troops, but guaranteed from all attack from without. It is thought that a state of things will arise which will open the eyes of the Papal adherents in France and of Roman Catholics in general to the impossibility of reconciling ecclesiastical administration with the progress of the age, and that the solution of the Roman question could then be brought about.[49]

This seemed to be the French way of expressing the Italian policy of moral force as a solution of the Roman tangle.

During the first week of June 1862 many bishops from all of Europe gathered in Rome at the invitation of the Pope. Among them were many French who had left home after having assured the Minister of Worship that their mission was religious in character. On 9 June the Pope addressed the cardinals and bishops in Consistory. He scathingly reviled all men, governments, and ideas which did not support the Papal claim to temporal authority over all his former possessions.

You and the other bishops of the Catholic world, and the faithful assigned to your care, you must not cease to soothe and assuage the agony and bitterness with which We are overwhelmed.

The bishops decided to reply to the Pope's allocution on the following day, and in reply they expressed in even more violent form their detestation for the Italian Government.

We see you . . . despoiled of these provinces . . . , and that by the detestable crime of those men who use the word liberty only as a veil for their excesses.

We recognize that the temporal sovereignty of the Holy See is

[49] Cowley to Russell, Paris, 5 June 1862, *F.O., France,* 1440: no. 747.

an institution necessary and manifestly established by divine Providence, and we do not hesitate to declare that in the present state of human affairs, this sovereignty is absolutely necessary for the just and free government of souls.[50]

The reaction among Italians was as violent as the attack upon them. In the Chamber an address to the King was voted which again claimed Rome for Italy's capital, criticized the bishops as foreign ecclesiastics who went beyond the bounds of religion to make political assertions, and charged the Pope's Government with responsibility for the disorders in South Italy. The only opponents to this address were those in favor of the inclusion of a declaration against French occupation. Since the majority ruled out any reference to French occupation, these few, twenty-four in number, drew up and published their own address.

It is against this [occupation], much more than against the words of the bishops that it is our duty to protest. . . . And we protest in the name of the moral conscience of humanity . . . in the name of liberty through popular suffrage . . . in the name of our independence . . . in the name of our unity. . . .[51]

France was receiving only another illustration of the growing impatience of the Italians in regard to Rome. Thouvenel later sent a protest to Rome criticizing the Vatican for precipitating such a demonstration and declaring that he had only allowed the departure of the French bishops with the understanding that the mission was to be purely religious.[52]

It was in the midst of this heated controversy that La Valette had to approach the Vatican with the French demand for reconciliation and threat of withdrawal. Vimercati reported that Thouvenel hoped and thought that Rome would remain immovable. He declared Thouvenel to have observed that "bishops and cardinals seemed paid to further our cause."[53] La

[50] *Journal des Débats,* 16 June 1862.

[51] Arbib, *loc. cit.,* pp. 691-692. *Aff. Etr., C.P., Italie,* 354: p. 274.

[52] Thouvenel to La Valette, Paris, 26 July 1862, *Aff. Etr., C.P., Rome,* 1021: pp. 55-63. Antonelli had given this assurance to La Valette. Maurain, p. 603.

[53] "Vescovi e cardinali sembravano pagati per far le cose nostre." Vimercati to Rattazzi, Paris, 12 June 1862, "Da Aspromonte a Mentana," *loc. cit.,* pp. 20-21.

Valette had an audience with the Pope on 20 June and interviews with Antonelli several times before and after his audience. Out of all these came the clearcut expression of the Vatican's policy. Instead of being pleased that France consulted him first, Antonelli said that France should first arrange an agreement with *Piedmont*. Then he would examine it seriously but would not promise to accept it. Antonelli did not value the guaranty of the Powers when those same Powers had not lived up to their promises made in Vienna to guarantee all the Papal States to the Pope. He claimed that to let Italy pay part of the debts would be recognizing Italy's possession of the lost provinces. Furthermore, to depend on a civil list from the Catholic Powers would make the Holy Father dependent rather than independent. Whenever there should be an ecclesiastical controversy between Pope and Sovereign, the latter would immediately discontinue his contribution to the civil list. Finally the Cardinal Secretary declared that the Pope could reform his government only when he had all his stolen territory returned to him. All this was reported to Thouvenel in the private correspondence between himself and La Valette.[54] With a view to publicity Thouvenel then drew up a model dispatch for La Valette to send from Rome, and after referring it to the Emperor for additions and corrections, forwarded it to Rome. La Valette rewrote, signed, and returned it as dispatch no. 78 which was eventually published in the *Livre Jaune*. It is significant that the Emperor and Thouvenel had La Valette say in conclusion:

When France scarcely six months ago invited the Holy Father to come to an understanding with her, in principle and without any definite stipulations, on a transaction destined to assure his independence, her overtures were rejected by an absolute veto. Her solicitude has not been wearied, however. The Government of the Emperor has just formulated and submitted to the Holy See the most explicit

[54] La Valette to Thouvenel, Rome, 20 June 1862, *Aff. Etr., C.P., Rome,* 1020: p. 214. In regard to Antonelli's suggestion to go first to Piedmont there is a marginal note written at the time of the Convention of 15 September 1864 which says: "This is an excellent answer to those who blame France for having concluded with Turin the Convention of 15 September instead of having first treated with the Pope."

proposals. Instructed to transmit them, I affirm, with the same regret, that they have met the same fate.[55]

On 26 June La Valette presented Montebello to the Holy Father and at that time inquired whether he was to take Antonelli's statements as final. "His Holiness declared to me that he entirely approved of them, and that he had nothing to add or retract."[56]

To use the words of Cavour, the supreme moment for Italy seemed to have again arrived, but this time the moment came without Cavour at the head of the Government. France had finally been persuaded to take independent action. The French Council had been converted; Parliament was amenable; public opinion was indifferent; pro-Italian La Valette had been substituted for Gramont and anti-Italian Goyon had been replaced by Montebello. Rome had repeatedly refused French proposals and France was again preparing the public for a further step in the matter. Under such favorable circumstances it must have been heartrending to the Italian statesmen to see Garibaldi for the second time begin a revolutionary movement which should cause this delicate preliminary scaffolding to fall to the ground.

Garibaldi, who had been stopped in his rash plans against the Austrian Trentino, began at the end of June to plan a campaign for Rome. The Italian King tried to interest him in the Balkans where he would not embarrass the Government in its relations with the Catholic powers. But Garibaldi wrote Victor-Emmanuel:

> The Greek affair is musty; so I'll talk about it with Your Majesty when we are in Rome.[57]

Garibaldi, who had already gone to Sicily supposedly to find followers for the Greek uprising, began, however, to inspire the Sicilians with the rallying cry of "Rome or death."

[55] La Valette to Thouvenel, Rome, 24 June 1862, *Aff. Etr., C.P., Rome,* 1020: pp. 236-248. For the slight variations suggested by the Emperor see *ibid.,* p. 249. *Livre Jaune,* (1862), pp. 9-14.

[56] La Valette to Thouvenel, Rome, 26 June 1862, *Aff. Etr., C.P., Rome,* 1020: pp. 252-253.

[57] July 1862, "Da Aspromonte a Mentana," *loc. cit.,* p. 22.

The move caused a veritable panic in the Italian governmental circles. The Emperor had insisted that Italy be quiet so that France's evacuation would arouse no alarm in France. Just at the moment when there was the least alarm and the best preparations, Garibaldi again occupied the stage and threw the lulled French into another scare. The problem of Rome was becoming an endless succession of Garibaldian fireworks and Papal icicles which in their turn either scorched the hands of diplomats or froze them to numbness. The first months of 1862 having been spent in thawing the Vatican, they would now spend the last months of the same year in quenching Garibaldi. In the end they were to be exactly where they started.

General Durando, the Italian Minister of Foreign Affairs in Rattazzi's cabinet, was optimistic enough to hope that the defeat of Garibaldi would convince France of Italy's strength at home and thus solve the "first step" in the question. Filled with such ideas he ventured incautiously to reassure the Italian Chamber on 20 July.

> Be patient, be steadfast as you were valiant and of one accord and I dare almost promise you, moved by that profound faith which has animated me for over thirty years of a political career, perhaps not entirely useless to Italy, I dare promise you, I say, that in a not far distant time you shall be in Rome.[58]

In a debate of the 25th Rattazzi took a firmer stand against Garibaldi. But at the same time he gave out a veiled hint that the Italian Government might eventually do the same as Garibaldi was plotting to do.

> Gentlemen, I declare that, if the only voice which can suggest war, if the voice of the King, when our Roman brethren should rise up, should appeal to us to aid our brethren; if he alone, who has the right to begin war, called us to arms, there would be no distinction whatever among us, neither among the members of the Left, nor among the members of the Right, nor among those of the Center; we would all answer the call and go to the defense of our brethren. But, gentlemen, until that voice is heard, which has the sole right to declare war . . . , I am confident that those who belong to the Left, as those who sit at the Right and Center, none of you will move

[58] *Atti ufficiali,* Chamber, 20 July 1862, p. 3000. Arbib, *loc. cit.*, p. 698.

from your places . . . ; none will dare to raise the standard which would be the standard of insurrection; none would dare to disobey the Constitution which we have all sworn to respect.[59]

Although Thouvenel approved of this attitude by Rattazzi, he gave no hope of French evacuation and for the first time showed that this new Garibaldian enterprise was delaying the long-sought solution.

It certainly would be out of place . . . at the time of such a crazy enterprise, which we wish to prevent and which we may have to repress, to negotiate even incidentally on the Roman question.[60]

On 3 August the Ministry had the King issue a stirring proclamation against the movement in South Italy:

Italians!

At the moment in which Europe renders homage to the wisdom of the Nation and recognizes its rights,[61] it saddens my heart that inexperienced and deluded youths, forgetful of their duty, and of their gratitude for our best ally, make the name of Rome a war-cry. . . .

Faithful to the Constitution, sworn to by me, I hold high Italy's banner sanctified by the blood and glorified by the valor of my people. No one follows this banner who violates the laws and attacks the liberty and welfare of the country by making themselves judges of its destiny.

Italians, avoid guilty impatience and heedless agitations. When the hour for the accomplishment of the great work shall arrive, the voice of your King will be heard among you. Any call which is not his, is a call to rebellion, to civil war.

The responsibility and the rigor of the laws shall fall on those who do not heed my words.

Acclaimed as King by the Nation, I know my duties, I will be able to preserve the integrity of the Crown and Parliament in order to have the right to call on Europe for full justice for Italy.[62]

Rattazzi was immediately interpellated in the Chamber and he was asked whether the King referred to Garibaldi in the

[59] Arbib, *loc. cit.*, pp. 699-700.

[60] Thouvenel to Chargé in Turin, Paris, 26 July 1862, *Livre Jaune,* (1862), pp. 45-46.

[61] Although this could well have referred to France's slow progress toward a withdrawal from Rome, yet it had more direct reference to the recognition by Russia which had been brought about through the efforts of France. See Rattazzi's speech in the Chamber, *Atti ufficiali,* 11 July 1862, p. 2871.

[62] Arbib, *loc. cit.*, pp. 700-701.

words of the proclamation. He replied firmly that since the actions of Garibaldi had brought him under the terms of the proclamation, therefore it was aimed at him as much as at any other. The Minister hoped Garibaldi would heed the King's warning, but in case he did not, the Government was ready to act to have the laws obeyed by everybody. The order of the day approving the Government's action was passed by an almost unanimous vote.[63]

Silvestrelli, who was the representative in Turin of the anti-Clerical Romans, was asked by his constituents what should be their conduct toward the new Garibaldian movement. He thought that they ought to revolt and gain their liberty before Garibaldi's arrival in order to make the liberation of Rome seem a work of the Romans themselves. Before sending this advice, however, he consulted Rattazzi. Rattazzi discouraged even this plan and he showed Silvestrelli a letter from the Emperor in which Napoleon indicated that Montebello was instructed to be more severe against internal revolts in Rome. This discouraged Silvestrelli and his Romans from beginning an insurrection.[64]

But there were rumors of Italian action against Rome by others than Garibaldi. The French chargé in Turin reported that many Italians were thinking of collecting a "fabulous" number together to march on Rome as an overpowering demonstration for Rome. Prince Napoleon himself had suggested such a demonstration to Rattazzi who rejected the idea. The French chargé concluded:

> At first this plan appeared . . . as an extravagance. Yet on second thought, considering how easily the Italian character became excitable, it is believable that its realization is not impossible. . . .
>
> Everybody in fact, but from different points of view, is pressing the Government for a solution of the Roman question: its friends, because Mr. Cavour promised them Rome; its adversaries, to embarrass it; Garibaldians and Mazzinians, to see the Pope out of Italy; even a large part of the clergy, because they hope for some

[63] *Atti ufficiali,* Chamber, 3 Aug. 1862, pp. 3229-3231.

[64] Silvestrelli to Ricasoli, Turin, 7 Aug. 1862, *Ricasoli lettere,* VII, 93-96.

good from an excess of evil. Thus it is with different aims that each faction is trying to influence the Government.[65]

It seemed, however, that nothing could be done by the Romans, the Italian demonstrators, or the Garibaldians unless the Emperor's tacit acquiescence could be gained, such as Cavour had obtained at Chambéry. With the pressure of those various factions behind him Rattazzi finally decided to try Cavour's method. Since the Emperor this time was not coming near the Italian border, Rattazzi conceived the idea of a secret mission to Paris by Pepoli, the Minister of Agriculture and Commerce and distant relative of the Emperor. Pepoli was supposed to be on his way to London to an exposition but he was to stop on his way for a short time and try to accomplish something in gaining French coöperation. Durando wrote Thouvenel asking that he receive Pepoli and give him some assurance of a solution if Garibaldi is stopped. Otherwise a crisis would occur in Italy. Rattazzi also wrote Prince Napoleon to arrange an interview between Pepoli and the Emperor.[66]

Pepoli saw Thouvenel first and requested an audience with the Emperor. Since no Chambéry nor Plombières could be accomplished with an Imperial minister, Pepoli did not try to negotiate to any great extent with Thouvenel. The French Foreign Minister, however, obtained for him an audience with the Emperor.[67]

The interview, which took place on 15 August, was one of the most interesting which will have to be considered in the history of this period. Pepoli mustered all the daring which Cavour might have displayed and by one bold stroke after another in utter desperation he attempted to drive the Emperor into the inescapable corner of the evacuation of Rome. Cavourian methods in the hands of a more fantastic, egotistical, and radical Pepoli could not possibly have the same effects on the

[65] Massignac to Thouvenel, Turin, 9 July 1862, *Aff. Etr., C.P., Italie,* 354: pp. 308-311. Rattazzi to Nigra, Turin, 10 Aug. 1862, "Da Aspromonte a Mentana," *loc. cit.,* p. 22.

[66] 11 Aug. 1862; Rattazzi to Prince Napoleon, Turin, 12 Aug. 1862; "Da Aspromonte a Mentana," *loc. cit.,* pp. 23-24.

[67] Cowley to Russell, Paris, 16 Aug. 1862, *F.O., France,* 1444: no. 1000.

Emperor. Pepoli's own account does not deprive us of any of the dramatic elements of the meeting.

The Emperor kissed me and expressed regret that I had been sick.

I thanked him and handed him immediately the King's letter. He read it and then thereupon asked me how things were going.

I did not conceal the truth from him. I disapproved Garibaldi's words and acts; I expressed the hope that we would master the situation; but I did not refrain from telling him that that would be done only at a great loss to our own strength. I added afterwards that once Garibaldi was defeated, we would still be faced with his same ideas but presented in a more vigorous form than before, and that the government through its victory would have assumed the obligation of solving the Roman question in a very short time. If the Government should fail to do so, it would be miserably ruined, ruined without dignity, deprived of all moral authority, and the cause of the Monarchy would have been lost in just the same way.

EMPEROR. But what can I do? A nation like France does not surrender to the threats of a Garibaldi! He threatens me with death. . . .

I (interrupting him). Sire, you are mistaken. Garibaldi is excessive in expression, Garibaldi lowers himself to unjust vituperations against you, but Garibaldi is incapable of raising against you the assassin's dagger. . . .

EMPEROR. But he has said words to that effect. Anyway I can not leave Rome now. I shall welcome with great relief an appropriate occasion for leaving, but now I can't. I am duty-bound to guard the Pontiff. Garibaldi is the evil genius of the Roman question. If he had delayed his Sicilian expedition for two months, the French army would no longer have been found in Rome. Now if he was not moving toward some senseless enterprise, I was disposed to sign a treaty with Italy.

I. But if the Government of the King gets the situation in hand, it seems to me the moment will be propitious for opening negotiations.

EMPEROR. You begin with that and then we'll see. We might have a Congress.

I. Italy would not accept it because they all would be against us except perhaps you, Sire, and England . . . and besides we can not wait and the King's Government must show Italy that it wants to solve the Roman question.

EMPEROR. But what could I do?

I. There is in Napoleonic history a fact that has struck me especially. The Emperor[68] preferred exile to civil war, he preferred to have his dynasty perish at the hands of foreigners, because he saw that in that way his descendents would have returned . . . and

[68] Meaning Napoleon I.

they did return. Well, we have got to save the principles of Unity and Monarchy, and to save them we prefer to see them perish at the hands of foreigners rather than by internal wars. That's the King's and the Ministry's program. And in this way the Union will issue from the present crisis more splendid than ever.[69]

EMPEROR. But with what foreigner do you wish to make war? You would be crazy to make war on Austria today.

I. No. All Italy will march on Rome and we will see whether Your Majesty would have them fire on us.

EMPEROR. Yes, I would order it.

I. Those orders are more easily given than executed. Your Majesty would not do it: I am convinced of that from within.

EMPEROR. *(Gets up, lights a cigar, and did not answer at once: then in a loud voice).* And why always Rome, why do you not prepare for Venice?[70]

I. Because Rome is our capital; because there is a general idea that we will find a way to organize the country in Rome; because Rome can make all hearts beat in unison; because—and I hope Your Majesty will allow me to speak openly—because your presence in Rome causes suspicion. Italy is accusing Your Majesty falsely. But they fear that you do not want Unity, and that you stay there to find a chance to dissolve it. They are calumnies, I repeat, but calumnies substantiated by facts, such as the letter published by my uncle and the program of the newspaper *La France*. . . .

EMPEROR. They certainly are calumnies. I was for a federation, it was a wiser course, but I accept the Union. . . . But I can not leave Rome. The religious question is very serious in France.

I. It will not become more serious by your departure from Rome. The priests detest Your Majesty just the same and they will never forgive you. Rome is the source of every intrigue against you. It is to your interest to hit clerical Rome hard. We are your best friend. Be assurred that it is only our gratitude for you that prevents us from committing some sublime folly.

EMPEROR. I know Rome is my enemy, I know Italy loves me, but I can not find a way to leave Rome. I search in vain and I do nothing but keep going in search of a quick solution.

I. Decide at least on a fixed time when you will abandon Rome.

EMPEROR. But I can not hand over Rome to you.

I. Hand it over to the Romans then.

EMPEROR. That's the same thing. Something must be done. I have no interest in, nor desire of, leaving Rome to the priests. I think that useless. But I can not give you the Pope and his destiny myself.

[69] The Rattazzi Ministry was evidently making it no easier for France than had Ricasoli.

[70] The Emperor was evidently agitated because just previously he had called an attempt against Austria a *follia*. The Quai d'Orsay was always discouraging any action against Austria.

But while Garibaldi is menacing us, it is useless to think of it.

I. But what should I say to the King?

EMPEROR. Tell him to be strong. Tell him to keep all his authority firm.

I. Yes! But he'll tell me that Your Majesty brought about the Second of December to save France from socialism, but that afterwards to consolidate it you acted the part of a good socialist.

EMPEROR. That is true.

I. Well, the King, after having put down Garibaldi, will be forced to act the part of a good Garibaldian and go to Rome against whoever may be there.

EMPEROR. Then you are in favor of a war with France?

I. No. But we shall make the French fire on us, just as the Russions fired on the Poles. And certainly that did not benefit Emperor Alexander.

EMPEROR. *(Very much alarmed, gets up and says).* Italy won't dare do it.

I. Oh yes she will, Sire. If not the present ministry, another. If not the Government, the Nation.

EMPEROR. But that's the same as war. It is the pressure of the masses. It is still war and France will never let anyone impose on her.

I. It is the pressure of justice and liberty.

EMPEROR. *(Is silent, then says):* Something will have to be done. But the evil is that I see that I must deal with public opinion and not with the Government.

I. That's true.

EMPEROR. Well that makes the negotiations difficult and arduous. . . .

I. Fare you well, Sire, . . . Rome. . . .

EMPEROR. Put down Garibaldi and then . . .

This is the gist of my dialogue. The Emperor said many things which I leave out for sake of brevity.[71]

Nothing more was accomplished by this mission than what the last two lines of the dialogue indicate. The Emperor would do nothing until Garibaldi was suppressed, and he would not even indicate what that something might be until the time had come to act. The Emperor was evidently displeased with this rough encounter. His suggestion that he would have to deal with the people rather than with the Government would seem to indicate a sudden coolness toward Pepoli and Italy. This incident

[71] Pepoli to Rattazzi, Paris, 15 Aug. 1865, "Da Aspromonte a Mentana," *loc. cit.*, pp. 24, 25-27. L. Carpi, *Il Risorgimento italiano, biografie,* (Gioacchino Pepoli), (Milan, 1884-1888), III, 382-383.

lingering in his mind while he was at Châlons may also explain to some extent his future attitude toward Thouvenel.

A little earlier Ricasoli had written a letter to the French senator, Pietri, which he intended to have shown to the Emperor. In it he reiterated that France helped his overthrow and now must suffer for it by the situation in Italy. He said France's and Italy's only salvation was to leave Rome in the hands of the Romans.[72] Pietri acknowledged receipt of the letter and arranged a rendezvous with Ricasoli at Marseilles for 23 August. There he explained that the Emperor had seen Ricasoli's letter and had indicated to Pietri his policy on the Roman question at that time. Garibaldi must be stopped. After that the Emperor would be willing to leave Rome to the Romans provided that Italy gave a promise not to touch Roman territory unless called on by the people themselves.[73] This would resemble his answer to Pepoli and throws some light on his eventual agreement with Italy.

Garibaldi landed in Calabria on 25 August and Cialdini was ordered immediately to suppress the movement with vigor. Garibaldi and his followers were surrounded in the mountains near Aspromonte and they finally surrendered on 30 August. Unfortunately at the last moment Garibaldi was wounded in his foot from a shot from the Royal army while he was trying to prevent his men from firing. His wound caused even greater emotion among the Italians.

Victor-Emmanuel and his government were in a more precarious position than ever before in regard to public sentiment. The King immediately telegraphed the Emperor that his act of firmness would now need its reward from France. But Napoleon's reply indicated that the warm August sun of Biarritz had not melted his increasing frigidity for the existing Italian Government.

> I share all the deep feeling of Your Majesty. With firmness you will overcome your difficulties.[74]

[72] Brolio, 30 July 1862, *Ricasoli lettere,* VII, 86-89.

[73] Ricasoli to Bastogi, and C. Bianchi, Marseilles, 23 Aug. 1862, *ibid.,* pp. 114-115.

[74] Biarritz, 1 Sept. 1862, "Da Aspromonte a Mentana," *loc. cit.,* p. 27.

Thouvenel, on the other hand, had not experienced the bold front of Pepoli as had the Emperor. Therefore with the defeat of Garibaldi the French Foreign Minister began to think seriously about acceding to Italy's wish for a French-Italian settlement. As a furtherance of this idea the French chargé at Turin during Benedetti's absence was writing continually to Paris of the need of some progress on the question. The Italian Ministry needed the appearance of progress as proof of the wisdom of their action against Garibaldi. Thouvenel's inclination toward a liberal settlement was confided to Pepoli, Gramont, Flahault, and Cowley.[75]

Thus it would appear that all chances of a solution had not been lost because of Garibaldi. The Italians had gradually reconciled themselves to obtaining the French evacuation as a first step instead of the immediate possession of Rome by Italy. The French Government and people even seemed still prepared for an agreement on this basis. In fact such a result might have been obtained had not the Governments of Italy and England by very ill-considered measures embarrassed Thouvenel's position and prevented the natural course of events.

At first after Garibaldi's check at the hands of the Italians, Russell was inclined to remain aloof from affairs between France and Italy. He claimed to be heeding Cowley's and Thouvenel's warnings that a British interference only paralyzed French action.[76] But at the climax of Italian demands on France at the end of September Palmerston pushed Russell to send a very ill-advised communication to the Quai d'Orsay.[77] The note showed many evidences of the blustering manner of Palmerston. The English did not remain within the realm of possibilities by requesting evacuation or the delivery of Rome to the Romans. In this note they openly demanded Rome as Italy's capital.

[75] Cowley to Russell, Paris, 8 Aug. 1862, *F.O., France* 1443: no. 962. Pepoli to Rattazzi, Paris, 16 Aug. 1862, "Da Aspromonte a Mentana," *loc. cit.*, p. 24. Thouvenel to Gramont, Paris, 22 Aug., 6 Sept. 1862; Thouvenel to Flahault, Paris, 1 Sept. 1862; Thouvenel, *Secret*, II, 367, 384-385, 379-383.

[76] Russell to Hudson, Gotha, 13 Sept. 1862, *R.P.*, CX.

[77] Russell told Cowley: "Palmerston [was] the real author of my despatch." Woburn Abbey, 6 Oct. 1862, *R.P.*, CV.

In the opinion of Her Majesty's Government the apparently mad enterprise of Garibaldi was only a local outburst of the feverish feeling which pervades the whole Italian nation who are burning with impatience to establish the seat of Italian Government in that city which their most cherished traditions point to as the natural and indispensible capital of an Italian Kingdom. In fact a Kingdom of Italy without Rome would be like a Kingdom of Greece without Athens.

The exclusion of the Italian nation from Rome by the overbearing Power of the Army of France keeps the whole of Italy in a political ferment. . . .

In utter disregard for the tenable position which Thouvenel was trying to have accepted, the British note continued by denouncing the temporal power, declaring for Italy's guardianship of the Pope, accusing France of depriving the Romans of their liberty, and concluding with a warning that France was losing Italy's friendship.[78]

Thouvenel's reception of this note was, as it might easily be expected, a refusal to receive it or communicate it to the Emperor. To Flahault he said:

The principal Secretary of State invites us to deliver over to Italy her legitimate capital. . . . The surest way of popularizing here the maintenance of our occupation in Rome is to let it be known that England desires its end. . . . Forms have a certain value in human affairs and that's what Lord Russell too often forgets.[79]

In the end, although Russell insisted on his former assertions, he suggested that Cowley "use the arguments which may tell and omit those which may offend."[80] But the harm had been done and still more harm was being done in the same manner by the Italians at almost the same time.

In addition to Victor-Emmanuel's dispairing pleas to Napoleon and Massignac's warning, Durando began to impress on France through Nigra and the French chargé the necessity of some immediate step in regard to Rome. His difficulties, he declared, would be insurmountable if he could not bring "some

[78] Russell to Cowley, London, 29 Sept. 1862, *F.O., France,* 1427: no. 962, (rough draft in Russell's own handwriting).

[79] 4 Oct. 1862, Thouvenel, *Secret,* II, 423-425. See also Cowley to Russell, Chantilly, 30 Sept. 1862, Paris, 3 Oct. 1862; *R.P.,* LVIII.

[80] Woburn Abbey, 6 Oct. 1862, *R.P.,* CV.

positive assurance [to the reassembling Chamber] or at least some favorable prediction of the approaching solution of the Roman question."[81] Thouvenel's reply to this was only a mild request of patience on the part of the Italians until complete calm should be restored[82] and until the Emperor should return from Biarritz.

So far nothing had been compromised, not even by the English note. But Durando, obviously unfitted for the direction of the Italian Foreign Office, unfortunately conceived the idea of drawing up a circular note of almost the same tenor as that of the English. There are even some indications that Rattazzi and England were coöperating to the extent of adopting similar positions.[83] After describing the events surrounding the Aspromonte affair, Durando claimed that the Italian people, Government, and army all showed by that crisis that they were strong enough and calm enough to validate any guaranties which they might make. But then the Foreign Minister took the fatal step of demanding Rome rather than French evacuation.

> But the watchword of the volunteers was this time, one must admit, the expression of a more imperious need than ever. The whole nation opposed Garibaldi's incautious move only because it was convinced that the King's Government would be able to fulfill the mandate which it received from Parliament in regard to Rome. . . . The European Powers will understand how irresistible is the movement which draws the entire nation toward Rome.[84]

As if to punctuate this policy the Italian Government allowed the following statement to be published in the official journal:

> The Monarchy can not but affirm openly that its existence is not complete, that the exercise of its rights is not unimpaired, and that

[81] Massignac to Thouvenel, Turin, 4 Sept. 1862, *Aff. Etr., C.P., Italie,* 355: pp. 118-119.

[82] Great excitement existed in Italy at this time because of the trial and possible sentence of Garibaldi and his companions.

[83] Hudson told Russell that "Rattazzi . . . entirely concurs [in your opinion] and is disposed to address a Diplomatic Note to the French Government . . . that they merely exercise a right when they request to be permitted to take exclusive charge of the Person of the Pope." Turin, 20 Sept. 1862, *R.P.,* LXIX.

[84] Durando to Representatives, Turin, 10 Sept. 1862, *Libro verde,* 18 Nov. 1862, pp. 1-3. *Aff. Etr., C.P., Italie,* 355: pp. 128-130. *Livre Jaune,* (1862), pp. 47-48.

its efforts are not entirely efficacious, without Rome as Italy's capital.[85]

The effect on Thouvenel was extremely unfavorable. Through Massignac and Nigra, both of whom felt keenly the inadvisability of the circular, Thouvenel let it be known that it would ruin France's chances of evacuation. So long as the French Catholics thought that the Italians would be satisfied with just French evacuation, they might acquiesce in it. But if it ever appeared, as Durando's circular suggested, that the Italians considered evacuation as only a step toward annexation, France's hands would be immediately tied. Both Durando and Rattazzi saw their mistake and began to search for some means of correcting it. Thouvenel told Flahault:

> They begin to feel that they have taken the wrong road by demanding *la capitale* and that it would be preferable to offer us guaranties of a nature to justify our evacuation. The result, I very much fear, will be almost the same, but forms have some value in human affairs. . . .[86]

The Emperor's immediate reaction to Durando's circular was to order that his note of 20 May 1862 to Thouvenel should be published in the *Moniteur*. Thouvenel told Cowley that the issue of General Durando's circular of 10 September. . .

> His Majesty looked upon in the light of a summons to himself to order the evacuation of Rome, and consequently as a gross affront. . . .

Thouvenel confided to Cowley that the Emperor had intended at the time to publish also a more positive manifesto defending the temporal power of the Pope. It was only with great difficulty that he was persuaded to withhold the more violent document. As it was, the note of 20 May was published so hurriedly that Walewski, who usually directed the Government publications in the *Moniteur*, being in the country, knew nothing of it until the next day.[87] It will be recalled that this note contained a passage which warned Italy against excessive demands while it chided the Pope for excessive obduracy.

[85] *Gazzetta ufficiale del Regno*, 17 Sept. 1862.
[86] 4 Oct. 1862, Thouvenel, *Secret*, II, 423-425.
[87] Cowley to Russell, Paris, 26 Sept., 21 Oct. 1862, *F.O., France*, 1445: no. 1136; 1446: no. 1209.

The publication of the Emperor's note had quite a sobering effect on Italy. Italian public opinion seemed surprised that the Emperor would not sanction the idea of Rome as Italy's capital, but Italy's statesmen thought that it still indicated a chance of obtaining an early evacuation by France.[88] After Garibaldi's defeat they could scarcely dream of any further delay. Both Victor-Emmanuel and Rattazzi approached Benedetti on the question of evacuation when he returned to Turin. They did not mention Italian occupation. After Nigra's suggestions from Paris that Italy should take one step at a time, Rattazzi determined to address another note solely to France which would attempt to counteract the evil effects of the circular by restricting the discussion to evacuation.[89]

The Durando dispatch of 8 October 1862 was the document which attempted to cover up his earlier circular. In it he omitted Italy's claim to Rome as its capital. He interpreted the publication of the Emperor's note to Thouvenel as an indication that France was willing to take up negotiations. He continued by showing how the occupation had failed in its main purposes of strengthening the Papal States and bringing permanent peace.

> It is evident in our opinion, that there is now no reason why we can not agree on an occasion for ending the occupation. That plan has already been tried out and has brought . . . neither conciliation nor reforms. . . .
>
> By leaving the Roman Court face to face with its own subjects we may hope to obtain what the long friendship of the Emperor has not been able to obtain by fourteen years of occupation and ineffectual negotiations.[90]

The full effect of Durando's former circular on the Emperor as well as the countervailing impression made by his October dispatch can not be fully appreciated until the story of the Emperor's adverse reaction is told in full. Then only will it be

[88] Benedetti to Thouvenel, Turin, 1 Oct. 1862, *Aff. Etr., C.P., Italie,* 355: pp. 176-180.

[89] Hudson to Russell, Turin, 20 Sept. 1862, *R.P.,* LXIX. Benedetti to Thouvenel, Turin, 26 Sept. 1862, *Aff. Etr., C.P., Italie,* 355: pp. 153-167. Cowley to Russell, Paris, 24 Oct. 1862, *F.O., France,* 1446: no. 1215.

[90] Durando to Nigra, Turin, 8 Oct. 1862, *Libro verde,* (18 Nov. 1862), pp. 3-6. *Aff. Etr., C.P., Italie,* 355: pp. 198-201. 8 Oct. 1862, *R.P.,* LXIX.

seen how disastrous were Aspromonte and Durando's circular to the Italian cause.

The Emperor's increasing hostility toward Italy is connected closely with his gradual assumption of a cool attitude toward his Foreign Minister. As far back as June 1861 when Thouvenel had proposed the recognition of Italy in the Council, his favor at Court had begun to decline. This had been particularly true in respect to the Empress' attitude. It is claimed, too, that at the time of the birth of Prince Napoleon's son earlier in 1862 the Empress began to importune the Emperor to be more generous to the Prince Imperial's godfather, Pius IX, lest harm befall him and this new-born child become the heir to the throne. Perhaps, if the rumored tale was true, the Empress' inability to present more children to the Imperial household added weight to her words. While the Emperor was not likely to be superstitiously religious, it seems as if this factor may account to some extent for the increased weight of the Empress' arguments.[91] When Thouvenel openly and vigorously opposed the Emperor's suggested solution in the spring of 1862, it is thought also that the Emperor harbored in his mind a resentment which was given free play when events began to embarrass Thouvenel's pro-Italian attitude.[92] There is little doubt that His Majesty was considerably ruffled by Pepoli's rough usage in that striking interview of August. Soon after that the Emperor at a military review at Châlons showed himself, as Thouvenel told Cowley, to be *très monté* against Garibaldi and very determined to protect the Pope.[93] Immediately after Aspromonte Thouvenel noted that the Emperor's "attitude was very hesitating and clerical influence at this time seems to predominate. . . ."[94]

It was just at this time (early September) that the Emperor went to Biarritz and there he seemed to allow his disgust for Italy and Thouvenel to increase. The Durando circular came in the midst of these unfavorable moods and it required all Thou-

[91] Cowley to Russell, *F.O., France,* 1446: no. 1209.
[92] Same to same, *ibid.,* no. 1215.
[93] Same to same, *ibid.,* 1444: no. 1042.
[94] Thouvenel to Flahault, Paris, 1 Sept. 1862, Thouvenel, *Secret,* II, 379-383.

venel's persuasion to prevent an excessive outburst on the part of Napoleon. No doubt this restraint only convinced the Emperor all the more of the fact that Thouvenel was not as severe on Italy as the occasion required. Perhaps he sincerely felt that Thouvenel's favor had encouraged the Italians to take the extreme position assumed in Durando's circular, and hence, that Thouvenel's inclinations would lead him to entertain Italian proposals which might exceed appreciably the Emperor's intentions.

If these were Napoleon's thoughts, it explains to a considerable degree his curt reply to Victor-Emmanuel and his conversation with Fould. While Fould was his guest at Biarritz, the Emperor discussed with him the possibility of substituting Mr. Drouyn de Lhuys for Thouvenel at the Foreign Office. Fould claimed that he did not discourage this proposal because he thought it was not seriously entertained and also because he was the Emperor's guest and did not wish to oppose the confidential views of his Imperial host.[95]

The Emperor had also noticed that the same indifference which appeared in the *procureurs*' reports in January and April continued in July. He interpreted this attitude as favorable to occupation. To Nigra he declared that "he had trustworthy reports which convinced him that the country at large approved of the continued occupation of Rome."[96] Napoleon could well have felt himself nearer to the spirit of public opinion while Thouvenel was gradually alienating himself from it.

Finally the impertinent British demands for Rome as Italy's capital, made at the same time as Durando's circular must have appeared as especially irritating.. In fact their almost simultaneous arrivals could be interpreted as an attempt at joint pressure on a France sensitive to Palmerstonian brusqueness.

Thouvenel accounted for the change in the Emperor in an interesting conversation with Cowley.

Mr. Thouvenel attributes the sudden change, partly to the violence of the Italian press, partly to the threats of assassination which

[95] See above note no. 91.
[96] See above note no. 92.

reached the Emperor,[97] and partly to the pressure put upon His Majesty by Her Majesty's Government. It was, however, . . . General Durando's circular of the 10th September . . . which brought matters to an issue.[98]

Thouvenel's activity in September and early October 1862 showed that he and the Emperor were drifting further and further apart. Almost as soon as Garibaldi's check at Aspromonte had occurred, Thouvenel began to forsee the necessity of a solution with Italy. While the Vatican hoped to see Garibaldi win so that Italy would break up and the Pope would retrieve his lost possessions from the ruins, Thouvenel on the other hand hailed the quick Italian victory as a proof of the value of future guaranties.

The development of Thouvenel's ideas at this time is reflected in his correspondence with his Ambassador at Vienna. Thouvenel began to suggest to Gramont a European congress to guarantee the Pope in his newly restricted possessions. Gramont agreed somewhat with Thouvenel's ideas and suggested a mixed occupation by troops of several Catholic powers. But by 25 September Thouvenel rejected the suggestion of a mixed garrison and proposed to Gramont a year's notice to the Pope before evacuation, a warning to Italy that a move against the Pope would be a *casus belli*, and a promise to the Holy Father that France would coöperate with the Catholic powers in considering any proposals of the Vatican. Gramont finally acquiesced in Thouvenel's last scheme provided that the Pope's army was able to defend his possession of Rome for four or five years so that it would not seem that France's evacuation was a direct cause of the downfall of the temporal power.[99]

As Thouvenel's ideas began to assume a definite shape, he

[97] A suggestion of the fear of assassination is seen in his conversation with Pepoli. The correspondence in the *Aff. Etr., C.P., Italie* are filled with police reports from Italy of attempted plans to take the Emperor's life. If it is true that Orsini brought Napoleon to Plombières, similar threatened attempts might easily be a factor in the situation.

[98] See above note no. 91.

[99] Thouvenel to Flahault, Paris, 1 Sept. 1862; Thouvenel to Gramont, Paris, 6, 25 Sept. 1862; Gramont to Thouvenel, Vienna, 12 Sept., 2 Oct. 1862; Thouvenel to Mercier, Paris, 11 Sept. 1862; Thouvenel, *Secret,* II, 379-383, 384-385, 406-408, 390-405, 419-421, 388.

put them down in the forms of a draft note to La Valette for the Vatican and a tentative treaty with Italy. In the Archives of the French Foreign Office are found these two unexecuted documents which reveal the final position of Thouvenel on the Roman question. In the note to La Valette he expressed regret at the Pope's reiterated *non-possumus* and wished to have the Holy Father informed of France's determination in such an eventuality to consult her own interests in the matter of seeking a solution.

> The energetic attitude of the Turinese Cabinet has warded off the danger, the insurrection has been put down, and the most violent persons today understand the impossibility of eliminating by violence or of deciding by a surprise that serious and menacing problem which we call the Roman question.
>
> The indefinite period of our occupation then permits hopes and conjectures alike erroneous and dangerous, and His Majesty has decided that his troops should return to France by the first of June of next year. . . . The frontier of the Papal States will be nevertheless protected by a formal declaration that any attack directed against her will be considered as a cause of war.

In the meantime the Pope was expected to organize a force for the preservation of internal order.[100]

The terms of the proposed treaty with Italy which were drawn up a little later provided, 1) that the King of Italy should *respect* the present territory of the Pope and to prevent an aggression upon it with all the means at his disposal; 2) that no restriction should be made by Italy against the movement of population or commerce from or to the Pope's territory; 3) that Italy should assume her share of the Papal debt for the annexed provinces; 4) that Italy should not object to a raising of a Papal force in Rome for keeping domestic peace; 5) that Italy should promise to attend a congress on the Roman question; 6) that France, considering the above promises, "reserves to herself [the right] to make known to the court of Rome its intention to determine a date for the end of the occupation of the Papal territory by her troops."[101]

[100] Proposed note from Thouvenel to La Valette, Paris, Sept. 1862, *Aff. Etr., M.D., Rome,* 124: (Sept. 1862).

[101] *Ibid.* (Oct. 1862).

A comparison of the two proposed documents with the eventual Convention of September 1864 will reveal some evident reasons why the Emperor would not agree with his Foreign Minister. One year would be too short a time for the Pope to organize a sufficient force. Aspromonte would not be a very reassuring guaranty. The *casus belli* meant really a potential reoccupation which would hardly relieve the situation should Italy enter Rome after a successful Roman insurrection. Article II of the treaty would be an interference with Italy's internal affairs. Lastly, France did not give Italy a definite enough promise about the date of evacuation. If these were the grounds of the Emperor's disagreement, he could be in a sense justified in abandoning his minister.

The Emperor returned to Paris on about 9 October. On the next day a meeting of the Council was held. Thouvenel's account to Benedetti gives a very good idea of the delicate situation.

> My dear friend, while you have been on the grill, I have been in the frying-pan, and it would be impossible for me to say whether or not we shall be eaten when well done. On the eve of the Emperor's return they were saying that I would be eaten raw, and the name of my successor, Mr. Drouyn de Lhuys, was being pronounced by those who thought they knew. Mr. Persigny, according to the 'inner circle,' would alone share my fate, which was to be announced to me at the first Council meeting. Three colleagues, of whom I am not over proud, Messrs. Baroche, Fould, and Rouher, (I flatter myself that Billault might have done the same had he been in Paris), insinuated by some trustworthy channel that a complete solidarity existed between them and me on the subject of the Roman question and that my retreat would be a signal for theirs.
>
> Whether this warning caused the reflection that things were less advanced than Count Walewski might have hoped, the Council meeting took place and the word *Rome* was not pronounced. Before the meeting I saw the Emperor for a few minutes. I rapidly informed His Majesty of what had happened recently in Turin, and read him the notes which Mr. Nigra, who arrived the night before, had hastened to bring to me.[102] I took care to say that there were two phrases, one where it is a question of "the demands of Italian na-

[102] Durando's second note written only to Nigra. See above note no. 90.

tionality,"[103] of which I would demand a modification, to say nothing of some corrections of detail and form.

The Emperor listened to me with the greatest attention and these are his very words: 'That's certainly better than in the past.' I informed him of Mr. Nigra's desire to see him just as soon as possible. His Majesty received the Italian this very day and I shall go to Saint Cloud Monday morning.[104]

. . . .

The Empress seemed uneasy and discontented. On the contrary Count Walewski had lost none of his poise. He had spent all day Thursday at St. Cloud and he went back yesterday after the Council meeting. To say the least I would bet no more on him than on myself.

Whatever may come of it, thanks to your advice, which proves that I was right in sending you back to Turin, Mr. Rattazzi has put into my hand a weapon which I will use to the limit.

The demand for Rome was a mistake under which Italy would remain unmistakably crushed. The demand for the evacuation of Rome by our troops made in diplomatic terms and accompanied by an offer of negotiations, that's a stand on which it is legitimate and natural for Turin to be placed, and on which I can in turn, establish myself resolutely.

. . . .

P.S. Mr. Nigra, who has just come from the Emperor, has just told me about his audience. In brief the Emperor replied that the note brought from Turin by the Italian Minister, with the exception of a few amendments to be discussed with me, constituted 'a new basis.' His Majesty added that at the same time this communication came very soon after the unfortunate circular of General Durando, and that everybody would call it a sham (*crierait à la comédie*). That's the kind of argument I will have to meet Monday. In such a situation Mr. Rattazzi or the King himself should, from my point of view, appeal to the patriotism and loyalty of General Durando and ask him to sacrifice himself silently. The new note signed by another than General Durando would have another value entirely.[105]

Thouvenel was in conference with the Emperor on Monday, the 13th, and at that time it is quite likely that he showed the Emperor his proposed note to Rome and that draft treaty for Turin. If he did not, he at least revealed a policy in line with

[103] This reference said that Italy would be willing to consider any plan "which, while reassuring the Catholic consciences, satisfied at the same time the legitimate demands of Italian nationality." See above note no. 90.

[104] The Council meeting evidently took place on the 10th. Monday was the 13th.

[105] 11 Oct. 1862, Thouvenel, *Pages d'histoire,* pp. 391-395.

those documents. Then it was that the Emperor unmasked himself to his Foreign Minister. What the Emperor said can be easily sensed from Thouvenel's own report to Flahault immediately thereafter.

We are certainly on the eve of a crisis which I foresaw. The Emperor, without taking up with his ministers the examination of the serious pending questions, seems determined to invite them all to hand in their resignations and then to reconstruct the cabinet under the influence which Count Walewski represents. Prince de La Tour d'Auvergne or Mr. Drouyn de Lhuys may be my successor.[106]

On Wednesday, the 15th, Thouvenel received the final news of his fate in a gentle and considerate note from the Emperor.

My dear Mr. Thouvenel, political considerations have compelled me to dismiss you from the Ministry of Foreign Affairs, but in deciding to separate myself from a man who has given me so many proofs of his devotion, I wish to tell him that my esteem for him and my confidence in him are in no way altered. I am persuaded that in all the positions which you will occupy I shall be able to count on your counsel as well as your attachment, and I beg of you, on your part, to always believe in my sincere friendship.[107]

In the person of Thouvenel the Italians had had a consistent friend. To them his dismissal meant a real loss. Their past heedlessness was to cost them much. If Rattazzi was himself compromised by joint responsibility with Durando for the circular to the extent that he could not see Durando retire alone as a consequence, then the Emperor would at least have to punctuate his disapproval by removing his own moderately pro-Italian minister.

The Emperor indicated to Cowley later that it was as much in the hopes of gaining a more conciliatory attitude in Rome that he had changed Ministers.

He (the Emperor) replied that he had hoped by a change of men to inspire the Pope with greater confidence and so to obtain concessions which might be some satisfaction to Italy.[108]

Along with Thouvenel went two of his intimate colleagues. Benedetti, disgruntled by an attempt to transfer him to Brus-

[106] Paris, 13 Oct. 1862, Thouvenel, *Secret,* II, 427-428.
[107] St. Cloud, 15 Oct. 1862, Thouvenel, *Secret,* II, 438-439.
[108] Cowley to Russell, Compiègne, 2 Dec. 1862, *R.P.,* LVIII.

sels, asked to be put on the reserved list.[109] La Valette, who had linked himself closely with Thouvenel and who had threatened to resign on an earlier occasion, now naturally gave up his post in Rome.

Later on, occasion will be taken to discuss fully the policy of the incoming Minister of Foreign Affairs. It may be well, however, as attention is momentarily turned to another quarter to know in brief his attitude. In a short interview with Cowley, Drouyn de Lhuys was reported as follows:

> His return to the Foreign Department did not imply any change in the Imperial policy. What had occurred was this: there were two parties in the Government, the one which believed that every means of settling the Roman question by friendly counsel had been exhausted, and that the time was come when an ultimatum must be pronounced, the other which still thought that every hope of a conciliatory arrangement ought not to be entirely abandoned. The Emperor, having to choose between these parties, sided with the latter and in this decision he (M. Drouyn de Lhuys) entirely concurred.[110]

The difference between the two opinions, however slight, was important. A policy such as the one indicated by Drouyn de Lhuys would certainly carry out the Emperor's intention of reassuring the Pope, but on the other hand it would cause great consternation in Italy.

Another interesting result growing out of the Aspromonte incident was one involving England in a plan to aid the Pope to flee from Rome. Since a great controversy arose between the Vatican and England over who originated the idea, it would be well to follow carefully the steps of an affair of considerable interest if not of great significance.

Odo Russell had been sent to Rome as England's agent. He was neither an ambassador nor a minister, and he had never been recognized by the Vatican as an accredited diplomat. Nevertheless, on the day of the feast of St. Peter and on the anniver-

[109] See above note no. 91. Drouyn de Lhuys to Benedetti, Paris, 25 Oct. 1862, *Aff. Etr., C.P., Italie,* 355: p. 242. Ideville, *Journal,* I, 283-285. How Persigny, who was also slated for dismissal, happened to remain is revealed somewhat in Baroche's papers reproduced in Maurain, pp. 620-623.

[110] Cowley to Russell, Paris, 21 Oct. 1862, *F.O., France,* 1446: no. 1208.

sary of the Pope's accession (21 June) it was the custom of the various diplomats accredited to the Roman Court to ask for audiences with the Holy Father. In January and June of 1861 and in January of 1862 Odo Russell had likewise requested audiences but they had consistently ignored his applications. He had repeated his request in June of 1862 more out of consistency and in order to show no disrespect toward the Pope rather than with any expectancy of fulfillment. As usual no reply was made to his request.[111]

However, during July Garibaldi began to make preparations in Sicily against the Pope in Rome. The Pope became alarmed over the attitude of France and her possible protection. Thouvenel and La Valette had just recently shown their lack of sympathy for the Pope's unyielding attitude. Then too, the French preparations caused suspicion. French warships had been stationed at Civita-Vecchia and French troops were being transferred from the Naples border to the region nearer Civita-Vecchia. It all looked to the Pope as if the French were going to concentrate on the port where Garibaldi was not likely to attack and leave undefended a region where Garibaldi was sure to come. It was interpreted as the beginning of another "Chambéry." The Vatican was also irritated at that time because France had obtained the recognition of Italy from Russia, Prussia, and Portugal.

In view of Garibaldi's activity and the recent French attitude the Pope began to think of flight. France as a place of exile was immediately eliminated. Austria and Spain would hesitate to receive Pius IX for fear of offending France. Neither could he go to Belgium or Bavaria without crossing France or Austria. He therefore had only England and Turkey to whom to look for aid. The latter because of its religion and weakness would be an impossible asylum. Consequently there remained only one power benevolent and powerful enough to protect His Holiness in flight.[112] With some such thoughts as these, accord-

[111] Odo Russell to Russell, Rome, 13 Feb. 1863, *F.O., Rome,* 89B: no. 24.

[112] Same to same (autograph), Rome, 14 Feb. 1863, *F.O., Rome,* 89B: no. 25.

ing to Odo Russell's surmise, the Pope directed Antonelli to arrange an audience with the British agent. Since Mr. Russell was considered a private person, the message was delivered through the Grand Chamberlain. On the evening of 25 July on arriving home Russell found the invitation awaiting him.[113]

At noon on the 26th Odo Russell was ushered into the Pope's presence and had a long conversation with him alone. The Pope seemed in a very good humor and was very benevolent in attitude. He was in the act of reading an article by Sir James Hudson describing the bad conditions in the territory ruled over by the Pope. The Holy Father complained of Hudson's unfair statements and jokingly said that Hudson had not helped the agricultural situation by "planting carrots" (an Italian expression meaning to exaggerate).

> After a few words on my part in defence of Sir James Hudson's views, His Holiness interrupted me to say that he had heard I was going to England on leave of absence and that he had sent for me to wish me a pleasant journey and to ask when I should return to Rome. He then went on to speak of my mother's late illness and observed that since I had done so much for *la madre* in Rome, could I not do something for *il Papa* in London?[114]
>
> The Pope said he was now forsaken by every Government in Europe; all were against him and probably even Spain would recognize the Kingdom of Italy. The recognition of Italy by Russia was the work of France. He had received several curious letters from St. Petersburg on the subject, which left no doubt in his mind that Prince Gortchakoff's new Italian policy was the price paid for certain concessions on the part of France in the East.
>
> Those concessions were contrary to British interests and Eng-

[113] Antonelli claimed that the audience had not been requested by the Pope but that it was in reply to Odo Russell's request of the month before. The Pope had been preoccupied with the bishops (see above) and had also been ill in the meantime. Thus the reply to the request of June had been unavoidably delayed until July. Antonelli to Chigi, Rome, 14 Feb. 1863, *Aff. Etr., C.P., Rome,* 1022: pp. 241-243.

[114] Antonelli later denied that the Pope knew of Odo's plan to go to London and in fact suspected that his early trip to London was in response to a joking reference of the Pope to British aid in exile. (Antonelli to Chigi, Rome, 27 Dec. 1862, *Aff. Etr., C.P., Rome,* 1022: pp. 220-224). This account of Odo's was written immediately after the interview before he knew that there would be a controversy over the origin of the interview and over the question of previous knowledge of his plan to return to London (see above note no. 111). Likewise it will be noticed that the Pope's joking phrase was definitely connected with his statement that he knew Odo was planning to go soon to London.

land, forsaken by her present ally, would have to reëstablish her old alliance with Austria, an alliance which could meet with his full sympathies.

The Pope went on to show that he too was opposed to Orthodox Russia in the East and that the Catholic Church would be one of the most advantageous allies for Great Britain if they could only eliminate their antagonism.

The French Emperor, [the Pope] continued, after making the late extraordinary and unacceptable propositions to him through Mr. de La Valette, had evidently organized the present Garibaldian movement, with the Cabinet of Turin to establish the basis of an excuse for handing over Rome to the Piedmontese.

The whole of Mr. de La Valette's and Mr. de Montebello's proceedings for the defence of Civita-Vecchia, the last place Garibaldi would think of attacking were a farce (*une comédie*); it might therefore become the Pope's duty to leave the Holy See, and it was evident he could not seek protection from the Catholic countries who, notwithstanding the proclaimed principles of the Church, had recognized the Kingdom of Italy. Spain would follow their example. Austria there were other objections to. Did I, under these circumstances, think that he could go and live in peace in England?

The Pope wished to be assured that he would not be molested by Protestant fanaticism and that he would be able to carry on the functions of a Pope (*faire le Pape*). Mr. Russell assured him that he would be treated hospitably and allowed to carry on his holy duties as long as he observed the laws of the land.

The Pope continued the audience by hoping for Russell's personal conversion to Catholicism and only at the end alluded lightly to his earlier request by remarking: "I shall expect you to protect me if I go to England. So *vi benedico* (I bless you)."

On leaving the Pope's chamber Russell met Cardinal de Mérode, Papal Secretary of War, "who held similar language to me." Then he called "according to custom" on Antonelli, "whom I found equally disposed to expect great things from England in consequence of the supposed Franco-Russian alliance for Eastern affairs."

To show that Odo Russell was not duped by the move made by the Vatican and also to throw some light on the sincerity of

England's subsequent action the last paragraphs of Odo's dispatch are worth reading in full.

In all probability the Pope's intention is, that I should repeat what he has said and that the French Government should feel the necessity of taking measures to ensure his remaining in Rome, as his flight to England would have a bad effect in France.

I have, therefore, not mentioned the Pope's conversation with me to anyone.[115]

Odo Russell immediately wrote down the long account of his momentous interview but did not dare to send it in the usual channels of communication. In a private letter he told Lord Russell that an interview had taken place and added: "I will send you an account by the first safe opportunity that I can find."[116] There seems to be no evidence either in the *Russell Papers* or in the dispatches of the Foreign Office to indicate that Odo Russell was called home immediately as a result of this interview. On the other hand it seems quite likely that the Foreign Office did not know of the significance of this interview until Odo Russell's arrival in London. Dispatch no. 100 which was written on 26 July was received at the Foreign Office only on August 18th.[117] It might even be possible that Odo Russell took it to England himself and discussed it verbally with Palmerston and Lord Russell.

The action which the British Government decided to take is reflected by an order issued ten days later to the Secretary of the Admiralty.

Earl Russell . . . request[s] that . . . Vice-Admiral Martin should have orders to accede to any request of the Pope to send a ship to Civita-Vecchia to convey him to Malta.[118]

Other details were no doubt worked out at this time and Odo Russell was sent on his way to Rome again about the first of October. While in Paris he wrote back to Russell:

[115] Odo Russell to Russell, Rome, 26 July 1862, *F.O., Rome,* 86B: no. 100.

[116] Odo Russell to Russell, Rome, 29 July 1862, *R.P.*, LXXVI. In a later letter Odo Russell stated that "my account which your Lordship has read in my despatch no. 100 of the 26th July was written immediately after the audience." See above note no. 111.

[117] See above note no. 115 and Foreign Office notation at the head of dispatch no. 100.

I read your new instructions with deep interest and rejoice at the prospect of carrying them out; it will be curious to watch their effect on the Vatican.

But what will the Emperor, Thouvenel, and Lord Cowley say to them? I expect they will raise objections.[119]

Many thanks for giving me such interesting work. I long to be at it again.[120]

What instructions Odo Russell referred to is not shown in the Foreign Office correspondence unless it is the enclosure to the dispatch no. 130 to Cowley. But on 25 October definite written instructions were sent to Odo Russell in Rome for his use at the Vatican. Lord Russell chided the Pope for his refusal to treat with Italy, blamed the Pope for the brigandage in Italy, and claimed that Rome was the rightful capital of the new Kingdom. If the Pope still felt justified in claiming Rome and the temporal power, he should retire temporarily and let the Romans decide. Then with a favorable decision he could return with increased strength. But the British avoided offering an asylum in England itself. It seemed safer and also more appropriate to protect the holy exile in an Italian community not far from Rome. Hence Malta was offered as the place of refuge.

In such a case the Admiral of Her Majesty in the Mediterranean would convey the Pope to Malta, to Trieste, to Marseilles, or to Valencia, and if His Holiness should choose to remain in Malta, Her Majesty's Government would there provide a mansion fit for his reception.

There His Holiness might be surrounded by his chief Cardinals and most trusty counsellors. He would not be asked to subscribe to any conditions repugnant to his conscience. Civil war would cease in Italy, and the Italian people would be at liberty either to enjoy the complete possession of their own territory, or again to assign to the Pope, if they saw fit, a temporal dominion. At all events . . .

[118] Layard to the Sec. of the Admiralty, London, F.O., 28 Aug. 1862, *F.O., France,* 1476: enclosure with no. 130. *Parl. Papers* (1863), LXXV, 332.

[119] This is a significant passage which may indicate the British purpose as one of embarrassing France further in the sight of her Catholics. Certainly if the Pope fled, the French could do little else than withdraw. But should the Pope not flee, this British move would be likely only to strengthen the French grip on Rome. It was a dangerous and uncertain move and could at most only expect to sicken the French a little more of their obligations to the Pope.

[120] Odo Russell to Russell, Paris, 3 Oct. 1862. *R.P.,* LXXVI.

when the storm was overpast, the Pope might return to Rome, owing to love and affection that homage would be paid to his sacred character which would be justly due to his exalted personal virtues.

You are directed to speak in the sense of this dispatch to Cardinal Antonelli, and to give him a copy of it to be submitted to the Pope.[121]

Russell's opinion of the British offer is found in a private letter written to Odo Russell.

I shall be glad to hear how you get on with Antonelli. My opinion is that the Pope may wait some time before he gets so good an offer.[122]

The delivery of the note took place on 11 November and Odo Russell confided to Russell that

the communication of your despatch to Cardinal Antonelli seemed to please him immensely, and he snatched the copy out of my hands and crammed it into his bosom and buttoned it up as if it had been a bag of golden scudi.

. . . The more I think over the measure and the more I read your despatch the more I feel that it was a good move in every respect.[123]

Antonelli delayed in giving a definitive reply until he could consult the Pope although he inferred that as long as France would protect the Pope in Rome, it was imperative for him to remain. After Mr. Russell saw him again on 28 November, he reported that His Eminence had replied

that he had communicated Your Lordship's despatch to the Pope the day after I had given him a copy of it, namely, on the 12th of November, and that His Holiness fully acknowledged the friendly spirit in which the communication had been made; but that, since it was his manifest duty to remain in Rome so long as he could do so with advantage to the spiritual interests of the Church, he could but thank Her Majesty's Government for their intentions, but he could not share their opinions, nor could he avail himself of their hospitable offers at present.[124]

[121] Russell to Odo Russell, London, 25 Oct. 1862, *F.O., Rome,* 85: no. 46. *Parl. Papers* (1863), LXXV, 1-2.

[122] 17 Nov. 1862, *R.P.,* CXI.

[123] 19 Nov. 1862, *R.P.,* LXXVI. As in this document so in most of the correspondence on this affair there seems to be, on the part of both England and the Vatican, a ring of insincerity. The reason for this becomes more apparent as the plot develops.

[124] 11 Nov. 1862, *F.O., Rome,* 86B: no. 108. *Parl. Papers* (1863), LXXV, 6-7. *Aff. Etr., C.P., Rome,* 1022: pp. 203-207, copy eventually transmitted by England to France.

Antonelli declared that he was sure Napoleon would not leave home without the Pope's consent.[125]

As Odo Russell had suspected in July, the Vatican seemed desirous of using the British offer to spur France and Austria to greater concern for the interests of the Pope. When Antonelli assured Mr. Russell in December that he intended to keep the English offer a secret, the latter reported home:

> I naturally concluded from this declaration that [Antonelli] must have given a copy of it to some friend. . . .

Odo Russell soon found that Antonelli had given a copy in fact to the Austrian Ambassador who in turn had sent it to Vienna by the way of Paris in order to let France also know of it. Antonelli had told Bach, the Austrian Ambassador, that the Pope might have to accept the English offer in the future.[126]

By 19 December Drouyn de Lhuys was well informed of the contents of the British invitation. He declared to Cowley that he had known nothing of it until the Austrian Ambassador at Paris, Metternich, had informed him.[127] On hearing the news "in an indirect way" Drouyn de Lhuys had a conference with the Papal Nuncio, Chigi, who confirmed the report. "While avoiding to appear to take it very seriously," Drouyn de Lhuys expressed the hope that if the Pope was ever obliged to flee, he would chose France rather than England. Soon after this con-

[125] 28 Nov. 1862, *F.O., Rome,* 86B: no. 118. *Parl. Papers* (1863), LXXV, 7. *Aff. Etr., C.P., Rome,* 1022: pp. 209-210.

[126] Same to same, Rome, 16 Dec. 1862, *R.P.,* LXXVI. The Pope told the French Ambassador that "Mr. Odo Russell himself had spoken of the note to one of the diplomats accredited to the Holy See." La Tour d'Auvergne to Drouyn de Lhuys, Rome, 27 Dec. 1862, *Aff. Etr., C.P., Rome,* 1021: pp. 462-475. Antonelli declared that "he had desired to keep the [English note] secret and that although he had had it translated into Italian, he had not communicated it to anyone and had always kept it in his room. . . ." On the other hand Odo Russell denied that he had mentioned the matter to anyone else. He said that he had been told of it by another diplomat and an Italian gentleman before he had breathed a word but he had not given an additional fact to those already known. Odo Russell to Russell, Rome, 13 Feb. 1863, *F.O., Rome,* 89B: no. 24. Russell persisted in the declaration that Antonelli had revealed the news when he thought the right moment had arrived.

[127] Cowley to Russell, Chantilly, 19 Dec. 1862, *R.P.,* LVIII. It certainly was not rumored around Rome very much or La Tour d'Auvergne would have found out and informed Drouyn de Lhuys. As a matter of fact Drouyn de Lhuys informed his own ambassador of the British invitation.

ference the French Foreign Minister informed his Ambassador in Rome, La Tour d'Auvergne, on the subject.[128]

Of course La Tour d'Auvergne immediately investigated the report and is purported to have obtained an explanation from the Pope himself.[129] Antonelli knew of D'Auvergne's dispatch describing the Pope's explanation and tacitly approved of its contents. But the statements of the French Ambassador carry certain facts which do not conform to Odo Russell's account. It claimed that Odo Russell had asked for the audience, that the Pope only mentioned jokingly the possible need of English protection as Odo was about to leave the audience chamber, that Russell had taken the suggestion seriously and had turned around to make sure of the Pope's seriousness, that the Pope reassured him that he had no apprehension for the moment and had not the slightest idea of leaving Rome. The French Ambassador's report (supposedly from Pius IX himself) went on to say that on hearing of the nature of the interview the English had recalled Odo Russell to London and had sent him back two months later with the offer to the Pope. Finally the French account declared that on a later occasion, when Odo Russell had learned that the Vatican would not accept the British offer, Odo had said that he had learned from a private letter from Lord Russell that he was sure the Pope would soon need to take advantage of the offer. The Pope also seems to have declared that Odo Russell told the Vatican they could make use of the note as they pleased, and the Pope had hurriedly assured him that he had no intention of using it. But the French report went on to say that Odo Russell himself began to spread the news of it among the other ministers and ambassadors at Rome. A very similar report was sent by Antonelli to Chigi which showed that

[128] 20 Dec. 1862, *Aff. Etr., C.P., Rome,* 1021: p. 428. *Livre Jaune* (1862), pp. 28-29.

[129] Antonelli told Odo Russell that "Prince de la Tour d'Auvergne's account of my (Russell's) interview with His Holiness had been communicated to the Ambassador by the Pope himself shortly after His Excellency's arrival in Rome on December last." Odo Russell to Russell, Rome, 13 Feb. 1863, *F.O., Rome,* 89B: no. 24.

the Pope, Antonelli, and D'Auvergne seemed to have concerted together on their accounts.[130]

Thus the whole import of the French account was that England had created the occasion, had made a serious affair out of the Pope's jest, had definitely plotted to embarrass France, and finally had spread the rumor since the Vatican was keeping the whole affair quiet. The French Government had this account published in order to have it appear to the French people that the Pope was still grateful to France and that England was trying to cause a misunderstanding between Rome and Paris.

When the English became aware of the French version, they began immediately to prepare a refutation. Odo Russell, of course, denied the "misstatements" of the French account.[131] Mr. Russell's original account of July was written right after the interview and without any premonition of the future controversy. Neither this account nor his two later notes of justification were published and consequently would be expected to be more accurate and sincere than the published notes of France and the Vatican after the controversy had begun. Thus Russell's account showed that the Pope's jest of *madre* and *papa* had come at the beginning of the interview at which time he had talked seriously and at length on the possibility of English protection. He had also mentioned it again before Odo Russell's departure. In this same July report, written before there was a question of whether Odo Russell had been called home purposely to plot with the British Foreign Office, it is found that the Pope had said "he had heard I (O. Russell) was going to England and he had sent for me to wish me a pleasant journey."[132] Then too, the Pope's account in the French dispatch had said that "Mr. Russell, who was on the point of going home on leave, asked for an audience."[133] Thus the fact that Odo Russell received a telegram giving him permission for his leave of absence

[130] La Tour d'Auvergne to Drouyn de Lhuys, Rome, 27 Dec. 1862, *Aff. Etr., C.P., Rome*, 1021: pp. 462-475; *Livre Jaune* (1862), pp. 36-37. Antonelli to Chigi, Rome, 27 Dec. 1862, *Aff. Etr., C.P., Rome,* 1022: pp. 220-224.

[131] See above notes nos. 113, 114, 126.

[132] See above note no. 115.

[133] "Qui se disposait à prendre un congé." See above note no. 130.

does not indicate that the British agent was suddenly recalled for the purpose of consultation. It was quite evident that the Pope knew before the audience that Odo Russell was about to leave for London. It is also apparent that Odo Russell was not allowed an audience the other years but on the occasion of the Garibaldi incident his request was granted after considerable delay.

The final remark in the French Ambassador's report about a later private letter from Lord Russell predicting a new danger to the Pope in the near future seemed to be an additional argument used by Antonelli to alarm the French. To have it appear that the English were still trying to frighten the Pope would convince the French still more that the English were definitely conspiring to cause a breach between France and the Vatican. The only private note appearing in the *Russell Papers* was "that the Pope may wait some time before he gets so good an offer."[134] No document of the nature related by Antonelli appeared in the *Russell Papers* in December. It can not be determined definitely what Odo Russell may have said to Antonelli in December but it is likely that he expressed some sentiment similar to Russell's in the November letter, in which case Antonelli either consciously or unconsciously elaborated it and presumed that the English letter had arrived in December. Antonelli persisted in this statement when he met Odo Russell again and the latter reported: "This I denied and I don't see how he could have so recollected."[135] Lord Russell published a dispatch to Cowley in which he denied the facts which were inconsistent with Odo Russell's dispatch and sent France a copy of the British offer. Odo Russell also sent two vigorous justifications to London which were not intended for publication and therefore would seem to be more sincere.[136]

Antonelli's excuse for the disparity between his and the Brit-

[134] See above note no. 122.

[135] See above note no. 111.

[136] Russell to Cowley, London, 29 Jan. 1863, *F.O., France,* 1476: no. 130. *Parl. Papers* (1863), LXXV, 7-9. *Aff. Etr., C.P., Rome,* 1022: pp. 195-197. See above notes nos. 111, 112.

ish account was to minimize Odo Russell's authority. Twice he referred to the fact that Odo Russell was an unaccredited agent. It would thus be inferred that the word of a Cardinal Secretary of State and a Sovereign Pope should be more trustworthy than that of a mere intriguing individual. "I am surprised . . .," said Antonelli, "that the facts were so altered and that Mr. Russell's reports, being nothing more than purely private correspondence because of the absence of any diplomatic character of the author, were published in the official correspondence."[137] Again Antonelli declared to Odo Russell that he confided more often to him because of his unofficial character than to the regular diplomats, but if the English were going to publish these confidences, he would have to discontinue them.[138]

It was interesting to see how both Rome and Paris tried to blame each other for the inaccuracies of their accounts when the English published their *pièces justificatives.* Cowley reported that

> Drouyn de Lhuys is a little ashamed of the fuss he has made about Odo's interview with His Holiness and feels that neither the Pope nor Antonelli told the French Ambassador the truth.[139]

A month later Cowley saw the Papal Nuncio "who gave me (Cowley) to understand that the version published by his government of the interview was forced upon them by the French." Cowley suggested that the English had been generous by not publishing all their documents on the question. "The Nuncio acquiesced in this observation."[140]

After surveying the whole situation, one can not help but feel that there was a great deal of insincerity on the part of both the Pope and England. When the British offer arrived, the danger of the Garibaldi invasion was passed. Yet the Malta invitation seemed just as welcome to Antonelli. That it did alarm France and Austria is shown by what followed its revelation. But the English were not without their intrigue. Odo Rus-

[137] See above note no. 113.
[138] Odo Russell to Russell, Rome, 16 Feb. 1863, *R.P.*, LXXVI.
[139] Cowley to Russell, Paris, 3 Feb. 1863, *R.P.*, LXXVI.
[140] Same to same, Paris, 2 March 1863, *F.O., France,* 1487: no. 269.

sell spoke as if England had some concerted plans when he said, "It will be curious to watch their effect on the Vatican. But what will the Emperor, Thouvenel, and Lord Cowley say to them?"[141] After the French had been alarmed by the Vatican's betrayal of the English and then disillusioned by England's betrayal of the Vatican, Russell wrote Odo, "You have done very well with your Pope, and I hope to set you right with the enlightened public without committing you. . . ."[142]

There was one sure result to come from this play of cross-purposes: the French would become more and more disgusted with their duty of occupying Rome. They would therefore become increasingly willing to find and seize upon an opportunity for evacuation.

The period in which Thouvenel and Rattazzi had directed the Franco-Italian negotiations on the Roman question had ended in failure as had the periods of Cavour and Ricasoli. The most important French condition in all the negotiations had been a suitable Italian guaranty backed by a strong, firm Italy. Cavour's death had bereft Italy of the only acceptable guaranty in the early period. Political divisions and uncertainties had developed at the time of Ricasoli's ministry because of his over-zealousness and his uncompromising attitude toward Rattazzi. These had undermined the confidence of the French in the efficacy or sincerity of any Italian guaranty in the early months of 1862. Hence no settlement could be seriously considered until Ricasoli had been succeeded by another. Thereupon the French with some justified or unjustified feeling of responsibility for the change in ministry, began to take more serious steps toward a final settlement. Just as the hesitant Emperor, the wary Parliament, and the sensitive French public were being brought to a favorable attitude for the negotiation; just when the Pope had been manœuvred into a very unpleasant position and plans were being definitely discussed; then it was that Garibaldi moved toward Rome and again prevented what he was most desirous to achieve, the French evacuation of Rome. Garibaldi's venture,

[141] See above note no 120.
[142] 2 Feb. 1863, *R.P.*, CXI.

Pepoli's conference, and Durando's circular along with many other influences finally convinced the Emperor that the French were proceeding too rapidly with an irresponsible Italy. A reaction set in and this time, to impress upon the Italians the error of their ways and to reassure the Pope so as to encourage him out of his immovable attitude, the Emperor sacrificed his own foreign minister. The effect of this change on Italy and on the course of the unfinished negotiation will be a part of the relation of the next chapter.

CHAPTER VI

PLAYING DEAD AND COUNTER-IRRITANTS

AT THE same time that England was offering the Pope Malta as a place of refuge, she was exerting pressure again on France through stern communications to the new French Foreign Minister. Russell wrote Cowley:

> We shall have to consider with his (Thouvenel's) successor all the pending questions except that of Rome. Upon the Roman question I shall probably direct you to read the dispatch at which Thouvenel was so much alarmed and to give a copy of it if desired.[1]
>
> I do not see any use in doing more; as Drouyn de Lhuys is an old friend, I suppose he will either write to me or send me a message. I shall be quite disposed to act cordially with him and I feel strongly the paramount necessity in the present state of the world that Great Britain and France should indulge no sentiments of national rivalry or pique but disappoint all those who would seek to profit by their quarrels.[2]

Cowley had a conversation with Drouyn de Lhuys toward the end of October at which time the latter indicated that he was going to demand from both Italy and the Vatican a statement of the basis on which each of them would treat. If both or either were satisfactory to France, he would try to reconcile them and settle the question. "Should, on the contrary, the Italian Government make satisfactory offers and they were refused by the Pope in spite of the counsels of France, he should be released from all further obligations to His Holiness."

Cowley observed that at the Congress of Paris in 1856 France had objected to foreign occupations in Italy and had given it to be understood that France remained in Rome only because of the presence of the Austrians in Bologna and yet now the French were still in Rome. "Mr. Drouyn de Lhuys did not reply to this observation. . . ."

When Cowley pointed out that France by her occupation

[1] Dispatch of 29 September 1862, see above Chapter V, pp. 202-203, note 78.

[2] 15 Oct. 1862, *R.P.*, CV.

was both losing Italian sympathy and aiding reaction, Drouyn de Lhuys countered with the observation that England maintained the Ottoman Empire in spite of its cruel and bad government. Cowley replied that the British had no army in Turkey and that the Sultan was attempting to make some reforms, however unsatisfactory, while the Pope was refusing to do even that.

Drouyn de Lhuys ended the conversation by reaffirming that the Emperor had no *arrière pensée* behind his occupation and would leave as soon as he could be sure that the Pope would not be harmed.[3]

In a private letter Cowley added that Drouyn de Lhuys had also said that if the Pope could have a large army of his own, this might help France to withdraw. It was Cowley's impression that Drouyn de Lhuys had "been so long out of office that he appears quite uninformed on most subjects."[4]

Odo Russell was just at that time passing through Paris on his way to Rome to make his Malta offer. He had a talk with the new French Foreign Minister who minimized the bad state of the Papal Government. He thought the Turkish Government to be much worse and that Rome would make reforms at the instance of a friendly French Government. He felt too that a large majority of the permanent residents of the Papal States were devoted to the Pope. Odo Russell, like Cowley, came to the following conclusion:

> He . . . spoke [on the Roman question] for rather more than an hour without interruption, and in the end he succeeded in convincing me that he knew little or nothing about it.[5]

In view of the attitude taken by Drouyn de Lhuys toward Rome in his first interview with Cowley and in his circular note to all the Powers, Lord Russell seized the opportunity to write another note to France. Seemingly taking his cue from the changed tone of Italy, he also omitted to demand Rome as

[3] Cowley's memorandum, Paris, 28 Oct. 1862, *F.O., France,* 1446: (no number; see under date).
[4] 29 Oct. 1862, *R.P.,* LVIII.
[5] Odo Russell to Russell, Paris, 30 Oct. 1862, *ibid.,* LXXVI.

Italy's capital and restricted himself to a demand to leave Rome to the Romans. With arguments very similar to those in his earlier September dispatch he recommended that this be brought about through French evacuation.[6]

When Cowley saw Drouyn de Lhuys, the latter declined to accept a copy of the note at that time. The French Minister said that because France and Great Britain disagreed on this minor matter, they should not allow it to affect their relations in other respects. He felt that, after all, England could have no direct interest in the Roman question and had, as a matter of fact, acquiesced in the French occupation in 1848. Cowley replied that the Roman question certainly would not affect the French-British relations on other matters; that England had a right to be interested in the Roman question from the point of view of the peace of Europe, Italian commercial and industrial stability, and the principle of non-intervention; and lastly that conditions had changed since 1848 which would justify Great Britain's objection to a policy previously approved.[7]

However, in addition to his remarks to Cowley, Drouyn de Lhuys drew up a note to be transmitted to Russell by Cadore, the new French Ambassador at the Court of St. James. Here again he deplored the fact that Anglo-French relations were being marred by a question which did not directly concern England. But he added a clause that would appear to imply that England was in no position to criticize France's conduct:

> Yes, no doubt the desire of the Romans for reforms is meeting delays and adjournments; but Rome is not the only country where such delays are a result of similar steps. There are certainly other countries where the suffering of the people is more real and still more worthy of the sympathy of the Christian Powers.[8]

He evidently again had reference to Turkey which he hoped to use as a stone against the British glass house.

[6] 31 Oct. 1862, *F.O., France,* 1428: no. 1077. *Aff. Etr., C.P., Angleterre,* 722: pp. 147-148. *Parl Papers,* (1863), LXXV, 2-3.

[7] Cowley to Russell, Paris, 7 Nov. 1862, *F.O., France,* 1447: no. 1253. *Parl. Papers,* (1863), LXXV, 3-5. Same to same, Paris, 9 Nov. 1862, *R.P.,* LVIII.

[8] Drouyn de Lhuys to Cadore, Compiègne, 25 Nov. 1862, *Aff. Etr., C.P., Angleterre,* 722: pp. 198-204. *Livre Jaune,* (1862), pp. 19-23.

It became quite evident to the British that Drouyn de Lhuys was an entirely different man to deal with than Thouvenel had been. Instead of agreeing with England and regretting the impossibility of action, the new Foreign Minister disagreed with the British and was inclined to criticize their interference.

But Russell did not immediately withdraw from the contest. Having given up the demand for Rome as Italy's capital, he now became more silent on the demand for delivering Rome to the Romans. Instead he complained of the brigandage and laid the blame at the door of France. The Pope and the bishops had declared that Rome must be "the seat of a temporal authority, independent of any other; 'the center, as it were, of universal concord; a place where no human ambition breathes; where no one ever intrigues for territorial dominion.' " The bad situation caused by the inexcusable brigandage proved the temporal rule in Rome to be quite the contrary. If brigands issued from Switzerland into Italy, Switzerland would immediately make amends or Italy could attack her. But Rome neither makes amends nor can Italy protect her own rights by a just war because of the presence of the French. The French could stop the brigands by a word and it is up to them to do so.[9]

During the last days of December and the month of January 1863 Drouyn de Lhuys took steps to satisfy the British modest demands on brigandage. Without denying that some brigandage started in Rome he pointed out that South Italy had always had brigandage, that much of it was so far into the interior that it could not have begun in Rome, and that the reports reaching the British were often exaggerated. He warned Russell that some brigands were threatening South-East Italy from Corfu. The responsibility rested on England to stop this. Nevertheless, he declared that France was taking immediate steps to stop brigandage, to suggest reforms, to demand the departure of Francis II, and to coöperate with the Italian army to check brigandage. These hopeful signs were enough to satisfy the

[9] Russell to Cowley, London, 27 Dec. 1862, *F.O., France,* 1430: no. 1325. Earl John Russell, *Speeches and Despatches* (2 vols., London, 1870), II, 360-363.

British temporarily, especially since some of the leading brigands were being apprehended. Francis II could not be dislodged from Rome, however, since he insisted on the right to reside in his own palace.[10]

Recalling Drouyn de Lhuys' declared intention to demand of Rome a basis of negotiation and reforms in its government, let us now turn to a consideration of the French efforts in that direction.

Drouyn de Lhuys had a conference with Monsignor Chigi, the Papal Nuncio, on 31 October. At that time he expressed regret that the Pope had refused reconciliation. He said that the Pope should aid France in combating her critics by initiating reforms in the Papal Government. He argued that just because the Pope did not have his former territories was no reason why he could not reform the government of what he actually possessed, and he gave the Nuncio to understand that France would not undertake the recovery of what had been lost. If the Pope insisted on the return of the Marches and Umbria purely because of his responsibility to the Faithful, could not the responsibility of the Catholic Powers relieve him of that burden?[11]

Such was the tone of Drouyn de Lhuys toward the Vatican. It did not differ greatly from Thouvenel's, but it was felt that he was more sympathetically inclined. This would tend to make the Vatican more receptive and perhaps to feel that the new minister would be the last one from whom they might expect the few French favors which might be still forthcoming.

Lallemand's first approach to the Pope did not bring very promising results. Antonelli was pleased with the appointment

[10] The following is the correspondence with Great Britain on the French efforts in respect to reforms and order in and about Rome: Cowley to Russell, Paris, 30, 30 Dec. 1862, 2 Feb., 7 May, 27 June, 7 July 1863, *F.O., France,* 1448: nos. 1445, 1446; 1485: no. 138; 1491: no. 540; 1493: nos. 742, 792. Cowley to Russell, Chantilly, 27 Nov. 1862; E. D'Azeglio to Russell, London, 7 May 1863; *R.P.*, LVIII, LXXI. Drouyn de Lhuys to Cadore, to D'Auvergne, and to Gros, Paris, 1 Jan. 1863, *Aff. Etr., C.P., Angleterre,* 723: pp. 9-16; Paris, 30 May 1863, *Rome,* 1023: pp. 268-274; Paris, 8 June 1863, *Angleterre,* p. 44.

[11] Lhuys to Lallemand (chargé in Rome), Paris, 31 Oct. 1862, *Aff. Etr., C.P., Rome,* 1021: pp. 252-256. *Livre Jaune,* (1862), 16-19, (this is not a complete copy).

of Drouyn de Lhuys. The Pope, too, was pleased with the new French Foreign Minister although he was reported to have declared that it perhaps only meant that he would have to be abandoned by a friend instead of by an opponent.[12] Lallemand took advantage of these good dispositions to press very earnestly the cause of conciliation and reform. But the replies were invariably the same as in the past.

> The territorial question does not then appear, I say it with regret, of a nature to be negotiated by the three interested parties together . . ., for I am strongly led to believe that the Holy Father will remain absolutely outside of any arrangement which may aim at the consecration of his present condition of possession.

In regard to the question of reforms Lallemand summarized the Pope's attitude in the following words: "Give me back my territory and my subjects and I will then publish my reforms."

Lallemand suggested that France negotiate with the Catholic powers the stabilization of the Pope's temporal power and that the Pope would acquiesce in it without approving or recognizing it. As a matter of fact the Pope had indicated to Montebello a month before that "perhaps that would be the best thing after all."[13]

Although on 15 November Drouyn de Lhuys asked Lallemand to make no proposals, on 6 December he instructed the latter to ask Rome to reform its government, if not to make the French leave sooner, at least to make the Pope stay longer.[14] Lallemand's reply was to the effect that the Emperor ought to impose reforms and that the Pope would not object since he is now embarrassed by both radicals and reactionaries. These reforms should be in the form of limited self-government in financial matters, and lay officials. The greatest opposition to the present system came from those laymen who could not hold office because of the priestly monopoly.[15]

With the arrival of La Tour d'Auvergne as the regular

[12] Lallemand to Lhuys, Rome, 8 Nov. 1862, *Aff. Etr., C.P., Rome,* 1021: pp. 262-263.

[13] Lallemand to Lhuys, Rome, 10 Nov. 1862, *Aff. Etr., C.P., Rome,* 1021: pp. 270-272. Same to same, Rome, 14 Nov. 1862, *ibid.,* pp. 280-281.

[14] 6 Dec. 1862, *Aff. Etr., C.P., Rome,* 1021: pp. 373-374.

[15] 18 Nov., 6 Dec. 1862, *Aff. Etr., C.P., Rome,* 1021: pp. 295-296, 375-381.

French Ambassador to the Vatican, negotiations for reform took more definite shape. Odo Russell reported home rumors of extravagant plans which were on foot. First, the Empress was working as best she could to persuade the Emperor to occupy Umbria and the Marches in return for Papal reforms. This would seem to be in line with the Pope's reiterations that he could not institute reforms without more territory. On the other hand Antonelli and those close to Austria seemed to be working for the establishment of a confederation in Italy. By offering France this preferable form of government and giving her membership in the confederation for Corsica and by allowing Austria membership also for Venetia, they were supposed to be able to gain support for the idea.[16] If these plans ever existed, they were so fantastic that nothing ever came of them. It is known that Austria seemed inclined to second France's requests for reform, but Austria's Ambassador was not at all enthusiastic about fulfilling those duties in Rome.[17]

On the occasion of the presentation of his credentials the Pope seemed so cordial to La Tour d'Auvergne that the latter began immediately a discussion in regard to reforms. The Pope declared at first that he had long ago made ready a set of reforms but soon after that he had lost three-fourths of his territory which made it foolish to proceed with the little that remained. These reforms arranged for an election of the municipal council which would in turn elect provincial councils who would again elect councillors of state who could take charge of the finances. The Pope explained that now no considerable income came from the provinces but only from the Faithful directly to the Pope. This fund was only for the Pope and not for the council to dispose of. However, before the audience was ended, the Pope agreed that reform in some shape ought to be considered. Nothing was said about an arrangement with Italy.[18]

[16] Odo Russell to Russell, Rome, 16 Dec. 1862, *R.P.*, LXXVI.

[17] Gramont to Lhuys, Vienna, 15 Nov. 1862, *Aff. Etr.*, *C.P.*, *Autriche*, 482: pp. 232-236. D'Auvergne to Lhuys, Rome, 2 Dec. 1862, *Aff. Etr.*, *C.P.*, *Rome*, 1021: pp. 418-423.

[18] D'Auvergne to Lhuys, Rome, 16 Dec. 1862, *Aff. Etr.*, *C.P.*, *Rome*, 1021: pp. 418-423.

Finally on 20 and 24 December Paris learned that definite reforms were to be undertaken. The *Osservatore romano* announced that elections would be held for municipal offices, that commercial, criminal, and civil codes would be drawn up, and passport restrictions between the Papal States and Italy would be made less rigid. It was also understood that the Vatican was planning to undertake some projects of public construction in the matter of railroads and the enlargement of the port of Civita-Vecchia.[19]

This was the most which La Tour d'Auvergne thought that France could expect at this time from the Pope. The matter of a settlement with Italy would have to wait for the future.[20] Drouyn de Lhuys was not deluded by the apparent reforms by the Pope. He told Cowley on two different occasions

> that they (the reforms) would be of little value except that something like the principle of election was, it seemed, to be introduced into the formation of the *Consulta,* and of the Provincial Councils and that this principle might be extended later.[21]

Nevertheless the French Foreign Minister did all he could to exhort Rome to continue the new policy. He reported the alarm which was being caused in Italy by the reforms and observed that the excitement came from the fear that reforms would mean the loss forever of Rome as Italy's capital.[22] It was the French policy to counter the Pope's demand for his old territory before giving reforms by saying that he would be able to keep what he still had only by instituting reform. Any appearance of alarm in Italy would serve as proof for the French contention.

If Thouvenel's dismissal caused considerable excitement in Rome and London, it can most assuredly be said that Drouyn de Lhuys' appointment caused nothing less than consternation

[19] D'Auvergne to Lhuys, Rome, 16, 20 Dec. 1862, *Aff. Etr., C.P., Rome,* 1021: pp. 424-425, 430-437.

[20] See above note no. 19, second document.

[21] Cowley to Russell, Paris, 18, 30 Dec. 1862, *F.O., France,* 1448: nos. 1396, 1446.

[22] Lhuys to D'Auvergne, Paris, 18 Jan. 1863, *Aff. Etr., C.P., Rome,* 1022: pp. 64-66.

in Turin. Even before the change came, when Nigra was reporting home the earlier rumors, Rattazzi was telling Benedetti that he "had never had the courage to wonder what [they] could do in such an unfortunate eventuality."[23] When Thouvenel announced the fatal news to Benedetti, his first thought was of the effect it might have on Italy.

I (Thouvenel) earnestly hope that they may not be too alarmed in Turin, that they may continue along the moderate path which they had just taken in regard to Rome, and if possible, that the great interests of Italy may bring together the important men into the King's councils.[24]

The last hope of Thouvenel seemed to hint at a change in the Italian ministry. The precarious situation certainly did not seem to be far from the fulfillment of such a hope. Hudson's description of the effects of the news on Rattazzi's cabinet is striking.

This morning at half past ten I found Rattazzi, Pepoli, and Depretis looking very much as if they had been assisting at their own funeral. Three more crestfallen gentlemen it has never been my fortune to meet. Thouvenel was out.

The only policy they could suggest was that Great Britain should use her good offices with Austria for a settlement of the Venetian question. In other words they were ready to guarantee anything provided they could avenge themselves on France. . . .

Durando whom I saw later in the morning was moved almost to tears at the situation.

In the midst of this political distress comes the minister of finance and presents his little bill of 15 millions (sterling) deficit. . . .

Whether the King will still persist in thrusting office on Rattazzi, I can not say. But I rather think he is revolving in his mind the expediency of sending for La Marmora if the Chamber of Deputies refuses a vote of confidence to Rattazzi.

In the country generally, believe me, the credit of the Government is zero. . . . The general opinion here is that Drouyn de Lhuys will split Italy into three divisions and will attempt to create an Italo-French kingdom in the Neopolitan Provinces.[25]

[23] Benedetti to Thouvenel, Turin, 15 Oct. 1862, Thouvenel, *Secret,* II, 437-438.

[24] Thouvenel to Benedetti, Paris, 16 Oct. 1862, *ibid.,* p. 440.

[25] Hudson to Russell, Turin, 17 Oct. 1862, *R.P.,* LXIX.

However ill-founded such apprehensions were, they go a long way to explain the sobering effect which the French ministerial change had on those of advanced tendencies. They felt Italy to be in the presence of a common and aggressive danger. The new situation closed their ranks a little more and it was possible later as will be seen, for a new ministry to gain support without promising much in regard to Rome.

It can be imagined then with what eagerness the Italians awaited Drouyn de Lhuys' first announcement of policy. Although his circular assured them that there would be no change of policy in regard to Rome and that France did not wish to remain there much longer,[26] still, his conversations with Nigra and his instructions sent to Massignac (chargé in charge of the legation after Benedetti's retirement) were not in the least reassuring. He appeared to dwell almost entirely on Durando's first circular and to pass over with very little attention the later dispatch. From the first the French Minister came to the quick conclusion that nothing could be done immediately with such a divergence of opinion.

> In the presence of that solemn statement and of the peremptory demand any discussion seems to me useless, and any attempt at settlement illusory. I observe with sincere regret that the Italian Government, by its absolute statements, to which I have just referred, has taken a stand where the permanent and traditional interests of France . . . forbid us to follow.

In conclusion, however, the new Foreign Minister said he would be glad to consider any wise proposal which the Italians might eventually offer in regard to Rome.[27]

The bitterness of the Italians after this severe curtain-lecture knew no bounds. Not only did they have to give up hope but in addition they had to sit and meekly see a foreigner dictate their fate. The fact that Rattazzi and Durando had brought it on themselves was almost forgotten for the moment.

[26] Lhuys to French diplomatic representatives, Paris, 18 Oct. 1862, *Livre Jaune,* (1862), p. 15.

[27] 26 Oct. 1862, *Aff. Etr., C.P., Italie,* 355: pp. 246-251. *Livre Jaune,* (1862), pp. 51-56. *Libro verde,* (18 Nov. 1862), pp. 6-11. See also Cowley to Russell, Paris, 21 Oct. 1862, *R.P.,* LVIII. Marco Minghetti, *Discorsi parlamentari* (8 vols., Rome, 1888-1890), IV, 14-15.

It was just at this juncture that Russell sent a note and a letter to Hudson in which he exhorted the Italians not to be led around by France nor to tremble at the Emperor's slightest frown. Italy should make no agreement with France. Let her know that there will be no fight while the French are in Rome but after their departure Italy should not promise to refuse to answer the call of the Romans.[28]

The reaction of the Italians to the above exhortation can easily be appreciated by reading the following extracts from Hudson's reply.

> No two men—not even a brace of godfathers at the font—ever promised and vowed with more unction than did Rattazzi and Durando this day to follow the precepts laid down in your dispatch and private letter of the 27th ult.
>
> They both, I must say, took the lead in the conversation, and as I had no previous communication with them I confess to having been agreeably surprised at the sound state of mind in which I found them as to the Roman question. . . . He (Rattazzi) therefore discussed the Roman question fully and patiently and arrived at the same conclusion as yourself. . . . He begged me to thank you warmly, very warmly, he said, for the kind thoughts, clear language, and sound opinions he had the pleasure of receiving from you and which he professed his readiness to follow.
>
> I suspect a great change has come over this cabinet. The fact is they have been following that will-o'-the-wisp, Prince Napoleon, who has landed them in the Serbonian bog of the Tuileries.
>
> They feel they must now extricate themselves as best they may, and they naturally accept with gratitude the helping hand you hold out.[29]

The diplomatic terms which the Italians used to interpret the above feelings to the French do not conceal their real thoughts. Massignac reported home that

> the Italian Government . . . seems to see some hope in the latitude which the Government of the Emperor leaves it to take the initiative of propositions moderate in form as well as content. For the moment all Mr. Rattazzi's attention is given to domestic questions and to the obvious preoccupations which the approaching assembling of Parliament causes him.[30]

[28] 27 Oct. 1862, *R.P.*, CX.
[29] Hudson to Russell, Turin, 3 Nov. 1862, *ibid.*, LXIX.
[30] 3 Nov. 1862, *Aff. Etr.*, *C.P.*, *Italie*, 355: pp. 257-258.

Before this, Rattazzi's greatest preoccupation on the eve of the assembling of Parliament had been the Roman question. Now he was obviously taking the French at their word and refusing to discuss the Roman question.

A week or so later a note from Prince Napoleon to Rattazzi seems to confirm the latter in the wisdom of aloofly ignoring France and the Roman question. The Prince said that because of the appointment of Drouyn de Lhuys the Italians should reduce their relations with France to the minimum. They should "play dead" (*faire la mort*), keep "absolutely calm and completely silent," and send one note of protest every month. "It would thus be the dignity and silence of a man justly considering himself hurt, but too weak himself to have justice done."[31]

But as Parliament met toward the end of November, it became more and more evident that Rattazzi would have to go. The King called Pasolini and asked him to form a coalition ministry without regard for parliamentary majorities and leaders. Hudson thought that the King wanted Pasolini to refuse so as to have an excuse to take Rattazzi and dissolve Parliament.[32] Pasolini did refuse and suggested the selection of a prime minister from the leaders of the majority opposition. The King did not dissolve Parliament and recall Rattazzi, but sent for Minghetti and Peruzzi. Having heard their exposition, he appointed Farini as Prime Minister, and he in turn selected Pasolini as Foreign Minister, Peruzzi for Interior, and Minghetti for Finance.[33]

In the interval while they were negotiating for the composition of the new cabinet, Hudson had an interview with Victor-Emmanuel (about 30 November). The former related that the King was greatly incensed. He squeezed the British Minister's

[31] 14 Nov. 1862, "Da Aspromonte a Mentana," *loc. cit.*, p. 31.

[32] Later the King told Sartiges: "I hope the new cabinet will not meet the same opposition in the Chamber as did the preceding one. If my predictions were mistaken, I would not hesitate to dissolve it." There were therefore thoughts of a dissolution in the mind of Victor-Emmanuel. *Aff. Etr., C.P., Italie,* 355: pp. 298-303.

[33] Hudson to Russell, Turin, 13 Dec. 1862, *R.P.*, LXIX. Giuseppe Pasolini, *Memorie del conte Pier Desiderio Pasolini* (2 vols., Turin, 1887), I, 321-323. *Aff. Etr., C.P., Italie,* 355: p. 342.

hand savagely while Hudson returned squeeze for squeeze. Several times the King repeated, "I didn't think you were so crafty." To which the Minister replied, "Nor did I think your ministers could be so clumsy." Hudson claimed that the King hoped through Rattazzi to bring about complications in the Balkans which would eventually gain Venice. Rattazzi's downfall, attributed to the English, stirred the King.[34]

On about the same day the new French Minister, Sartiges, presented his credentials and had a long conversation with the King. The King still asked that the Emperor do something on the Roman question. Sartiges pointed out that France had left the door open for any suggestion from Italy. The French Minister continued, however, by suggesting that Italy's difficulty was not at Rome but at home in financial matters. The French position was practically that as stated in the Emperor's note to Thouvenel of 28 May 1862. At the interview the King continued to insist that Rome lay at the root of Italy's principal troubles.[35]

On 3 December Rattazzi made his valedictory speech in the Chamber in which he justified his policy toward France and the Roman question. He denied that his attitude had been one of servility toward France and gave evidence of the "playing dead" policy.

> Gentlemen, as to the Roman question we should strengthen ourselves so as to be able to solve it. We must be prepared so as to be able to take Rome ourselves. Can we say to France, 'Give us Rome,' when Rome does not belong to France, when Rome belongs to Italy? (*Bravo!*).[36]

Pasolini, at the time of his appointment as Foreign Minister, was commended to France by both Sartiges and Arese. Sartiges wrote Drouyn de Lhuys that Pasolini was considered very highly by moderate men in Italy, and Arese wrote the Emperor in praise of the whole ministry and especially of Pasolini. The Emperor replied in a very gracious way to Arese. He tried to as-

[34] Hudson to Russell, Turin, 30 Nov. 1862, *R.P.*, LXIX.

[35] Sartiges to Lhuys, Turin, 30 Nov. 1862, *Aff. Etr., C.P., Italie,* 355: pp. 298-303.

[36] *L'Italie,* 3 Dec. 1862.

suage the disappointment which Arese had felt after his mission to the Emperor in 1861 by expressing great pleasure at a reopening of correspondence and inviting such "a beloved friend" as he to come and see him during the coming year. In the letter was also the comment that "the opinion you have of the Italian ministry gives me great pleasure." The Emperor reasserted his interest in Italy and his desire to leave Rome and hoped for strong, wise men in Italy with whom to deal.[37]

There was therefore a great deal of curiosity in both France and Italy as to the position the new Italian ministry would take toward the Roman question. It was of course difficult for Farini and Pasolini to make a positive statement until they should be in office long enough to become fully acquainted with the situation. Hence it was that Farini's first statement in the Italian Chamber was to cautiously suggest the impossibility of an immediate solution of the Roman question.

> We believe we are reflecting a sentiment of common dignity by abstaining from promises from which quick results will not follow, and we find in our own faith the right of declaring to Italy that she must expect the final accomplishment from the development of events and from occasions prepared and attained without illusions and without disappointment.[38]

The declaration seemed to indicate that the Cabinet would not push the Roman question immediately.

During the period in which the Italian Foreign Office was occupied in formulating its new policy it was greatly aided by a long note of information and advice from Nigra in Paris. This able and indispensable minister traced the history of the Roman question in French-Italian relations from the times of Cavour and Ricasoli right up to the downfall of Rattazzi. He pointed out the fact that the French divided the problem and would treat only on evacuation and not on Italian annexation. He showed the inadvisability of the Durando circular and pointed

[37] Sartiges to Lhuys, Turin, 10 Dec. 1862, *Aff. Etr., C.P., Italie,* 355: pp. 334-339. *Livre Jaune,* (1862), p. 56. Arese to Napoleon III, 11 Dec. 1862; Napoleon III to Arese, Paris, 2 Jan. 1863, Bonfadini, *Arese,* pp. 302-303, 304. Grabinski, *Arese,* pp. 199-200.

[38] *Atti ufficiali,* Chamber, 11 Dec. 1862, pp. 3633-3634.

out its relation to the Thouvenel dismissal. Finally he stated fearlessly his opinion on the future plan of action.

It would therefore appear advisable not to undertake new negotiations for the time being. But in any case it would not only be honest but also politically useful to provoke no illusions, and to excite no vain hopes. The country and Parliament should know that France is in no way disposed at the present time to leave Rome, and that the unity of Italy is running a grave danger if preoccupations about foreign affairs hindered the internal reorganization of the state.[39]

This attitude was very close to the idea of "playing dead" suggested by Prince Napoleon. It had been adopted by Rattazzi toward the last and now seemed to have been taken up and continued by the new ministry. Minghetti, who eventually succeeded Farini as head of this ministry, said in his memoirs:

When therefore we entered the government on 8 December 1862, the situation was so unfortunate that a worse could not be imagined. To begin negotiations again at such a time, to make a new attempt would have been to invite disdainful repulses, or at least unpleasant replies. For that reason we thought to let a little time pass, and to await a more favorable opportunity to take up the discussion again.[40]

In this recorded recollection we see reflected the feeling of resentment which prevailed in Italian councils after the fall of Thouvenel. This feeling explains the attitude subsequently held by Italy in its relations with France.

The policy of remaining silent on the Roman question was impressed upon the French Minister at Turin on every convenient occasion by Pasolini, Farini, Minghetti, and even by Victor-Emmanuel. Pasolini himself told Sartiges that

he was abstaining from discussing questions of the future and that at present he and his colleagues restricted themselves to the circle determined by their program, silence on the Roman question.[41]

Also in a circular dispatch Pasolini emphasized that the new Italian Government would turn its attention to its domestic

[39] Pasolini, *Memorie,* I, 325-328. Minghetti, *Convenzione,* p. 13.
[40] Minghetti, *Convenzione,* p. 13.
[41] Sartiges to Lhuys, Turin, 19 Dec. 1862, *Aff. Etr., C.P., Italie,* 355: pp. 392-393. Same to same, *ibid.,* pp. 366-367; 356: pp. 4-7.

problems with a view to gaining greater respect for the country among the other Powers without at the same time renouncing any of its rights and claims. These Drouyn de Lhuys was forced to admit to Nigra were "fine thoughts in fine language."[42]

Strangely enough this attitude of "playing dead" was taken up by Parliament and the Italian press with enthusiasm. La Marmora complimented Pasolini on organizing the country instead of trying to hurry the Roman question. Sartiges reported that when Musolino interpellated the Government on the Roman question, the Chamber "declared that it did not intend to determine a day for the reconsideration of the Roman question." Also this same French Minister remarked that the papers were so favorable to this silence on the Roman question that he could but feel that Italy was really on the contrary intending to open a discussion on the question in the near future.[43]

This policy of "playing dead" of course had much of the elements of the old diplomatic trick of ignoring some one when you find that you are losing his attentions. The reaction on the second party is often one of a renewal of interest for the one who had felt himself slighted. Italy did this again to France by joining the Triple Alliance in 1882. Texas used that method with the reluctant United States in regard to annexation. To a certain extent the reaction in France on this occasion was what might have been calculated by the Italians. The French began to emphasize the fact that they had not left the door closed and that they were ready to listen to any sensible proposals from Italy.[44] The Italian reply invariably was that they did not have the slightest idea of burying the Roman question, but out of their profound regard for the Emperor they thought they would desist from annoying him with continual demands on that subject.

[42] Pasolini to Italian representatives, Turin, 20 Dec. 1862, *Aff. Etr., C.P., Italie,* 355: p. 396. Nigra to Pasolini, Paris, 22 Dec. 1862, Pasolini, *Memorie,* I, 325.

[43] La Marmora to Pasolini, Naples, 13 Dec. 1862, Pasolini, *Memorie,* I, 323. Sartiges to Lhuys, Turin, 19, 19 Dec. 1862, *Aff. Etr., C.P., Italie,* 355: pp. 384, 392-393.

[44] Sartiges to Lhuys, Turin, 10, 13 Dec. 1862, *Aff. Etr., C.P., Italie,* 355: pp. 347-352, 366-367.

When the "playing dead" attitude was more definitely sounded in the *Opinione*, a paper thought to be in close touch with the Ministry, Sartiges went so far as to remonstrate with Pasolini. The *Opinione* had said that "between France who denies Rome to the Italians and Italy who irrevocably insists on it, there is no possible agreement."[45] Sartiges reported:

> I thought I ought to consult incidentally Mr. Pasolini on the meaning which might be attributed to it. The Foreign Minister began by declaring that there was no paper in the country which had the right of speaking in the name of the Government or to claim to be inspired by it. He made no difficulty of recognizing the declaration once made that the Roman question should be allowed to sleep for the present, that question had been discussed altogether too much in both the Chamber and the press; but at the same time he admitted that he and his colleagues shared the opinion of the country that Rome was the natural capital of Italy. He added that that was the inheritance from Mr. Cavour which every Italian ministry had to accept; that General Durando had reaffirmed it; that when he proposed to the Government of the Emperor to negotiate, it was on the basis of Rome to the Italians, and that the only difference between the program of the present cabinet and the former one was the refusal to make new overtures to the Imperial Government who felt that it could not agree to negotiate on that same basis. 'But,' I said to Mr. Pasolini, 'that's a regular *non-possumus* which you are pronouncing, while we are inviting you to come to an understanding with the Court of Rome on the basis of conciliation, don't you think it hazardous to tie your hands in advance without knowing whether events will not bring in their wake combinations for which it will be profitable to open new negotiations?'
>
> Mr. Pasolini objected to the much too absolute interpretation which I attached to his words, and he explained that the present ministers were continuing to follow with the greatest interest the march of events and that the day when they thought it possible to take up this negotiation with the Imperial Government without displeasing it, they would hasten to do it.

Pasolini wished that France might allow the Roman people to vote on their destiny. Sartiges pointed out the dangerous precedent for European dynasties, the Savoyard included, if the people could always put to a vote their preference in regard to their traditional sovereign as he was suggesting in regard to the Pope and the Romans. Pasolini closed the discussion by re-

[45] *L'Opinione*, 21 Dec. 1862.

affirming his gratitude for what the Emperor had done and his hope for his coöperation in the future.[46]

Drouyn de Lhuys, not wishing to appear to be soliciting Italy and also not wishing to have it appear at home that he was the cause of this change in Italy, replied, and published the reply, that Sartiges had better not dwell any longer on the press statements and that he (Drouyn de Lhuys) was glad to note a more moderate attitude on the part of the Italians.[47]

In view of the publication of Sartiges' note Pasolini published another which he purposely sent to Nigra and in which he denied the absolute *non-possumus* inferred in the French document. To attempt to throw the blame back on the French, he added in closing that "since no proposition was formulated in the interview in question, I did not have to pronounce my position on the consequences which could result from [the French intervention in Rome]."[48]

When eyes were being turned toward public opinion, it is to be expected that the Emperor consulted the *procureurs*' reports in January 1863 to see what effect his change at the Quai d'Orsay had had on the French public mind. As a matter of fact the reaction in France seemed quite salutary. There was little or no opposition to Drouyn de Lhuys' appointment and in liberal quarters there appeared either a lack of interest or silence. At Besançon, native country of Lallemand, the thinking people generally applauded the appointment of Drouyn de Lhuys. In Bourges the new attitude of the French Government "obtained general assent." From Normandy came word that "the political situation already satisfactory was still more improved by Drouyn de Lhuys' nomination." Many people in Montpellier who had been wavering in their support of the Em-

[46] Sartiges to Lhuys, Turin, 25 Dec. 1862, *Aff. Etr., C.P., Italie,* 355: pp. 419-423. This document was published by the French for public and parliamentary consumption in a very garbled form early in 1863. The purpose was to show that the Emperor was justified in selecting Drouyn de Lhuys because of the *non-possumus* of Italy. See *Livre Jaune,* (1862), pp. 57-58.

[47] Lhuys to Sartiges, Paris, 26 Dec. 1862, *Aff. Etr., C.P., Italie,* 355: pp. 427-428. *Livre Jaune,* (1862), pp. 58-59.

[48] 22 Jan. 1862, *Libro verde,* (29 May 1863), pp. 2-3. *Aff. Etr., C.P., Italie,* 356: pp. 68-69.

pire had quickly shown new loyalty after the ministerial change. Likewise in Paris itself many Conservatives who had begun to desert the Imperial Party were now returning to its support. At Agens, Aix, Bordeaux, Lyons, and in Brittany there seemed to be an entire silence and apathy with neither strong disappointment with the departure of Thouvenel nor keen joy at the arrival of Drouyn de Lhuys. The Emperor was so interested in the reports that he had a summary made which showed strongly the conclusions quite in favor of the new orientation. The Italians would have found little encouragement among the French in January 1863.[49]

In the French Senate this year one of the most important incidents was Thouvenel's speech justifying his policy. Making clear from the outset that he had not, and did not, feel himself responsible to the Senate—ministerial responsibility should always be to the Emperor—still he wished to use his right in the Senate to express his views. He quoted the Senate's reply to the Emperor's speech of the previous year and declared that in his policy he had adhered strictly to that position. In closing he charged that the new ministry in their three months of office had not been able to do more than he. He feared that the new element in control would tend to lead the Emperor into a blind servitude to the irreconcilable Holy See.[50]

Nevertheless, in spite of published documents and French parliamentary debates the Italian Government adhered to its sullen silence on Rome almost until the eve of the final negotiations of the Convention in 1864. In February Sartiges reported:

> The Italian Government up to now has scrupulously kept its word by letting the Roman question sleep, and for the moment it does sleep, officially at least, in the Chambers and on the surface of the country.[51]

[49] *Rapports des procureurs,* extracts, 368; Besançon, 14 Jan. 1863, 373: v. 7; Bourges, 9 Jan. 1863, 374: v. 3; Caen, 10 Jan. 1863, 375: v. 4; Montpellier, 9 Jan. 1863, 380: v. 4; Paris, 3 Feb. 1863, 384: v. 9; Agens, 7 Jan. 1863, 370: v. 4; Aix, 9 Jan. 1863, 370: v. 5; Bordeaux, 13 Jan. 1863, 374: v. 3; Lyons, 29 Dec. 1862, 379: v. 5; Rennes, 12 Jan. 1863, 386: v. 4.

[50] *Moniteur universel,* (Senate), 30 Jan. 1863.

[51] 9 Feb. 1863, *Aff. Etr., C.P., Italie,* 356: pp. 102-103.

While England and Italy were pouting in silence over the Roman question and the Pope was apparently granting a semblance of reform, the Poles were carrying on a struggle against Russia. France's sympathy had been always with the Poles. However, just at this time Emperor Napoleon III and the Tsar were on particularly friendly terms. Thus French policy found great embarrassment in forming and following a direct and firm policy in regard to the Poles.

Austria, too, was in a peculiar position. She was Russia's rival in the Balkans and the Near East, but on the other hand any Polish uprising might bring about the loss of Austria's Polish possessions as well. Hence Austria might be inclined to be sympathetic to Russia in regard to Poland, at least, and would hesitate to increase Russia's embarrassments.

In such a situation it gave the Emperor another opportunity to develop his characteristically extravagant dreams of a remodelling of the map of Europe. One of the first indications of a general plan was made by the Empress to the Austrian Ambassador, Metternich. According to the Empress the increased number of dissatisfied areas in Europe was really making more and more necessary a European congress to settle matters definitively and peacefully. She then proceeded to confide to Metternich the definitive plan which she claimed to be the one which both she and the Emperor approved. It contained two paragraphs in particular which involved Austria and Italy:

> Austria was to cede Venetia to Piedmont, a part of Galicia (Lemberg and Cracovie) to Poland, and was to take a long line of new frontiers through Serbia along the Adriatic, Silesia, and all she wanted south of the Main.
>
> Piedmont was to have Lombardy, Venetia, Tuscany, Parma, Piacenza, Bologna, and Ferrarra, but was to restore the Two Sicilies to the King of Naples, who was to enlarge the territory of the Pope (*arrondir le Pape*).[52]

[52] Metternich to Rechberg, Paris, 22 Feb. 1863, (from *Haus, Hof, und Staatsarchiv,* Vienna), quoted from Herman Oncken, *Die Rheinpolitik Kaiser Napoleons III. von 1863 bis zu 1870 und der Ursprung des Krieges von 1870-1871* (3 vols., Stuttgart, 1926), I, 4-5.

Only four days after the Empress' conversation with Metternich Emperor Napoleon approached him with the proposal of an alliance between France and Austria to the same end. Austria would have to make some sacrifices but would get in return great compensations.

> Is it not more worth while not to be hypocritical and tell you what's in the back of my mind? It is enormously to my advantage if I can arrange the Polish and Italian questions. I have tried to come to agreements with Russia and England, and I have not succeeded. I say it frankly, I will join whatever Power will assist me and I do not conceal the fact that it is with Austria that I would prefer to make an agreement because our interests are identical.

Metternich, who reported home this conversation, added that Lord Cowley had heard that England would discourage this project of the Emperor but would try to decline the proposals in an inoffensive way.[53]

About a week later the Emperor saw Metternich again. This time his offer to Austria was quite definite.

> In case events in Poland force you to evacuate Galicia, I offer you exclusive preponderance in the East and material compensations to be designated by yourself. . . . If the definitive settlement of the Italian question (King of Naples, Pope, and Piedmont)[54] required the surrender of Venetia, I would support your attempts at preponderance in Germany. . . .

Metternich objected that this arrangement was much too favorable to France. It provided for specific sacrifices by Austria while offering her only vague concessions in the form of support for uncertain projects. Furthermore, it was not known that Austria would be compelled to lose Galicia or Venetia.[55]

Finally on 9 March Metternich and the Emperor agreed on a tentative formula of understanding which the former sent home for consideration with little faith in its eventual acceptance. It was worded in part as follows:

[53] 26 Feb. 1863, *ibid.*, I, 7-8.

[54] These were Metternich's parentheses and would seem to indicate that the Emperor spoke to him in the same manner in regard to the Italian arrangement as had the Empress previously.

[55] Same to same, Paris, 5 March 1863, *ibid.*, I, 11-12.

The Governments of France and Austria see from now on the necessity of entering into the most confidential communications in regard to the combination of their efforts in the double aim which they have proposed; reserving to themselves, should the occasion arise, to give their common action the guaranty of an offensive and defensive alliance whose stipulations would be drawn up by agreement.[56]

Metternich later in March went to Vienna with the proposals. Rechberg, the Austrian Foreign Minister, in his conversation with Gramont, the French Ambassador, practically but gently discouraged the project. He said he did not like to use the word "never"[57] but so many things, changes, and compensations were necessary before that cession (Venetia) could become possible that he could hardly find a word other than "never" to express his opinion.[58]

It is quite unlikely that Italy knew of the Emperor's negotiations with Austria early in March. But it was Italy's policy to attempt to gain something out of every European complication and the Polish question could not but have excited the Italian Ministry by the potential combinations which might be made through it for the obtaining of Venetia. To stress Venice would also keep them more consistent with their policy of silence on Rome.

The Emperor's kind letter inviting Arese to come to see him and the Emperor's apparent good opinion of the new Italian ministry may have encouraged Arese to make plans early in March 1863 to go to Paris to revisit his friends. There is some indication, however, that his visit was inspired by the Italian Foreign Office. He was in Turin during the last of February and the beginning of March and the burden of his thoughts at that time was that Italy should take advantage of the Polish question for advancing her cause in Venice and Rome. He spoke to the French Minister several times in this regard.[59] It is there-

[56] Same to same, Paris, 9 March 1863, *ibid.*, I, 15.

[57] Metternich in commenting on the irreconcilable position of the Pope had remarked: "Il ne faut jamais dire jamais."

[58] Gramont to Lhuys, Vienna, 26 March 1863, *Aff. Etr., C.P., Autriche,* 483: pp. 265-268.

[59] Sartiges to Lhuys, Turin, 14 March 1863, *Aff. Etr., C.P., Italie,* 356: pp. 222-223.

fore quite likely that he also had conversations with his friend, Pasolini, about the same matter. Later he went to Genoa and wrote Pasolini that he was going to Paris and would be glad to be used as the channel of any communications which he might wish to make to the Emperor.

Whether this Genoa letter was written purposely to give the mission the appearance of a private visit can not be made certain. At least Pasolini took advantage of Arese's offer to make some far-reaching proposals to Napoleon III. After thanking Arese for his "obliging offer," he outlined in a letter the nature of the communication which he wished to be made to the Emperor. Pasolini wished Arese to impress on Napoleon the fact that the present ministry was not anti-French. Its silence on the Roman question was for the purpose of keeping Italian attention on the program of internal organization and strengthening of the state. Also it was thought that silence on the Roman question for a time was conformable, and not contrary, to the wishes of the Emperor himself. Arese was to show that the present program was entirely in line with Cavour's plans. The Farini ministry considered itself the real heir of Cavour's policy. Italy was quite willing to be patient and not hastily precipitate the completion of its unity. However, Pasolini felt that the Polish and Greek questions together with favorable attitudes in Prussia, England, and Austria might make it a convenient time to take some common action in some direction. Pasolini would suggest no definite plans since the Emperor better than anyone else knew what would be the best conduct to follow. He only wished to pledge Italy's full coöperation with France in whatever plans might be evolved. As a last remark he voiced a warning of the danger to France and Italy should Italy be denied participation in the events and changes which might take place. It would turn the Italians toward the extremists in their search for the fulfillment of their hopes.[60]

In addition to this general letter Pasolini armed Arese with a memorandum of details which he might use if the Emperor

[60] Pasolini to Arese, Turin, 9 March 1863, Bonfadini, *Arese,* pp. 309-311. Grabinski, *Arese,* pp. 206-207. Pasolini, *Memorie,* I, 345-347.

should launch into a plan of action. These more definite points might be summed up briefly as follows: 1) the need to solve the Roman and Venetian questions with the least possible disturbance; 2) the financial weakness of Turkey and Austria might make it possible for Italy to purchase parts of Bosnia and Herzegovina for Austria in return for Venetia; 3) Italian willingness to suppress all anti-Austrian agitation; 4) a preliminary agreement to deal with the Roman question and the election of a successor should be made between France and Italy before the death of Pius IX; 5) in that event French troops keep order, allow peaceful demonstrations, and frighten the new Pope and the Conclave out of their unrelenting attitude; 6) danger of Roman and Garibaldian excesses if some arrangement is not made to head them off; 7) the Emperor could defend this policy on the ground of his traditional loyalty to the Church and to the principle of universal suffrage.[61]

Arese arrived in Paris on 13 March, was given a very warm welcome, and was pressed to make his abode in the Tuileries. The next morning, when the news of his arrival reached Turin, the announcement in the newspapers was the first news which Sartiges had of the mission. The French Minister was considerably chagrined that he had been kept in the dark. He sent Mr. de Bonnières to Pasolini to remonstrate and ask an explanation. Pasolini said that Arese was just going to Paris on private business and had asked whether Pasolini might have any errands for him to perform while there. Pasolini had merely replied:

> Tell them over there that we are a well-behaved (*honnêtes*) people, that we have proved that, and we especially want them to know it in Paris. Come back as soon as you can and tell us what they may have said about us.
>
> In spite of this reply (Sartiges continued) I believe that Count Arese has been sent to the Emperor on a mission dealing with the Polish and Roman questions. . . . It is not to the French Government but to the Emperor that he is sent.[62]

[61]Memorandum of Pasolini to Arese, Turin, 9 Mar. 1863, Bonfadini, *Arese,* Appen. A, pp. 432-435.

[62] Sartiges to Lhuys, Turin, 14 March 1863, *Aff. Etr., C.P., Italie,* 356: pp. 222-223.

Considering that the French Minister, Drouyn de Lhuys' more direct representative, was not informed in advance, that he was given a very brief and casual explanation in contrast to the long and serious instructions sent to Arese, and finally that the Italians disliked Drouyn de Lhuys, all these facts would seem to indicate a tendency to continue the "playing dead" in regard to him while reopening negotiations with France through the Emperor.

At the very time when Arese was arriving in Paris, Nigra and Pasolini learned of the French alliance proposal to Austria and of Metternich's return with it to Vienna. These facts of course threw the Italians into a flurry of excitement. Pasolini telegraphed Arese that "we have the greatest interest to know what there is to it so that we can determine a suitable rôle for ourselves." Nigra, in transmitting the telegram, sent a note to Arese to make arrangements for a confidential conversation on the same matter.[63]

Two days later Arese was able to draw from the Emperor the fact that "Metternich took away with him proposals about Poland which were vague and uncertain depending on circumstances and developments (*come circonstanze e notizie*)." Pasolini, having received this meagre news by telegraph, replied: "However vague and uncertain the proposals may be, we must know them in order to be able to adjust ourselves. Am writing."[64] In his letter of the same date Pasolini showed he was not satisfied with the few words of explanation by the Emperor. He felt that the Emperor had definite plans and that these should be known to Italy to aid her to conform to the French position. He wanted Arese to find these out if possible and incidentally to sound out Napoleon on the possibilities in the questions of Hungary, Serbia, and the Danubian Provinces.[65]

[63] Pasolini to Arese, Turin, 14 March 1863; Nigra to Arese, Paris, 14 March 1863; Bonfadini, *Arese,* pp. 312-313.

[64] Arese to Pasolini, Paris, 16 March 1863; Pasolini to Arese, Turin, 16 March 1863, *ibid.,* pp. 313, 315.

[65] Pasolini to Arese, Turin, 16 March 1863, *ibid.,* pp. 315-316. Pasolini, *Memorie,* I, 347-348.

Arese's dispatch gives us a clearer idea of just what the Emperor was willing to have Italy know. Arese reported:

> From the long conversations which I have had with the Emperor I think I can conclude that if he can depend on England, or at least on Austria, it would not be long before the din of battle (*branle-bas du combat*) would be heard, and as to this they would count on us. This last phrase was said and repeated explicitly, for there is the perspective of Venice for us. We spoke a great deal about the Roman question, and I am convinced that on that the Emperor has no definite idea. He accepted your project, although he classed it as absurd, and promised to examine it and give me an answer. I know, however, that he has written to Rome recently to get definite news on the health of the Pope, and that he has asked for information on the cardinal who should be supported and those who should be excluded.[66]

He wanted a cardinal to be the next Pope who was as Italian and liberal as could be expected of a cardinal. The Emperor wished to know whom the Italians would advise. Arese had also seen Drouyn de Lhuys who assured the Italian again of France's intention and desire to have Italian coöperation in any future step. Arese in closing observed that he thought that France was following a day by day policy similar to that of Italy.[67]

Naturally nothing which the Emperor said to Arese would lead him to suspect the division of Italy which he and the Empress had suggested to Metternich. On the other hand he said nothing which would be entirely contrary to his conversations with the Austrian Ambassador. In his final paragraph of his last written communication to Arese on this occasion he came the nearest to recognizing the unity of Italy as it was in 1863.

> If the Italian Government consolidates its authority in the annexed provinces, if it reëstablishes its credit, if it boldly brings to an end all demagogic extravagances, it will obtain a moral strength most efficacious in assuring its destinies. If, on the contrary, it wants to keep its neighbors in a constant state of alarm, irritating and disastrous in results, it runs the risk of eventually seeing the great advantages already obtained compromised.

[66] As a matter of fact the request for further information on the Cardinals had been sent out only two days before Arese's account (14 March 1863). Lhuys to D'Auvergne, Paris, *Aff. Etr., C.P., Rome,* 1022: pp. 356-357.

[67] 16 March 1863, Bonfadini, *Arese,* p. 313-314. Grabinski, *Arese,* pp. 210-212. Pasolini, *Memorie,* I, 348-349.

There was nothing in this statement, however, contrary to his plan as explained to Austria. The Emperor expressed a desire to withdraw from Rome after the Pope had received serious assurances for the *status quo*, and here again he indicated his willingness to see happen what may in Rome provided that France was sufficiently separated from events. The Emperor again wanted to know Italy's candidate for the next Pope. In addition he complained of Italy's constant demands for Rome as capital. He said that only retarded a solution.[68]

Pasolini instructed Arese to suggest Cardinal Boffondi as Italy's choice of a successor, and replied to Napoleon's chiding of Italy for her continued demands for Rome by declaring that "I do not believe anyone could have been less blustering and more reserved than I have been on the Roman question." In the light of his "playing dead" policy nothing was more true. The Italian Foreign Minister, having just received a request from England to join with other Powers in a remonstrance against Russia for Poland, wanted to know France's attitude so that Italy could back France by assuming the same.[69]

The Emperor assured Arese that his remarks about Italy's impatience referred more particularly to the former ministry—with the present ministry he was much more satisfied. In regard to the English proposal Drouyn de Lhuys suggested that Italy could better decline coöperation on different grounds than France by denying that Italy had had any participation in the decisions of the Congress of Vienna of 1815.[70]

Arese's mission ended on the very day when a very important change took place in the Italian Ministry. He had kept up or perhaps renewed Italy's intimate contact with France,

[68] Arese to Pasolini, Paris, 18 March 1863, Grabinski, *Arese,* pp. 214-215. Bonfadini, *Arese,* pp. 317-318. D'Ambès, *Memoirs,* II, 274-275. D'Ambès tells us that both he and Conneau were present at some of the conferences between Arese and the Emperor. He remarked that Drouyn de Lhuys was there also, "the Lord only knows why." Pasolini, *Memorie,* I, 252-253.

[69] 20 March 1863, Pasolini, *Memorie,* I, 251-252. Bonfadini, *Arese,* p. 318.

[70] Lhuys to Sartiges, Paris, 26 March 1863, *Aff. Etr., C.P., Italie,* 356: pp. 287-289. Arese to Pasolini, Paris, 24 March 1863, Pasolini, *Memorie,* I, 352.

but he had not gone very far in furthering the purposes of his mission as indicated in his original instructions. Mr. Grabinski remarked that "Arese stayed in Paris until 24 March. The Emperor told him nothing more which could encourage him to sustain the hopes of the Turin Cabinet."[71] These observations characterize very well the failure of the second Arese mission.

Farini, who had been one of the outstanding leaders in the Italian unification movement and co-delegate with Cialdini at Chambéry, had been chosen to head the conservative cabinet after Rattazzi's resignation. About 1 March 1863, however, it became apparent that he was becoming more and more incapacitated by softening of the brain. Since Pasolini had taken the Foreign Office under protest, he even began to think of taking this occasion for resigning so as to enable the King to retire Farini quietly.[72]

Although nothing was done immediately, the situation was brought to a crisis by Prince Napoleon's speech in the French Senate on 19 March. On that occasion the Prince had declared himself violently against Russia and showed unrestrained sympathy for Poland. Toward the close he declared that the situation "is not war, but neither is it peace."[73] This speech had a very bad effect on Farini, causing him to lose his mind completely. On reading the news reports from Paris, he hastened to the King and called on him to lead the army against Russia. The King, embarrassed and attempting to calm his minister, asked how Italy should get to Russia without crossing Austria and Prussia. When Farini mentioned something about the recent improvements in methods of travel, Victor-Emmanuel became convinced of the need of another prime minister. Minghetti, Pasolini, and Peruzzi were called, and it was decided to send Farini to a sanatorium.[74]

In the negotiating for the reorganization of the ministry

[71] Grabinski, *Arese,* p. 217.

[72] Hudson to Russell, Turin, 1 March 1863, *R.P.,* LXX.

[73] Emile Ollivier, *L'Empire libéral* (18 vols., Paris, 1895-1902), VI, 167-170.

[74] Hudson to Russell, Turin, 28 March 1863, *R.P.,* LXX, Pasolini, *Memorie,* I, 355-358.

Pasolini insisted on his own retirement. It was therefore decided that Minghetti should take the Presidency of the Council and, after some hesitation, it was also decided to appoint Visconti-Venosta, the young General Secretary of the Ministry of Foreign Affairs,[75] as Pasolini's successor. There was a great deal of murmuring at first over the advisability of this choice, but after Visconti-Venosta had defended the ministerial foreign policy on Poland in the Chamber on 26 and 27 March in firm and statesmanlike accents, his critics became more reassured. Then it was that this young statesman began that excellent career which extended over a period of almost fifty years.[76]

With the change in ministry the Parliament and people in Italy began to show a little impatience that nothing was being done about Venice and Rome. The Minghetti government had time and again said that they would give attention to internal affairs while waiting for European complications which might give Italy a chance to do something about Venetia or Rome. Europe had now become hopelessly complicated in the Polish question, and it was asked how Italy would take advantage of it for her own benefit.

In February 1863 Prussia and Russia had made a reciprocal military alliance to aid each other against the Polish uprising. Although Austria did not join that alliance, she took a benevolent attitude and felt less need of outside support against complications with her own Polish subjects. This alliance had weakened the English and French who were sympathetic with the Poles but who also respectively wanted to keep on good terms with Austria and Russia. It had also led France, England, and finally Austria to join in sending notes of protest to Russia asking her to grant the Poles the Constitution stipulated in the Treaty of 1815. Gortchakoff, realizing that he had Prussia's support and that England and Austria had coöperated with France only because they did not wish to give France the

[75] Visconti-Venosta at this time was only 34 years old.

[76] Minghetti to Contessa Pepoli, Turin, 25, 27, 28 March 1863, R. de Cesare, "Visconti-Venosta," *Nuova Antologia,* (Jan. 1915), CLXXV, p. 11. Sartiges to Lhuys, Turin, 24 March 1863, *Aff. Etr., C.P., Italie,* 356: p. 252.

credit for being the sole champion of the Poles, did not hesitate to refuse the advice of the petitioning Powers.

The Italian Government saw an opportunity now of continuing to neglect the Roman question but at the same time of becoming active for Venice by trying to create a European alliance against Russia. This alliance would be built up primarily around an Anglo-French union. To this end Minghetti and Visconti-Venosta on 16 July 1863 sent Pasolini on a mission to London and Paris. He was to try to bring England and France together and have them draw Austria and Sweden into an alliance of five including Italy. Austria, Sweden, and France would try to obtain Prussian neutrality, and then a war would be begun with Russia. In case of victory the Duchy of Warsaw would be made independent, Italy would get Venetia, Austria would get Moldavia and Wallachia, Sweden could have the Aaland Islands.[77] Stopping in Paris only long enough to confer with Nigra, Pasolini went immediately to London. After spending over a month in England (20 July to 27 August), he was only able to reveal a benevolent attitude by the English toward Italy. They seemed to require some evidence from the Emperor of a desire for an English alliance before they would take it up seriously.

On 17 August Minghetti suggested that Pasolini go to Paris and see whether he could get the initiative for such an alliance from the Emperor. Pasolini arrived in Paris on 27 August. He had a long conference with the Emperor on 6 September at which time Napoleon began to talk about the Roman question. He admired the advance which had been made toward order and strength, and remarked that he would be glad to take up the Roman question again as soon as he was sure that Italy could give acceptable guaranties.

It was quite evident that the Emperor was trying to draw Italy out of her silence. But Pasolini immediately changed the subject to European combinations. The Emperor declined to consider the proposal of an English alliance during the present

[77] *Carteggio tra Marco Minghetti e Giuseppe Pasolini.* Edited by Guido Pasolini. (3 vols., Turin, 1928-1929), III, 288-289, note.

period of uncertainty. The Frankfort Congress was in session, Austrian action against Denmark seemed imminent, and the combinations which that might call for demanded that France keep her hands free. Thus the (first) Pasolini mission to London and Paris ended in failure, and Pasolini himself returned to Italy on 21 September.[78]

Thus two missions to Paris, those of Arese and Pasolini, had failed to gain any step toward Venice. But on 4 November 1863 Napoleon invited all European Powers to a congress to revise the arrangements of 1815 in such a way as to conform with the present situation and to solve peacefully the present pressing questions, that is: Poland, Denmark, Danubian Provinces, Rome, and Venetia. Although both the Pope and Italy accepted the congress, England declined the invitation because she thought that neither Austria, Italy, nor the Pope would give up their respective claims. The congress would therefore engender more bitterness than it would promote peace. France was not only disappointed by the British refusal which would mean the end of the congress plan, but also she was irritated by the abruptness of the English reply. The fact that the reply to the Emperor came from Russell instead of from the Queen only increased the Emperor's resentment toward England. Austria, who had by that time cast its lot with Prussia in the Danish question, also declined the congress proposal because she feared the loss of Venetia.[79]

Strangely enough it was the Emperor himself who suggested that Pasolini try the same mission again to see whether Palmerston would accept an alliance with France on the Polish question now that he had refused the Congress. Pasolini immediately returned to France and had a long conversation with Napoleon at Compiègne on 8 December. Here the Emperor expressed the desire that the same proposals be made to England again as had

[78] For details of this mission see *Carteggio Pasolini-Minghetti,* III, 288-357. Pasolini, *Memorie,* I, 370-377.

[79] For the congress proposals see Ollivier, *Empire libéral,* VI, 355-367; *F.O., France,* 1483: no. 1226; 1499: no. 1160; *Aff. Etr., C.P., Angleterre,* 727: pp. 89-99; *ibid., Rome,* 1025: pp. 129-132; *ibid., Italie,* 358: p. 372; *Aff. Etr., M.D., Italie,* 37: p. 176.

been made in August but this time Pasolini could indicate the Emperor's hearty approval. However, the Emperor wanted it to appear that he had approved the combination before England refused the congress.

With this last difficult simulation added to his burden Pasolini hurried to London and saw both Palmerston and Russell. After a long conversation on European affairs in general, Pasolini recorded:

> I asked [Palmerston] frankly if there was nothing we could do to reunite England and France in a common policy, and he told me that he saw nothing at the present time. When I saw Russell I began with this same question, and he told me likewise that he saw nothing that Italy could do in that direction (*che per ora non vede nulla*).

Although Pasolini stayed in London until January 1864, he accomplished nothing toward the fulfillment of his original aim.

He returned to France and had a long conversation with the Emperor. Here he told of England's refusal of an alliance with France for the present, and England's opposition to a war against Russia while Europe was in its present precarious situation. At this conference Pasolini found a chance to say that Italy must do everything she could to complete her unity. The Emperor agreed and wanted Pasolini to tell the King that he was going to think it over carefully, but he did not want war at present. Italy must remain quiet and look for a good opportunity to act. Thus ended the second Pasolini mission, as had the first, with nothing tangible accomplished.[80]

With the entrance of Drouyn de Lhuys in the French Foreign Office, Italy had tried to keep a very evident silence on the Roman question. To offset the activity in that direction she tried to strengthen her internal force and had succeeded appreciably. But with the arrival of complications in Poland, Italy took up the counter-irritant of Venetia so as to be able to still

[80] Material on Pasolini's second mission to France may be found in the following references: *Carteggio Pasolini-Minghetti,* III, 379-427. Pasolini, *Memorie,* I, 390-393, 396-397, 406-407, 410-412. Elliot to Russell, Turin, 12 Dec. 1863; Russell to Elliot, Pembroke Lodge, 27 Dec. 1863; *R.P.,* LXX, CX, *Aff. Etr., C.P., Angleterre,* 727: pp. 212-214, 221-223; *ibid., C.P., Italie,* 358: p. 515.

keep quiet on Rome. When this brought no results after one Arese mission and two by Pasolini, Italy briefly played with the Danish counter-irritant with the same results.[81]

There can be no doubt that Italy's silence on the Roman question and her attention to her internal reorganization had a very favorable effect on the Emperor in inclining him to undertake discussions again on Rome. While the direct results of the complications from the Polish and Danish questions seem to have brought no appreciable gains to the cause of Italy in Venice, it is quite likely that indirectly, as will soon be seen, these two European questions contributed much toward hastening a French-Italian agreement on Rome.

[81] Some references to Italy and the Danish question are as follows: *Ricasoli lettere,* VII, 186; *F.O., France,* 1525: no. 246.

PART III

THE CONVENTION OF 15 SEPTEMBER 1864

CHAPTER VII

THE NEGOTIATION OF THE CONVENTION

NAPOLEON III had hoped that under his rule Paris would again become the diplomatic hub of Europe. While the Congress of 1856 had appeared to be the first indication of a future French hegemony, subsequent events hardly fulfilled the ambitious dreams of the Emperor. To be a leader in diplomacy you must be at least one jump ahead of your adversary. Napoleon's foreign ministers, on the other hand, were generally several jumps behind their contemporaries, and Napoleon himself was more often at the "led" end of the halter than at the "leading."

By his active sympathy for the Poles the French Emperor had driven his friend, the Tsar of Russia, into a hostile combination with Prussia and Austria. When Napoleon, with England's aid, bungled the Danish question badly, the Austro-Prussian coalition became still more firm. Because he persisted in the occupation of Rome and because he constantly accused Albion of perfidiousness in respect to Poland, Denmark, and the congress invitation, the relations between France and England became devoid of all cordiality. In the face of an anti-French campaign in the Italian press and Parliament, and a Mazzinian plot in Paris against the Emperor's life, the Quai d'Orsay likewise awoke to the realization that it was fast losing its only possible Mediterranean ally. Thus it came about that without any national catastrophe, as in 1870, but purely through a lack of directive force, France drifted into a state of inglorious isolation.[1]

Such an abandonment was a serious menace to French prestige and glory, and a great danger to the ruling dynasty. Isolation has always been the *bête noire* of the French foreign office.

[1] References to French isolation and the Roman question can be found in the following collections: Cowley to Russell, Paris, 5 Dec. 1863; same to same, Paris, 7 Jan. 1864; *F.O., France,* 1499: no. 1160; 1522: no. 48. Sartiges to Lhuys, Turin, 14 June 1863, *Aff. Etr., C.P., Italie,* 357: pp. 203-204. *Perseveranza* (of Milan), 28 Sept. 1863. Ollivier, *Empire libéral,* VI, 110-124, 312-329.

Hence, when France had to face this alarming prospect, most of her objections to the solution of the Roman question vanished. The tendency to seek relief in the Roman question was natural for two reasons: first, the road to Rome would connect France again with the roads to both London and Turin; and secondly, French opinion at that moment seemed less excited about Italy and the Pope.

Indeed French public opinion and the internal political situation from 1862 to 1864 also had a very large share in deciding Napoleon to attack the Roman problem. It was evident that the opposition to the Empire was ever spreading so as to include many more groups. The enthusiasm of the unquestioned Bonapartists had been considerably dampened and the number of allied supporters on whom they could depend was becoming more and more restricted.

The parliamentary election of June 1863 revealed the unfavorable internal political situation in no uncertain fashion. It was found that the opposition included the industrialist bourgeoisie and a large share of the Clericals, in addition to the usual Legitimist, Orleanist, and Republican groups. The bourgeoisie was not only disgusted with the Government's foreign policy, but it also was protesting against the partial abandonment of protection as exemplified by the Cobden Treaty with Great Britain. The disruption of French cotton manufacturing by the American Civil War also aggravated the industrial dissatisfaction. Although the appointment of Drouyn de Lhuys was supposed to be a move favorable to the Clericals and although the Government supported many Clericals as official candidates, yet the Clericals as a whole offered a large share of the violent opposition in the election. In many regions of France the clergy violated the Concordat to lead attacks on the Government. The "regret clause" of 1862, the Government's opposition to the activities of the Society of St. Vincent de Paul, and the exclusion of Keller, a prominent Clerical, from the list of official candidates stirred the Clericals.

The ominous campaign was followed by the even more alarming election returns. All of the Paris district went over to the opposition. Eight Republicans and one Orleanist (Thiers) were elected. In the provinces all the large industrial and commercial cities joined the opposition. Only the rural regions and the smaller towns appeared to remain loyal to the Government. But even the apparent support in the country was largely attributed to the closer surveillance which the local government officials could exercise over the individual voter. In comparison with the election of 1857 the Government received 163,000 less votes and the opposition 1,290,000 more.

Of the opposition groups only the Clericals suffered a diminution of membership in the Legislative Body. In addition to a loss of about ten seats they found that many of their remaining members were not those who could be depended upon to keep the religious questions uppermost on their program. Ollivier described it as a complete "rout . . . of the party of episcopal agitators."[2]

That the opposition to the Government persisted even after this election is shown in the reports of the *procureurs* of January and April 1864. They informed the Minister of Justice that the "appreciable revival of the spirit of opposition" was still apparent in Aix. The serious swing in Paris towards the opponents of the Government continued. "Marseilles was not far behind [Paris]" and in Toulon "the activity of the secret societies" was beginning again. In Bordeaux "the spirit of criticism and discussion took on proportions never before attained." Agitation in Bourges against the Government was growing. In Lyons "the Government's orators were listened to with disfavor and the masses were reserving their support for the opposition." In Orleans the election of the general council was won for the Government by a very narrow majority. In April, the hostile attitude of opinion was still apparent, especially in Paris, Bordeaux, Lyons, and Bourges. In Normandy and Savoy there was considerable sympathy for Poland but no desire for war. In many

[2] For accounts of the election of 1863 see: Seignobos in Lavisse, *France contemporaine,* VII, 26-32; Maurain, 634-676; La Gorce, *Second Empire,* IV, 119-240; Ollivier, *Empire libéral,* VI, 215-267.

instances the Roman question was not mentioned and in others it was only to remark that there was little or no interest in the subject.[3]

Thus the growing opposition to the Emperor's Government was connected with both its domestic and foreign policies. Indeed, within a year after Drouyn de Lhuys' appointment there was considerable agitation for his resignation. Grey said:

> The reason for his (Drouyn de Lhuys') retirement would, according to the public, have been the course adopted under his advice in the Polish question, a course which has resulted in a conclusion highly distasteful to the sensitive feelings of the French nation. . . . I hear from all sides the opinion expressed that the Emperor *must* do something for the dignity of France. . . . My own feeling is that Mr. Drouyn de Lhuys shares in this feeling.[4]

In the light of the increasing opposition it was evident to the Emperor that something would have to be done to stem its tide. An analysis of the election returns and the *procureurs'* reports showed that the Clericals were losing popularity and that the Roman question was not exciting as much French sympathy for the Pope as formerly. These two observations made the French Government more willing to solve the Roman question by a treaty with Italy. Such a step would reduce the opposition of the more popular anti-clerical Liberals and at the same time diminish French isolation by pleasing both Italy and England. Incidentally French nationalist sentiment, in whatever group it appeared, would be appeased by the improved French position in Europe. Foreign and domestic questions alike tended to push France on her road to Rome. Indeed, this veering in 1864 toward the anti-clerical Liberals in regard to the Roman question, in conjunction with the slight liberalization of the laws on labor organizations, seems to mark another step in the early stages of the development of the Liberal Empire.

[3] *Rapports des procureurs,* Aix, 11 Jan., 2 April 1864, 370: v. 5; Besançon, 12 Jan., 12 April 1864, 373: v. 7; Bordeaux, 20 Jan., 16 April 1864, 374: v. 4; Bourges, 8 Jan., 4 April 1864, 374: v. 4; Caen, 9 April 1864, 375: v. 5; Chambéry, 31 Dec. 1863, 30 March 1864, 375: v. 1; Lyons, 30 Dec. 1863, 26 March 1864, 379: v. 6; Paris, 15 Feb. 1864, 384: v. 9. In another collection of the Archives nationales, BB^{18}, 1686, A^4, 218: Orleans, 22 Feb. 1864.

[4] 2 Oct. 1864, *F.O., France,* 1496: no. 104.

In Italy also the course of events was leading to a new interest in Rome. Having failed in 1863 to obtain Venice through the Polish and Danish crises, her statesmen began to abandon their sullen silence on Rome. This revival of interest in the Roman question was enhanced by the political speculation accompanying the change from the Farini to the Minghetti ministry.[5] Minghetti's declaration on 18 June 1863 suggested that soon there would be an end to "playing dead."

> In regard to France it is thought opportune to begin again . . . negotiations. We are glad to treat; we are also ready to take the initiative, but we intend to choose the moment in which negotiations will offer us every possibility of approximating the solution of the great problem.[6]

Both Boncompagni and Rattazzi spoke in the Chamber. They regretted the policy of playing dead and hoped for a solution. Boncompagni was even willing to recognize the Pope's temporal power in return for his recognition of the new Italy. On 20 June the Chamber approved the new attitude of the government by a vote of confidence of 145 against 53.[7] The Italian press and public opinion kept in step with the recent shift in policy. Sartiges reported that

> all (Minghetti, Visconti, Boncompagni, La Farina, and the governmental press) consider the Roman question in its relation to the Emperor's Government as entering a new phase. The *Perseveranza,* the *Opinione,* and the *Stampa* announce it categorically, and showed that the Turin Cabinet was supported in that by a majority of public opinion.[8]

In much the same manner as the threat of isolation had moved France to act with Italy on Rome, the serious illness of the Pope impelled Italy toward the French camp in spite of the

[5] Sartiges said on the occasion of the Italian ministerial change: "[Pasolini's] departure from the ministry will diminish among its members the element of resistance to an entente with the Emperor's Government on the Roman question." Turin, 24 March 1863, *Aff. Étr., C.P., Italie,* 356: pp. 263-266.

[6] Minghetti in the Chamber, 17 and 18 June 1863, Minghetti, *Discorsi,* II, 345-353, 356-631.

[7] Sartiges to Lhuys, Turin, 18, 20 June 1863, *Aff. Etr., C.P., Italie,* 357: pp. 215-217, 231.

[8] 24 June 1863, *ibid.,* p. 248.

latter's apparent isolation. Italy was always ready to take advantage of any situation in Europe, whether she had to fight at the side of a victorious hero or play the good Samaritan to a proud outcast. Both France and Italy were fearful lest Pius IX should die before they had reached some agreement for common action in Rome.[9]

In January and May of 1864 the Pope had severe attacks of erysipelas. These caused great alarm, and false rumors got abroad that he had died and that the fact was being kept a secret. It can be imagined what uneasiness was felt by Italian and French statesmen in either case. La Marmora wrote to Minghetti: "The Roman question is urgent; immediate steps should be taken to solve it." La Marmora, although averse to revolution, felt sincerely that something should be done if the Pope died. He therefore assured Minghetti that if an Italian invasion of Rome had to be executed as a last resort, "you may count on me."[10] Malaret, the successor to Sartiges at Turin, wrote that moderate men in Italy were thinking of the possibility of France and Italy agreeing on former proposals if the Pope should die. Both Minghetti and Pepoli, who were to become the most active figures in the renewed negotiations, indicated that it was the Pope's uncertain health which led them to begin to treat with France again for a solution.[11]

The first step had already been taken by Italy before the scare over the Pope's illness. Visconti-Venosta on 4 July 1863 had sent a note to Nigra which contained a moderate demand for the French evacuation of Rome instead of an insistence on the Italian possession of the city. Non-intervention on the part

[9] For the French policy in the case of Pius IX's death see the following documents: *Aff. Etr., C.P., Rome,* 1021: pp. 489-495; 1022: pp. 93-95, 356, 357; 1026: pp. 134, 138, 172-177, 210-219, 247-264; *Italie,* 359: p. 191; 360: pp. 3-4.

[10] Jan. 1864, G. Massari, *Il generale Alfonso La Marmora. Ricordi biografici* (Florence, 1880), p. 287. Minghetti, *Convenzione,* p. 24.

[11] Reference to the Pope's illness and its effects on Italy are as follows: Massari, *La Marmora,* p. 287. Minghetti, *Convenzione,* pp. 24, 16-20. Piero Veroli, "Giocchino Napoleone Pepoli," *Rivista Europa,* XXX, (1882), p. 1196. *Aff. Etr., C.P., Italie,* 359: pp. 180-182; *Rome,* 1026: p. 300. Odo Russell to Russell, Rome, 30 March 1864; Elliot to Russell, Turin, 16 April 1864, *R.P.,* LXXVII, LXX.

of both France and Italy was to be the basis of this accord.[12] This offer was not followed up by either country because of their preoccupation over the Polish question. When Italy took the initiative again, she was under the pressure of the imminence of the Pope's death. But in spite of that danger Minghetti sent the later request unofficially through Vimercati to Rouher, who at that time headed the Imperial ministry. The Italian Prime Minister evidently still resented Drouyn de Lhuys' appointment, and, while willing to break silence, he was going to ignore the Emperor's foreign minister.[13]

Rouher's reply was couched in very benevolent terms. He thought that Minghetti was justified in reopening negotiations because of the likelihood of the Pope's death. As soon as the sessions of Parliament were over, he promised to "provoke the appreciations of the Emperor and . . . try to smooth out the obstacles to a lasting settlement."[14]

One month later Visconti-Venosta informed the Chamber that "if an attitude of reserve had been first dictated to us by circumstances, we have seized an opportunity of reopening the discussion, of recommencing an exchange of ideas of a nature to eliminate difficulties and to agree on terms for an honorable transaction."[15]

During the time of the exchange of letters with Rouher, La Marmora wrote Minghetti again urging him to begin negotiations. He added that although he had no definite plan, yet, "since the Emperor seems to be entertaining better dispositions, I take the liberty of offering to go myself to speak to him about it." La Marmora knew the Emperor personally from their contacts in the Crimean and Austro-Sardinian wars, and it seemed likely that such an emissary would have a great deal of weight in persuading the Emperor to take action. Minghetti accepted La Marmora's offer, but before his mission could be arranged, Garibaldi had returned from England, and Pepoli had begun con-

[12] 4 July 1863, *Aff. Etr., C.P., Italie,* 357: pp. 277-287, 290-298.
[13] Minghetti, *Convenzione,* pp. 16-20.
[14] 15 April 1864, Minghetti, *Convenzione,* pp. 21-23.
[15] *Atti ufficiali,* Chamber, 12 May 1864, pp. 2398-2403.

versations with the Emperor on his own responsibility. Garibaldi's presence in Ischia demanded La Marmora's attentions in Italy,[16] and Minghetti decided to wait until Pepoli's phase of the negotiations became "exhausted" before he sent the General.[17] However, on the contrary, the overtures begun by Pepoli led quite unexpectedly to the climax of the definitive negotiations themselves.

After the fall of the Rattazzi Government Pepoli had been sent as Italian minister to St. Petersburg. If they thought that such a mission would calm the radical tendencies in Pepoli, his superiors were to find themselves quite mistaken. The longer he remained in Russia, the more he became impressed with the effacement of his country. The remark by Lord Napier, the British Ambassador to Russia, that Italy's position would continue to be low in Europe as long as France continued to occupy Rome, stirred again Pepoli's impatience for Rome as capital. An article in a Russian paper to the effect that Victor-Emmanuel could not even "change his shirt without Napoleon's consent" also aroused Pepoli's indignation. From then on he seemed to have nursed the idea that Italy must get Rome as soon as possible, and that she must seize every opportunity to assert her independence from France. He constantly dwelt upon these ideas in his dispatches home during the years 1863 and 1864, and it may be that they had some influence in deciding Minghetti to negotiate through Rouher rather than through Drouyn de Lhuys.[18]

Perhaps hoping to be able to move the Ministry to action by his presence, since the Pope's illness also alarmed him, and perhaps also sincerely on account of his health, which was his declared reason; Pepoli requested a leave of absence from his post in St. Petersburg. This was granted to him and he came home toward the last of April, by the way of Paris. At the French capital he had an opportunity to interview the Emperor, his

[16] La Marmora had charge of the Italian troops in South Italy.

[17] References to La Marmora's proposed mission are found in Minghetti, *Convenzione*, pp. 25-27, 45-46.

[18] Pepoli to Visconti, St. Petersburg, 18 May, 18 Aug., 5 Sept., 5 Oct. 1863, Veroli, *loc. cit.*, XXX, 975-982.

relative, who asked him for a memorandum of a solution if one should occur to him.[19]

On his return to Turin, Pepoli considered seriously the content of such a memorandum and finally decided to send one on 12 May. In two letters, one to the Prince and one to the Emperor, he stressed the need of a prompt solution. "As you will see," he said to Prince Napoleon, "I have profited by your ideas as expressed to Count Cavour: the modifications which I have made are dictated by the different situation which exists." The modification seemed to make the French-Italian agreement contingent upon the death of the Pope. When the conclave would meet, the Emperor was to present the cardinals with the French-Italian agreement which would make them be careful to select a Pope who would not be hostile to France or Italy. Pepoli requested the privilege of coming to Paris to explain his proposal in person if the Emperor was favorably impressed.[20]

Simultaneously with the Pepoli overtures Visconti-Venosta instructed Nigra to open negotiations with France on the Roman question.

> We hope therefore that the Imperial Government will recognize that it is urgent to arrive at an accord with the Government of the King to prevent complications which must necessarily arise at a time whose date no one can definitely fix.[21]

Drouyn de Lhuys' reply of 3 June was very favorable to the suggestion, but he still insisted that Italy make the first positive proposal.[22] His *amour propre*, sensitive to Italy's earlier contemptuousness, required this modicum of satisfaction.

But on 28 May the Emperor, independently of his foreign minister, had already had Conneau communicate to the Italian Foreign Office his desire to take up the negotiation on the basis of the plan of 1861 with a three year period before evacuation.

[19] Veroli, *loc. cit.*, XXX, pp. 975-976. Minghetti, *Convenzione*, pp. 38-42. L. Carpi, *Il risorgimento italiano, biografie*, (Pepoli), (Milan, 1884-1888), III, 385-387.

[20] Pepoli to Prince Napoleon, to Napoleon III, Favorita, 12 May 1864, Veroli, *loc. cit.*, XXX, pp. 1197-1199, 1203.

[21] Visconti to Nigra, Turin, 27 May 1864, *Aff. Etr., C.P., Italie,* 359: pp. 352-354.

[22] June 1864, *Aff. Etr., C.P., Italie,* 360: pp. 53-55.

The project of 1861 had required that Italy respect the Pope's actual territory and protect him from any irregular attacks. France would then evacuate Rome.

The Emperor's note, coming through Conneau rather than through the French Foreign Office and being more favorable to Italy than that of Drouyn de Lhuys, led the Italian ministers to look to the Tuileries rather than to the Quai d'Orsay for their future field of action. Since it appeared that the Emperor's communication had been in response to Pepoli's proposal, the latter was able to persuade Minghetti and Visconti-Venosta that he should be the emissary for a preliminary conference.[23] Minghetti, in asking La Marmora to temporarily step aside in favor of Pepoli, declared that

> [Pepoli] was sure he could persuade the Emperor to accept his own ideas. So I think it would be inopportune for you to be there right now. It seems better to let this phase exhaust itself, especially since Pepoli's sojourn in Paris will be brief. . . . He knows nothing of your intended voyage. Nigra has been told to keep quiet on that.[24]

Pepoli arrived in Paris on 11 June, had dinner at Fontainebleau on the 13th, and returned again on the 14th to Fontainebleau to spend a week with the Emperor.[25] On about 15 June Nigra, Pepoli, and the Emperor had a long conference which Nigra reported carefully to Visconti-Venosta.

> Pepoli and I took up the argument about the eventuality of the death of the Pope. We told His Majesty that if the Pope died, we should come to some understanding for a common action, and since we could not promise the Romans an early departure of the French garrison, we would be unable to stop the Roman emigrants from crossing the frontier, that there would be demonstrations, and perhaps, plebiscites too, that there might be general or partial insurrections in the Papal States, especially where they were not occupied by French troops.
>
> Drouyn de Lhuys pressed us to counsel prudence and patience; but what authority could such advice have, if we do not hold a promise of evacuation? Certainly General Montebello has all the

[23] Minghetti to La Marmora, Turin, 4 June 1864, Minghetti, *Convenzione,* pp. 38-54.

[24] Minghetti to La Marmora, Turin, 10 June 1864, Minghetti, *Convenzione,* pp. 45-46, 47.

[25] Pepoli to Minghetti, Paris, 14 June 1864, Minghetti, *Convenzione,* p. 47.

necessary means to enable him to put down any uprising, but we do not think that it would be to the interest of the Emperor to have to go to such an extreme.

The Emperor replied protesting that he had always had, and still had, a strong desire to withdraw the French garrison from Rome, but he could not do it, unless he could be sure that the departure of the troops would not have as a *necessary and immediate consequence*[26] the downfall of the temporal power.

If Italy undertook the obligation, he said, of respecting and having respected the Papal territory, he had no reason to doubt that the King's Government would keep its word; but could this assurance be imparted to the minds of the mass of the Catholics? There is a vote of the Italian Parliament which proclaims Rome as capital. If I sign the treaty which you propose, they will say that it is all a farce (*si griderà alla comedia*).

Everybody thinks that the Italian Government only keeps its capital at Turin until it can transfer it to Rome.[26] To engender into Catholic opinion the conviction that the Italian Government will keep its promise of not attacking and of not allowing the Papal States to be attacked a *practical*[26] guaranty should be offered which will prove that your treaty is not a sham.

To these words Marquis Pepoli replied that he knew that the King's Government, *independently of the question under discussion,*[26] and for reasons of internal administration, had the intention of proposing to His Majesty moving the capital from Turin to some other city, and he asked if that fact would constitute in the Emperor's eyes the guaranty which he was looking for.

Here it is necessary to stop for a moment and consider this new element in the negotiation which had never before appeared in the French and Italian discussions on Rome. How did Pepoli happen to think of the capital transfer and suggest it so suddenly?

The suggestion of removing the capital from Turin was not a new idea. From the minute that the Italian unification had been brought about by additions to Piedmont, there was a danger that the spirit of the union would be killed by the dominance of the Piedmontese. From these "old provinces" came the dynasty, the constitution, many of the officers in the army, and a large share of the civil officials. Cavour as the diplomatic leader was a Piedmontese; Garibaldi as the source of martial inspiration was a Sardinian of Nice and Caprera. Finally Turin as capital

[26] These are the author's italics.

symbolized this natural but unwelcome leadership. The Piedmontese formed that element of Italy which seemed to have the genius for government and administration: Ollivier called them the Anglo-Saxons of Italy. But many who had been seeking *Italian* unity and a new *Italian* nation feared that only an overgrown Piedmont would result. Such sentiment was weakening Italy internally and was one of the mainsprings of the demand that Rome be the capital. But, because fulfillment of that aspiration seemed to become more and more remote, the opposition to Turin became almost stronger than the desire for Rome.

One of the earliest to oppose Turin, irrespective of Rome, was Prince Napoleon. Writing to Nigra soon after Garibaldi's invasion of the Neapolitan provinces in 1860, he said:

> Establish your provisional capital at Florence. . . . Avoid the danger of trying to piedmontize Italy, for which they often reproach you with some reason. Go to Florence until you can enter Rome.[27]

Again in May 1864 the Prince wrote Manteucci advising the Italians "to transfer the capital from Turin to Florence for by staying in Turin you will make Italy discontented."[28]

Another French suggestion came from a source close to the Emperor. On 20 February 1862 in the *Patrie* appeared an article over the name of De la Ponterie. As a matter of fact it was widely rumored that the real author was La Guéronnière, the press official of Napoleon III's Interior department and author of many celebrated pamphlets. In this article the suggestion of the removal of the capital from Turin was again offered.

> The Court of Turin will recognize . . . no doubt that satisfied with its triumphs, in which the liberty of Italy played such a memorable part, henceforth engaged in the immense work of organizing the Peninsula, it should turn its regards to some one of the illustrious cities worthy by so many titles of being the capital of Italy. It should give up removing the seat of government to Rome.[29]

In Italy Massimo d'Azeglio, himself a Piedmontese, had been advocating Florence in preference to Turin or Rome ever since

[27] 10 Oct. 1860, Comandini, *op. cit.*, pp. 190-191. Bollea, *Silloge*, pp. 252-254.

[28] Paris, 2 May 1864, *Rivista storica del Risorgimento italiano,* I, 182-183.

[29] *La Patrie,* 20 Feb. 1862.

the union began to take form.[30] An interesting document in the French Foreign Office Archives contains a report of 1 March 1863 from the French Secretary of Legation at Turin on Peruzzi's statement in Parliament about the location of the capital.

> Mr. Peruzzi went on to speak of the capital, and giving Turin the praise she deserved, he declared that *after careful consideration* he and his colleagues were persuaded that in no other Italian city could the seat of government be better placed until it should be transferred to Rome.[31]

The most important fact to notice is that after the formation of the Farini-Minghetti cabinet there had been *a discussion* on the advisability of removing the government from Turin. That the Government and people were purposely keeping quiet on Rome made the question of another city than Turin still more alive. Knowing also that so many officials in army and government were Piedmontese, many began to think that they were purposely delaying the solution of the Roman question for the benefit of Turin. Although the italics in the above quotation are the author's, yet, it is significant that the document had been penciled and underlined by the Quai d'Orsay. Thus the French appeared to have been noticing the discussion in regard to moving the capital.

Minghetti, three months later, made a statement in Parliament in regard to Turin which indicated that he and Peruzzi were in substantial agreement on the question of the location of the capital temporarily in Turin.

> Gentlemen, if they say that Italy will be really constituted only at Rome, I admit it; if they say that there will be some major difficulties in setting it up from a point at the far end of the Peninsula which would not be present from the center, again I agree; but if they mean to deny the possibility of establishing Italy except from some particular point in it, I positively disagree. (*Signs of approval.*)

[30] Eugène Rendu, *L'Italie de 1847 à 1865. Correspondance politique de Massimo D'Azeglio* (Paris, 1867), pp. 184-185; quoted from M. D'Azeglio, *Questioni urgenti,* p. 51. M. D'Azeglio to Minghetti, Florence, 8 March 1861, Chiala, *Cavour lettere,* VI, 690.

[31] Turin, 1 March 1863, *Aff. Etr., C.P., Italie,* 356: p. 175.

The topographical location of a city is not the predominant element in organizing the Kingdom, but the will of the people, the wisdom of the Parliaments, the firmness and the energy of the governing officials. . . .[32]

It is evident, too, that Pepoli, when he had returned to Turin in early May, had come into the midst of many discussions of a similar nature. In addition to his concern over Rome there grew upon him a conviction of the bad effect of the Piedmont predominance on the Italian union.[33]

Thus the question of the capital transfer had been under discussion since 1860. Almost as many suggestions had come from France as from Italy. Indeed, the French had appeared to be taking special notice of the growing controversy in 1863 and 1864. It is not likely, therefore, that it was entirely unpremeditated on Napoleon's part when he connected Turin with the Roman question and when he asked for some *practical* guaranty. Nor is it surprising that, after the Turin hint, Pepoli immediately thought of the transfer as a possible way out of the dilemma.

As a matter of fact Nigra in his official account seemed to infer that as soon as the demand for a guaranty *in fact* was injected into the negotiations, the transfer seemed the only possible reply. He said the Italian negotiators had definite instructions not to sacrifice any of the national rights of Italy. Consequently they could not promise as a practical guaranty to pass a resolution in Parliament renouncing all claims to Rome; neither could they accept a collective guaranty by the Catholic Powers of the Pope's territories; nor could they even agree to allow the French to remain in Civita-Vecchia after they had left Rome. Any of those three practical guaranties would have been contrary to the supposed Italian national right to succeed to the Pope's temporal power. Hence, Nigra continued, Mr. Pepoli proposed the transfer as the required positive guaranty. But he made it seem as if the Italian Government had already considered it from the point of view of administrative and military strat-

[32] Minghetti, *Discorsi,* II, 356-361. (17 June 1863).
[33] Veroli, *loc. cit.,* XXX, 1196. Carpi, *Biografie,* (Pepoli), III, 386-387.

egy.[34] Any appearance of French dictation would have been disastrous to its acceptance at home.

Nigra's earlier detailed and confidential account of the important interview goes on to describe the effect this transfer proposal had on the Emperor.

His Majesty, after several moments reflection, said that, should that fact prove true, it would seem to him to be of a nature to attain the scope intended, and to engender that confidence of which he had spoken, and he added that, that being the case, he saw no difficulty in signing the treaty.[35]

I (Nigra) did not conceal from the Emperor the fact that the idea of transferring the capital being no more than a simple intention of the Government, I could only take the arrangement *ad referendum*. . . . I added that this new fact was a rather serious matter; that it presented very grave difficulties and inconveniences; that it involved displacing the center of gravitation of the Government, and to take it away from a firm and stable element essentially accustomed to self-government, to transport it in the midst of a new element; that the very material difficulties of carrying it out were great and numerous.

I insisted, therefore, that entirely outside of the fact of the transference of the capital—an act which should be more especially considered in connection with the internal ordering of Italy—we might try to come to some accord for the present on some common action in the event of the Pope's death, an event which might happen suddenly at any time.

But the Emperor, while declaring that he could not fail to appreciate these considerations, confirmed what he had just said before; that is, that the pact of transferring the capital seemed to him the only one which, engendering confidence in the earnestness of our promises, would enable him to sign the treaty.

The same things were confirmed to Marquis Pepoli and myself by Mr. Drouyn de Lhuys in a conference which we had with him at Fontainebleau.

These events took place toward the middle of the month of last June.

[34] Nigra to Visconti, Paris, 15 Sept. 1864, *Aff. Etr., C.P., Italie,* 360: pp. 392-394.

[35] "Several moments reflection" seem a very short time for the Emperor to make up his usually uncertain mind on so important a question of guaranties. The question of guaranties had obstructed the negotiations during all the past three years. Certainly if the Emperor had not thought over that possibility long before, he could hardly have made such an acceptance after even "several moments of reflection." The suggestion would have to come from the Italians because it involved their domestic affairs, but it seems quite clear that the Emperor consciously guided the negotiations into that channel with a definite intention in mind.

Marquis Pepoli left for Turin on 23 June, and brought these things to the attention of Your Excellency and the President of the Council.[36]

When Visconti-Venosta and Minghetti received the detailed account from Pepoli, they were inclined to accept the capital transfer clause if that alone would bring about the treaty of evacuation. Visconti-Venosta told Nigra:

> And yet when the Emperor has confidence in no other guaranty, when this is the *sine qua non,* and when it involves the withdrawal of the French from Rome . . . , I believe it is difficult for any patriotic Italian to refuse the project.

Minghetti's opinion was almost identical with that of his Foreign Minister. If the treaty could not be made without that particular practical guaranty, then he favored such a concession.[37]

This decision once having been made, they then found it necessary to prepare the Turinese for the sacrifice. It was, therefore, very important for Minghetti to include La Marmora in the Ministry and have him as an additional advocate of the treaty because he was one of the strongest Piedmontese leaders. If the capital was to be taken from Turin, it would be well to have a Piedmontese at the head of the Government. Minghetti was from Bologna and Visconti-Venosta from Milan. While they might

[36] From this report it would seem that Nigra was rather taken back by Pepoli's quick and rash proposal. He seemed to be trying to discourage the idea. Napoleon's insistence would seem to suggest that perhaps he and Pepoli planned the little dialogue to impress and win over Nigra because his influence would be powerful in Turin. Minghetti's remarks on this point are significant. Claiming that the Government had not "seriously" taken up the question of changing the capital as Pepoli had said, he added: "I imagined that Pepoli spoke the way he did, either because that was his opinion, or because he was prompted by the Emperor himself so that the proposals might come spontaneously from Italy." If Minghetti was not trying to throw the blame of the proposal on Pepoli, his account would seem to confirm the concerted dialogue supposition. As will be seen later, Pepoli does not seem to claim that the suggestion was born in Turin, but at one time gave the Emperor the credit and at another time himself. Motives obscure the exactness of the situation but it rather points to a prearranged dialogue between the Emperor and Pepoli. For the Nigra account see Minghetti, *Convenzione,* pp. 53-59.

[37] Visconti to Nigra, Turin, 2 July 1864, Minghetti, *Convenzione,* pp. 68-70; Cesare, *Roma e lo Stato del Papa,* II, 252-253; Cesare, "Emilio Visconti-Venosta," *Nuova Antologia,* (1915), CLXXV, 13-14. Minghetti to Nigra, Turin, 8 July 1864, Minghetti, *Convenzione,* pp. 73-75.

retain their respective portfolios, it would be preferable to have La Marmora the President of the Council. Then too, La Marmora was one of the leading generals. If, from the military point of view, he considered some other city than Turin as preferable, the Turinese opposition would be appreciably weakened.

Consequently Minghetti wrote La Marmora on 6 July telling him of the chances of a successful negotiation on the basis of the Cavour project. He added, however, that the Emperor wanted some guaranty *de fait*, but he avoided mentioning the particular one which Pepoli had proposed. He sincerely hoped that La Marmora would come up to Turin where they could talk it all over at length. Minghetti tells us in his *Convenzione* that he tried to hint at the change in the Ministry without being too specific.[38]

La Marmora's reply on the 12th was to oppose the Cavour plan. He said that Italy could not prevent irregular groups from going across the frontier. Italy would therefore have the French and all Europe against her and might see Rome occupied again anyway. Still more interesting is the fact that when a guaranty *de fait* was mentioned, La Marmora immediately suspected the capital transfer.

> And what can *the act* be which the Emperor has been searching for so as to give the fine project *a serious character?* To my mind it can be nothing but the transfer of the capital, either to Florence or to some other city.

He objected to French dictation in such a matter and he feared the effect it might have on the internal stability of Italy.[39]

Then Minghetti requested Nigra to fix up another account of the interview at Fontainebleau which would have a greater appeal to La Marmora. The revised version was to minimize Pepoli's share in the negotiations because of La Marmora's lack of confidence in him. Nigra complied with this request on 21 July and in this second report revealed some further details of the first negotiations. Nigra mentioned that from the Em-

[38] 6 July 1864, Minghetti, *Convenzione*, pp. 48-50.

[39] 12 July 1864, Minghetti, *Convenzione*, pp. 51-52. Massari, *La Marmora*, p. 289.

peror's reference to a practical guaranty it "could only be applied to the hypothesis of the transfer of the capital." From this admission we can see grounds for understanding the Emperor's intentions in saying what he did, and also we can understand better why both Pepoli and La Marmora thought so quickly of such a clause. Nigra this time did not mention whether it was he or Pepoli who had suggested the capital transfer. All through the document there was very little mention of Pepoli. Toward the end Nigra added a report of a recent conversation with Drouyn de Lhuys in which the latter had made a very significant observation.

Mr. Drouyn de Lhuys approved without reserve, and added these words which I cite textually:

'Naturally the result of all this will be that you will end up by going to Rome; but it is important that between this event and that of the evacuation there should come such an interval and such a series of events as to prevent the establishment of any connection between them for which France might be held responsible.[40]

Minghetti and La Marmora met at Pasolini's home in Pegli from 26 to 31 July. Here the General was shown Nigra's specially prepared account which confirmed his premonition of the transfer clause. La Marmora opposed the clause which guaranteed the Pope's frontier, but, apparently free from provincialism, he offered less resistance to the moving of the capital if it could be done without the appearance of French dictation. If the Emperor insisted on both the frontier and capital guaranties, then La Marmora demanded that the boundaries between the Pope's territory and Italy be modified in Italy's favor so as to enable the latter to better enforce her frontier obligations. The General declined to undertake the presidency of the ministry because he was unused to parliamentary life and also because he and the King were not in entire agreement. But La Marmora concluded that if he could go himself to the Emperor, he was "convinced that . . . he might succeed in . . . restricting our promise to Rome, the Comarca, and Civita-Vecchia." He even suggested "that perhaps this conversation would change his own

[40] Nigra to Minghetti (for La Marmora), Paris, 21 July 1864, Minghetti, *Convenzione,* pp. 76-80.

present attitude and make possible the accomplishment of the ministerial combination."

Although Minghetti frankly stated that he was ready to accept the French proposal as it stood, he showed a willingness to give La Marmora a chance to confer with the Emperor. "The conclusion (at Pegli) was to let Pepoli complete his mission and decide afterwards on the advisability of [La Marmora's] visit to the Emperor."[41]

While Minghetti and La Marmora were still engaged in the Pegli conference, Visconti-Venosta was drawing up new instructions for Pepoli's second trip to Paris. Victor-Emmanuel, who knew of all the transactions with the exception of the capital clause, asked to have Napoleon promise aid against an Austrian attack. Pepoli was instructed to discuss this point with the Emperor and to request three other modifications: 1) France was to leave Rome as soon as possible instead of after two years, 2) Italy was to have six months in which to change her capital, 3) the clause providing for the transfer was to be secret. Later Visconti-Venosta sent more detailed instructions to Nigra on the last point. The clause for the removal of the capital should be worded carefully to avoid the appearance of French dictation and at the same time to prevent a charge that Pepoli had made the concession unnecessarily.[42]

Nigra and Pepoli were successful in gaining some minor changes in this second negotiation, but they failed to gain much on the most important points of their discussion. Nigra reported to Minghetti as follows:

Pepoli has just returned from St. Cloud (4 o'clock). He is leaving this very evening for Turin. I have only time enough to write you these few lines. It was impossible to obtain from the Emperor a delay of less than two years. But we were able to have omitted the words "foreign legion" and have inserted another important modification by which we promise, *not to assume* a part of the public debt, but to negotiate to assume, a change the full im-

[41] On the Pegli Conference see: Minghetti to Nigra, Turin, 6 Aug. 1864, Minghetti, *Convenzione,* pp. 85-86, 80-81. Pasolini, *Memorie,* I, 418-424. Massari, *La Marmora,* p. 289.

[42] Pietro Silva, *Nuova Antologia,* (16 May 1913), p. 281. Minghetti, *Convenzione,* pp. 87-91.

portance of which you will easily understand. The extension of the time limit is also compensated by having the clause dealing with the organization of the Papal army omitted, and by having substituted in its place the phrase of the former Cavour plan. It certainly would have been very important to obtain a shorter period of delay, but there was no way for us to do it. The Emperor was inflexible on that point. However, in spite of the establishment of the delay of two years, Pepoli and I are still convinced of the advisability of accepting the treaty. I hope you will all be of the same opinion. Therefore lose no time: put the matter before the King, and send Pepoli back with full powers for him and me.[43]

When Pepoli returned to Turin, Minghetti recorded that

Pepoli went through Turin on the morning of 11 August and brought me the draft of the convention in the terms by which it was drawn up by our negotiators. He added that respecting the guaranty of defence against Austria, the Emperor had thought he could not include it therein because it would be extraneous to the subject matter, but that if Austria attacked Italy, the King could count on French aid (*qu'il prendrait fait et cause pour l'Italie*) and in that event it could be arranged by an exchange of notes.[44]

Minghetti's reproduction of this draft treaty is unreliable. Just a swift reading of it would be sufficient to reveal that it was identical with the terms of the final treaty. But these two copies could not be the same, since there were to be several later modifications before the treaty was signed. For instance, Nigra in a note of *14 September* reported that article 3 of the draft had been changed. Minghetti's *August* draft contained this particular change which was not made until September.[45] One will obtain a better understanding of the draft treaty by adding the results of the two Pepoli negotiations to the original Thouvenel-Cavour plan.

On the next day (12 August) Minghetti presented the whole proposal including the transfer clause to the Council of Ministers. After a careful consideration of each clause the whole Ministry with but one exception endorsed the convention. Only General Della Rovere dissented. He told Minghetti that he would

[43] Nigra to Minghetti, Paris, 5 August 1864, Minghetti, *Convenzione*, p. 93.

[44] *Ibid.*, pp. 94-95

[45] Nigra to Minghetti, Paris, 14 Sept. 1864, *ibid.*, pp. 174-175. Then compare Article 3 in *ibid.*, pp. 94-95 with Article 3 in *ibid.*, pp. 170-180.

remain in the Ministry until the end of the negotiation, but that after the signing of the convention he would have to withdraw.[46]

Minghetti realized then that the "whole truth" would have to be told to Victor-Emmanuel. With considerable trepidation, therefore, he undertook the unwelcome task of persuading the King to abandon Turin.

> I spoke to the King on the morning of the 13th and the details of that conversation remain impressed on my mind. I began by going over again all the negotiations with which he was already acquainted; I read all the articles of which he fully approved, and coming to the point where it was necessary to define an act which could be considered as a guaranty, I pronounced the words, transfer of the capital.
>
> The King was astounded (*ne fu colpito*).
>
> 'Why that?' he asked. 'How do they happen to put those two things together?'
>
> 'Sire,' I said, 'the Emperor wants to be able to say to the Catholics: I have not left Rome without insuring the Pope against an aggression by the Italians. But the promise to respect the Papal boundary would be frustrated by the impossibility of their keeping the capital long at Turin. This impatience will impel them to transgress the boundary. If they transfer the capital somewhere else, that alone will take up time. Capitals are not changed like suits of clothes. And if under altered circumstances Italy should go to Rome, such an interval would have passed as to remove any semblance of French complicity.'
>
> The King was silent, then proudly replied: 'If the capital must be changed, I will do it spontaneously when I please, I do not want someone else to dictate to me.'
>
> 'Your Majesty,' I replied, 'it is not a foreigner who is dictating to you, but the opinion of the Italians themselves. Pepoli said in Paris that it was a step already decided by the Italian Government. That is not true, nothing could be decided without your assent, but the idea of transferring the capital is in the minds of many, of many more than it outwardly appears.'
>
> 'But what will Turin say? Is it not shameful to compensate her for so many sacrifices by imposing another sacrifice still more cruel?'
>
> 'Your Majesty, if the sacrifice which is being demanded had come from domestic disorders or dissatisfaction, it would really be terrible. But it rather loses its seriousness when such a sacrifice brings so important a result as the withdrawal of the French from Rome. It is a means of saving the country.'

[46] Minghetti, *Convenzione*, pp. 97-98.

'I can not accustom myself to that idea,' said the King.

And I: 'If Your Majesty could see my very soul, he would know how it pains me, too, to abandon such a good city as Turin, a city so devoted to the dynasty, and so worthy of the gratitude of Italy.'

Then the King, banging the table fiercely with his fist, exclaimed, 'And what is Turin to the rest of you? I am the one who will have his heart torn out by it, I am the one who has always lived here, who has all his childhood recollections, his familiar habits, his affections associated with her.'

The King was now walking back and forth in the room, visibly agitated, and there were tears in his eyes.

'Your Majesty,' I said, 'need not decide today: the negotiations have been going on for a long time, and they are not yet ended. Your Majesty can think it over as long as you wish. In the meantime, if you will permit me, I will call again tomorrow to discuss it with you.'

'I want to know, word for word, what Pepoli said at Paris; what they replied on this subject: I want to be informed of everything. Telegraph him (Pepoli) to come immediately.'

'Your Majesty will be obeyed and Pepoli will be here tomorrow morning at your command.'

Pepoli came and carefully explained it all to the King, telling him that he himself had proposed the change of capital. The King replied that he wanted to think it over a few days before he gave a decision.

Then Minghetti went again to see the King. The latter was still sad but no longer angry. They went over together phrase by phrase and clause by clause the other articles of the treaty. The King wanted a clause to prevent the harboring of brigands by the Pope; and he wanted a stipulation that the treaty would go into effect regardless of the Vatican's attitude. Minghetti recorded, "This seemed to me hardly necessary since France and Italy took obligations independently of the Pope and without consulting him." The King still insisted on a written clause for reciprocal action against Austria.

On the 15th the King finally touched on the transfer clause again. He said he would like first to send Menabrea as a personal representative to the Emperor in an attempt to eliminate or modify the transfer clause. Minghetti offered no objection to this wish and there the matter rested for a while.[47]

[47] Minghetti, *Convenzione*, pp. 98-101.

In the meantime steps had been taken to send La Marmora on his projected mission to the Emperor. As a result Menabrea's journey was temporarily postponed. Visconti-Venosta instructed Nigra to give full information to La Marmora on his arrival in Paris, to show him that he was wrong in thinking that the Emperor would agree to different boundaries or to a different time limit, and to help any effort toward accomplishing the French withdrawal sometime during the year of 1865. Nigra was also to suggest to the Emperor that he persuade La Marmora to accept the presidency of the Italian Ministry.[48]

La Marmora's instructions were rather contradictory. He was to try to obtain a shorter period of evacuation, "but," Minghetti added, "just the same . . . it seems to me the treaty ought to be accepted even as it is."[49] This indicated only too clearly to La Marmora that he would have very little home support in what he was undertaking.

His interview with the Emperor was arranged so soon after his arrival on 16 August that he had almost no time to learn the details of the negotiations from Nigra. However, he endeavored to convince the Emperor that Italy could not protect the Pope's frontiers without obtaining some more of the Church's territory. It was, of course, impossible for the Emperor to give away territory belonging to someone else. Hence, the only result of the conversation was the impression gained by the Emperor that the Italian Government was trying to make a promise which its own general admitted could not be fulfilled. La Marmora wrote to Minghetti, "I do not know whether I replied well or badly to the Emperor . . . , [but] I fear . . . from what he said that I did not suit him. In that case disavow me, as you see best; but take care, I pray you, to avoid ever putting me or any other in the false position in which I was today."[50]

La Marmora's fear was confirmed a little later by Drouyn de Lhuys in their interview. The latter reported the Emperor to have said that he "was not pleased with General La Mar-

[48] Minghetti, *Convenzione*, pp. 102-104.
[49] Minghetti to La Marmora, Turin, 15 Aug. 1864, *ibid.*, pp. 104-105.
[50] 16 Aug. 1864, *ibid.*, pp. 108-111.

mora."[51] Drouyn de Lhuys professed so strongly France's desire to leave Rome that it only convinced the General more than ever of the needlessness of great Italian sacrifices for something which the French wanted so ardently anyway. On the other hand Drouyn de Lhuys' earnest appeals for La Marmora's entrance into the ministry fell on deaf ears.

Then La Marmora began his arguments to Drouyn de Lhuys for a revision of the Italian-Papal boundary. This time he stressed particularly the fact that Italy could not possibly stop every individual who tried to enter the Church's territory. Drouyn de Lhuys' reply is very significant.

> He (Drouyn de Lhuys) said and repeated several times that they did not demand the impossible of us; that when we stopped groups from going over, if some went in one by one, if they then organized and attacked the Papal troops, we will be in no way responsible; and that if the Papal troops were then unable to resist, if they were overcome, and that for that reason the Pope should abandon Rome—'it would be a proof that the good Lord no longer favored the temporal power, and then let happen what may (*arrivera ce qui arrivera*).'[52]

This attitude might be in conformity with the letter, at least, of the proposed convention since Italy was expected to only repel attacks, which inferred migrations in groups. What is more interesting is the readiness of this supposedly pro-Vatican French foreign minister to make as light as possible the Italian commitments.

Minghetti replied to La Marmora's report on the audience with the Emperor by saying that he thought that Italy could enforce Article 1 by watching movements in the cities as well as on the frontier. He recognized that La Marmora could not enter the ministry under the present circumstances, but he predicted that there would soon be a ministerial crisis which would end in a ministry headed by the General.

La Marmora inferred from this last remark that Minghetti

[51] Minghetti, *Convenzione*, p. 119.
[52] La Marmora to Minghetti, 21 Aug. 1864, and memorandum of interview with Drouyn de Lhuys of 17 Aug. 1864, *ibid.*, pp. 111-114, 119-122.

suspected him of intriguing against the present ministry. Wishing to counteract any such impression, he immediately replied:

> If I had any ambitious motives, I would not have gone as far away as I am now from all politicians and from everything which pertains to politics. . . . Be convinced that if by the force of events I should one day stifle my repugnance for the ministry, I will have recourse to you as much as to anyone else.

In closing he announced his intention of going to Cherbourg, Châlons, Holland, Belgium, and the Rhine to inspect military fortifications. He asked leave to be absent from Turin until the last of September.[53]

Thus ended one general's mission without success and perhaps even with some harm done to the progress of the negotiation. Hardly had this been finished, however, before the Emperor and his Foreign Minister were faced by another Italian general on another mission to modify the terms of the proposed convention. This time it was Victor-Emmanuel's dispatch of General Menabrea with the hope of a last-minute conversion of the Emperor on questions of time limit and the capital.

When Pepoli heard of the proposed Menabrea mission, he was very much opposed. Although his *amour propre* may have been touched by this interference in what he considered his own negotiation, yet it may be said to his credit that he had other good reasons for voicing his objections. He knew from his own negotiations that little more would be conceded by the Emperor. Any further attempts would only antagonize the French. Besides, this fine idea of winning over individual Italian objectors by sending them up in single file one after the other against the Emperor purely to demonstrate the folly of their objections was like hunting deer with cannon. You might hit the deer but in the end there would be no game to take home. These critics might become convinced that their objections were in vain, but in the meantime the Emperor would tire of the whole affair.

Minghetti wrote Pepoli telling him that the Ministry was favorable to the treaty regardless of the Menabrea mission. He

[53] Minghetti, *Convenzione,* pp. 119-122. See also Massari, *La Marmora,* pp. 290 ff.

further reassured him by remarking that the King intended to send Pepoli with full powers for the final signature.[54]

Menabrea was sent on 21 August. His instructions were interesting.

> In fulfilling your mission do not lose sight of the fact that the Ministry is favorable to the treaty even with the (transfer) clause.

And yet

> it would be preferable, and in any case more in conformity with His Majesty's desire, to eliminate completely the idea of the transfer of the capital or to substitute another system. . . .

Menabrea was to show how bad it would be to inject the capital transfer into the midst of the Roman question and how necessary it would be to handle the old provinces with tact (*ménager*). They formed at that time the conservative nucleus, but by the transfer they might become radical in regard to the annexation of Rome.[55]

Finally Victor-Emmanuel wrote a personal letter to the Emperor.

> I thought, Sire, that you had forgotten me and with me the cause of Italy. I see it is just the contrary, from what Pepoli tells me, and I express my gratitude to you for it. The treaty will calm for a time the ardent aspirations of the Italians, and you will have their benedictions for it. There is, however, a rather serious difficulty which appears at the first glance in the capital transfer. . . . Hoping to find an easier solution . . ., I am sending General Menabrea to you, etc.[56]

Menabrea arrived in Paris on 23 August and obtained an immediate audience with the Emperor to whom he consigned the King's letter. On reading it the Emperor asked what changes Menabrea was instructed to propose. The General suggested either a delay of two years for the transfer, which would be the same delay for the evacuation, or the adoption of a nomadic

[54] Veroli, *loc. cit.*, pp. 1204-1208. Minghetti, *Convenzione*, pp. 126-128.

[55] Minghetti, *Convenzione*, pp. 124-126.

[56] 23 Aug. 1864, *Les origines diplomatiques de la guerre de 1870-1871, recueil de documents publiés par le ministère des affaires étrangères* (17 vols. to date, Paris, 1910-1928), [quoted hereafter as *Doc. Guerre 1870*], IV, 47-48. Minghetti, *Convenzione*, pp. 123-124. Ollivier, *Empire libéral*, VII, 159-160.

Parliament which would hold sessions at different times in the various Italian cities while the King and the administration remained in Turin. The Emperor did not object greatly to the first proposal but in the case of the second he naturally pointed out that it would make Italy seem less stable than ever. Furthermore, it would do just the opposite from assuring the Catholics that Italy was not intending to go to Rome. He had objected to Turin before because that seemed temporary, but a nomadic capital, instead of giving a greater semblance of permanency, would appear all the more transitory. The Emperor said he could not give an immediate answer. He wanted to talk with Drouyn de Lhuys first. Menabrea took leave after assuring the Emperor that he would wait to take his reply to the King.[57]

Events began to look more and more discouraging. Menabrea called on Prince Napoleon on 26 August and found him fully informed on the negotiations, probably by Pepoli. The Prince took the initiative in the conversation and warned Menabrea against delaying and objecting too much to the terms of the convention.

If you think you can get something more from the Emperor, you are mistaken. The Emperor's first impulse is the most extensive and most generous. If he is given time to reflect, he finds inconveniences where he had not seen them before. Be on your guard for delays and especially for the people who surround him. They know nothing yet; but just as soon as they suspect something, they will do all they can to paralyze this affair. The words 'capital transfer' which frighten the King so much does not mean as much as he thinks. . . . Lose no time then in negotiating, hurry the solution of this affair, and especially do not let the King compromise his popularity, do not let them say that he abandoned Rome for Turin. Besides, there are various ways of transferring the capital. You could leave the departments in Turin. It would be enough to have the King, the Parliament, and the Ministers in the city which you will designate as capital. The evacuation of Rome would be hailed with great favor . . . especially in England. This question solved would be enough in itself to reëstablish the English alliance to counteract the union of the Northern Powers. At the same time in spite of the interest which France has in this question, do not think you can

[57] Menabrea to Minghetti, Paris, 23 Aug. 1864, Minghetti, *Convenzione,* pp. 129-132.

prevail upon the Emperor whose calculations have been made, and who would not easily enlarge them further.[58]

It was beginning to look as if the Italians were letting another opportunity go by which would take the French from Rome. Nevertheless it is significant to see the international situation linked so closely with the solution of the Roman question.

Menabrea had still more reason to feel uneasy after Nigra dined with the Emperor on 28 August. On that occasion Nigra had loyally presented the same arguments which Menabrea had been instructed to use.

But the Emperor observed that that (transfer) was the very base of the negotiations and that it alone made them possible. 'Besides,' he said, 'even I recognize that the inconveniences pointed out by the King are serious. I can not deny it. Anyway you can get along somehow just as things are, and then we will see—'

The Emperor then dropped the subject altogether and began to talk about Tunis.

Nigra concluded that "the Emperor would not be sorry to find a pretext for remaining in the *status quo;* nor would Drouyn de Lhuys, who is already quite frightened by the possible consequences. . . ."[59] The Emperor thus seemed to be almost persuaded by the arguments of the Italians themselves that the convention was unwise and a danger to Italy. An Italian general most acquainted with frontier problems had even suggested that Italy could not carry out her guaranty. Of course it was good tactics on the Emperor's part to simulate a cooling of his ardor in order to frighten the Italians out of their bothersome tactics. On the other hand Drouyn de Lhuys' well known earlier dispositions, the Emperor's reputation for last minute retreats, and the danger of Clerical influence against the negotiations, all added a vivid reality and sincerity to the Emperor's recent tabling of the negotiations in his conversation with Nigra. Indeed, in order to counter the troublesome Italian demands, the Emperor and Drouyn de Lhuys began to insist on a better boundary for France east of Nice.[60]

[58] Same to same, Paris, 26 Aug. 1864, Minghetti, *Convenzione,* pp. 132-135.

[59] Nigra to Visconti, Paris, 28 Aug. 1864, *ibid.,* pp. 136-138.

[60] Visconti to Pepoli, Turin, 7 Sept. 1864, Carpi, *Biografie,* (Pepoli), III, 421-422.

Minghetti and Visconti-Venosta were greatly perturbed by these developments. The two telegrams, which Minghetti speedily dispatched, reflect Turin's alarm. To Menabria:

Dispatch from Nigra makes me suspect Emperor may take pretext to back out of concluded terms. Remember King has not refused, Ministry has accepted, and if worst comes to worst, convention drawn up by Pepoli must stand. You have full power to obtain this result.

To Nigra:

Look out not to lose an inch of territory we have won. To give up the treaty would be more serious for Italy than all the difficulties of its execution. King wants to improve it, but has not refused. We are decided to do everything possible to bring it to a successful conclusion.

This time Turin seemed to be seriously endeavoring to salvage the situation. But would it be too late? Menabrea's reply gave some encouragement without removing all cause of alarm.

Dispatch received. Wishes anticipated. Yesterday conference with Drouyn de Lhuys: I declared above all we accept treaty and King does not refuse, but wants modification to make it more enforceable. Prince Napoleon told me Emperor uncertain and perhaps willing to find pretext to withdraw proposal. My declaration has removed every pretext.[61]

Thus Menabrea revealed to the French the equivocalness of his position. He was in Paris purposely to plead the King's cause and he was at the same time undermining it by saying that Italy would accept the terms regardless of the success of his mission. It is no wonder that the French were disgusted and showed signs of abandoning the treaty. The depth of Menabrea's failure is shown in his telegraphic dispatch to Minghetti of 31 August.

Emperor gone without giving reply. Drouyn de Lhuys out of town. Am going to Chambéry, think useless to come back to Paris. However, if necessary, telegraph me.[62]

Menabrea was, however, in Paris until about 12 September. There he awaited the return of the Emperor with the expectations of another audience.

[61] Minghetti to Menabrea and Nigra, Turin, 28 Aug. 1864; Menabrea to Minghetti, Paris, 29 Aug. 1864; Minghetti, *Convenzione,* pp. 138-139.

[62] *Ibid.,* pp. 140-141.

On 8 September Minghetti again heard from Menabrea who had seen Rouher. The situation was as precarious as ever.

> Rouher advises hurrying signature of treaty to overcome contrary influences which may arise. It is presumed effect of treaty greater than is thought. He adopts my formula: capital transfer consists of transfer of royal residence, Parliament, diplomatic corps. The rest are internal details. . . . He would advise sending Pepoli to Paris at once with full powers. Rouher will try to have two year delay shortened. Once in Paris Pepoli will have to see him. He suggests my seeing Emperor before departure. He thinks guaranty against Austria natural consequence of treaty, but it does not seem it should be part of it (*objet de stipulations*).

The next day Menabrea again exhorted haste in concluding the treaty by the following warning:

> Drouyn de Lhuys is very much opposed, trying to make Emperor suspect our good faith. . . . Prince Napoleon insists that we hurry to finish it.

By the 11th Menabrea was able to have a final audience with the Emperor.

> He (the Emperor) wants, above all, declaration of capital transfer. As to mode of execution he leaves that to our good faith. His speech was benevolent. He seemed more than ever desirous of leaving Rome.[63]

By the 9th Minghetti had become absolutely convinced that the capital transfer would have to be accepted. If the King still would not agree to that clause, the treaty would be lost. In that case Minghetti felt that the main purpose of his ministry would have been nullified and he and his colleagues would be compelled to resign. He therefore put the question squarely before the King. At the same time he wrote Pepoli in Bologna asking him to come to Turin immediately.

The King finally replied that he could not agree to the capital transfer, but he asked his Prime Minister not to make his refusal a subject of resignation in the Council meeting which was to be held that morning. Just at this time Vimercati had an audience with Victor-Emmanuel. In a very diplomatic way the former recognized the feeling of dignity which impelled the

[63] 8, 9, 11 Sept. 1864, Minghetti, *Convenzione,* pp. 164-165.

King to refuse the transfer clause, but he showed how the country would ascribe the King's refusal to pure selfishness. Facing this unpleasant outlook, the King began to weaken just at the moment when a second note arrived from Minghetti which definitely threatened resignation. Then it was that Victor-Emmanuel, setting aside all his own personal affections, gave in. He remarked to Pepoli on his arrival that he would rather lose his crown than have the people think that he did not love the Union (*la Patria*).[64] Thereupon he notified Minghetti that he would accept the transfer clause providing Florence were chosen as Turin's successor.[65]

Pepoli was then sent off post-haste to Paris on 12 September with final instructions for both him and Nigra. Menabrea left Paris for Turin on the same day. Several important points were taken up in the final instructions. On the manner of including the capital transfer Minghetti and Visconti-Venosta asked: 1) that nothing should suggest outside pressure on Italy for the transfer, 2) that the transfer provision should be put in a secret protocol which would be destroyed as soon as the transfer had been passed by Parliament, 3) that France should publish nothing which might infer that the transfer was definitely connected with the treaty. Since there were reasons to suspect an Austrian attack as soon as the question of the capital transfer was undertaken, Turin again asked for an exchange of notes on joint defence against Austria. Furthermore, the Italian plenipotentiaries were to make it known that any foreign attempt to come to the assistance of the Pope by sending their troops into his territory would be considered as an act of war against Italy. Italy also wanted the assurance that France had not, and would not, make any arrangement which

[64] This statement by the King would seem to justify Minghetti in saying that the threatened resignation was not the principal cause of the King's change of mind. At least Minghetti would have been justified in saying that the threatened resignation was not the *only* cause for the King's acceptance. See Minghetti, *Convenzione,* p. 166.

[65] *Ibid.,* p. 166. Veroli, *loc. cit.,* pp. 1206-1208. Minghetti wired Menabrea: "To let you know King accepts treaty, provided capital is taken to Florence for exclusively strategical reasons. Pepoli leaves tonight with full powers. Tell Nigra." Minghetti, *Convenzione,* p. 166.

would weaken the force of this convention. Italy asked finally that France furnish an *act*, such as the removal of Francis II from Rome, which would reassure the Italians when the treaty went into effect.[66]

Pepoli arrived in Paris on Tuesday, 13 September, and the whole day was devoted to negotiations between Nigra, Pepoli, and Drouyn de Lhuys on the definitive terms of the convention. The first clause which read, "Italy engages *to respect* the present territory of the Holy Father," was changed to read, "Italy engages *not to attack*, etc."[67] The word *respect* might infer recognition; the word *attack* only involved a voluntary restriction on Italy's freedom of action. Article 4 on the Papal debt received another alteration. Previously it had read, "The Italian Government declares itself ready to enter into *direct* negotiations *with the Papal Government*. . . . " It was finally changed by omitting the above italicized words.[68] Other changes and decisions made in this important conference are well described in Nigra's report of the 14th:

> The wording of the treaty was definitively determined. The separate articles had already been agreed upon but to the third article was added the phrase *peace and order on the frontier*[69] to indicate the obligation of the Papal Government to prevent its territory and boundaries from becoming safety zones and encouragements for brigandage. . . . [The secret article] was made into a separate protocol in conformity with the Ministry's instructions. But the Emperor reserved for another time the question as to whether this document should be destroyed.
>
> It was understood with the Emperor and with Drouyn de Lhuys that, in the publications which the French Government should make in respect to the convention, it would be said that the Italian Government for reasons of strategy and internal administration had decided to transfer the capital of the Kingdom to another place, and that such a decision, having come to the knowledge of the French Government, facilitated the negotiations because it appeared

[66] Minghetti and Visconti to Nigra and Pepoli, Turin, 12 Sept. 1864, confidential instructions, Minghetti, *Convenzione*, pp. 167-173.

[67] M. B. d'Harcourt, *Les quatres ministères de M. Drouyn de Lhuys* (Paris, 1882), p. 160.

[68] Lhuys to Treelhard (?), Paris, 23 Oct. 1865, *Aff. Etr., C.P., Italie,* 363: pp. 184-185.

[69] This wording appeared also in Minghetti's earlier draft treaty and therefore leads one to question the exactness of his reproduction of that draft treaty.

of such a nature as to make it quite certain that the Italian Government was renouncing the use of all violent means for going to Rome. It was well understood that the treaty should mean no more nor less than what it said. . . .[70]

In the instructions Your Excellency requested that we ask a guaranty of our present territory against Austria in case she should attack it and that this guaranty could take the form of an exchange of notes. We had already on another occasion made a request to the Emperor in this regard and General Menabrea had also been instructed to make a similar request. The Emperor replied at one time, and later confirmed it again, that he could make no formal promise in this regard, but that Italy could in such an eventuality count on the traditions and tendency of his policy. This same language was confirmed again by the two ministers who were present at the St. Cloud conference.[71] As to the eventuality in which Spain or another minor power might decide to intervene in Rome, we declared very explicitly that we would consider that as a *casus belli,* and the Italian Government would take such action as would follow from such a decision. The Emperor asked: 'By what right?' We replied, 'By the right given to us by the principle of non-intervention, which Your Majesty is sanctioning at this very moment by a solemn treaty.'

Mr. Rouher strongly supported our reply, and the Emperor considered himself satisfied (*si tenne per satisfatto*). . . .[72]

But, having taken up every point in their official instructions, Nigra still found it necessary to discuss with Drouyn de Lhuys

[70] Pepoli likewise ended his account in even more specific terms than this: "It only remains for me to recall the declarations which we made verbally to the Emperor's Foreign Minister. It was thus agreed that the treaty says only what is written, that the transfer of the capital was a point of departure of the negotiations, but that it is an act dictated by strategical and administrative reasons; that the French Government declared that it sees in this fact a serious pledge of the intentions of Italy to give up the idea of occupying Rome as its capital by force; finally that Italy's policy can henceforth be summed up under two points:

"1. Inviolable respect for the principal of non-intervention.

"2. Constant and moral efforts to bring about a conciliation between the Pope and Italy on the basis of a free Church in a free State.

"Finally I am able to honestly affirm that neither the present Ministers nor the French Government could ever affirm that there exists one document written, or that there has been one word pronounced, by the Italian plenipotentiaries which might have given, explicitly or implicitly, to the capital transfer another sense than the one I have just attributed to it." Minghetti, *Convenzione,* pp. 176-177.

[71] These were Drouyn de Lhuys and Rouher.

[72] Thus the matters regarding the presentation of the transfer treaty, aid against Austria, the question of Spanish intervention, and the safeguarding of Italy's national aspirations were looked after to the extent that the French position would allow. Nigra to Minghetti, Paris, 14 (?) Dec. 1864, *ibid.,* pp. 174-175.

the question of the French demand for boundary adjustments near Nice. Pepoli reported as follows to Visconti-Venosta:

> The Foreign Minister wished at least that the line of the new boundary be designated in such a way that it go down from Sesia to Savona. But on Nigra's declaration that the Italian Government accepted this line in principle (*in massima*),[73] but that he did not want it stipulated in the treaty because it would be equivalent to the Imperial project already rejected, and after new and reiterated assurances which broke down all his objections, His Excellency, Drouyn de Lhuys, dexterously driven out of one trench after another, ended by leaving it entirely up to the decision of the Emperor.

Pepoli had already been granted a special audience with the Emperor for the morning of the 14th. This final conversation which he had with the Emperor at St. Cloud he reported that same evening to Visconti-Venosta as follows:

> Having been cordially welcomed this morning by His Majesty, I handed him the draft of the treaty, pointing out to him that since the opposition of his Foreign Minister had finally been overcome, all depended on him and that we all placed our hopes on his benevolence toward Italy.
>
> The Italian Government was disposed to make great sacrifices, but could not advance itself further without fear of compromising itself and the peace of the country.
>
> I renewed the declarations of Nigra to His Excellency, Mr. Drouyn de Lhuys, and I added that Italy would welcome the treaty with great enthusiasm; and that the extreme parties, enemies of the Government as they were of any rule of order, would find their weapons blunted which they intended to use to combat the authority of the Government and to decrease in the people its sympathy for the French Nation and its gratitude toward the Emperor.
>
> His Majesty, after having briefly looked over the treaty, reread carefully the additional modified articles and declared that he approved it, and it was determined that tomorrow the convention would be signed, and that it would be ratified as was stipulated.
>
> Thus were these difficult negotiations brought to an end. . . .[74]

That the Emperor did not insist on the Nice boundary adjustment may be an indication that he was using that question

[73] *In massima* in Italian may have two very different meanings: one, 'completely' or 'the maximum'; the other, 'in principle.' After consultation with several authorities on Italian the latter interpretation was accepted.

[74] 14 Sept. 1864, Carpi, *Biografie* (Pepoli), III, 422-423.

as a club over Italy's head to make her accept what had been originally in the treaty. But it is equally likely that he would have been glad to have had something to satisfy the French national sentiment at the same time.

Between the time of Menabrea's mission and Pepoli's return, however, a complete change had apparently occurred in the Emperor and Drouyn de Lhuys. From showing definite signs of dropping the negotiations, they had returned with benevolence, even enthusiasm, to the final adoption of the articles of the treaty. It is hard to account for changes in the moods of the Emperor or his ministers, but there is reason to believe that the Italian withdrawal of their demands and their recall of Menabrea had had some beneficial effect on the Emperor's attitude. Perhaps Pepoli by his return had been able to influence the Emperor to some extent. The English give us one suggestion, which, if it does not prove to be a possible cause of the favorable change in the Emperor, is at least worth mentioning. Grey, the British chargé, wrote to Russell the following account:

I have heard a curious story which I think worth repeating to Your Lordship as I have every reason to believe it to be quite true. It appears that when Prince Humbert came here (to Paris) the other day, Prince Napoleon thought it would be a good opportunity to have his boy christened, he having only been as yet baptized. King Victor-Emmanuel was to be one of the godfathers. Accordingly the Prince applied to the Archbishop of Paris to perform the ceremony but was met by a refusal, the Archbishop saying that he had positive instructions from the Pope not to christen the child if the excommunicated King was one of the godfathers. Upon this Prince Napoleon applied to the Emperor who wrote to Rome to ask that the Archbishop should be desired to perform the ceremony and the Empress also wrote to the same effect to the Pope himself. The result of these letters was that the Archbishop informed the Prince that he was now ready to christen the boy but upon one condition, viz., that the territories of which the Pope had been deprived should be restored to His Holiness so that the excommunication of Victor-Emmanuel might be revoked. Otherwise, the King being without the pale of the Church, it would be impossible to christen if his Majesty was godfather. There the matter remains, but it is said that it made the Emperor very angry and had no small share in clinching his determination to sign the convention.

I should mention that the details I have given above were obtained by Claremont from Prince Napoleon's own aide-de-camp yesterday.[75]

Matters of such a nature are known to have affected Napoleon, and it might have had some influence on his final decision to sign the convention. This seems more probable when it is considered that there was a general tendency in September to be unsympathetic toward the Pope. The French Foreign Office had a 73-page report drawn up to show how the Popes from 1831 to 1864 had consistently and repeatedly refused to carry out political reforms at the request of the French Government. This report ended with the following words:

> The last words of the Holy Father respecting the question of reforms, spoken to the French Ambassador in the month of September 1864, were these: 'Let them give me back my States and I will make reforms.'[76]

Drouyn de Lhuys had reference to this report when he wrote a severe note to the Vatican on 12 September. In this note he declared that the Vatican's political principles did not conform with those of France, and being assured of Italian guaranties, he was going to arrange with that Kingdom for the withdrawal of the French troops.[77] Although Sartiges was instructed not to deliver the note to Antonelli until the treaty had actually been signed, yet it is interesting to note that Drouyn de Lhuys had decided to go on and sign the treaty even before Pepoli had arrived for the final negotiations. The Pope's refusal to allow the christening of Prince Napoleon's son and his rejection of French requests for reforms may explain to some extent the Emperor's renewed benevolence toward Italy.

On the following day, Thursday, 15 September 1864, Nigra and Pepoli for Italy, and Drouyn de Lhuys for France, finally signed the Convention which had been in the process of negotiation for the greater part of three years and a half. The ceremony took place in the Quai d'Orsay after which Pepoli left as soon as possible for Turin.

[75] 29 Sept. 1864; Claremont to Cowley, Paris, 27 Sept. 1864; *R.P.*, LX.
[76] *Aff. Etr., M.D., Rome,* 124: (Sept. 1864).
[77] Lhuys to Sartiges, Paris, 12 Sept. 1864, *Doc. Guerre 1870,* IV, 127-134.

The terms of the short Convention of 15 September 1864 are given here in full with the appended protocol. The similarity of the terms to those negotiated with Cavour will be evident, and the modifications which were made in the negotiation of 1864 will also be noticeable.

Their Majesties, the Emperor of the French, and the King of Italy, having determined to conclude a convention, have named for their plenipotentiaries, to wit: (Drouyn de Lhuys, Pepoli, Nigra), who, after having communicated their full powers respectively, which were found in good and due form, have agreed to the following articles:

Article I. Italy undertakes not to attack the present territory of the Holy Father, and to prevent, by force if necessary, any attack on the said territory coming from without.[78]

Article II. France will withdraw her troops from the Papal States gradually and as fast as the army of the Holy Father shall be organized. Nevertheless, the evacuation will have to be carried out within two years.[79]

Article III. The Italian Government denies itself the right of protest against the organization of a Papal army composed even of foreign Catholic volunteers, sufficient[80] to maintain the authority of the Holy Father and order and peace in the interior as well as on the borders[81] of his States, provided that this force may not degenerate into a means of attack against the Italian Government.[82]

Article IV. Italy declares herself ready to enter[83] into an agreement for undertaking a proportional part of the debt of the former States of the Church.

Article V. The present convention will be ratified and its ratifications will be exchanged within fifteen days or sooner if possible.

In witness whereof the respective plenipotentiaries have signed the present convention and have set thereto the seal of their arms.

Made in duplicate in Paris, on the fifteenth day of the month of

[78] This was not exactly an Italian recognition of his right to rule over these states. It however obligated the Italians to stop any attack by any band of men by land or sea against the actual territory of the Pope.

[79] This suggested that appreciable evacuation might take place before the end of the two years.

[80] No definite number was mentioned out of deference to the independent status of the Papal Government.

[81] This would indicate a Papal obligation to prevent brigandage.

[82] This does not mean that the Pope might not use that force as a means of attack against the Italian Government, but that the Italian Government could protest whenever a force for such a use were organized.

[83] Italy insisted on determining her financial obligation for the future. She accepted the principle of an obligation and left it an open matter whether the negotiation would be with Rome or with Paris.

September in the year of our Lord one thousand eight hundred and sixty-four.

(L.S.) Drouyn de Lhuys
(L.S.) Nigra
(L.S.) Pepoli

Proctocol following the Convention[84] signed in Paris between France and Italy, respecting the evacuation of the Papal States by French troops.

The convention signed this day between their Majesties the Emperor of the French and the King of Italy will have executory value only when His Majesty the King of Italy shall have decreed[85] the transfer of the capital of the Kingdom in the place which will be later determined by His aforesaid Majesty. This transfer will have to be carried out within six months of the date of the said convention.[86]

The present protocol will have the same force in value as the above-mentioned convention. It will be ratified, and its ratifications will be exchanged at the same time as those of the said convention.

Made in duplicate in Paris, 15 September 1864.[87]

(L.S.) Drouyn de Lhuys
(L.S.) Nigra
(L.S.) Pepoli

[84] This protocol was made separate from the Convention so that it might not appear that Italy was negotiating with a foreign country in regard to a domestic matter. This was done as a result of the last instructions from Turin and became the final form of the Nigra-Minghetti correspondence on the subject.

[85] It was thought at first that according to the Italian Constitution the King had a right to decree the change of capital without Parliament. But to have transferred the capital without Parliament would have given the measure a semblance of a temporary expedient, and also would have ignored Parliament's control of appropriations. In Chapter VIII it will be seen that they decided to have Parliament determine the transfer through its appropriation power.

[86] Because of the delay caused in obtaining the Italian Parliament's approval this was changed (see Chapter VIII) so that the six-month and two-year periods began simultaneously with the date of the decree of the capital transfer after a favorable vote by Parliament.

[87] For printed copies of the convention and its protocol see A. de Clercq, *Recueil des traités de la France* (22 v. Paris, 1880), IX, 129-130; *Doc. Guerre 1870*, IV, 366-367; *Livre Jaune*, (1864), pp. 43-45; Minghetti, *Convenzione*, pp. 178-180.

CHAPTER VIII

THE CAPITAL TRANSFER AND INTERPRETATIONS

MINGHETTI had scarcely received news from Pepoli that the treaty was about to be signed when he began to take immediate steps for arranging the transfer of the capital in such a way as to have it appear a spontaneous action of the Italian Government. During the last days of the spring session in July an arrangement had been made with Mordini to speak in the Parliament in favor of the change of capital from Turin to some other place in Italy. This he had done, and it had had the advantage of making it appear that Italy was debating the question before the Convention had been drawn up and signed.[1] Now at the last moment Minghetti made plans to call a council of war and have the leading generals recommend the withdrawal of the capital from Turin and its establishment in Florence for purely strategical reasons. All of the generals, including La Marmora, were requested to be present at a council of war on Sunday, 18 September.[2]

La Marmora replied that it was impossible for him to be in Turin by that time and he would therefore plan to be back when his leave of absence terminated. The General was evidently taking advantage of his remoteness in order to keep an entirely hands-off attitude in respect to the Convention. One phrase in his telegraphic reply caused considerable comment: La Marmora added, "I rejoice with you that the King has accepted the project in question."[3] Some saw in this the General's approval of the Convention; others thought it was a rather sarcastic reflection inferring that they were to be congratulated upon being able to persuade the King to approve such an impossible treaty. Minghetti rejected both of the above inferences and did La

[1] Minghetti, *Convenzione,* pp. 61-62.
[2] Minghetti to La Marmora, Turin, 15 Sept. 1864, *ibid.,* p. 181.
[3] "Je me félicite avec vous de ce que le Roi a accepté le projet en question." *Ibid.*

Marmora the likely justice of accepting the statement as just a form of courtesy.[4]

The council of war met at the appointed time with Prince Eugene of Savoy as chairman. The generals decided unanimously that the capital should be transferred to Florence. The wording of the Prince's covering letter and the resolution of the council are significant. Prince Eugene's communication to Minghetti said: "The voting [was] unanimous in recognizing Florence as the only possible capital *at the present time (oggigiorno)* for Italy which would be the most strategical in a military sense."[5] This attitude of the possible temporary nature of Florence as capital was more specific in the actual report of the council.

> All the members of the committee are . . . unanimous in the belief that of all the principal cities of Italy, Florence, because of its central location, its protection by the Apennines, and its sufficient distance from the sea, is found to be in the best strategical position for transferring there the capital of the Kingdom *for the present (presentamente)*.[6]

On the next day, 19 September, the Government informed the King of the decision of the generals and asked him to call a special session of Parliament for 5 October to obtain the appropriations for the transfer of the capital. They took care to tell the King that they considered that no parliamentary ratification in addition to the royal ratification was needed for either the treaty or its secret protocol because those called for no appropriation of money. One statement, however, in the call for the Parliament is interesting for the veiled way the Italian statesmen tried to indicate the transfer to Florence as a step to Rome.

> Another result [of the transfer] will be that the effectiveness of the moral means which Italy will use towards Rome will be as much more sure, when the seat of the Government is nearer, as the re-

[4] Minghetti, *Convenzione*, p. 181.

[5] The italics of the above quotation are the author's and indicate the significance of the facts that the generals would not admit that Florence would *always* be "the only possible capital" or that they would venture on the subject beyond their *military* sphere.

[6] Report of the council of war, 18 Sept. 1864, Minghetti, *Convenzione*, p. 183.

lations will be more frequent and the community of interests and customs will be older and more intimate.[7]

In this paragraph there was not the slightest suggestion of the renunciation of Rome, nothing more than the renunciation of forceful means to that end.

During the period of negotiations the secret had been well kept in both Paris and Turin. Malaret, the French Minister in Turin, wrote home on 26 August that he noted a definite increase of interest in Italy on the Roman question, but there was not the slightest trace in his confidential dispatch of a suspicion that a convention was actually in the process of negotiation. Drouyn de Lhuys had not informed him, and there was evidently not even the slightest rumor in the Piedmontese city.[8] Pasolini himself declared that he had "never seen a political secret so well kept."[9] Later when the secret was revealed, Cowley remarked that the secret had been so well kept that even Rothchild was completely ignorant of it and had later come to him for information on it when rumors began.[10]

However closely the secret may have been kept during the negotiations, it was revealed almost immediately after the signature of the treaty. Pepoli arrived in Turin on the evening of the 16th and on the morning of the 17th was astounded to find news of it published in the *Opinione*. Minghetti and Visconti-Venosta were very much embarrassed over the fact that this revelation would interfere with their plan of procedure and it would also make it appear that the Italian Government had prematurely announced the news in spite of reciprocal promises by Italy and France to further secrecy.[11] But this first announcement does not seem to have conveyed the idea of the capital transfer.[12]

The news of the unauthorized announcement spread rapidly.

[7] Report to the King, 19 Sept. 1864, *Aff. Etr., C.P., Italie,* 360: pp. 329-330.

[8] Malaret to Lhuys, Turin, 22 Aug. 1864, *ibid.,* pp. 185-189.

[9] Pasolini, *Memorie,* I, 418-419.

[10] Cowley to Russell, Paris, 19 Sept. 1864, *F.O., France,* 1533: no. 80.

[11] Veroli, *loc. cit.,* XXXI, 102.

[12] Elliot to Russel, Turin, 17 Sept. 1864, *R.P.,* LXX.

On the 18th it was discussed in the Roman journal, *Gazzetta del Popolo*, and the news of the capital transfer began to circulate at almost this same time. It was later found by investigation that the head of the Bureau of Foreign Affairs[13] in Turin had revealed the contents of Nigra's report of the 15th to the editor (*direttore*) of the *Opinione*.[14]

News having spread from Italy about the Franco-Italian Convention, the French Government could not very well keep silence without drawing the suspicions of the French public upon it. Therefore Drouyn de Lhuys informed Turin as follows on the 21st:

> The premature revelations in the Italian press in spite of the mutually promised secrecy obliges us in turn to give to the public by means of the papers some explanations in regard to the concluded arrangement.[15]

Already on the 19th the *Constitutionnel* was allowed to prepare the way by a statement that although it had no official notice of the Convention, it was sure that the French Government had not considered the existing situation as permanent nor would the Government have abandoned the existing situation without "safeguarding" the interests which it had had for so long under its care.[16] The Government's announcements referred to in Drouyn de Lhuys' notice to Turin appeared in the *Constitutionnel* of the 22nd. It was published over the name of Paulin Limagrac. The article began by noting the better disposition in Italy which had abandoned its radical tendencies for a much more moderate outlook.

> Also when the Italian Government, concerned with the necessity of organizing the new state and for strategical, political, and administrative considerations thinking it necessary to decide on the choice of a capital, announced its decision to transfer the seat of the central authority of the Kingdom to another city than Turin; the

[13] Capo del Gabinetto degli Affari Esteri.

[14] Veroli, *loc. cit.*, XXXI, 102. *Doc. Guerre 1870,* IV, 141, note no. 4. Malaret to Lhuys, Turin, 19 Sept. 1864, *Aff. Etr., C.P., Italie,* 360: pp. 223-230; *Doc. Guerre 1870,* IV, 141-144.

[15] Lhuys to Malaret, Paris, 21 Sept. 1864, *Aff. Etr., C.P., Italie,* 360: p. 232. *Doc. Guerre 1870,* IV, 147.

[16] *Constitutionnel,* 19 Sept. 1864.

Government of the Emperor thought the moment had arrived to examine and discuss the conditions which would permit it to leave Rome in complete security.

The article continued to outline briefly the terms of the treaty without mentioning the protocol. The purpose of the protocol, however, was taken care of by the above quotation in regard to the intention to transfer the capital.[17]

The disappointment of the Turinese on hearing of the transfer clause, which Minghetti had feared might appear, far exceeded his most pessimistic apprehensions. Malaret well describes the early effect of this news upon the populace of Turin.

> If the perspective of the evacuation of Rome after a maximum delay of two years caused here a general satisfaction, such was not the case when it was known that this advantage, so earnestly desired for so long a time, was to cost the city of Turin even its title of provisional capital of the Italian Kingdom. In their hearts most of the men belonging to the old provinces thought surely that this 'provisional' would be indefinitely maintained and none were seriously prepared for the effort of patriotism which in the name of general interest, the King's Government and the King himself unexpectedly is asking of them today. . . . At the moment of writing it is certain that the city of Turin is very far from appreciating the diplomatic success which the Cabinet has just obtained and that the general feeling, at least in the public at large, is one of deep stupefaction and bitter deception.

The French Minister went on to describe the efforts of the Ministry to gain the addition of Lanza and Sella, both Piedmontese, to its number in order to make the project more acceptable to the local people. But these men, while offering to support the measure individually in Parliament, like La Marmora, declined to accept the proffered portfolios. The French Minister was assured, however, that the aid of these men to the cause would very likely be more valuable in the Parliament if they were not, than if they were, a part of the Cabinet.[18] The evidences of Turin's resentment on the 19th were mild in comparison to those which were to follow. On the evening of the 20th a crowd of about 2000 paraded the streets. Arriving at the Foreign

[17] *Constitutionnel,* 22 Sept. 1864.
[18] Malaret to Lhuys, Turin, 19 Sept. 1864, see above note no. 14.

Office they shouted, "Down with the Ministry!", accompanying their shouts with hisses and whistles. Then they moved over under the windows of Pepoli's rooms at Hotel Feder to shout, "Death to Marquis Pepoli!", with more hissing and whistling.[19]

Pepoli wrote to Prince Napoleon and the Emperor in great haste that they allow nothing to be published in the French press which would show any evidences of French pressure on the Italians in regard to the capital transfer. The Foreign Office made the same request through Malaret to Drouyn de Lhuys. The publication in the *Constitutionnel* of the 22nd showed an evidence of French care on that delicate matter.[20]

If the anger of the Turin populace was evidenced on the 20th only by demonstrations, it became aggravated on the evening of the 21st by actual rioting and violence. Armed with sticks and stones a mob tried to disarm some troops who were stationed on guard near the Piazza del Castello. Several soldiers were hurt and ten men and one woman were killed. Order was temporarily restored but what the ministers had never dreamed of in their blackest moods had happened: blood had been shed, and in the center of the "Anglo-Saxons of Italy."[21]

There were evidences of governmental lack of foresight and preparation. They had allowed the parading of the previous night; they had brought in very few extra troops for the emergency; and finally they had depended too much on the National Guard of Turin who responded in very few numbers and with no enthusiasm.[21] Further ineptness was to be noticed in the conduct of the Government before the crisis was over.

During the day of the 22nd all was quiet. Consternation from the ghastly results of the fighting caused a temporary lull. In this inauspicious interval the Municipal Council of Turin met. There was severe blame on the Government for the deaths

[19] Pepoli to Prince Napoleon, Turin. 20 (?) Sept. 1864; same to Napoleon III, Turin, 21 Sept. 1864; Veroli, *loc. cit.*, XXXI, 106-107. Malaret to Lhuys, Turin, 21 Sept. 1864, *Aff. Etr., C.P., Italie,* 360: p. 233; *Doc. Guerre 1870,* IV, 149.

[20] See references in note no. 19 above.

[21] Malaret to Luhys, Turin, 22 Sept. 1864, (11:00 A.M.), *Aff. Etr., C.P., Italie,* 360: p. 235. *Doc. Guerre 1870,* IV, 150-151.

of the evening before, and a decidedly disgruntled attitude toward the whole transfer arrangement. When Menabrea, as member of the Council, tried to speak in the name of the King, he was silenced by the presiding magistrate. It was claimed that in the Council he was only a councilman and not a minister of the King. This apparent lack of courtesy and the evidence of sympathy for the municipality was claimed to have encouraged among the more violent of the populace the attitude of resentment for the casualties of the previous evening.[22]

Thus began again on the evening of the 22nd what was to be the last and the worst of the Turin disorders. A large mob of excited Turinese began to enter the Piazza St. Carlo from the various corner entrances. More troops had been hurried into the town during the day, a part of which were stationed around the police headquarters (*questura*) which faces on this square. The mob began to hurl stones at the troops, who, manœuvering so as to prevent any more rioters from entering the square, found themselves divided on two sides of the public place. Apparently becoming panicky because of a lack of firm and skillful direction, the troops opened fire on the people from both sides of the square. The result was twenty-two dead; but worst of all, seventeen of the twenty-two were soldiers themselves. Evidently in their fright they had fired on each other from opposite sides of the square.[23]

Such violence could not continue very long with such evidences of clumsy direction among the forces of law and order without a reckoning for the responsible ministry which directed the public powers. The King, who had remained in the country during most of these disturbances, became convinced of the necessity for the resignation of the Ministry. Victor-Emmanuel's reflections on the situation were later expressed to Mr. Rothan in the following terms:

> They (the Turinese) acted rather badly and in so doing were in the wrong. But it's the Ministry's fault if events turned out so badly. I traced for them step by step an excellent course which would have

[22] Same to same, Turin, 23 Sept. 1864, *Aff. Etr.*, *C.P.*, *Italie*, 360: p. 253.
[23] Same to same, Turin, 23 Sept. 1864, (11:50 A.M.), *ibid.*, p. 253.

conciliated everybody if they had followed it. They did not wish to listen to me and they are suffering the consequences. . . .[24]

In this state of mind on 23 September after the tragedy of Piazza St. Carlo the King sent La Rocca to Minghetti asking him informally to have the Ministry resign. Minghetti resented the fact that the King had not addressed him directly and refused to resign without an express and direct command of the King. This the King gave immediately and the whole Cabinet resigned.[25] Thus within three years three Italian ministries and one French foreign minister had been compelled to resign because of the Roman question. Victor-Emmanuel quickly summoned La Marmora to form a new cabinet, which task the General obediently accepted. In accepting the resignation of the outgoing ministry the King benevolently observed

that in coming to the decision to do without their services, he had had no intention of disavowing what he had done in concert with them; that consequently the maintenance of the Convention of 15 September could not be questioned. But . . . as a result of events out of their and his control, the position of the cabinet had become difficult, and in certain respects, bad; that a new ministry could, while still carrying on the policy, avoid further bloodshed, and that it was solely in the interest of humanity that he had thought it better to call to his councils men, no more capable nor devoted, but less immediately compromised than they.[26]

After this important governmental change Turin became quiet and did not again disturb the peace until the following February after the transfer of the capital had been decreed. But there was a hostile reaction to this change in the provinces. Pepoli's observation from Bologna was that the news of the ministerial change was received as a shock. He feared that the November elections would be accompanied by cries of "Down with Turin." The French Consul in Milan reported that the ministerial change

has produced here the most unfortunate impression. Agitation is beginning to appear in the populace. . . . One should not be surprised in the present state of mind in Milan if they soon begin to shout

[24] Rothan to Lhuys, Turin, 31 Dec. 1864, *Aff. Etr., C.P., Italie,* 361: pp. 409-410.

[25] Malaret to Lhuys, Turin, 23 Sept. 1864, (6:34 P.M.), *ibid.,* 360: p. 254.

[26] Malaret to Lhuys, Turin, 25 Sept. 1864, *ibid.,* no. 85. *Doc. Guerre 1870,* IV, 174-177.

in the streets, 'Down with Turin,' 'Long live France and Rome. . . .' The result is to give the outgoing ministry an unexpected popularity and provoke in all the large cities of Italy a sentiment favorable to the Convention.[27]

Drouyn de Lhuys' first communication to La Marmora, even before the latter had been able to select his colleagues, was to the effect of arranging for the publication of the treaty. The French Foreign Minister felt that it was not advisable to keep the public in the dark as to the actual terms of the instrument.[28] This French suggestion would also seem to indicate a nervousness on the part of Drouyn de Lhuys as to whether La Marmora would continue the treaty. La Marmora's pessimistic attitude toward the treaty during his Paris mission was still fresh in Drouyn de Lhuys' mind. While the treaty remained secret, La Marmora might perhaps try to revise it at least. Once the treaty was published, he would be more or less committed to it. If this request did nothing more, it would at least draw a reply from the new Italian minister and reveal his attitude on the whole subject.

In a conversation with Malaret, La Marmora objected to the publication and hinted that he desired a slight modification to enable Italy to have more time to transfer her capital. Malaret immediately discouraged any alteration since such action would give false hopes to the resisting Piedmontese. La Marmora assured Malaret that he would take care of the Piedmontese, and he also stated that he would execute the entire treaty in spite of his opposition to some of the clauses. All he wanted was a slight extension of time before the capital was transferred.[29]

The Emperor's Foreign Minister was prompt in opposing any change in the Convention. To give in then would perhaps be only opening the door to further approaches and requests for revision.

[27] Same to same, Turin, 24 Sept. 1864; Defly to Lhuys, Milan, 24 Sept. 1864, *Doc. Guerre 1870,* IV, 168-172, 176 note. Pepoli to Prince Napoleon, Bologna, 23 Sept. 1864, Veroli, *loc. cit.,* XXXI, 108.

[28] Lhuys to Malaret, Paris, 26 Sept. 1864, *Doc. Guerre 1870,* IV, 179.

[29] Malaret to Lhuys, Turin, 27 Sept. 1864, *Aff. Etr., C.P., Italie,* 360: p. 286-296. *Doc. Guerre 1870,* IV, 188-192.

> It was the Court of Turin which told us on its own initiative that it intended to transfer its capital. It was the one which began conversations on the evacuation of the Roman territory. All the clauses of the Convention stand together. We could neither abandon nor modify any of them.[30]

Nigra, who had returned to Turin to confer with the new ministry, was sent back to Paris on 29 September to explain the Italian position to Drouyn de Lhuys. What he said to the French Foreign Minister was somewhat as follows: For the ratification of the Convention and the protocol the King's assent was sufficient since the protocol did not provide for the transfer but was only the hyphen between the Convention and the transfer. At the time of signing, the Italian negotiators had thought that the King alone could also decree the transfer of the capital. La Marmora, however, wanted Parliament's consent and needed Parliament's appropriation of funds for the transfer. Because of the ministerial change Parliament's meeting would have to be postponed from the first to the last part of October. This would reduce Italy's period of six months to arrange the transfer to one of five months and increase the administrative and political difficulties considerably. Therefore Nigra proposed that both the six month period for the transfer and the two year period for the evacuation be counted from the day when the capital transfer is decreed by the Italian Parliament. Nigra showed how this would not make it appear to the Italian Parliament that it was being rudely pushed in its deliberations. On the other hand, being anxious to obtain evacuation as soon as possible, the Parliament would not delay very long on the transfer question.

Drouyn de Lhuys being convinced of the reasonableness and sincerity of the Italian request, consented to the newly proposed interpretation in spite of his earlier opposition to any change.[31] This assent was made easier by the fact that the Convention did not really have to be altered. It only necessitated an agreed in-

[30] Lhuys to Malaret, Paris, 28 Sept. 1864, *Aff. Etr., C.P., Italie,* 360: p. 298. *Doc. Guerre 1870,* IV, 193.

[31] Lhuys to Malaret, Paris, 3 Oct. 1864, *Aff. Etr., C.P., Italie,* 360: pp. 317-318. *Doc. Guerre 1870,* IV, 214-215. *Livre Jaune,* (1864), pp. 51-52.

terpretation of the time clause. This interpretation was taken care of by the following declaration signed by Drouyn de Lhuys which thereby became an integral part of the Convention:

In the terms of the Convention of 15 September 1864 and of the annexed protocol the period for the transfer of the capital of the Kingdom of Italy had been determined as six months from the date of the said Convention, and the evacuation of the Roman States by the French troops was to be carried out within a period of two years from the date of the decree which would have authorized the transfer.

The Italian plenipotentiaries supposed then that this measure could be carried out by a decree which would be made immediately by His Majesty the King of Italy. In this hypothesis, the beginning of both periods might have been almost simultaneous, and the Italian Government would have had the six months judged necessary for transferring its capital.

But on the one hand the Turin Cabinet thought that such an important measure needed the approval of the Chambers and the passage of a law; on the other hand the ministerial change in Italy caused a delay in the meeting of Parliament from 5 to 24 October. In these circumstances the beginning of the period formally agreed to would no longer leave sufficient time for the capital transfer.

The Imperial Government, desirous of assisting any arrangement which without altering the terms agreed to on 15 September, would be helpful in facilitating their execution, consents that the period of six months for the transfer of Italy's capital, as well as the period of two years for the evacuation of the Papal territory, begin at the date of the royal decree sanctioning the law which is going to be presented to the Italian Parliament.

Made in duplicate in Paris, 3 October 1864.

(Signed) Drouyn de Lhuys[32]

La Marmora was contented with this declaration. He wrote Minghetti:

I do not believe we can expect any more from the French Government; and I confess that if I had thought that the Emperor intended to explain himself so clearly, I would have been more easily reassured about the possible difficulties to be encountered in executing the Convention.[33]

[32] Additional declaration to the Convention of 15 September 1864. *Aff. Etr., C.P., Italie,* 360: pp. 319-320. *Doc. Guerre 1870,* IV, 367-368. *Livre Jaune,* (1864), pp. 52-53.

[33] It is possible that he also had reference here to Drouyn de Lhuys' assurances that Italy would not be held responsible for individual escapes across the frontier. La Marmora to Minghetti, Turin, 4 Oct. 1864, Minghetti, *Convenzione,* p. 182.

While this declaration was under discussion in Paris, La Marmora had succeeded in forming his Cabinet. He himself took the Ministry of Foreign Affairs while three other Piedmontese, including Lanza, Sella, and Petitti, took respectively the ministries of Interior, Finance, and War.[34] Thus a predominantly Piedmontese Cabinet was to accept and enforce the Convention, fulfilling Minghetti's desire but under circumstances unfortunate for himself.

On the same day that the Ministry was announced (30 September) a formal declaration was published in the *Gazzetta Ufficiale* which made it very clear to the Turinese that the new government intended to accept the recent Convention in its entirety.

> On assuming the direction of public affairs in the midst of such grave circumstances the new Ministry feels the obligation of informing the Nation in the clearest and most explicit terms its intentions regarding the predominating question . . . of public opinion.
>
> It accepts the Convention recently stipulated with the Imperial French Government for the withdrawal of the French troops from the Papal territory together with the condition for the transfer of the capital to another place.

The announcement continued by favoring help to Turin for any losses incurred by the sudden change as long as such aid did not take the form of "extending the period fixed by the Convention for the evacuation of the French troops from the Papal territory."[35] This was a palatable way of saying that such aid would not be in the form of delaying the transfer, since the beginnings of the intervening periods before the transfer and the evacuation were identical.

In the interval between the formation of the new Italian Ministry and the meeting of the Italian Parliament the Vatican was given the occasion to learn of the Convention and react to its contents. With the premature revelation of its terms in Turin Drouyn de Lhuys instructed Sartiges to present his note of 12 September to the Vatican Government which announced the ne-

[34] *Aff. Etr., C.P., Italie,* 360: p. 314. *Doc. Guerre 1870,* IV, 204-205.
[35] *Gazzetta Ufficiale,* Turin, 30 Sept. 1864.

gotiation of that treaty. "The oral comments which you will add will have to be worded in benevolent, friendly terms devoid of recriminations."[36]

Sartiges executed his instructions first in an interview with Cardinal Antonelli on 23 September. On this occasion, as also on the occasion of the audience with the Pope, it can not be said that the French Ambassador avoided entirely the use of unnecessarily harsh and unsympathetic language. Both conversations were in the nature of lectures to the ruler of the Papal States and his advisor. In breaking the news "gently" to the Cardinal Secretary of State, Sartiges declared:

> All Europe has been waiting now for thirty years for internal reforms in Rome; France for fifteen years through her legislature and her ambassadors has constantly asked you to grant them.
>
> 'To be more exact,' the Cardinal interrupted, 'you should say that we have promised reforms as soon as we receive again the Legations.'
>
> [Sartiges] Since 1859 the Emperor had at one time proposed the presidency of an Italian Confederation to the Pope . . . , at another time the guaranty of his reduced territory. You have imposed impossible conditions to the execution of reforms, you have said *no* to the offer of the presidency, *no* to guaranties offered time and again, you have announced that you will always say *no,* and that you have time to wait, we have not; France can not have her strength and her action scattered to the four corners of the earth. She can not remain in a state of semi-hostility toward powers whose interests and sympathies are so similar to her own and who accuse her of staying in Rome for selfish reasons.[37] We are stationed here to defend the temporal power; now that we think it carefully safeguarded by the important fact of the transfer of the capital of the Kingdom of Italy from Turin to Florence and by the guaranties in the Convention of 15 September, we say to you in a friendly spirit[38] that it seems to us, and we hope it seems to you, that the time has come for us to get out.[39]

Antonelli nevertheless expressed his surprise and bewilderment, thought that Italy would not live up to her word, looked to

[36] Lhuys to Sartiges, Paris, 20 Sept. 1864, *Doc. Guerre 1870,* IV, 144-145.

[37] This shows a desire to have the Pope think at least that France needed to keep the friendship of Italy and England to preserve her diplomatic influence. Evidence seems to indicate considerable sincerity in such a statement.

[38] ?

[39] Sartiges to Lhuys, Rome, 23 Sept. 1864, *Aff. Etr., C.P., Rome,* 1028: pp. 79-86. *Doc. Guerre 1870,* IV, 157-161. D'Harcourt, *Quatre ministères,* pp. 192-196.

Providence for the return of the lost territory, and ended by saying that he would give his official opinion after the Pope and Cardinals had given the matter their consideration.[39]

On the following day the French Ambassador had a chance to harass the erysipelatic Pontiff in a manner to cause one to marvel at the self-control of an old man so given to fits of anger.

I (Sartiges) repeated to the Holy Father, who listened to me with attention and kindness, the observations contained in Your Excellency's dispatch; at the same time I presented to His Holiness a copy of the document, which he began to read aloud, stopping from time to time to give the following comments. Thus at the mention that at the beginning of 1859 he proposed to end the occupation at the end of that year, he stopped to say: 'That's true, but they told me then that the presence of the French and Austrians would cause a European war and naturally I agreed to the departure to avoid that eventuality.' He went on reading. At the paragraph which spoke of intervention being against one of the principles of public law, he stopped, looked at me smiling in a questioning manner, and said: 'Against your modern public law.'

The Pope doubted the good faith of Italy, in spite of Sartiges' insistence that it was backed by the word of France. He saw no possibility of raising an army sufficient to protect himself because of his low financial situation. Sartiges said that the debt clause of the Convention would relieve His Holiness of a great financial burden which would enable him to increase his army. The Pope here refused to negotiate with Italy on the debt because of the tacit renunciation of his states contained in such a procedure.

'But, Holy Father, what a situation you would be in if the Italian Government, through the mediation of France, put at the disposal of the holders of the Roman debt 15 or 20 million francs which you would refuse to accept while the clergy continued to go from thatched hut to thatched hut gathering in your name the widow's and orphan's pence . . . !' This thought seemed to make a marked impression on the Pope and he had nothing to say. . . .

Sartiges went on to tell the Pope that Catholic opinion still revered him personally and favored the principle of the temporal power but they were not concerned over the extent of the territory.

In the course of the conversation the Holy Father said again: 'I know the condition of Europe, it is deplorable, I admit the exigencies of certain situations,[40] I am still grateful to the Emperor for all he has done for me in the last sixteen years, and for all that he will certainly still do for me, but I admit that this news came like a bolt out of a clear sky. Still we have two years ahead of us. That's a lot. We'll have to see what becomes of Italy [during that time].'

'What are the words which Your Holiness authorizes me to write to Paris as the résumé of the interview which you had deigned to grant me?'

'Write,' he replied, 'that the Pope can not give ground for great hopes, but he will study carefully the question once he knows it more in detail than he does at present, and that he will avail himself of the advice of his Cardinals, and that then he will let you know his opinion on the Convention if you still request it, for up to now all has been done without my knowledge, and I will thank you to continue its execution without my participation.[41] I would prefer to remain like a man on his balcony watching it pass by.'[42]

Drouyn de Lhuys' reply to Sartiges was an attempt to moderate his gruff attitude toward the Roman Court.

Do not demand nor provoke a reply. Give benevolent explanations. Avoid polemics. Do not expose yourself to recriminations or explicit protests by trying to get their approval.[43]

Following the above telegraphic dispatch went another detailed dispatch by mail which expressed the same sentiment. This added, however, a desire that the Pope consult his Cardinals individually rather than in Consistory. There was a fear of a Papal consistorial allocution which would disturb French public opinion.[44]

On the occasion of another interview Antonelli complained because Rome was not consulted but recognized the possibility of France negotiating with Italy on the debt in the place of the Vatican. Sartiges explained that France and Italy had negotiated the treaty without the Vatican because neither the Vatican could recognize the *status quo* by negotiations between them-

[40] French isolation (?).

[41] This was thought to be a suggestion for France to arrange the debt payment with Italy.

[42] Sartiges to Lhuys, Rome, 24 Sept. 1864, *Aff. Etr., C.P., Rome,* 1028: pp. 88-96. *Doc. Guerre 1870,* IV, 163-167. D'Harcourt, *Quatre ministères,* pp. 196-200.

[43] Lhuys to Sartiges, Paris, 28 Sept. 1864, *Doc. Guerre 1870,* IV, 192.

[44] The full document is reproduced only in the following places: *Aff. Etr., C.P., Rome,* 1028: pp. 118-120. *Doc. Guerre 1870,* IV, 210-212.

selves, but by a Franco-Italian negotiation they could all acquiesce in it without committing themselves.[45]

The "man on his balcony" evinced a desire, however, to sit as a spectator of the Italian debates before he gave any indication of approval or disapproval of the Convention. If the Italians then openly renounced Rome as capital, he would be convinced of their sincerity. France seemed to approve heartily this expectant attitude, but warned the Pope that the debates might still talk of Rome because it was too soon for all that discussion to die down. On the other hand France made all kinds of efforts to quiet such talk in Turin, and La Marmora consented to keep quiet unless forced to make an out-and-out statement. When, by the exchange of notes, France and Italy agreed to reserve their respective freedom of action in case of a revolt in Rome, the Pope and Antonelli both expressed more satisfaction with the Convention but felt sure that the freedom of action meant French interference on behalf of the Pope in case of such internal revolt.[46]

France did not encourage this unsolicited interpretation, however, and on the next occasion Sartiges told Antonelli

> that once the French troops were withdrawn, the Papal Government would henceforth be held responsible for its own acts; that His Holiness and his Prime Minister had both ruled long enough to know the material, moral, and political needs of the country and that the task of doing what would need to be done in the interest of the Papal Government would fall to them alone; and finally that our rôle as affectionate and respectful advisors would cease on the day when we assured the Holy See the security of its frontiers from without and its full and complete freedom of action from within.[47]

As a result of the whole affair the Pope was not greatly reassured. When the French Auditor of the Rote tried to assure the Pope of the continuously benevolent dispositions of Drouyn de Lhuys toward the Holy See, the "man on the balcony" began

[45] Sartiges to Lhuys, Rome, 1, 8 Oct., 1864, *Aff. Etr., C.P., Rome,* 1028: pp. 121-127, 152-156. *Doc. Guerre 1870,* IV, 230-232.

[46] *Aff. Etr., C.P., Rome,* 1028: pp. 161-164, 165-169, 178-179, 182-184, 196-197, 217; *Italie,* 360: 348-353. *Doc. Guerre 1870,* IV, 241-243, 243-246, 258-259, 254-258, 320-321, 322-324, 336.

[47] Sartiges to Lhuys, Rome, 8 Nov. 1864, *Aff. Etr., C.P., Rome,* 1028: p. 212. *Doc. Guerre 1870,* V, 12.

to express fear of the next possible scene which might "pass by." "But who will be your foreign minister when the time comes to execute the instrument?"[48]

Austria also was adversely impressed by the news of the Convention. Its Paris Ambassador, Mr. Mülien, was instructed to object to the negotiations of the Convention without having consulted Rome and the Catholic Powers. Furthermore, he was to object to the fact that France was actually recognizing Florence as a part of Italy since Austria was still interested in the cause of the deposed Duke of Tuscany.

Drouyn de Lhuys replied that nothing was negotiated in the Convention but what touched purely French and Italian affairs. Therefore it was not expected that France would consult others especially since Austria had frequently declined to coöperate in a solution of the Roman question. If Rome objected that she had not been consulted, it was for her to approach France on the matter. In regard to Florence

> I begged Mr. Mülien to be kind enough to notice that for four years the Italian Government has been carrying out *de facto* all the acts of sovereignty in Florence and that the position *de jure* of any person was not changed because a Government transferred its capital to a city where it enjoyed the exercise up to that time of only a delegated but an equally sovereign authority.[49]

In the face of a quick, firm reply from France, Austria acquiesced in the French point of view.[50] But again she joined with Spain and Rome in proposing a four-sided agreement to guarantee to the Pope his actual possessions. France replied in the negative. She considered that such a proposal cast reflections on France's good faith in the Convention of September and for France to join in such an agreement would be doubting Italy's good faith in respect to the same Convention.[51]

The French Foreign Minister did not fail to take advantage

[48] Ideville, *Journal,* II, 217.

[49] Lhuys to Gramont, Paris, 26 Sept. 1864, *Aff. Etr., C.P., Autriche,* 487: pp. 124-127. *Doc. Guerre 1870,* IV, 180-184.

[50] Gramont to Lhuys, Vienna, 30 Sept. 1864, *Aff. Etr., C.P., Autriche,* 487: pp. 128-134.

[51] Lhuys to Malaret, Paris, 7 Oct. 1864, *ibid., Italie,* 360: pp. 331-335. *Doc. Guerre 1870,* IV, 226-228.

of this offer, however, to let Italy know that any appearance of neglect in the fulfillment of her obligations might lead to an alliance against her. La Marmora was struck by this eventuality, and, reassured by France's refusal, he was more determined than ever to execute the Convention faithfully.[52]

In some quarters it was definitely feared that the Convention had weakened Austria's position in the question of the Duchies. Not desiring to be involved in the Schleswig trouble when Venice might become Italy's next object of negotiation or attack, and when France seemed to be approaching Italy and England, Austria began to take steps to end the war without perhaps determining the full disposition of the conquered territory. The French Consular Agent at Kiel wrote home that

here (at Kiel) they think that the recent Convention concluded between the Imperial Government and the Italian Government will have favorable results for the Duchies. They say that Austria wishes to disengage herself from the German-Danish question, that she is going to push the conclusion of peace . . . so as to be able to resume her full freedom of action in Italy.[53]

It is significant that just one month and a half after the signature of the September Convention, Austria signed the treaty of peace in regard to the Schleswig war (30 October) without definitely determining the disposition of that territory with Prussia.

It was perhaps after witnessing the excessive alarm on the part of Austria that Napoleon III went so far in reassuring that Empire as to declare:

If at the time Marquis Pepoli told me of the transfer of the capital to Florence, I had immediately given my troops orders to depart, I would understand your suspicion [that France and Italy were not acting in good faith]. But here is the decision I made: I keep a margin of two years so as to convince myself thoroughly of the intentions of the Italian Government. Either Italy will organize what she has and will be able to hold down the revolutionary groups and then we shall leave Rome; or, on the contrary, if the Italian Government can not subdue its passions, then the breakup [of the union] will begin and our troops will stay in Rome. . . . I want

[52] See above note no. 51 and Malaret to Lhuys, Turin, 10 Oct. 1864, *Aff. Etr., C.P., Italie*, 360: 343-347. *Doc. Guerre 1870,* IV, 236-240.

[53] Méroux de Valois to Lhuys, Kiel, 27, 29, Sept. 1864, *Doc. Guerre 1870,* IV, 187, 197-198

Italy to possess what she has, *no more nor less.* . . . Italy would undertake a war against you at her own risk and peril.[54]

The Emperor had gone as far as to envisage a situation in which he would not observe his own treaty obligations, but that situation was the remote and almost impossible one of the actual disappearance of the other contracting party.

Before the meeting of the Italian Parliament it would be well to see what was the general Italian sentiment in respect to the Convention and the capital transfer. The reports, as they began to come into Turin, seemed to indicate a growing favor and enthusiasm for the new arrangement. Pepoli's description of Bolognese resentment toward Turin has already been discussed. In Milan much the same situation existed. The French Consul reported on 27 September that

on receiving the news of the resignation of the Minghetti cabinet, several municipalities of Lombardy had consulted Milan to inquire whether it would not be good to send an address to the King to ask him to maintain the Convention with France. The syndic of Milan advised them to abstain from any demonstration. The advice was followed; but a large number of senators, deputies, provincial and communal councilmen, journalists, professors, lawyers, and workers met at the headquarters of the Patriotic Society on 26 September, and voted an address to La Marmora in which they demanded the immediate assembling of Parliament, 'sole judge of national questions,' and the adoption of measures 'that the national representation may be called to deliberate under conditions which assure its full liberty of action.'[55]

Other cities and provinces were manifesting so similar a spirit that Elliot was able to report that even

the Turin papers admit with much bitterness that the great majority of the country approves the French Convention and that it is certain to be ratified.[56]

No doubt the reports from all parts of the Peninsula had as much influence in calming Turin as did the appointment of La Marmora to head the Ministry.

[54] Metternich memorandum of a conversation with Napoleon III, 1 Dec. 1864, *Aff. Etr., C.P., Italie,* 361: pp. 245-246.

[55] Defly to Lhuys, Milan, 27 Sept. 1864, *Doc. Guerre 1870,* IV, 191-192, note no. 2.

[56] Elliot to Russell, Turin, 28 Sept. 1864; Odo Russell to Russell, Turin, 29 Oct. 1864; *R.P.,* LXX, LXXVII.

The Italian Parliament began its sessions in Turin on 24 October. At that time La Marmora presented the law for the transfer and some documents dealing with the negotiation of the Convention. In his speech he reasserted his determination to accept and carry out the Convention because between its disadvantages and its advantages, the latter "were found to be much the greater." He favored Florence because of its location and believed that strategically Turin could not remain the capital. On the other hand he hoped that Turin would nobly rise again to this occasion of sacrifice, and in return he hoped that the nation in appreciation would gladly provide for any harm which the sudden tranfer might work upon the present capital city.[57]

The bill providing for the transfer was worded as follows:

Article 1. The capital of the Kingdom will be transferred to Florence within six months from the date of the present law.

Article 2. To defray the expenses of the transfer there shall be opened in the extra-ordinary sections of the domestic budget and in a special chapter, a credit of 7,000,000 livres divided as follows:

Available in 1864..................2,000,000
Available in 1865..................5,000,000

Article 3. The Ministers of Interior, Finance, and Public Works are specially charged with the execution of the present law.[58]

This bill was sent to committee where it remained until about 3 November.

In the meantime, before the debate in the Chamber and Senate began on the capital transfer, another international diplomatic debate took place in the form of an exchange of notes between France and Italy. It was caused by the publication of Nigra's full official report of the negotiations of the Convention for the benefit of the Italian Parliament. In this report Nigra, summarizing the clauses, gave the impression that they were like those in the Cavour negotiations with slight alterations. In speaking of Article 3, Nigra pointed out that the Papal army would have to guard his frontiers against brigandage. Finally on the question of national aspirations he said:

[57] La Marmora in the Italian Chamber, 24 Oct. 1864, reported in *Aff. Etr., C.P., Italie*, 360: pp. 371-373, 398-399.

[58] *Ibid.*, p. 399.

It was well understood in our conferences with the French plenipotentiaries that the Convention should, and could, mean neither more nor less than it said, that is that by the Convention Italy promises to renounce all violent means.

We have equally declared that this Convention is the result of the principle of non-intervention; to the extent that the future policy of Italy, in regard to Rome, will henceforth consist of observing and having observed the principle of non-intervention and employing every means of a moral nature to obtain a conciliation between Italy and the Papacy on the basis proclaimed by Count Cavour of a free Church in a free State.[59]

Drouyn de Lhuys immediately took exception to the particularly Italian point of view of Nigra's comments. He stressed the differences instead of the similarities between the Convention and the project which had been under discussion with Cavour. These differences were the transfer protocol, the two year period before complete evacuation, and the lack of a limit on the size of the Pope's army. The French Foreign Minister also pointed out that Italy had an equal responsibility along with the Pope in keeping order on the frontiers. Finally in regard to the Italian national aspirations he declared that France would never allow the interpretation that a continuance of the right to use moral force in the Italian claim on Rome meant the right to obtain Rome by some roundabout way. It meant nothing more than the right to reconcile Italy and Rome.[60]

There was evidently a misunderstanding in regard to the shades of meaning in the clauses and the various accompanying declarations. Therefore Nigra conferred again with Drouyn de Lhuys and Napoleon III from which conferences it resulted that it was recognized that Nigra's note was correct in what it said but it left room for inaccurate interpretations because of what it did not say. Nigra said that he had not mentioned the use of moral force in case of a revolt in Rome because that was not an eventuality which should be foreseen in a Franco-Italian treaty. Therefore moral means could only apply to the other

[59] Nigra to Visconti, Paris, 15 Sept. 1864, *Aff. Etr., C.P., Italie,* 360: pp. 392-394.

[60] Lhuys to Malaret, Paris, 28 October 1864, *Aff. Etr., C.P., Italie,* 360: pp. 407-409. *Doc. Guerre 1870,* IV, 309-313.

eventuality of reconciliation. Hence, on any other eventuality, France and Italy reserved to themselves the right to determine their conduct without any reference to the stipulations of the September Convention. Nigra and the French agreed to seven points which would clarify the articles of the Convention: 1) Renunciation by Italy of violent means included a renunciation of the use of revolutionary agents. 2) Moral means did not include anything which would excite insurrection but was limited to the forces of civilization and progress. 3) Aspirations were to refer to a desire to be reconciled with the Pope. 4) The capital transfer was "neither a provisional expedient nor a step toward Rome." 5) This Convention differed from the project negotiated with Cavour. 6) It did not provide for the case of a revolt in Rome, and France reserved full freedom of action in such an eventuality. 7) Italy adhered to Cavour's declaration that Rome would not be annexed or become Italy's capital without the consent of France.[61]

On 5 November, Drouyn de Lhuys took it upon himself to publish these later negotiations of interpretations. This embarrassed La Marmora just at the moment when the debates began in the Chambers on the transfer bill. Consequently he published Nigra's account which stressed the fact that the Emperor and Drouyn de Lhuys recognized the validity of Nigra's first report. Together with this La Marmora published a note which he had sent to Nigra purposely for publication. In this note the new Italian Prime Minister declared: 1) He regretted that France should suggest that Italy had any *arrière pensée* beneath the words "moral means." Italy certainly had none. 2) If Italy accomplishes her national aspiration, it will not be by violating the Convention. 3) Italy's national aspirations are a part of her conscience and can not form a part of a negotiated treaty. 4) How long in the future Florence is to be Italy's capital is a question of the future and therefore as in the question of revolts in Rome, Italy reserves to herself full freedom. 5) Italy

[61] Lhuys to Malaret, Paris, 27, 28, 30 Oct. 1864, *Aff. Etr., C.P., Italie,* 360; pp. 402, 407-409, 423-429. *Doc. Guerre 1870,* IV, 303, 309-313, 324-327. Nigra to La Marmora, Paris, 30 October 1864; *Staatsarchiv,* VII, 317-318.

also reserves to herself full freedom of action in regard to future eventualities in Rome.[62]

The fact that the choice of a capital was a domestic question and that Italy could remove it from Florence at will was an incontrovertable fact, and it was only natural that Italy's freedom of action was as great as that of France in unforeseen eventualities not provided for. La Marmora's declarations rallied greater support to his bill for the transfer since the French could not, and did not, challenge them. Russell remarked: "I didn't see that the last despatches have altered the Convention of September 15."[63]

During the deliberations of the Italian parliamentary committee there was an attempt to insert the word *provisional* before *capital,* but this failed.[64] The members of the committee were Borgotti, Pessina, Bixio, Boncampagni, Bonghi, Poerio, de Felippo, Silvestrelli, and Mosca. Mosca was the reporter of the committee before the Chamber, and the report, which was presented on 3 November, gave the following opinions:[65] 1) The committee considered both the Convention and the transfer bill. 2) It approved of the Convention. 3) The renunciation of the use of force against Rome was not a renunciation of Rome but the limitation to moral force. 4) International law would compel Italy to respect the Pope's boundaries without the treaty. 5) The treaty determined nothing and forbade nothing in case of an uprising in Rome. 6) Italy has won the application of non-intervention to Rome. 7) The capital transfer did not constitute an interference in Italy's internal affairs: it is the cause of the treaty and is not caused by it. 8) "Nothing indicated expressly that the Government is transferring the capital temporarily to another city, nor was there anything to indicate that the new capital is definitely chosen." 9) The debt clause did not make

[62] La Marmora to Nigra, Turin, 7 Nov. 1864, *Gazzetta Ufficiale,* 7 Nov. 1864. Massari, *La Marmora,* pp. 296-300. *Aff. Etr., C.P., Italie,* 361, pp. 55-56.

[63] Russell to Grey, Alderly Park, 7 Nov. 1864, *R.P.,* CVI.

[64] Malaret to Lhuys, Turin, 28 Oct. 1864, *Aff. Etr., C.P., Italie,* 360: pp. 411-420.

[65] *Atti ufficiali,* Chamber, 3 Nov. 1864, pp. 3691-3692.

this treaty a financial one because Italy only promised to negotiate. The result of the future negotiation will bring about another treaty which would be presented to Parliament. 10) Therefore the Convention need not be ratified by Parliament. 11) It was recommended that approval of the transfer bill was sufficient to approve of the whole transaction. 12) The passage of the proposed transfer bill was recommended since Florence was the best city for the location of the capital *under the present circumstances* (*nelle circonstanze presente*).

The first important speech in the debate was by Deputy Ferraris who claimed that the Convention itself should be ratified by the Chamber for two reasons: 1) because by recognizing the Pope's possession of Rome, the Convention relinquished Italian territory, 2) because by promising to negotiate on a debt question, Italy was already assuming financial obligations.

Pessina replied for the committee that the eventual debt treaty would be presented to Parliament for ratification and that Rome was not a territory under the *Statuto* and therefore could not be subject to a vote of Parliament. Hence the motion to allow Parliament to ratify the treaty should not be sustained.

Mr. Boggio countered these arguments by saying that the transfer of the capital was the guaranty of the Convention, therefore the Convention itself should be ratified.

La Marmora closed that day's discussion by noting that Nigra's first report is still accurate and the fact there had grown up a diversity of interpretations was not his fault since that often happens. He indirectly recognized the newly established interpretations.

On the following day, 8 November, the discussion was renewed. Lanza spoke this time against the motion to consider the Convention itself since no territory nor money was involved. The motion was put to a vote and was rejected.

Beginning the discussion on the transfer bill, Miceli, one of the radicals, declared that to promise protection to the Pope was traitorous since the Pope was an avowed enemy of Italy. Visconti-Venosta came to the defense of the measure by stating that the Pope could never have an army large enough to menace Italy. He further argued that France did not promise aid to the Pope in case of internal revolt because that would encourage tyranny in the Papal Government. By reserving her freedom of action France gave Italy a chance to do the same.

The words of Boncampagni, who spoke on 9 November, were extremely significant. First he declared that France had recognized that Italy had a special interest in Rome by negotiating the treaty with her alone. But his next argument was even more remarkable:

> Well, I shall declare my opinion fairly and squarely: I believe that we are establishing a permanent capital (*murmurs from the Left*). . . . In fact, when one talks of governmental decrees, acts, and laws; what distinguishes a permanent act from a temporary one? A permanent act is from its nature perpetual, and this perpetuity occurs every time its effect is not limited by an express time. But, in the name of heaven (*Dio mio*), the perpetuity of human laws are very different from the perpetuity of divine laws. The perpetuity of human laws is permanent until another takes its place (*laughter from the Left*); by giving the capital transfer law a permanent character, Italy does not renounce her faculty to transfer it to Rome when Rome may become a part of the Kingdom, she does not renounce the vote which proclaimed that that should be the capital.

La Marmora spoke on the 12th in a very serious vein. He admitted that he had been against the treaty at one time but on coming into office he had found it accepted and he was going to take it up and enforce it for the honor of Italy.

> I saw it was a serious treaty and that for the first time Italy was making an international treaty of such importance. This treaty is signed at the same time by King Victor-Emmanuel and by the Emperor: it is a serious matter. The change was such within me, I repeat, that I decided to accept the task immediately which His Majesty wished to confide in me and I set out to form a ministry with the fixed idea of accepting the treaty.

He went on to explain that the principal reason he had opposed the treaty was because he feared it would divide Italy.[66] On the

[66] This may be true but during the negotiation he did not bring that one forward. It will be remembered that he insisted on the impossibility of preventing raids on the Papal frontier.

contrary he found that it had united Italy more than ever. He could, therefore, do no more than favor such a measure.

The discussion was taken up again on Monday the 14th and Pepoli explained again how no other practical guaranty could be offered by Italy. He answered the argument that France was trying to get more control over Italy by the Convention by showing that England heartily approved of the Convention.[67] Certainly England would not approve it if it gave France more control.

On the 15th Lanza spoke again and suggested that in case of a revolt in Rome France and Italy could intervene jointly. He reiterated that the transfer to Florence was intended to be permanent.[68]

Minghetti, the person who had been responsible for the acceptance of the treaty, did not speak at all for it. Although he gave as the reason his desire to hurry the vote, the real reason was very likely the embarrassment he would cause to the Government in the face of the Piedmontese deputies.[69]

The vote in the Chamber took place on 19 November and the transfer bill became a law, 317 to 70. It was an exceptionally large majority and it is significant to know that of the seventy opponents forty were Piedmontese. The national will was almost unanimous for the Convention and the transfer.[70]

In the Senate Massimo D'Azeglio's speech in favor of the transfer bill was one of the most famous. Unable to read it himself he had his friend and colleague, Senator Moscuzza, read it for him. He reminded the Senate of his advocacy of Florence as capital four years before and he insisted that the transfer to Florence should be absolutely permanent. They should never go to Rome. His closing words contained a wealth of feeling:

When the new bride goes forth from the home where she was born, her parents consent to it, they really wish it to be so; but

[67] See below, pp. 431-432.

[68] For the debates of the Italian Chamber see *Atti ufficiali,* Chamber, 7 Nov. to 15 Nov. 1864, pp. 3710-3734, 3762-3764, 3776-3778, 3789-3791.

[69] Minghetti to Galeotti, Bologna, 25 Nov. 1864, M. Minghetti, *Lettere a Leopoldo Galeotti* (Bologna, 1903), p. 52.

[70] Malaret to Lhuys, Turin, 20 Nov. 1864, *Aff. Etr., C.P., Italie,* 361: p. 202. *Doc. Guerre 1870,* V, 74-78.

if when the occasion comes, their very hearts seem to be breaking, who would wish to condemn them? (*Fine, fine*).

Thus since the nation wills it, since an unfortunate treaty is less of a danger to the present condition of our affairs than a divided opinion, even I with a sad heart accept it. (*Fine, good*).[71]

The measure likewise in the Senate obtained an overwhelming victory. The vote was 134 to 47.[72] The capital transfer on which the Convention depended needed only the King's decree to make it a law. This was given on 11 December and La Marmora informed France through Nigra as follows:

This day, 11 December (1864), the law for the transfer of the capital, already approved by the Chamber of Deputies in its session of 19 November 1864 and by the Senate of the Kingdom in its session of 9 December 1864, was sanctioned by the King.

His Majesty has likewise signed this day the Royal Decree by which the Convention concluded in Paris on 15 September 1864 is put into force.

I beg Your Honor to kindly bring the above to the knowledge of His Excellency the Imperial Minister of Foreign Affairs.[73]

Thus went into force a measure the negotiation of which had been in progress ever since April 1861. By 11 June 1865 Italy's capital would be in Florence; by 11 December 1866 no more French troops would remain on the Italian Peninsula. However much the Convention of September may have eventually failed in gaining for the Italians their hoped-for goal, it can be truly said that this treaty was a very important measure in the history of the Roman question. The days of 15 September and 11 December 1864 mark the end of one and the beginning of another very important period in the history of the seemingly endless and insoluble Roman question.

To trace this Convention to its end in 1870, to observe its course of eventual execution, the accompanying complications, and the discouraging failure requires another volume and can not further swell the pages of this one. But before bringing the story of the Convention's negotiation and formulation to an end,

[71] *Atti ufficiali*, Senate, 3 Dec. 1864, pp. 1153-1155.

[72] Pasolini, *Memorie*, I, 423.

[73] La Marmora to Nigra, Turin, 11 Dec. 1864, *Libro verde, documenti presentati da La Marmora*, p. 5.

it would be well to give some brief attention to the immediate effects of its conclusion.

First, in that nation across the channel, what was the reaction to the terms of the Convention in that country whose interest in Italy had time and again led her to exert pressure directly or indirectly, frankly or surreptitiously, on France for evacuation? The English press hailed the treaty with favor while Palmerston, Russell, and Gladstone, all three, not only heartily approved of the evacuation clauses but also favored the selection of Florence as capital, which they hoped would remain such in spite of any future disposition of Rome.[74] More significant than all this polite approval were the words of Russell to Grey in Paris:

> I think it is a great step to the cordial alliance between England and France that the Emperor should have made the Convention of 15th September. I hope he will not draw back from it, and we on our part, shall do everything possible to make it easy for him to execute it.[75]

One of the motives of this positive action on the part of Napoleon was to gain some real friendship from some European power. England, now somewhat chagrined by her failure to mediate in the Danish-German question, seemed glad for an opportunity to repair her wire to Paris.

It is interesting too to see how Bismark might have been preparing to take advantage of the new situation. Austria knew that both England and France were favorable to the Italian annexation of Venice. She saw that Italy would now be quiet on Rome and hence might turn her attention to Venice. It has been already noted that she hastily made peace along with Prussia in the Schleswig war, and Bismark did not seem averse to take advantage of Austria's weakness. To gain Austrian support he did not need to make concessions in Schleswig; he only needed to offer benevolent neutrality. Likewise in his relations with France, Bismarck realized that with increased Austrian hostility

[74] For the many expressions of opinion see: *Aff. Etr., C.P., Angleterre,* 731: pp. 76-77, 84, 91, 122-123, 127-128, 148-156; *Autriche,* 487: pp. 217-222. *Doc. Guerre 1870,* IV, 358. Minghetti, *Convenzione,* pp. 204-205. Bollea, *op. cit.,* pp. 448-449.

[75] 2 Oct. 1864, *R.P.,* CVI.

toward France, Prussia was in a more advantageous position. For France's negative support he no longer would have to offer compensation on the Rhine—his own benevolent neutrality would again be all that he would have to pay. The French consul at Kiel realized it only too well. When such calculations were being rumored, he inclosed an article from a Kiel journal which ended with the suggestion that for Prussia "Venice has become the boulevard to the Rhine."[76] Later in December, when Bismarck made a visit to Paris, the Austrians became extremely alarmed. Rumor in Vienna, reported Gramont, has it that "it is with the Emperor's consent that he (Bismarck) is undertaking his new campaign of annexing Lauenburg, then Holstein, and then Schleswig to Prussia."[77]

If Austria was concerned over the possible fate of Venice as a result of the September Convention, so were the Venetians. Consul Pillet in Venice wrote the following interesting report home to Paris:

> [The Venetians] observe that . . . [the Convention] instead of giving them (Italians) the Papal States, obliges them to respect and even defend them; that this advantage could be a guaranty of the actual possessions and very probably a promise of help in the day when they think they can redeem Venice, either by friendly arrangement or by force of arms; and they invoke in favor of these hopes the evident embarrassment of the Austrian papers and officials, who certainly were not in on the secret. If, they say, it had been the Emperor's intention to make Italy renounce Venice, he would have used the fact to gain favor with Austria, and the latter would be gloating now instead of worrying.[78]

In addition to making Venice uneasy and the other cities of the Peninsula more united to the new Kingdom, the newly formulated Convention had a very unhealthful effect on Turin and Piedmont. Radicals in Italy were usually known by their impatient attitude toward the question of establishing the capital at Rome. Turin and Piedmont always formed the nucleus of the stable and conservative sections. General Fleury recorded his

[76] Méroux de Valois to Lhuys, Kiel, 19 Oct. 1864, *Doc. Guerre 1870*, IV, 274-276.

[77] Gramont to Lhuys, Vienna, 2 Dec. 1864, *Aff. Etr., C.P., Autriche*, 487: p. 226.

[78] Pillet to Lhuys, Venice, 25 Sept. 1864, *Doc. Guerre 1870*, IV, 177-179.

impression of the change which took place in Piedmont as the result of the Convention.

> The change of capital had come to modify the attitude of the Piedmontese. When it once had been admitted that the seat of the Government could no longer remain in Turin, a great number of them had more or less sincerely proclaimed that it should be taken to Rome. The most extremely conservative men were then seen to become the followers of the most radical solutions of the Roman question, and the language held by the most influential members of its representation immediately after the Convention had helped to alarm the timorous souls.[79]

French opinion seemed to respond almost as unanimously and favorably to the Convention as did the Italian. The reports of the *procureurs* sent in in October came too soon to show exactly the effect that the measure had had on the French public mind. By January, however, opinion had had plenty of opportunity to inform itself and reflect on the extent of its meaning. The January reports represented almost unanimous lack of concern. While there was at first a little alarm over the safety of the Pope, that had been calmed by the later interpretations. There was also a continuous enthusiasm among a small minority of radicals, but the great mass of the people including the conservatives once reassured showed little interest either by favor or hostility. Only in Franche-Comté was there a tendency to be alarmed unduly but little opposition was offered. What was particularly significant was the absence of the vindictive attack on the Government which appeared in the reports of October 1863 and January 1864. If the Convention had not created something positive in French opinion, at least it seemed to have had the hoped-for negative effect of aiding in diminishing the striking dissatisfaction with the Imperial policy of 1863.[80]

In spite of the long period of negotation, the strenuous efforts of both the French and the Italians, and the widespread interest which welcomed the Convention's appearance, it was

[79] Fleury, *Souvenirs,* II, 300-301.

[80] *Rapports des procureurs,* Agens, 31 Dec. 1864, 370: v. 4; Aix, 6 Jan. 1865, 370: v. 5; Amiens, 7 Jan. 1865, 371: v. 5; Besançon, 11 Jan. 1865, 373: v. 7; Bordeaux, 15 Jan. 1865, 374: v. 4; Bourges, 6 Jan. 1865, 374: v. 4; Caen, 11 Jan. 1865, 375: v. 5; Lyons, 28 Dec. 1864, 379: v. 6; Montpellier, 11 Jan. 1865, 380: v. 5; Paris, 14 Nov. 1864, 384: v. 9; Rennes, 14 Jan. 1865, 386: v. 5.

admitted from the start that it was not a solution of the Roman question. That solution lay in a rapprochement between Italy and the Pope on the basis of some future arrangement. It was only one step toward the solution of that thorny problem. In the ten year period in which the French occupation formed the major problem in the greater question of the disposition of Rome the September Convention stands as a half-way mark, before which attention centered around negotiations of an agreement, and after which thoughts concentrated on its execution.

By a careful study of the sources one is convinced of the sincerity of the French Government in desiring to withdraw. That it took them almost five years to agree to an arrangement for the evacuation of Rome is accounted for by the various forces opposing that step. French public opinion showed too great a concern for the Pope to allow France to accept such an arrangement without assurances and guaranties. The death of Cavour, the precipitate impatience of Ricasoli, the ineptness of Rattazzi and Durando, and finally the rash enterprises of Garibaldi tended to destroy the necessary assurances and make any guaranties valueless. The French adverse reaction to these reverses led finally to the substitution of Drouyn de Lhuys in the place of the mildly pro-Italian Thouvenel. This not only caused a setback in French readiness to treat, but it also caused in Italy a resentment which took the form of a long period of silence on the Roman question. In the process of "trial and error" of the interregnum period the errors predominate and terminate the trials and thereby prolong the discussion.

In favor of the continuance of the negotiations was the constant British pressure. This force became all the more outstanding when in desperation France, facing an imminent isolation, had recourse to Rome in order to arrive at London. As time became more and more distant from Garibaldi's expedition, French Catholic feeling gradually subsided. The existence of the *procureur* reports and the evidence of the attention given them bear witness to the influence of the French public's quiescence on the Emperor's determination to reopen negotiations and conclude a treaty. Another encouragement for the temporary settlement was the return of Italy under moderate leadership to a sober and conservative policy. Aspromonte and her "playing dead" gave evidence of the self-control necesary to reassure the Emperor and the French. The impending death of Pius IX was the final precipitating factor.

The concluded arrangement was so similar to the project negotiated with Cavour, and during the interregnum the statesmen so often returned again and again to that project, that one is compelled to recognize that the beginning of the Convention of 1864 is found in the year 1861. Thus the author of the earlier becomes indirectly, while even out of office, the author of the later. Hence Thouvenel was largely the one to conceive the terms; in 1862 it was he who altered his own orginial plan to include the clause which provided for a three- or two-year delay before evacuation. He could at least have the satisfaction of observing that the man who succeeded him had been compelled to adopt, not only his own policy, but even his very terms themselves.

If the Convention indicated that it was only the prelude to the next and final step of the solution by a reconciliation between Italy and the Vatican, the Italians did not generally agree that reconciliation was necessarily that final step. However definitively they may have established the Government in Florence, the Italians had not renounced their determination of obtaining Rome and of making it their capital. In fact they had just been able to join Turin's wholehearted support to the Roman cause. But the only hope left for the Italians was the success of a purely internal revolt in Rome, a year or so after French evacuation, the establishment of an independent Roman government by the Roman people, and by plebiscite their request for annexation by Italy. This eventuality, remote because of the political inertia of the Romans, was nevertheless presented by the French to the Italians time and again to bear witness to the Emperor's lack of enthusiasm for the temporal power and his sincerity in seeking to evacuate Rome.

BIBLIOGRAPHY

Bibliographies

Bastgen, Hubert. *Die römische Frage. Dokumente und Stimmen.* 3. v. Freiburg i. B., 1917-1918, II, 841-846; III, Part I, 331-332; Part II, 223-224.

Catalogo generale delle pubblicazioni edite dallo Stato o col suo concorso (1861-1923). Rome, 1924.

Catalogo metodico degli scritti contenuti nelle pubblicazioni periodiche italiane e straniere della Biblioteca della Camera dei Deputati. First Series, 7 v., 1885-1907; New Series, 2 v., Rome, 1914-1928.

Guide to Historical Literature. Edited by W. H. Allison, S. B. Fay, A. H. Shearer, H. R. Shipman. N. Y., 1931.

Huntington, T. W., Jr. *The Italiana Bibliography.* N.Y., 1928.

Part V. contains English books on modern Italian history.

Lemmi, Francesco. *Il risorgimento. Guido bibliografiche.* Roma, 1926.

See especially pp. 272-283.

Bibliographie des travaux publiés de 1866 à 1897 sur l'histoire de France. Published under the direction of P. Caron. Paris, 1907-1912.

Répertoire méthodique de l'histoire moderne et contemporaine de la France. Compiled under the direction of G. Brière and P. Caron. 8 v. Paris, 1898-1910.

For the years 1910-1919 the *Revue d'histoire moderne et contemporaine* must be consulted.

Répertoire bibliographique de l'histoire de France. Compiled by P. Caron and H. Stein. 2 v., Paris, 1923-1927.

Revue des bibliothèques (1922).

Catalogue of the *Livres Jaunes* for the years up to 1922 compiled by M. René Doré.

Rivista storica del risorgimento italiano, II, 762-797.

Bibliography on Cavour to 1897, compiled under the direction of Signor Bazziconi.

Salata, Francesco. *Per la storia diplomatica della questione romana.* 2 v., Milan, 1929-1930.

Bibliographical notes at the end of the volumes.

Seignobos, Charles. *Le déclin de l'Empire et l'établissement de la Troisième République.* Volume VII of Ernest Lavisse's *Histoire contemporaine de la France depuis la Révolution jusqu'à la paix de 1919*. Paris, 1921.

See especially pp. 103-104.

Manuscript Collections

Archives du ministère des affaires étrangères (France). *Correspondance politique. Correspondance circulaire. Correspondance consulaire. Mémoires et documents.*

The official correspondence of the French Foreign Office. The collections used principally were those of the *Correspondance politique (C.P.)* and *Mémoires et documents (M.D.)* concerning Italy, Rome, and England. The dispatches sent and received were placed chronologically together in the volumes. The page numbers used are those stamped on the pages by the French Foreign Office. In case of no page numeration the exact or approximate dates are given.

Archives nationales (France). *Rapports politiques des procureurs-généraux. Ministère de Justice.* (BB^{30}).

This collection, only recently made available, contains the very valuable reports of the French district-attorneys to the Ministers of Justice. They contain either monthly, semi-annual, or quarterly accounts of the political opinion of each judicial district in France from 1849 to 1875. All the reports from 1860 to 1865 of twelve judicial districts out of the twenty-six were studied thoroughly. These twelve were selected so as to include urban and rural sections; those of the north, east, south, and west; those with industrial and commercial as well as agricultural interests; and finally those well known for their clerical and anti-clerical sentiments. The twelve chosen were the following: Agens, Aix, Amiens, Besançon, Bordeaux, Bourges, Caen, Chambéry, Lyons, Montpellier, Paris, Rennes. Within the cartons and volumes the reports were arranged chronologically but were not always consistently numbered. In addition to the date, therefore, the carton number and the volume number are both given. Bibliographical notes for this series are to be found in *Cambridge Modern History,* XI, 927; in Maurain, *Politique ecclésiastique,* p. xxiii; in Charles Schmidt, *Les sources de l'histoire de France depuis 1789 aux Archives Nationales*. Paris, 1907, pp. 249-250; and in Charles Seignobos, "Les documents inédits des Archives Nationales sur la réaction de 1848-1858," *Bulletin de la société d'histoire moderne,* (June, 1907).

Papiers de Cerçay.

This important collection includes the private correspondence of many French officials of this period, especially that of Thouvenel, La Valette, Gramont, La Tour d'Auvergne, Barrot, Montebello, Rouher, Flahault, Talleyrand, Benedetti, and Persigny. These papers, deposited in the Archives of the French Foreign Office, are not yet available for historical research although some of the more important correspondence has been already published in various works. A catalogue of these papers is found in *Doc. Guerre 1870,* XII, 408 ff.

Public Record Office. British Foreign Office Correspondence.

Official British correspondence arranged chronologically and numbered, but the pages are not numbered. For clarity the names of the countries concerned are mentioned in the footnote references instead of the Foreign Office numerical designations.

Public Record Office. Russell Papers.

Private letters of Earl John Russell, British Secretary of State for Foreign Affairs. His correspondence with Cowley, Hudson, and Odo Russell, the British representatives at Paris, Turin, and Rome respectively, were especially consulted. The letters are not numbered but they are arranged chronologically within the volumes.

Published Source Material

(Anonymous). "Sulla via di Roma. Da Aspromonte a Mentana," *Nuova Antologia,* Series IV, LXXXV (Jan. 1900), 7-33; LXXXVIII (June 1900), 593.

The writer of these articles contributed many important documents written to and by Rattazzi. The contributor is not known nor the source of the documents, although it is likely that they were drawn from Rattazzi's private letters or (less likely) from the official government files. The *Nuova Antologia,* were unable to inform the author of the identity of the original contributor because of no information to that effect in their files. They hastened, however, to "guarantee the authenticity of the documents." Giuliobiola to the author, Rome, 16 April 1930.

Archivio storico italiano. Published by Regia deputazione toscana di storia patria. Florence, 1842 ff.

Atti ufficiali del parlamento italiano (1861-1874).

Official report of debates in the Italian Parliament.

Bastgen, Hubert. *Die römische Frage. Dokumente und Stimmen.* 3 v., Freiburg i. B., 1917-1918.

Especially good on the Roman question in the European press.

Bianchi, N. *La politique du comte de Cavour de 1852 à 1861. Lettres inédites avec notes. Correspondance particulière avec le marquis Emmanuel D'Azeglio.* Turin, 1885.

Bianchi, N. *Storia documentata della diplomazia europea in Italia 1814-1861.* 8 v., Turin, 1865-1872.

Volume VIII is the only one which contains material on the subject of the present work. The documents deal almost exclusively with Italian-Vatican relations.

Bollea, L. C. *Una silloge di lettere del risorgimento di particolare attinenza all' alleanza franco-italiana, alla guerra del 1859 ed alla Spedizione dei Mille* (1839-1873). Turin, 1919.

After a considerable controversy Mr. Bollea was able to publish these documents which he had arranged for editing after consulting the originals in the *Archivio di Stato di Torino.*

Carreresi, Allessandro. *Lettere di Gino Capponi e di altri a lui.* 6 v., 1883-1890.

See especially volumes III and IV.

Il Carteggio Cavour-Nigra dal 1858 al 1861. A cura della R. Commissione Editrice. Vol. IV, *La liberazione del Mezzogiorno.* Bologna, 1929.

Official publication of Cavour's correspondence taken from the *Archivio di Stato di Torino.*

Cavour, Camillio. *Discorsi parlamentari raccolti e pubblicati per ordine della Camera dei Deputati.* 11 v., Turin, 1863-1872.

Chiala, Luigi. *Lettere edite ed inedite del conte Camillio di Cavour.* 7 v., Turin, 1883-1887.

Comandini, A. *Il principe Napoleone nel risorgimento italiano.* Milan, 1922.

Documents drawn largely from the Bonaparte archives at Prangins Villa and from other archives in Italy.

Le Constitutionnel.

The Paris journal frequently inspired by the Government.

D'Ambès, Baron. *Intimate Memoirs of Napoleon III.* (English translation by A. R. Allison). 2 v., Boston, 1912.

Volume III has memorandums of important incidents connected with the Roman question after 1861.

D'Hauterive, Ernest. *Napoléon III et le Prince Napoléon. Correspondance inédite.* Paris, 1925.

Letters taken directly from the Bonaparte archives at the Villa of Prangins. They appeared in serial form in the *Revue des deux mondes,* Période VII; XIX, XX, (1924). English translation by Mr. Herbert Wilson under the title of *The Second Empire and its Downfall.* N.Y., 1927.

Fleury, Général comte de. *Souvenirs.* 2. v., Paris, 1897.

Gazzetta ufficiale.

A Turin paper in which many of the Italian Government's communications were made.

Halt, Robert (ed.). *Papiers sauvés des Tuileries.* Paris, 1871.

Ideville, H. d'. *Journal d'un diplomate en Italie 1859-1862; 1862-1866. Note intimes pour servir à l'histoire du Second Empire.* 2 v., Paris, 1872-1873.

Italia, Roma, e Papato nelle discussioni parlamentari dal 1860 al 1871. A cura di Benito Mussolini. Rome, 1930.

Libro verde.

27 June 1861 *Riconoscimento del Regno d'Italia.*

20 Nov. 1861 *Questione romana.*

12 July 1862 *Alcune questioni italiane.*

29 May 1863 (Documents presented by Visconti-Venosta).

12 Dec. 1865 (Documents presented by La Marmora).

The collection of official Italian documents presented to the Italian Parliament.

Livre jaune. (1860, 1861, 1862, 1864).

The collection of official French documents presented to the French Parliament.

Masson, Frédéric. "L'Italie libérée. Lettres et dépêches au Prince Napoléon de Victor-Emmanuel II et de Cavour, 1857-1862," *Revue des deux mondes,* Période VII, (1923), XIII, 39-73, 550-575, 845-861; XIV, 365-390.

Letters taken from the Bonaparte Archives at the Villa of Prangins.

Minghetti, Marco. *La convenzione di settembre. Un capitolo dei miei ricordi.* Pubblicato per cura del principe di Camporeale. Bologna, 1899.

One of the important sources for the negotiation of the Convention of September; it includes Minghetti's memoirs on the subject as well as a wealth of dispatches.

Minghetti, Marco. *Discorsi parlamentari* 8 v. Rome, 1888-1890.

(Minghetti, Marco). *Carteggio tra Marco Minghetti e Giuseppe Pasolini.* Per cura di Guido Pasolini. 3 v., Turin, 1924-1929.

Letters from the correspondence of Minghetti and Pasolini conserved in the *Archivio Pasolini* at Ravenna.

Moniteur universel.

French official journal for governmental decrees and the reports of debates in the French Parliament.

(Napoleon III). *La politique impériale exposée par les discours et proclamations de l'Empereur Napoléon III depuis 10 décembre 1852 jusqu'en février 1868.* Paris, 1868.

Oncken, Herman. *Die Rheinpolitik Kaiser Napoleons III. von 1863 bis 1870 und der Ursprung des Krieges von 1870-1871.* 3 v. Stuttgart, 1926.

Contain documents drawn from the Austrian *Haus, Hof, und Staat Archiv* and from the Prussian Archives.

Origines diplomatiques de la guerre de 1870-1871. Recueil de documents publié par le ministère des affaires étrangères. 17 v., Paris, 1910-1928.

Documents largely from the Archives of the French Foreign Office.

Pantaleoni, D. *L'Idea italiana della soppressione del potere temporale dei Papi.* Turin, 1884.

Parliamentary Papers. (*British Blue Books*).

Further Correspondence respecting the Affairs of Italy. Parts II-IX, 1860-1861.

Further Correspondence relating to the Affairs of Italy. Part VII, May to Dec. 1860, 1861, [2757], LXVII, 101 ff. Part VIII, June to March 1861, 1861, [2787, 2788], LXVII, 341 ff.

Papers respecting the French Occupation of Rome, 1862, [3024], LXIII, 479 ff.

Further Papers relative to the Affairs of Rome, 1863, [3074], LXXV, 331 ff.

Correspondence relative to the Affairs of Rome, 1860, [3080], LXXV, 335 ff.

Pasolini, Conte Pier Desiderio (ed). *Giuseppe Pasolini, Memorie raccolte da suo figlio, 1815-1876.* 2. v., Turin, 1887. (English translation by Lady Dalhousie, London, 1885).

From the *Archivio di Pasolini* at Ravenna.

Questione romana negli anni 1860-1861. Carteggio del conte di Cavour con D. Pantaleoni, C. Passaglia, O. Vimercati. A cura della R. Commissione Editrice. 2 v., Bologna, 1929.

An official publication by the Italian Government containing most of the previously unpublished documents in the *Archivio di Stato di Torino* and the archives of the Italian Foreign Office at Rome.

Rendu, Eugène. *L'Italie de 1847 à 1865. Correspondance de Massimo D'Azeglio.* Paris, 1867.

Ricasoli, Barone Bettino. *Lettere e documenti del Barone Ricasoli.* Pubblicati per cura di Marco Tabarrini e Aurelio Gotti. 11 v., Florence, 1887-1896.

Russell, Earl John. *Later Correspondence 1840-1878.* Edited by G. P. Gooch. 2. v., London, 1925.

Selected correspondence taken from the *Russell Papers* in the Public Record Office.

Russell, Earl John. *Speeches and Despatches.* 2. v., London, 1870.

Staatsarchiv. Sammlung der offiziellen Aktenstücke zur Geschichte der Gegenwart. Hamburg, 1861- .

The first seven volumes contain material on the subject of the present work.

Thouvenel, L. (ed.). *Pages d'histoire du Second Empire d'après les papiers de M. Thouvenel, ancien ministre des affaires étrangères.* Paris, 1903.

Thouvenel, L. (ed.). *Le secret de L'Empereur. Correspondence confidentielle et inédite échangée entre M. Thouvenel, le duc de Gramont, et le général comte de Flahault, 1860-1863.* 2. v., Paris, 1889.

Published Writings

Alberti, M. degli. "Napoleone III e B. Ricasoli," *Il Risorgimento italiano,* I, (1908).

Alfiere, Contessa. "Il conte Cavour e la questione romana," *Nuova Antologia,* I, (1866), 815-820.

Ambrosi de Magistris, R. and Ghiron, J. *Roma nella storia dell'unità d'Italia.* Turin, 1886.

Andriulli, G. A. *Pio IX nel risorgimento italiano.* Milan, 1928.

Arbib, A. "Sulla via di Roma. La questione nel Parlamento (1860-1862), "*Nuova Antologia,* (16 Feb. 1900).

Argenti, N. "Una fase poca nota nella questione romana," *Nuova Antologia,* (1 Sept. 1911).

Artom, E. *L'Opera politica del Senatore I. Artom nel risorgimento italiano.* Bologna, 1906.

Bianchi, C. "Cavour e la questione romana," *Nuova Antologia,* XV, (Nov. 1870), 642.

Bonfadini, R. *Vita di Francesco Arese.* Turin, 1894.

Boncampagni, C. "Relazioni tra la Francia e l'Italia dal 15 novembre 1864 al luglio 1871," *Nuova Antologia,* XX, (May-June 1872), 46 ff., 299 ff.

Bourgeois, Emile and Clermont, Emile. *Rome et Napoléon III (1849-1870), étude sur les origines et la chûte du Second Empire.* Paris, 1907.

An able review of the September Convention considering the limited sources available at the time of publication.

Cadorna, C. "Cavour e la sua politica nelle relazioni fra Chiesa e Stato." *Nuova Antologia,* LXII, (April 1882), 637 ff.; LXIII, (May-June 1882), 444 ff., 649 ff.

Calvi, E. "Progetti rivoluzionari in Roma per la morte preveduta di Pio IX (1864)," *Rassegna storica del risorgimento italiano,* (1916), 181 ff.

Carpi, L. *Risorgimento italiano. Biografie* (di Pepoli). Vol. III. Milan, 1885.

Chiala, Luigi. *Pagine di storia contemporanea dal 1858 al 1892.* 3 v., Turin, 1892-1893.

Volume I is very valuable for material on the Italian press and the Parliamentary debates from 1858 to 1878.

Comandini, A. "Roma capitale e la sua nemica (l'Imperatrice Eugenia)," *Il secolo XX,* (1 Sept. 1920).

Corti, E. C. "Les idées de l'Empératrice Eugénie sur le redressement de la carte de l'Europe d'après les rapports du prince Richard de Metternich," *Revue des études napoléonienne,* II, 147-155.

Curatulo, Giacomo Emilio. *La questione romana da Cavour a Mussolini.* Rome, 1928.

Debidour, Antonin. *Histoire diplomatique de l'Europe. Series* I. 2 v., Paris, 1891.

Debidour, Antonin. *Histoire des rapports de l'Eglise et de l'Etat en France de 1789 à 1870*. 2nd ed., Paris, 1911.

De Cesare, Raffaele. *Roma e lo Stato del Papa dal ritorno di Pio IX al veinte settembre (1850-1870)*. 2 v., Rome, 1907.

English translation by Helen Zimmern with the title *The Last Days of Papal Rome*. N.Y., 1909.

De Cesare, Raffaele. "Emilio Visconti-Venosta. Storia e ricordi," *Nuova Antologia,* Series V. CLXXV, (1915).

Diamilla Müller, D. E. *Politica segreta italiana (1863-1870)*. Turin, 1891.

Dupanloup, Félix. *Lettre à un catholique (réponse à la brochure 'Le Pape et le Congrès')*. Paris, 1860.

Dupanloup, Félix. *Seconde lettre à un catholique*. Paris, 1861.

Dupanloup, Félix. *Lettre à M. le vicomte La Guéronnière en réponse à la brochure 'La France, Rome, et l'Italie'*. Paris, 1861.

Durand-Moribau, Henri. *La question romaine depuis le traité de Paris (1856) jusqu' au 20 septembre 1870*. Paris, 1901.

A seemingly biased and pro-Catholic study of the September Convention with few references to important source materials.

Durando, C. *Episodi diplomatici del risorgimento italiano dal 1856 al 1863*. Turin, 1901.

Faccio, G. C. "Tentativi di Cavour per risolvere la questione romana nel 1860-1861," *Nuova Antologia,* (1 June 1912).

Falloux, A. F. P. comte de. *La Convention du 15 septembre 1864*. Paris, 1864.

A partisan tract written in opposition to the Convention.

Gallavresi, G. "Le marquis Visconti-Venosta," *Revue des deux mondes,* Période VI, XXV, (1915), 64-73.

Giacometti, G. *L'Unité italienne 1861-1862. Aperçu d'histoire politique et diplomatique*. Paris, 1898.

Grabinski, Comte Joseph. *Un ami de Napoléon III. Le comte Arese et la politique italienne sous le Second Empire*. Paris, 1897.

Harcourt, M. B. d' *Les quatres ministères de M. Drouyn de Lhuys*. Paris, 1882.

One-fourth of the book deals with the September Convention and several important documents are reproduced.

Hancock, E. K. *Bettino Ricasoli and the Risorgimento in Italy*. London, 1926.

Isaia, D. Antonio. *Negoziato fra il conte di Cavour ed il cardinale*

Antonelli conchiuso per la cessione del poter temporale del Papa. Turin, 1862.

La Gorce, Pierre. *Histoire du Second Empire.* 7 v. Paris, 1894-1905.

La Guéronnière, L. E. A. vicomte de. *Le Pape et le Congrès.* Paris, 1859.

La Guéronnière, L. E. A., etc. *La France, Rome, et l'Italie.* Paris, 1861.

This was really written for the Emperor by Persigny. La Guéronnière was under Persigny in the Ministry of Interior as supervisor of the press.

La Guéronnière, L. E. A., etc. *L'Abandon de Rome.* Paris, 1862.

Lando, Magini. *Roma capitale al primo parlamento italiano. Discussioni e voto 25, 26, 27 marzo 1861.* Florence, 1895.

Leroy-Beaulieu, A. *Un empereur, un roi, un pape.* Paris, 1879.

Leti, G. *Roma e lo Stato Pontifico dal 1849 al 1870.* 2 v., 2nd ed., Ascoli-Piceno, 1911.

Massari, G. *La vita ed il regno di Vittorio Emanuele II di Savoia, primo re d'Italia.* 2 v., Milan, 1896.

Massari, G. *Il generale Alfonso La Marmora. Ricordi biografici.* Florence, 1880.

Massei, C. *L'Italia e la politica di Napoleone III durante e dopo la guerra dell'indipendenza.* 3 v., Livorno, 1872.

Matter, Paul. *Cavour et l'unité italienne.* 3 v., Paris, 1922-1927.

An excellent work whose third volume shows a careful use of sources for the years 1856-1861.

Maurain, Jean. *La politique ecclésiastique du Second Empire de 1852 à 1869.* Paris, 1930.

An excellent and exhaustive study "limited," in the words of the author, "to internal policy." It furnishes a splendid background, however, for foreign affairs by describing the internal situation in France. Dr. Maurain has made a thorough examination of the manuscript sources in the Paris archives.

Mazziotti, Matteo. "Un fervido amico dell'Italia in Francia. Enrico Conneau," *Nuova Antologia,* Series VI, CCXX, (16 Sept. 1922).

Mazziotti, Matteo. *Napoleone III e l'Italia.* Milan, 1925.

Mazzoni, Ida. *I moti di Torino per la Convenzione di 15 settembre 1864.* Poggibonsi, 1929.

Merimée, Prosper. *Lettres à Panizzi (1850-1870).* 2 v., Paris, 1881.

Minghetti, Marco. *Lettere a Leopoldo Galeotti.* Bologna, 1903.

Monti, A. *Pio IX nel risorgimento italiano con documenti inedite ed illustrazioni.* Bari, 1928.

Mosciaro, Filippo. *Il trasferimento della capitale del regno, ossia la Convenzione del 15 settembre 1864 tra l'Italia e la Francia.* Aversa, 1865.

(Napoleon, Jerome). "Sei lettere inedite del Girolamo Napoleone a Manteucci," *Rivisto storica del risorgimento italiano,* I, 179-184.

Ollivier, Emile. *L'Empire libéral.* 18 v., Paris, 1895-1912.

Volumes, V, VI, and VII are particularly valuable.

Oriani, Alfredo. *La lotta politica in Italia. Origini della lotta attuale.* Turin, 1892.

Pagano, C. "Napoleone III, Eugenia di Montijo, e Francesco Arese in un carteggio inedito," *Nuova Antologia,* (1 Jan. 1921).

Pantaleoni, D. *L'Ultimo tentativo del Cavour per la liberazione di Roma nel 1861.* Florence, 1885.

Pantaleoni, D. (Forçade). "La question romaine," *Revue des deux mondes,* (15 Aug., 1 Sept. 1861).

Quintavalle, F., *Il risorgimento italiano (1814-1870).* Milan, 1926.

Roux, F. C. "La Russie et la politique italienne de Napoléon III," *Revue historique,* CV, (1910-1911), 35-62, 277-301.

Russell, Earl John. *Recollections and Suggestions 1813-1873.* London, 1875.

Salata, Francesco. *Per la storia diplomatica della questione romana.* 2 v., Milan, 1929-1930.

Seignobos, Charles. *Le déclin de l'Empire et l'établissement de la Troisième République (1859-1875).* Volume VII of Ernest Lavisse's *Histoire contemporaine de la France depuis la Révolution jusqu'à la paix de 1919.* Paris, 1921.

Silva, Pietro. "La convenzione di settembre secondo nuovi documenti," *Nuova Antologia,* (16 May 1913), 271-294.

Tivaroni, Carlo. *Storia critica del risorgimento italiano, 1735-1870.* 9 v., Turin, 1888-1897.

Vaccalluzzo, M. "La crisi di un uomo politico. Massimo D'Azeglio ed il trasferimento della capitale," *Nuova Antologia,* (1 May 1923).

Veroli, Piero. "Gioacchino Napoleone Pepoli," *Rivista Europa,* XXVIII, XXIX, XXX, XXXI, (1882-1883).

Material taken from Pepoli's own *relazione.*

INDEX

Nigra again hurried to Cowley with the same story that something must be done before the Italian Parliament convened. Cowley's reflections to Russell suggest that he discouraged Nigra's hasty methods:

I do not suppose that any objection would be made here to overtures from the Italian Government to that of Rome, but I do not think that the French Ambassador will be permitted to take charge of them.

I fear, however, that Baron Ricasoli's persistence will not make the Emperor more amenable to his wishes, and that it may increase the desire which is said to be felt here that he should be superseded by Mr. Rattazzi.

I believe that Nigra, who is convinced that the Roman question can not be terminated without the aid of France, has written to advise great caution on the part of the Italian Government.[95]

Rayneval reported from Turin that there seemed to be very little effort there to keep even Ricasoli's propositions secret. Everybody knew almost all about them. If Hudson in Turin was told as much as Cowley in Paris, it is likely that the English were one source for outside information. Yet any divulgation would make Rome suspect that the proposals were only made to put the Pope in a bad light.

On receiving the announcement from Nigra that France might wait until she had sounded out the Vatican, Ricasoli sent a long reply advising strongly against such a step and included a veiled threat to France. The significant part ran somewhat as follows:

You told me it was your opinion that the French Government, before accepting the task of being the instrument of our communications to the Pope, wishes to feel out the ground in order to be sure of the Roman Court's consent to receive them through the medium of the Imperial Embassy. I certainly do not wish that to happen, and I confess to you that I do not see any serious reason for that preventative inquiry. Perhaps the Imperial Government fears a refusal, and sees in that refusal a slight or an embarrassment. If the Roman Court declined to receive from the Imperial representative the communications under discussion, it would be giving just another

[95] This would seem to indicate that Nigra's resolution to caution Ricasoli came after his interviews with Thouvenel and Cowley. The predicted note by Nigra was written on 27 Sept. 1861. Cowley to Russell, 20 Sept. 1861, *F.O., France,* 1396: no. 1141.

proof of its ill-will, its obstinacy, and its ingratitude toward France. But the French Government far from receiving rebuff would profit by having given a great satisfaction to the sincere or timorous Catholic opinion. . . . But proceeding with the plan which you pointed out to me the Imperial Government would obviously run the risk of having this last (*supremo*) attempt become abortive at its very inception, and of causing those unfriendly to it to insinuate that it was sorry to find an occasion to withdraw its troops from Rome, and that therefore she intended to remain there indefinitely and for ulterior motives. . . . That hope (of negotiations) having been lost, [the Italian Government] can do no less than give the national opinion the satisfaction of seeing how it has not been negligent nor inactive on this burning question . . . [by] publishing the negotiations attempted by it and the reasons which caused their failure. . . . But preliminary inquiries made to the Roman Court would very probably be the occasion for preventing the negotiations from even being started.[96]

The threat to publish the documents in case of failure and to cause both the English and the Italians to suspect France of having ulterior motives is quite obvious. But it also revealed that Ricasoli's state of mind was bordering on to desperation and that by using the bludgeon at so early a stage he only revealed a lack of diplomatic finesse for which his predecessor was famous.

Nigra's letter of caution, which Cowley predicted, was sent in reply to this latest outburst of Ricasoli. He said he had talked and argued with Thouvenel but the latter insisted on awaiting reports from La Valette. The Emperor would not be in Paris until the 30th and Prince Napoleon would not be back until the middle of the next month. He advised Ricasoli to let the matter drop for a while. If he would not be in a hurry, he might gain many points without as many conditions and concessions.[97] Ricasoli's reply was almost a repetition of his earlier dispatches. He regretted the French silence:

I believe that even personally I ought to have had a better correspondence. . . . If France does not think she can second our project, if she does not believe she can give us her support, we must consider well what means we should take by ourselves.

[96] 24 Sept. 1861, *Ricasoli lettere,* VI, 171-174.
[97] Paris, 27 Sept. 1861, *ibid.,* pp. 180-181.